Music as a Chariot

Music as a Chariot offers a multidisciplinary perspective whose primary proposition is that theatre is a *type* of music. Understanding how music enables the theatre experience helps to shape our entire approach to the performing arts.

Beginning with a discussion on the origin and nature of time, the author takes us on an evolutionary journey to discover how music, language and mimesis co-evolved, eventually coming together to produce the complex way we experience theatre.

The book integrates the evolutionary neuroscience of the human brain into this journey, offering practical implications and applications for the auditory expression of this concept—namely the fundamental techniques artists use to create sound scores for theatre.

With contributions from directors, playwrights, actors and designers, *Music as a Chariot* explores the use of music to carry ideas into the human soul—a concept that extends beyond the theatrical to include film, video gaming, dance, or anywhere art is manipulated in time.

Richard K. Thomas is Professor of Visual and Performing Arts at Purdue University with over 100 credits as a composer, sound designer, author, playmaker, and educator. He is a Fellow of USITT, and winner of the 2018 Distinguished Achievement Award in Sound Design and Technology.

Music as a Chariot

The Evolutionary Origins of Theatre
in Time, Sound, and Music

Richard K. Thomas

Routledge
Taylor & Francis Group

NEW YORK AND LONDON

First published 2018
by Routledge
711 Third Avenue, New York, NY 10017

and by Routledge
2 Park Square, Milton Park, Abingdon, Oxon, OX14 4RN

Routledge is an imprint of the Taylor & Francis Group, an informa business

Library of Congress Cataloging-in-Publication Data
Names: Thomas, Richard K., 1953– author.
Title: Music as a chariot : the evolutionary origins of theatre in time,
    sound, and music / Richard K. Thomas.
Description: New York : Routledge, 2018. | Includes bibliographical
    references.
Identifiers: LCCN 2017038214 | ISBN 9781138295469 (hardback) |
    ISBN 9781138295773 (pbk.) | ISBN 1315145634 (ebook)
Subjects: LCSH: Music in the theater. | Theaters—Sound effects. |
    Music—Philosophy and aesthetics.
Classification: LCC MT960 .T48 2018 | DDC 781.5/5—dc23
LC record available at https://lccn.loc.gov/2017038214

ISBN: 978-1-138-29546-9 (hbk)
ISBN: 978-1-138-29577-3 (pbk)
ISBN: 978-1-315-14563-1 (ebk)

Typeset in Sabon
by Apex CoVantage, LLC

Dedicated to all my students
Who helped me build the class upon which this book is based.
Who challenged me when I was wrong,
And forgave me when I was right.
Who laughed with me at the endless insanity of the human condition,
And sat with me in "silent wonder" for a moment at the beauty
of our predicament.
But most of all, who became the lifelong friends and colleagues
I'll cherish and admire
For the rest of my days.

CONTENTS

FOREWORD

In the summer of 1988, I had just completed an undergrad degree in electrical and computer engineering at Purdue University that also included a fair amount of classwork in acoustics and music theory. I was set to start grad school in the fall, also at Purdue, to study acoustics in the School of Mechanical Engineering. But, as the summer progressed, I began to question my plans and bounced between a fascination with acoustics and engineering and a deeper desire to explore the more creative aspects of music and audio.

Tension between the analytical and the expressive, between things engineered and things created, was not entirely new to me. An influential and prescient teacher in my senior year of high school summed it up in a note on my final essay of the year: "You will always wrestle with a tug of war between the analytical and the creative."

With summer passing and grad school approaching, I was running out of time if I was going to change course. Fortunately, I found a path forward with the help of two tremendously supportive and generous people: Stuart Bolton, my professor for acoustics and noise control, and Helen Brown, my professor for music theory and composition.

To this day, I am grateful that they supported me to expand my outlook beyond traditional engineering, which, among other things, included introducing me to Rick Thomas, a professor in Purdue's Theatre Department. Rick encouraged me to enter his graduate sound design program and helped me through a compressed application process. That fall, I was accepted into the M.F.A. program in the Theatre Department at Purdue.

One of my first interactions with Rick reflects what I came to appreciate about him as a teacher and an artist, and also reflects one of the core ideas in this book. Rick said, "You know a lot about engineering, but we need to teach you about the human condition."

These were inspiring words, but putting them in practice at the start of the school year was more terror than inspiration thanks to Rick, who had decided that "learning about the human condition" was best achieved by putting me—an uptight engineer—in the first-year undergraduate acting program. "Fish out of water" doesn't begin to describe how out of place I was among actors, but fortunately my peers and professors both had an abundance of empathy and goodwill. The craft and principles that I learned with them for creating and performing art as part of a team have served me over three decades of work in technology and entertainment.

During grad school, I had the privilege to help Rick teach sound design classes, which both drew upon and built on his evolving ideas about the nature of music in theatre. The curriculum for these classes was my first exposure to the fundamental connection that Rick saw between the visual and the auditory. The idea that size in the visual world could be thought of as volume in the auditory world, that lines and shapes in physical objects could correspond to melodies and harmonies in music, that the texture and color of a surface could be thought of as the timbre and tone of an instrument—these were foundational to me.

After completing my M.F.A., my career took a direction away from the theatre, and I began working on and designing video games. It turns out that putting on a play and making a video game have more in common than one might think. Both video games and theatre seek to immerse the audience in a fabricated moment in space and time and take them on an emotional journey. Both involve working as part of a diverse and collaborative team, and both depend on harnessing technology to tell a story and captivate the viewer.

Rick would lead his students through a process of deconstruction followed by synthesis: a process of getting to the root and core of something and then exploring how its pieces could be manipulated to make something new. I believe that process is echoed in his approach to this book. We can better understand how music incites emotions and creates mood if we start with a model of how our brains process sound waves. We can better understand the role of music in any art form if we go back through time and trace the connections between music, language, stories and performance.

Today, the Theatre Department at Purdue is housed in a wonderful collection of purposeful and modern facilities. During my tenure, things were more improvised and cramped, and Rick was gracious enough to share his office with his graduate assistants. A file cabinet in the corner of that office housed Rick's growing collection of notes and papers, many of which were my first exposure to his thinking about the connection between artist and audience and how we each uniquely experience music and theatre.

Rick continues to be a mentor and friend, and I know that he has put a career's worth of thinking and experience into writing this book, which should speak well to sound designers, composers, musicians, directors, actors, engineers, and anyone who has ever sat in the audience of a live performance.

Matt Booty
June 2017
Matt Booty is a corporate vice president at Microsoft,
where he works in the Xbox division and leads the
Minecraft video game franchise.

ACKNOWLEDGMENTS

I've been putting off writing these acknowledgments for pretty much the whole time I've been writing this book. When it takes your entire life to write a book, you leave behind an incredibly long trail of people to whom you are deeply indebted. I don't want to leave anyone out, but this section too, must have a finite length. Regrettably, I will not be able to mention everyone to whom I am deeply indebted. Instead, I'll try to make sure I cover everyone in groups, and just hope no one is too offended that I didn't have space to name them personally.

First, let me thank the people who specifically helped my make this book: Al Pounders for his lovely cover art; Matt Booty for his awesome foreword; Carnegie Mellon sound design professor, Joe Pino; and my dear lifelong friend and collaborator, Carrie Newcomer, for their endless patience and endurance in reading this book in its formative stages and providing so many helpful comments and suggestions along the way. Thanks also to my Honors 499 class who helped me test this version of the book in spring 2017, and to the Honors College for funding the project. These were brilliant students never afraid to tell me when they thought I was off my rocker, or really needed to explain something better, and I think the book is much better for that. Many thanks to Robert Meitus, who helped me navigate all the legal hurdles that one has to leap to get a book published. I also need to acknowledge the many specialists in their own respective fields, who actually made most of the discoveries revealed in this book. Hopefully, I have gotten their conclusions right. Finally, thanks to the good people at Routledge, who've shown incredible faith in my work and ability to bring this project to fruition.

Let me also thank my colleagues.

First, thanks to the many mentors who have helped me shape my theatre aesthetic over these many years, especially Van Phillips, Jim O'Connor, Dale Miller, Joel Fink, Dick Forsythe, Caryl Matthews, Abe Jacob and especially my dear friend Maurie Mogridge, who, after 40 years of "Tuesdays with Maurie" lunches, still provides wonderful insights and inspiration.

This book is partly autobiographical, but doesn't overtly reflect what I've learned and the great companionship I've shared with so many composers and sound designers, engineers and technicians over the years. They've influenced this book more than they will ever know. I met these wonderful people through the many theatres and universities in which I've worked and visited, and some extraordinary organizations: The United States Institute for Theatre Technology (USITT), not just the Sound Commission, but especially the believers in the organization whose primary discipline was not sound, but understood its importance nevertheless. They empowered my career and our field by believing that sound design and music composition was an important art form. I am indebted to the International Organization of Scenographers, Theatre Architects and Technicians (OISTAT) and the amazing friends and family I've found and cherish there from all over the world; my friends and colleagues in the National Theatre Conference (NTC) who have allowed me to pontificate and explore the function of sound and music in theatre beyond the confines of design and technology; and the newly founded Theatrical Sound Designers and Composers Association (TSDCA). Another group of colleagues that has been indispensable to both my own personal development and the field of sound design for the theatre are the many manufacturers and other professional organizations who have assisted my work, become great friends, and with whom I have had the great privilege to collaborate over these many years.

Let me take time to thank Purdue University, which actively embraces its role as a Research One institution, and has supported my research *and* creative endeavor for over 40 years. From top to bottom, I could not have found a more wonderful place to spend my career. The Dean's Office, particularly our current Dean David Reingold and Associate Deans Joel Ebarb and Melissa Remis, made this book possible through two sabbaticals and subvention funds for image acquisition, for when a picture really could say a thousand words. The head of our Patti and Rusty Rueff School of Visual and Performing Arts and Harry Bulow, who has unfailingly supported my work even when it seemed destined to fly off the deep end. I've had the tremendous pleasure of working with many great faculty and staff from departments, schools and colleges all over campus in deep and meaningful ways: my many friends and colleagues in the Music and Dance Divisions and the Art and Design Department; my long-standing collaborations with Hall of Music Productions and Steve Hall; WBAA, Film and Visual Studies, the Electrical and Computer Engineering and Multidisciplinary Engineering programs in the College of Engineering; the Purdue Polytechnic Institute, especially the Department of Electrical and Computer Engineering Technology. But especially, I want to thank my second family, the faculty and staff of Purdue University Theatre. Like any family, we love, fight and challenge each other on a daily basis, but I wouldn't trade them for the world. My deep appreciation to our staff, who routinely go so far out of their way to accommodate my seemingly harebrained ideas. This incredible group of colleagues has helped to make me a better artist and person. They are a family like no other, and I cherish the time we've spent together.

I'm blessed to have so many friends, and I want to thank all of them, but especially the ones who held my hand through the last two years of this arduous book-making process: Carrie Newcomer and Robert Meitus, Maurie Mogridge, Al Pounders and Loren Olson, my dear friends Larry and Rita Smeyak, and my concert buddies, Alex Chorosevic and John Hermes. And, as long as I'm mentioning my friends, I must thank the roommates I've had over the many years, who taught me valuable life lessons, and became a lifelong friend thereafter.

Finally, I am deeply indebted to my family whom I love so dearly. In their own way, they've helped make possible the production of this book: Buz and Judy, Tom and Bonnie, Jay and Tammy, TJ and Leah. Finally, I must never forget my mom and dad, Harry and Lillian, who sacrificed everything to build one of the most wonderful families in the world.

CHAPTER 1

WHY THIS BOOK?

Of the nature of the soul . . . let me speak briefly, and in a figure. And let the figure be composite—a pair of winged horses and a charioteer. Now the winged horses and the charioteers of the gods are all of them noble and of noble descent, but those of other races are mixed; the human charioteer drives his in a pair; and one of them is noble and of noble breed, and the other is ignoble and of ignoble breed; and the driving of them of necessity gives a great deal of trouble to him . . . the soul which has seen most of truth shall come to the birth as a philosopher, or artist, or some musical and loving nature.

—Plato, *Phaedrus*

Know thou the self as occupier of the chariot, but the body as the chariot itself; but know thou the intellect (buddhi) as charioteer, and also the mind (manas) as rein. The senses (indriya) they call the steeds, the objects of sense the resorts (gocara) for them; him that is yoked (yukta) with self, senses, and mind, the wise call by the name enjoyer.

—*The Katha-Upanishad*

Introduction: An Ear-Opening Experience

I was a junior in high school in 1969, a nerd at a time when nerds could not have been less fashionable. Every day brought another embarrassment and humiliation. But I had found music early in my life, and music, it would turn out, would be my salvation.

One day, after a particularly traumatic experience—which, curiously I can't even recall now—I came home, and went up to my bedroom to sulk. I can't ever remember being so despondent and overwhelmed. I pulled out a new record that I had just bought a couple of days ago. It was a new band I had recently encountered, Pink Floyd. I put on side three of *Ummagumma*, an experimental departure from their earlier albums.

I lay down on my bed as the grand and pompous first movement of *Sysyphus* started. Somehow it was exactly what I was feeling: angry, oppressed, overwhelmed. The second movement, a piano solo, calmed me down quite a bit, and was much more reflective, although quite melancholy, which was now how I was feeling. The third movement led me into a world that was funky but unpredictable, a bit scary and chaotic, again very much like my life. It built to a huge climax, and then released into this quiet, reflective but deeply unsettling world.

By this point I was only semi-conscious, but somehow deeply connected to the music, my moods changing with the album tracks.

A crashing, raging sound momentarily shook me from my reverie followed by an eerie dissonant and slowly building section before the monolithic oppressive chords made their final climactic re-entrance. It left me in a very calm place, immersed in a world of birds singing and insects buzzing around, and eventually a very simple, peaceful acoustic guitar seemed to take away all my pain. This gave way to the final movement on that spinning bit of vinyl, *Several Species of Small Furry Animals Gathered Together in a Cave and Grooving with a Pict*. The piece is among the most whimsical in popular music. It left me . . . happy.

As I awoke from this experience, I was astounded. How was it that less than a half an hour ago I had lay down on my bed overwhelmed by despair and hopelessness? And now I was . . . happy!? Nothing in my world had changed, except that I had listened to music. How was it possible that music could possibly have that kind of influence on me?

A little over three years later, I was going into my junior year at Michigan State University, when I landed a job as an assistant director with one of our faculty members, Peter Landry, at the Calumet Summer Theatre, in one of the most northern points in Michigan. We were mounting a production of Emlyn Williams's classic psychological thriller, *Night Must Fall*.

The rehearsal process was uneventful until about two weeks before we opened. Peter received news that his father had passed away. He told me that he would need to leave for about a week for the funeral, and I would have to take over directing the play. Picture this: I'm barely a junior, and all the people in the company are either grads or the senior star actors at Michigan State. And I'm going to "direct" them! Now, I'm an opportunist as much as anybody else, so I was like "yeah, sure I'll do that, no problem."

Then Peter said, "Oh, and while I'm gone could you find some sound effects? Door creaks and thunders, things like that." This is a murder mystery, right? It's about a gardener who comes to visit this really, really old lady in a wheelchair, and it's one of those creepy, spooky, great summer stock entertainment kind of shows. So, he left, and I started to put together some sound effects from these Electro Voice sound effects records they had—thunders, door creaks, all the sounds I thought the show might need—and commenced to directing the production. And I directed, and I directed, and I directed, and every day the show just got progressively . . . *worse*. It never got *better*. Every direction I gave made the show *worse*. It kept going down and down and down and down and down . . .

So now I'm really embarrassed, and Peter comes back from his father's funeral about a week later, and the show is as deadly boring as you can possibly imagine. Not at all scary, my creepy sound effects are not doing anything. We all gathered, and Peter pulled out this reel-to-reel tape recorder—in those days it was a Wollensak. He sat down, and said, "well I'll tell you what, let's just run through and see what we've got." We started running through the show, and while Peter was gone, he had put together a soundtrack of film composers such as Bernard Herrmann, classic music from fifties suspense thrillers. And the show went from "I can't bear to watch this" to frightening, chilling and riveting. The tempo and rhythms of the actors magically fell into place; the music *commanded* and *transformed* the acting. I experienced the show like it was my very first time and it totally blew me away.

Suddenly I realized how music could fundamentally transform theatre.

Old School Aesthetics

So began a journey that has lasted my entire life, a combination of discovering how sound and music work in the sound scores I composed, and of sharing those discoveries with students in sound design classes over 40 years.

These are the discoveries I hope to share with you in this book, but before I do, it's important that we understand something about art and artists. We are all unique and different. That is as it should be. Who would want to live in a world in which all of the art followed the same set of rules, in which all of the art somehow turns out the *same*, because we all follow the same rules? Every maker of art and every person who experiences art has a separate and unique *aesthetic*.

Aesthetic. That word can mean a lot of things to a lot of people. It has changed quite a bit from its original use. The origin of the term aesthetic comes from the Greek term *aisthetikos*, which means "perceptible things," or from *aisthesthai*, meaning to "perceive by the senses." However, it was resurrected and appropriated in the mid-eighteenth century to mean what it generally means now, our general sense of beauty and art (Oxforddictionaries.com 2016). But this earlier definition precisely fits our needs in this book. So, we will use the term exclusively in this book in the Greek sense. When we use the term aesthetic in this book we will mean *how we perceive the world through our senses, especially our senses of hearing and sight*. Using the term in this way allows us to immediately bypass value judgments in perceiving art. Quite the contrary, it validates every individual's own valuation of art. If it moved you, then it's a valuable piece of art.

Oh, and by the way, in 2003, *Stylus* editor Ed Howard reported that the general consensus about the *Ummagumma* tracks I had been listening to was that they were "something lower than shit" (Howard 2003). Other people's aesthetic. Go figure.

At the same time, we are very concerned in this book with how we *connect* with each other using music, especially when we use it in the more highly specialized discipline of creating sound scores for theatre. How our audience *perceives* music is critically important in understanding how we connect with one another, even more so when we attach ideas to music like we routinely do in theatre. We will find that using the term "aesthetic" in the Greek sense will be much more helpful in improving our ability to create and understand music composition and sound design for the theatre.

In using the term "aesthetic" in this manner, we go much further than avoiding often less than useful valuations of artworks that undermine and inhibit creativity. If you create music in your art work, this book makes no attempt to evaluate the quality of your art. Instead, this book will hopefully give you a fundamental understanding of the interconnection between composer, performer and audience. To do that, it helps to understand how human beings perceive the world through their senses. But do not confuse that with me trying to convince you to like music that I like, or theatre that I like, or that I think you should compose or design in a certain way. I will show you some fundamental tools we use along the way, and help you understand how we use them and why they work. What you do with them is gloriously your own business. In that sense, my hope is that my aesthetic will *inform* your aesthetic, not that I will convince you that I have attained some ultimate truth that you must blindly adopt as if it were a religion.

When Sound Gets Divorced from Music

As an example, let's consider how I have typically composed sound scores for theatre over the last 40 years. I like to work more like the composer of a musical would work: we compose pretty much the entire score, and the director then stages the entire production allowing the preexisting music which dictates tempo, dynamics, vocal colors and so forth. I've been fortunate to work with an extraordinary director, Joel Fink, together in this manner for many, many productions both in Chicago and at the Colorado Shakespeare Festival, and we've developed an amazingly intuitive relationship where we instinctively know how each other "perceives the outside world through their senses," each other's aesthetic. On any number of productions, Joel has walked in to the first cast read-through with my complete soundtrack, to which he will stage the production. Yes, there are many changes and adaptations we will make along the way to address mistakes I made in the composition, nuances that the actors bring to the performance, and the tremendous conception that Joel develops in the realization of each production. Working in this manner puts a tremendous responsibility on my shoulders to come to a complete and full understanding of exactly how music works in the production. There have been instances where Joel has listened to my initial compositions and said "lovely piece, Rick, but this music is for a different show." But for the most part, the score is largely composed in advance of the rehearsal process.

Composing the score in advance of rehearsals, like a musical, has become a large part of my theatre aesthetic.

But it isn't the only viable aesthetic out there. Most directors will argue for a different aesthetic, and with very valid arguments. While working in this manner has its advantages, as evidenced in the dominance of preexisting scores in musical theatre and opera, working in this manner also has its decided disadvantages. In particular, an existing score tends to undermine the journey of discovery undertaken by the actors. Including music very early in a production tends to dictate the actors' pacing and rhythms—it's very hard to fight against it. Many directors are very leery about introducing sound too early in the rehearsal process, and some prefer not to introduce it until the actors' pacing and rhythms have been clearly set. Scenic artists typically develop the space in which the events of the play unfold. Once this space has been created, directors then learn how to reveal actions that take place in time. Since sound is primarily a time art, it makes sense to orchestrate those actions after the actors' action has been staged. Doing this helps to accommodate the rhythms imposed on the actors' performance imposed by the scenery. This is another very common way of working, especially in smaller theatres with limited budgets. Most films are also created in this manner. The composer receives a relatively complete edit of the movie and then composes the score to support the rhythms and pacing of the actors and the film editor.

Working in this manner places its own challenges on composers and sound designers: their process can't really start until the other processes are complete. In film, this often means very compressed time schedules squeezed between the "rough cut" and the release of the film. In theatre, this often means that the composer/sound designer can't really begin to work on a show until the technical rehearsals—a time-honored tradition made all the more pragmatic by salaries that compel sound artists to restrict their effort to very short time periods. Still, this approach can work amazingly well provided that the amount of orchestrating required is doable, and, conversely, that the sound team has developed the extraordinary ability to create workable sound quickly and efficiently, often while waiting for lighting designers to perfect their own contributions.

If composing the sound score before the show goes into rehearsal is one approach, and composing the sound score during the technical rehearsals is another, there remains but one more aesthetic in the creation of sound scores: composing the sound score *during* the rehearsal process. It seems that this is, for practical reasons the most common approach, but perhaps the one that is the most fraught with potential problems when the sound score is composed simultaneously, but separately from the rehearsal process. The problems with this approach will require a bit of explanation, but is so important that it serves as one of the underlying themes of this book, so bear with me.

Joe Stockdale is considered by many to be the "father" of Purdue Theatre. He came to Purdue in 1951 and directed productions there until spring of 1976, three months before my tenure at Purdue began. He led the LORT Purdue Professional Theatre and directed 140 shows that included such notable artists as William Saroyan, Academy Award winner Anne Revere and James Earl Jones. His students included such legendary figures of the American stage as Peter Schneider and Tom Moore (Williams 2007). Later in life I had the privilege of discussing some of my then emerging ideas about the function of music in theatre, and Joe graciously offered these thoughts in an email to me:

> At the end of the sixteenth century in a Florentine academy, opera was "invented" as part of the rediscovery of classical theatre. The creation of opera was based on an interpretation of Aristotle's writing about music as a constituent part of tragedy. However, in opera, the libretto [plot's text] was secondary to music because operas were sung throughout and therefore music composition and its relation to character was the natural focus rather than music's relationship to plot described by Aristotle.
>
> Throughout the centuries that followed plot and its relationship to character continued to be the focus in drama except for interludes of musical prominence such as Ben Jonson's court masques (1605–1625), Gay's *The Beggar's Opera* (1727), Rousseau's *Pygmalion* (1770), Diderot's discussion of fitting prose to music, music's popularity in underscoring the text of melodrama, Richard Wagner's thoughts on the unification of the theatrical elements of opera, musical background for early silent films, then TV soap operas, and eventually genuine musicals such as *Show Boat, Oklahoma, South Pacific, Gypsy*, and *West Side Story* and now the triumph of the musical revue on Broadway which pretty much eliminates plot and dialogue.
>
> (Stockdale 2009)

Joe's disdain for the modern Broadway musical aside, there is a very real problem with Joe's snapshot history for me: it only considers instrumental and sung music. It doesn't include music's profound influence in theatre that is neither instrumental nor sung music.

For example, it doesn't include the *prosody* of the actors' dialogue. Prosody is the part of speech that doesn't use signs or symbols like language does; it involves the rhythms with which the actors speak, the stresses and dynamics, the speech melody. It's how we tell a question from an exclamation from a command, even when the words spoken are all exactly the same. Consider the many ways of saying the simple statement "I'm going to the store." It could be filled with the excitement and anticipation of having just won the lottery. It could be filled with frustration and anger, like how I would say it after I discovered for the third time that I was missing a part to repair my leaky faucet. It could simply be filled with indifference because I'm bored and need something to do. Or it could be bursting with the excitement and anticipation of going shopping for that new flat-screen television. It's a form of music that we as orchestrators cannot ignore.

Beyond the music inherent in the actors' speech, there are also inherent rhythms and dynamics of the actors' physical performance. In another art form, we would consider these to be a form of dance. But can we ignore these when we create sound scores for the stage?

The plot of the play also has its own musical structures. Traditionally this structure follows the form inciting event, rising action, climax and resolution. But modern theatre provides us with many alternative forms. In order to draw us into the world of the play we implement very specific rhythms, tempos and dynamics. These musical elements bring together the prosody of the actors' voices, and their physicalizations into a larger musical structure that also includes scene changes, blocking, projections, lighting and more. One of the most common problems I encounter in younger student composers and designers is their inability to conceive how the individual elements of the production combine to form a larger whole, in the same manner that a composer develops a theme in a sonata into an exposition, a development and a recapitulation. These are critically important musical structures.

You may argue that I am defining music unnecessarily too wide. But I will argue in the course of this book that this wide definition of music is justified anthropologically, neurologically, evolutionarily and historically, and one way or another is essential to creating the dramatic experience of the audience. Hopefully by the time you finish reading this book you too will never think of music so narrowly again, that is, solely confined to instrumental and sung sounds that we *hear*.

Let's briefly discuss how the problem of sound scores becoming disconnected from the music of the actors and the play came to manifest itself in theatre. Electronic theatre sound design as we now know it came to the theatre table pretty late. Electronic pioneers started experimenting with sound in the theatre in the 1930s and 1940s. One of the earlier means of cueing recorded sound into a performance relied on a sound operator dropping the needle onto a spinning disc rotating at 78 revolutions per minute. A valuable operator was one who could produce the desired sound in a relatively precise way—"If the dog could bark somewhere around here, that would be great!"[1] As you can imagine, this precluded the ability to perform in a musical manner that had the same precision as, for example, a pianist who could play ahead of the beat, on the beat or off the beat—millisecond differences that have great musical meaning in performance.

However, the musicality of a lot of these sound "effects," as they were probably rightly called, was not so important. Sound was being used iconically; that is, the sound performed was being used as an icon for the real thing to let the audience know some specific fact about the story (e.g., that a dog had barked). As long as the audience understood that the sound they heard was supposed to *represent* a dog, all was well. And, of course, it was easier to play a recording of a dog than to have a real dog located offstage and convince it to bark on cue. Never mind that the dog barked in the acoustic environment of the backstage area, not the actual acoustic environment of the scene. Ditto for a train. The prominence of dramatic realism in the twentieth century paradoxically empowered this iconic approach to sound over musicality.

By the time I started "designing" sound in the early 1970s, and for quite some time after, everyone referred to sound as "the newest design element," if they were willing to consider it as a design element at all. Because sound was so often considered in its iconic function rather than its musical, a whole process developed for incorporating sound into a production that was modelled after lighting: stage managers calling cues, sound operators located in glass booths, and loudspeakers located where the lights were, creating sounds that emanated outside of the dramatic space. Sound often became a Band-Aid to address other problems: scene and costume changes that went on way too long, instilling mood where none had surfaced in the rehearsals. As I once overheard an artistic director say to a struggling director: "Put some music under it. It will mean *something*." Of course, as my sound design friend Joe Pino put it, "that's the problem. It always means *something*. There's no way that you can prevent that" (Pino 2017).

And, most significantly, there was little to no perceived need to bring in the sound team early in the process to create the music *with* the team. Back in the day, some directors' idea of sound design was that they would provide a list of sound effects, and the sound technician would go to their sound effects library and find several versions of the required sound. The director would then pick out the best one. This was sound design? No wonder people were saying "sound design? There's no such thing as sound design, it will never be an art form." So we played the sound effects back at something resembling the right moment, mostly because the audience needed to know something, for example, that a dog barked—backstage.

By the time theatrical style changed to demanding a more musical theatre, the processes were so firmly in place to *prevent* the musical integration of sound into a production that change would often be an uphill battle. Today the sound team often goes away on its own and develops the sound score that seems appropriate for the script and the director's interpretation. But this approach that divorces the composer and designer from the other "musics" of the production often leads to fragmented, trivial, oversimplistic sound scores that more often distract listeners rather than pull them deeper into the performance. This process often results in the creation of two *musics*, the music that drives the performance itself, and the audible music and sound that attempts to somehow match, dictate, correlate or illustrate that internal music.

Such a process of composing the sound score simultaneously, but separately from the composition of the music of the actors, seems to be rather hit or miss. Ideally, we would compose the sound score simultaneously *within* the rehearsal process. But as I said before, that is pragmatically difficult for a variety of reasons. To overcome what is pragmatically working against us, we need a fundamental understanding of how sound and music work in theatre that could then empower us to utilize their full power to engage and transport audiences into our dramatic worlds. What we need in production is an aesthetic informed by the experience of music in theatre, that transports the audience into the world of the play. It is my hope to build the foundation for such an understanding in this book.

Who Should Read This Book

Even in the preceding examples, many production teams have achieved extraordinary results using any of the three processes described without the benefit of this book! This is no accident. Music is primal; it's a biological component of human physiology and psychology. Music is so fundamental to our being that we take it for granted that we understand it. Everybody can listen to music and be moved by it. You don't have to have any training whatsoever. That is quite different from language. An intuitive approach also applies to making music. Many of the world's most beloved musicians have no formal training whatsoever. They can't read a note of music; they have no formal training on their instrument. They play from the heart, from deeply ingrained intuition, allowing their emotions to flow through their instrument. Ask them how or why they play notes in a certain way, and they will be at a loss to explain. It just happens.

A similar situation exists with directors and actors and other artists expressing themselves through music. For example, a director may say to an actor, "If you put a beat right there in that line, you'll get the laugh you're looking for," and sure enough, the actor puts the beat there—just a little pause, just a little cadence, a musical thing right there, and there's a laugh. The actor turns to the director, and says "how did you know that?" The director responds, "I don't know," or "I've been doing this for 40 years." But ask the director why, why musically is that right? They can't tell you. It's intuitive. Music is very intuitive. It's one of the arguments about music being biologically and evolutionarily driven. It's really intuitive. All cultures have it. All time periods have it.

For many, this intuition is enough. For the rest of us, there will come a time when we need to effectively communicate, and we will want to have a command over our tools in order to connect with our audience effectively. Nearly everyone can communicate to a certain degree using their native language. However, the best communicators are those that also study their language, who understand and learn the nuance of meaning, syntax, phrasing, efficiency and precision. It is similar with music. In every artist's life, there are hills and valleys; hills of magnificent inspiration that come from who knows where, and valleys where we seemingly don't have a creative idea to offer. We don't need to understand how music works in theatre to get us through the hills, we need to understand how music works to provide a craft that leads us to success in the valleys. In this book, I will argue that the art we need to understand, that will lead us to better craft, lies in understanding music holistically. The more we understand how music works, the more we will understand how theatre works, because theatre is a type of music.

You'll notice that I keep using the term "connection" in describing our work as composers and sound designers for the stage. This implies a distinct bias that I have as a playmaker, that also applies to my target audience: that music is fundamentally not the same as communication, in which *information* is transferred from one entity to another. We'll see that music doesn't usually work that way. Instead we use music to manipulate the audience's perception of time, and in the process, stimulate emotions in them. It's a careful distinction, one that will hopefully become much more necessary as we move forward in this book.

But this process of connecting with an audience still involves transmission, mediating and reception. My objective is to transport the audience to a balanced blend between a world we as a production team choose, and a world the audience creates in their imaginations. Because of this, I tend to carefully balance how much I leave to chance. There are many fine artists out there who are perfectly content to simply express themselves as artists and let the audience make of it what they will. Pure composers often encounter this problem when they first attempt to write for the stage—it's not enough to be able to express oneself in a moving manner. Expression in theatre is tied to a larger conception, and must support that larger conception in what is experienced by the audience. So, while we will discuss the careful balance we must achieve between what we give the audience as playmakers and what we require the audience to supply themselves, this book is intended for those who want to improve their ability to connect with an audience, their ability to consciously manipulate design elements to affect an audience in a very specific and predetermined way.

Given these caveats, I hope that this book will prove an invaluable source of inspiration for composers and sound designers alike, regardless of whether you have formal training in music. For years, I called my course "Composition for Non-composers," but, in practice, I have found that formally trained composers have found great benefit in it also. Forty years' experience teaching this subject in classes does provide some hope that this material will help you become a better composer and designer. But I've discovered something else along the way: there is tremendous interest in this subject beyond composers and sound designers for theatre and film. Musicians, directors, playwrights and actors have found their way into my class and enriched the dialogue tremendously. Visual artists interested in exploring the element of time in their works have also participated and found value in these discussions. Even those with just an avocational interest in how they are being manipulated when they go to the theatre have found the discussions contained herein intriguing. There's something to be said for the idea that one gains even more enjoyment from experiencing a work of art when one is able to simultaneously analyze the experience one is having. It is the intention of this book to provide some tools to do just that too.

Overview of the Book

In this book, then, we'll attempt to identify the core principles of music that apply not just to instrumental and sung music, but to art in general, and more specifically to theatre, including playwriting, directing, acting, visual design, and, of course, sound design and music composition.

We'll make the argument that theatre is specifically a development of music, a specialized form of music. Our thesis is very simple:

Music = Time Manipulated
Song = Music + Idea
Theatre = Song + Mimesis

We start with time and define that. What is music, then? Music is just time manipulated. We will define music in a very broad way to include the prosodics of speech and visual music such as dance. What is song? Song is simply when you add the communication of ideas to the fundamental connection provided by the music. And then finally, what is theatre? It's when you take a song, and you add imitation to it (or more specifically, mimesis, which we'll explore quite a bit in later chapters). Instead of singing *about* something, we *become* that something. It's that simple, and we shall see that this is exactly how theatre developed.

The most important principle for which we will be building a case is that theatre is a very specific type of music. You can have music without theatre; you cannot have theatre without music, especially as we define music in its broad sense. Once we understand how music works in its broad sense, how music works in its more traditionally understood aural form will hopefully become much clearer.

To get to the most basic principles we use in creating sound scores for theatre, we'll need to narrow our subject down quite a bit. We will do this by separating culturally acquired characteristics of music and theatre that change significantly from one time period to another and from one culture to another. Such an investigation would be overwhelming, and it would not get us where we want to go. There have been thousands and thousands of volumes written on the historical and cultural forms theatre has taken. We are not interested in supplanting those; we are simply interested in exploring the foundation upon which those forms are built. We want to identify core principles, and to do that we need to identify elements and principles of music and theatre that have not changed for tens of thousands of years. They worked the same way for the Greeks as for cave dwellers. They work the same way for us. Timeless principles are a great place to start when building an aesthetic of music and sound in theatre. If you are going to build a foundation for learning how to use music to connect with an audience in theatre, what better place to start than things you know to be true for everybody? So we will study music as an evolutionary adaptation. Why evolution? Evolutionary changes take place over thousands and millions of years. If a trait applies to our ancestors and also applies to us, we're pretty certain that we've identified a fairly fundamental principle of the human condition that we can learn to manipulate. By identifying those principles, we can assure ourselves that the principles that we discover will apply to all periods of sound and music, and to all cultures, not just white Anglo-Saxon Protestant males in the United States.

As we shall see, music is simply a word we use to describe how we consciously manipulate our perception of time. In order to understand music, then, we will need to understand how time works. We'll start there, at the beginning of time and the universe, looking for clues in the fields of physics and astrophysics. We'll specifically look at the physical differences between sound and light and their relationship to matter. Then we'll trace how we came to be able to perceive time and space, and the specialized evolution of our ears and eyes to do both. We'll investigate how evolution led to important pretheatre activities such as ritual and dreaming and connect those to our understanding of how time and space work. We'll see how rhythm evolved around the same time that primitive man began to walk on two legs and look at the relationship between rhythm and bipedal locomotion.

We'll consider the complementary evolution of music and language, especially in the evolution of the human brain, and in particular, the relationship of music to language in song. This will lead us into discussions about the neurological evidence showing fundamental brain functions that haven't changed in thousands of years. Michael Thaut wrote one of the outstanding books on this subject, *Rhythm, Music and the Brain*, and explains the reason this inquiry is so helpful in this way:

> Music has received an unprecedented research focus in the brain sciences over the previous two decades. This came as a surprise to many artists and scientists alike; it was an unlikely development

for music, as an aesthetic medium and art form, to become a focus of many serious brain scientists' major research efforts. Furthermore, music received an almost exclusive and privileged position in brain research compared to other artistic fields. No other art form has received anything close to this level of attention.

. . . We now know that by studying the physiology and neurology of brain function in music we can actually obtain a great deal of knowledge about general brain function, in regard to the perception of complex auditory sound stimuli, time and rhythm processing, differential processing of music and language as two aural communication systems, biological substrates of learning versus innate talent in the arts, and processing of higher cognitive functions related to temporality and emotion. Music has become a very useful model for brain research in perception and cognition.

It has become quite clear in recent years that one of the most interesting and provocative suggestions coming out of these efforts in music and brain science is the realization of music as a biologically deeply ingrained function of the human brain. The brain has neural circuitry that is dedicated to music.

(Thaut 2005, vii–viii)

We'll look into the relationship between this neurological evidence and the evolution of art as a human endeavor. We'll connect psychological theories to this evolution, specifically related to the evolution of music, how and why music incites interest in its audience, and the role that memory, a close ally of music, plays in art.

We'll see how music and song contributed to the first great civilizations and how, when combined with mimesis, they begat the art form we now know as theatre. In conclusion, we'll consider the development of one specific strain, the first truly *autonomous* theatre of ancient Greece, as a case study. We'll investigate how Greek theatre developed out of music, and explore their uncanny understanding of how humans perceived both. Aristotle said that tragedy developed from the dithyramb and comedy from the phallic song. What's the importance of this statement? The importance of this statement is that Aristotle specifically suggests that theatre developed out of a musical form. It's not a minor detail. It's a major consideration that supports the major underlying theme of this book—especially when one considers the role that Greek theatre played in the subsequent development of Western civilization.

Ten Questions

1. Define the term "aesthetic" as we will use it in this book.
2. What is the purpose of this book, and what does that have to do with our definition of aesthetic?
3. Describe three ways in which sound designers create sound scores for theatre.
4. What is prosody?
5. Name three forms of music besides instrumental and sung music in plays.

6. What does it mean when we use sound "iconically"?
7. What is the great danger of creating the sound score during but independent of the rehearsal process?
8. State the thesis of the book in its most simple way.
9. What is the most important fundamental principle underlying this book?
10. What types of principles will this book hope to explore, and which types will it hope to avoid?

Things to Share

1. Tell us a story about the first time that music profoundly moved you, that moment when it changed your life. Play us an excerpt of the music, so we can more fundamentally appreciate that moment. When you tell your story, consider when and how you will introduce the music. How will you set up the story in such a way that when you play the music, and we hear the music, we will have something like the same experience you had when you first encountered the music?
2. Tell us about your music aesthetic. How do you perceive music through your senses? Tell us about what kinds of music you like, and see if you can look deep into your life to help us understand why you are attracted to this music. Find a way to help us connect to this music in the same way you do. Then play an amazing example of this music for us to experience.

Note

1 See David Collison's outstanding book for a detailed and delightful history of sound in the theatre: Collison, David. *The Sound of Theatre.* 2008. Eastbourne, UK: Professional Light and Sound Association.

Bibliography

Howard, Ed. 2003. "Pink Floyd-Ummagumma." September 1. Accessed January 15, 2016. www.stylusmagazine.com/articles/on_second_thought/pink-floyd-ummagumma.htm.

Oxforddictionaries.com. 2016. "Aesthetic." Oxford University Press. Accessed January 15, 2016. www.oxforddictionaries.com/definition/learner/aesthetic.

Pino, Joe, interview by Rick Thomas. 2017. *Personal Interview*, March 9.

Plato. 2009. "Phaedrus, by Plato." The Internet Classics Archive. Accessed December 31, 2016. http://classics.mit.edu/Plato/phaedrus.html.

Stockdale, Joe. 2009. *A Couple of Thoughts from Joe*, August 17.

Thaut, Michael H. 2005. *Rhythm, Music, and the Brain.* New York: Routledge Taylor & Francis Group.

Whitney, W.D. 1890. "Translation of the Katha-Upanishad." *Transactions of the American Philogical Association* 21: 88–112.

Williams, David M. 2007. "Centennial Curtain Call: Celebrating 100 Years of Purdue Theatre." *Liberal Arts Magazine* Fall: 12–16.

PART I

THE NATURE OF TIME

■■■■

CHAPTER 2

LET THERE BE A BIG BANG

Introduction: If a Tree Falls in the Universe . . .

About 13.7 billion years ago, the universe exploded into existence with the Big Bang. As far as we know, there was very little music and theatre at that particular moment. There is quite a bit of controversy about what came before the Big Bang. One line of thought says, "nothing," which is hard to wrap our brains around. But we do call it the "dawn of time." Before the Big Bang, there was no time. There was no matter. Or if there was something, it is irrelevant, because it cannot possibly have any effect on the present moment. This monumental event set into motion everything that came after it, not from a deterministic point of view in which every future moment is inevitable, but from the vantage point that all the rules of the universe, including how sound and music work, proceed from this singularity, this singular moment in time.

Now, the Bible also says in Genesis 1:3, "And God said, let there be light: and there was light." Notwithstanding that the surrounding verses paint a decidedly different picture of creation, the Bible has a good point. The Big Bang must have been quite a spectacular burst of light, but could it have made a sound? In my very first Introduction to Sound Design class in the spring of 1977, I offered two distinct definitions of the word "sound." I got the first out of David Collison's 1976 book, *Stage Sound*. At the time, it was really the only book devoted to sound for the theatre outside of Harold Burris-Meyer's 1959 book, *Sound in the Theatre* (Burris-Meyer 1959). Collison's definition states: "sound is essentially the movement of air in the form of pressure waves radiating from the source at a speed of about 1,130 feet (350 meters) per second" (Collison 1976, 10). The second definition came from Howard Tremaine's *Audio Cyclopedia*: (sound) "is a wave motion propagated in an elastic medium, traveling in both transverse and longitudinal directions, producing an auditory sensation in the ear by the change of pressure at the ear" (Tremaine 1969, 11). Besides the obvious difference in technical specificity between the two definitions, I couldn't help but notice a critically important distinction: one definition insisted that it's not a sound if no one hears it; the other, not so much. A light bulb went off, as I realized that the answer to the age-old question about whether a tree falling in the woods makes a sound if there is no one around to hear it, depends on how you define sound! Even in my first classes, I became aware of how important definitions were in making your case. This may sound like a small thing now, but we will return to the importance of it in Chapter 4 when we define music, and in Chapter 12, as we bring together many of the ideas of this book into a hopefully consistently argued and well-supported thesis about the origins of theatre in music.

Leaving aside the "if a tree falls in the woods, and no one is around to hear it, does it make a sound?" cocktail party chestnut, we are still left to deal with any definition of sound that describes it as a vibration that propagates through a medium, such as air. While the singularity that produced the Big Bang was infinitely dense, the next moment and all the subsequent moments produced a lot of empty space. And sound doesn't travel in a vacuum. So, it's pretty debatable how big a "bang" there actually was. As a pragmatic reality, while the potential for sound existed throughout the universe since the dawn of time, it would not be until about 9 billion years later when the earth formed that sound would begin to have a practical significance.

Now this might seem like nit-picking, but in actuality it reveals an incredibly significant difference between light and sound that has tremendous implications for this book and for the art we create. Light and sound provide two of the most important stimuli to our senses that help us apprehend the external world. In theatre, they are almost solely responsible for providing the sensory input that informs our aesthetic. If we consider theatre to be an art form in which we seek to divine the great secrets of the universe, then we must accept that we will be doing this primarily through these two senses. Before we can understand how we use these senses in the creation, mediation and experience of theatre, it will help tremendously to first understand a bit more about them and how they reveal our universe to us.

In this chapter, we will investigate the fundamental differences between light and sound and how evolution advanced so that we could perceive them. We will see how light transmits through electromagnetic waves that are perceived by the eye as primarily spatial and secondarily temporal, and how sound transmits through mechanical waves that are perceived by the ear as primarily temporal and secondarily spatial. Understanding these differences is essential to understanding the role that time and music play in theatre. We will investigate that role in later chapters.

The Nature of Light and Sound

When I first started teaching about sound design back in the mid-1970s, there was great pressure to think, and therefore teach, about sound like it was visual design, for example, scenery, costumes and lights. Sound as a design element, when anyone considered it at all, was thought of as "the fourth design element," similar to the other three. My job quickly became to provide lectures on sound design in introductory scenography classes based on this premise.

In one of the beginning scenography classes, taught by my major professor, Van Phillips, and legendary Broadway lighting designer, Lee Watson, we investigated fundamental elements of visual design: line, color, mass, rhythm, space and texture. It wasn't a far leap for me to find strong equivalents of these elements in sound. I liked the process Van and Lee used, and developed my own course based on their class. I've been developing these ideas ever since, and they not only serve as the foundation for this book, but also my workshops and class projects based on this book. I am indebted to them both for planting the seed that would later become my life's work.

Finding a common language to talk about both visual design and sound design seemed surprisingly easy. Much later in life I would discover why. Sound and light provide our senses with clues to the nature of the universe in the form of waves that emanate from matter in that universe. These waves might come from a distant star, or that molten eruption on our forming earth. Waves are vibrations that transfer energy from one place to another. There are two relevant media that transmit waves: space and mass. Generally speaking, light waves are electromagnetic vibrations that transmit through space, and sound waves are mechanical vibrations that transmit through mass. In order for us to know anything about the universe that surrounds us, we'll have to take in energy that has been transmitted to us through space and mass.

Waves transmitted through space and mass share a great number of similarities. They have wavelengths and frequencies that are determined by the speed with which they travel through the medium. They share properties of *reflection* (the angle of incidence equals the angle of reflection), *diffraction* (the ability to bend around objects), *absorption* (typically turning the energy into heat, like your microwave), *transmission* (going right through an object) and *Doppler shift* (a phenomenon in which the received frequency changes from the source frequency because either the source or the receiver or both are moving). So, from the vantage point that sound and light are both wave transmissions that share similar properties, it makes perfect sense that we would want to consider sound design as similar to our visual design counterpoints, scenery, costumes and lights. I suspect, however, that in my beginning scenography classes and the larger theatre in general, this was more of a marriage of convenience than a matter of scientific inquiry.

But the waves that travel through space and those that travel through mass also have significant differences. In an effort to separate the differences between sound and light, I developed the practice of starting each guest lecture by writing Einstein's famous equation, $E = mc^2$ on the chalkboard. "This is also how theatre works," I would say; "dramatic energy is equal to mass put into motion by 'c' which is space and time, light and sound." I really knew nothing about Einstein's theories, but for some reason, the equation seemed to fit. Only much later would I realize the significance of this statement, and much of this book will lay out the argument for including this concept in one's aesthetic.

Electromagnetic waves that travel through space, such as light, transmit themselves using the massless photon which streams from the source to the receiver. This type of transmission allows electromagnetic waves to travel at the fastest speeds possible in our universe, 186,300 miles per second.[1] This lack of mass allows photons to oscillate at superfast frequencies—311,000 to 737,000 gigacycles per second for light, with wavelengths of 16–38 millionths of an inch. The tiny wavelengths of a light wave typically reflect in all directions when they encounter an object, which is responsible for making objects visible from many directions simultaneously. But those same tiny wavelengths only travel in a straight line, meaning that the receiver must be pointed at the source of the light in order to perceive the streaming mass of photons. This does have its advantages, however: it allows the receiver to precisely determine the direction of the incoming source of light. Light is very well-suited to reveal the spatial characteristics of mass. Why? Because light involves extremely fast vibrations that can convey a tremendous amount of information about the spatial characteristics of a source, especially direction and shape.

Mechanical waves that travel through mass, such as sound, work quite the opposite of the fast oscillations of light. They are much closer to the sense of touch, which requires direct contact between the source and the receiver. Mechanical

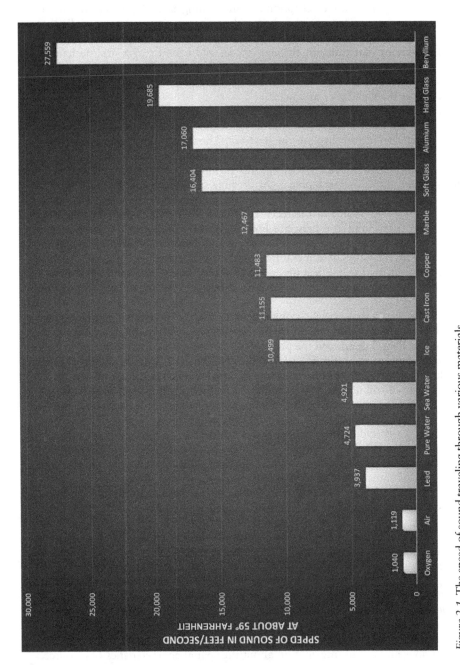

Figure 2.1 The speed of sound traveling through various materials.

Credit: Davis, Don. Carolyn Davis. 1987. *Sound System Engineering.* Indianapolis: Howard W. Sams. 149.

waves generated by the source vibrate the molecules of their neighbors in all directions, and these molecules vibrate their neighbor, and so on, continuing in this fashion until they are absorbed, or the wave has reached the receiver, and, in turn, vibrates the receiver. This type of transmission takes a lot more time to happen than for light. Sound transmits much, much slower than light, about 1,130 feet (344 meters) per second in air.

The types of vibrations that can be transmitted through mass work best at very low frequencies, less than 20,000 vibrations per second for sound, and have wavelengths as long as 50 feet! As frequency increases, the mass medium itself absorbs more and more, often turning the wave into heat before it effectively reaches the receiver. Mechanical waves transmit best at short distances, much closer to the zero-distance requirement for touch.

Sound waves that travel through mass constantly change perceptibly over time. The wavelengths that reflect off of objects do not provide detailed spatial characteristics about the source itself. The mass through which sound transmits also degrades the ability of the sound wave to provide detailed information about the spatial characteristics of the source. Unlike light, sound sources emit waves over a wide spherical area, especially at lower frequencies; the receiver does not need to be oriented in any particular direction in order to receive information from the source. This "omnidirectionality" tends to compromise the receiver's ability to localize to the specific direction of the source, especially at low frequencies. Sound does provide the receiver with amplitude information that varies in time in an analogous manner to the way the source vibrated, but at a later time than the source because the vibrations are traveling at substantially less than the speed of light. Sound waves provide less detailed information regarding the spatial characteristics of the source, but very detailed temporal information.[2] Therefore, sound waves are very well-suited to revealing the temporal properties of mass, that is, how mass vibrates in time.

In this way, electromagnetic vibrations such as light complement the mechanical vibrations such as sound in such a way as to provide a more detailed picture of four primary dimensions of our universe than either one does individually. Potsdam is either 40 kilometers or 30 minutes from Berlin; if you know both, you know more about the journey to Potsdam than if you only know one. Scientists use the speed of light, 186,300 miles per second, to determine the precise length of a meter. They first developed our concepts of time (hours, minutes and seconds of a day) based on the spatial position of the sun in the sky (ibn-Ahmad al-Bīrūnī 1879, 148). We understand then, that light reveals space by defining it relative to time, and sound reveals time by defining it relative to space[3] (Thomas 2010; Landau 2001).

Consider how magnificently light and sound complement each other and how important they have been to our survival. Our 4-billion-year-old earth must have had its share of spectacular storms producing lightning and thunder. While the photons emitted from the lightning flash provided very specific information about the spatial direction of the lightning, the time it took for the sound to travel to the receiver would also provide important information about how imminent the danger was. From an evolutionary vantage point, it would certainly make sense for organisms to develop an ability to perceive both electromagnetic waves that transmit through space and mechanical waves that transmit through mass. Organisms that did this would stand a much better chance of surviving.

The Evolution of Hearing and Seeing

It would take another half billion years or so before life would begin to appear on earth, about 4 billion years ago. Scientists are pretty sure that these organisms didn't sing, dance, play music or go to the theatre, being single-celled creatures. But they did develop a rudimentary nervous system, that is, the ability to sense vibrations from the outside world. The prokaryote, one of the earliest forms of life, evolved in the oceans of the earth. It had mechanoreceptor cells that sensed motion, mechanical vibrations that varied over time (Fritzsch and Beisel 2001, 712).

Notice the ultra-primitive connection to sound? Eventually single-celled organisms evolved into multicelled organs, and then groups of these cells started to specialize, resulting in multi-organ creatures like jellyfish, perhaps the oldest multi-organ animal on earth dating back 600–700 million years ago (Angier 2011).

These organisms also developed the ability to perceive a small frequency band of the electromagnetic spectrum that penetrated water, what we now call visible light. Early eyes were only able to tell light from dark, but that was enough to develop a sense of direction based on where the light was. Perception of time via these primitive eyes was pretty much limited to circadian rhythms, the slowly changing 24-hour light transmissions of the moon and stars at night and the sun during the day. At this earliest stage of evolution in the animal kingdom,

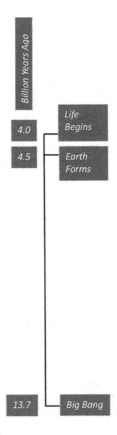

Figure 2.2 Origins of earth timeline.

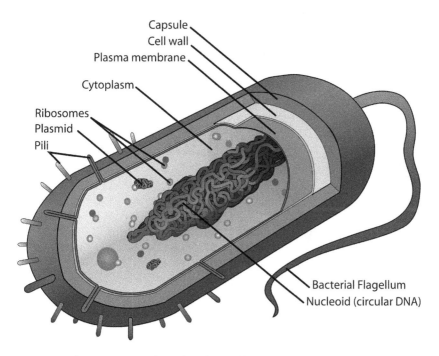

Capsule
Cell wall
Plasma membrane
Cytoplasm
Ribosomes
Plasmid
Pili
Bacterial Flagellum
Nucleoid (circular DNA)

Figure 2.3 Prokaryote, one of the earliest form of life.

Credit: Illustration by LadyofHats.

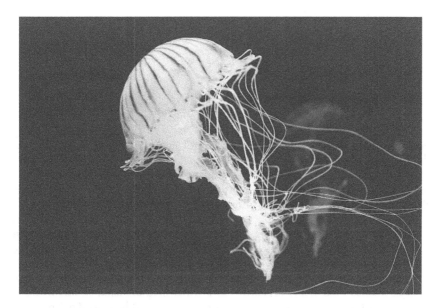

Figure 2.4 Jellyfish.

Credit: Photo via Visualhunt.

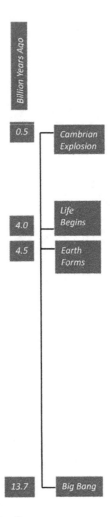

Figure 2.5 Cambrian explosion timeline.

electromagnetic waves provided spatial information (light from above) that allowed animals to perceive time (circadian rhythms), while mechanical waves provided temporal information (low frequency waves) that allowed animals to perceive space (e.g., the boundaries of their environment). Again notice the complementary relationship between primitive perception of time and space.

Another significant development during this early period that would affect how we perceive the world was evolution's symmetrical approach to developing organisms that would eventually result in two eyes, two ears and two halves of the brain (among many other features) (Martindale and Henry 1998). Two eyes provide either the advantage of increased depth perception when located at the front of the head like many predators, or a wider field of vision when located on each side of the head like many prey. Two ears seem to have evolved primarily to allow creatures to discern temporal differences that helped localize a sound source. At first the brain appeared as a cluster of neurons near the ears and eyes, but it too would evolve two symmetrical sections (New Scientist 2011). Those two symmetrical halves of the brain will play an important role later in this book.

About 500 million years ago there was a sudden, tremendous spate of evolutionary development called the Cambrian Explosion, sometimes referred to as the "Big Bang" of evolution. Evolutionary biologists argue that the catalyst for this was the sudden evolution of eyes that were able to perceive space much better—direction more precisely, shapes more clearly, and color, especially reflections in the blue-green wavelengths of light that transmit through water, more diversely. This all happened in the relatively short time span of about 1 million years, and was a huge game changer, resulting in the sudden explosion of *phyla*. Phyla is the term scientists use to describe the broadest categorization of animals. Most of the 37 phyla that exist today evolved in this preciously short time period.

One extraordinary characteristic common to some lucky creatures in the 37 phyla was the unique ability to synchronize pulses together rhythmically. Rhythmic movement is commonplace in the animal kingdom; how would animals move through their environment without it? But two animals synchronizing their movements with each other is much rarer; it requires that each animal perceive the intervals between beats in such a way as to be able to predict where the next beat will occur. A number of insects have figured this out; for example, a group of fiddler crabs looking for love have figured out that they are more likely to attract females if they all sound together in joint repetitive signaling, thus amplifying their sound in what is called the beacon effect. Ditto for North American meadow crickets. Once females join the group, then the males start competing for their favor. Smart male insects adjust their timing so that their signal occurs just slightly before other males. The females will orient toward the male that signals first, or plays "ahead of the beat" (Merker, Madison and Eckerdal 2009, 5).[4] Ants, crickets, frogs and fireflies all seem to have evolved with this common ability to synchronize their sound or light (in the case of fireflies) to each other. Hard to imagine that this ability to synchronize to a beat—the same ability some of us display so marvelously on the dance floor—is found in many other species in the animal kingdom. But it does tell us something about how important the ability of animals to "organize time" is in the animal kingdom. We'll explore the human version of this phenomenon, called entrainment, more in Chapters 5 and 6, but it's worth pointing out now that its basis may lie in our most distant past, over 500 million years ago.

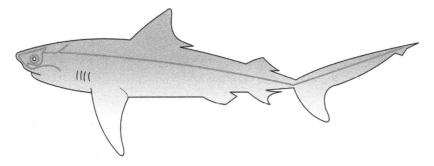

Figure 2.6 Fish with lateral line.

Credit: Illustration by Chris Huh.

Our particular branch of evolution descends from the phylum chordata, the subphylum of which is *vertebrata*, or vertebrates, that include our human predecessors: boney fish (Parker 2011). The ability of these fish to sense mechanical vibrations continued on a much more linear course than the evolution of eyes. The mechanoreceptors responsible for sensing external vibrations developed into the *lateral line*.

The lateral line is an organ containing hair cells that run lengthwise down each side of the fish, allowing the fish to detect movement, that is, vibrations in time (DOSITS 2016). The lateral line only sensed vibrations lower than 160–200 Hz (think bass; fish would love hip hop!), but only at a distance of a couple of body lengths. It allowed fish to sense other creatures nearby and perhaps any atmospheric disturbances that made their way through the water. Not much by human standards, but one could imagine these two primitive senses proved very

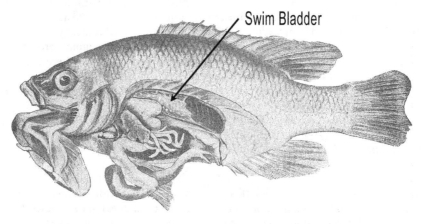

Figure 2.7 Swim bladder.

Credit: University of Washington Freshwater and Marine Image Bank.

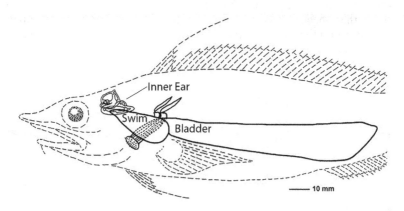

Figure 2.8 Fish inner ear.

Credit: Reprinted from *Deep Sea Research* Part I: *Oceanographic Research Papers*, Vol 58, Issue 1, Xiaohong Deng, Hans-Joachim Wagner, Arthur N. Popper "The Inner Ear and Its Coupling to the Swim Bladder in the Deep-Sea Fish Antimora Rostrata (Teleostei: Moridae)," 27–37, Copyright 2011 with permission from Elsevier.

useful in helping a fish pursue its single most critical need (finding food) and avoid its single most critical mistake (becoming food).

In fish, we again see a distinct difference in how early creatures perceived time and space. Fish eyes sensed space as the simultaneous reflections of light on an infinite number of objects upon which the fish must focus its eyes one at a time in space to perceive something. Its lateral line, however, perceived space as time, a disturbance that occurred suddenly, probably did not last long, and ended just as quickly. Certainly, the eyes became the most useful organ to perceive space after the Big Bang of the Cambrian Explosion. Cambrian eyes provided animals a much better ability to perceive space than the lateral line. The lateral line could only provide spatial information about the general direction and size of a wave, but very little information about the object itself, in a "who made that sound?" sort of way.

Still, the ability of the lateral line to perceive temporal relationships between objects in space had its uses. Since light waves travel in a straight line, fish eyes evolved to focus in a particular direction; a lateral line could prove very useful in alerting about a potential predator in a different direction than where the eyes were focused (e.g., from behind). Eyes were somewhat useless once the sun went down, or if the water was murky, but fish sensed mechanical vibrations in the water 24/7 and regardless of how murky the water was (Butler and Hodos 2005, 194). So there were good reasons for the lateral line to continue to evolve. Still, mechanisms for sensing mechanical vibrations evolved slowly; if eye evolution was to be the hare of the Cambrian Explosion, ear evolution would certainly be the tortoise (Parker 2011, 328).

Some fish evolved a swim bladder that literally provided them with buoyancy, the ability to stay afloat in the water.

It turns out that the swim bladder was also very receptive to mechanical vibrations (Jourdain 1997, 9). Eventually fish evolved an *inner ear* around the same time as the lateral line, some arguing that the inner ear evolved from the lateral line, some arguing that they both evolved from a common ancestral structure (Popper, Platt and Edds 1992). The inner ear had similar hair cells to those of the lateral line that allowed fish to sense somewhat higher frequencies, but still less than about 1,000 Hz, not exactly what we would call high-fidelity.

But if the swim bladder was located close to the inner ear, higher frequency reception improved, as the bones of the fish conducted the vibrations of the swim bladder to the inner ear. This increased frequency resolution would provide greater information about the organisms generating the sound waves.

Because water has about the same density as fish bodies, sound passes right through the fish's body and into its inner ear (DOSITS 2016). That was all well and good, but about 365 million years ago, fish started wandering out of the water and onto dry land. Now, there were problems because the mechanical vibrations were in air, and vibrations don't like to change densities when going from one medium (air) to another (the animal's body). These *tetrapods*, as they were called (literally "four feet") needed to adapt their hearing apparatus to accommodate this change of density—at least the ones that wanted to survive!

To help out, a single bone from the jaw of the earliest tetrapods migrated to become attached to the inner ear (Clack 1994). This bone, which we would eventually refer to as the *stapes*, better matched the impedance (resistance to vibrations) between the air and the fluids of the inner ear.

About 200–250 million years ago, some tetrapods developed an eardrum, a thin vibrating layer of tissue that connected the outside air to the stapes (Manley

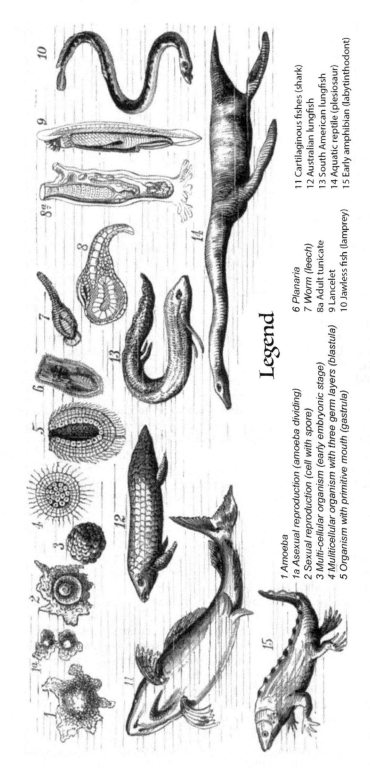

Figure 2.9 Evolution of tetrapods, from *The Modern Theory of the Descent of Man* by Ernst Haeckel, 1874.

Credit: Haeckel, Ernst. 1876. "Haeckel on the Human Pedigree." *Scientific American* 34 (11): 167. Adapted by Richard K. Thomas

Legend

1 Amoeba
1a Asexual reproduction (amoeba dividing)
2 Sexual reproduction (cell with spore)
3 Multi-cellular organism (early embryonic stage)
4 Multicellular organism with three germ layers (blastula)
5 Organism with primitive mouth (gastrula)

6 Planaria
7 Worm (leech)
8a Adult tunicate
9 Lancelet
10 Jawless fish (lamprey)

11 Cartilaginous fishes (shark)
12 Australian lungfish
13 South American lungfish
14 Aquatic reptile (plesiosaur)
15 Early amphibian (labytinthodont)

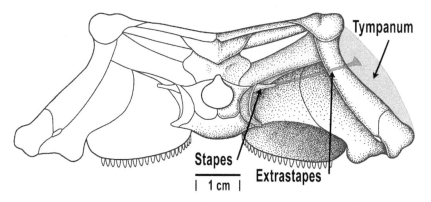

Figure 2.10 Müller and Tsuji investigated a transitional "terrestrial parareptile" *Macro-leter poezicus*, from about 250 million years ago. Their reconstruction draw-ing, viewed from the back and lower part of the skull (occipital view), shows a stapes connected to a tympanum.

Credit: Müller J., Tsuji L.A. 2007. "Impedance-Matching Hearing in Paleozoic Reptiles: Evi-dence of Advanced Sensory Perception at an Early Stage of Amniote Evolution." *PLOS ONE* 2 (9): e889. Accessed July 20, 2017. https://doi.org/10.1371/journal.pone.0000889. Adapted by Richard K. Thomas CC-BY-2.5. https://creativecommons.org/licenses/by/2.5/deed.en. Adapted by Richard K. Thomas.

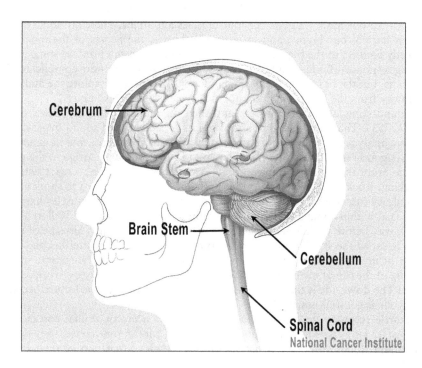

Figure 2.11 The major parts of the brain.

Credit: From the National Cancer Institute, Alan Hoofring, Illustrator. Adapted by Richard K. Thomas.

and Köppl 1998). Now when the eardrum vibrated, the stapes vibrated, and that, in turn, vibrated the inner ear. Slowly evolving in this inner ear was the *basilar membrane*, the part of the inner ear that transduces the mechanical vibrations of sound into the electrical pulses of neurons. The basilar membrane is a long structure that tends to vibrate in different parts depending on which frequencies are exciting it via the middle ear bones (see Figure 7.10 for a drawing of the human version). The hair cells along the basilar membrane vibrate in turn and generate electrical impulses that correlate to the original source wave, with different frequencies stimulating different parts of the stiff, resonant structure. Tetrapods with eardrums and more highly evolved inner ears could sense temporal changes such as frequency and envelope (how a sound unfolds in time) much better on land than animals without one.

The Evolution of the Brain Leads to the Ability to Express Emotions

As tetrapods evolved, their brains grew in size and complexity. The tetrapod brain had long ago acquired its *brainstem* and *cerebellum*. The brainstem sits at the top of our *spinal cord*, the cerebellum right behind it.

The brainstem provides the nerve impulses back and forth between the body and the brain. It plays a central role in our most biologically fundamental functions such as breathing, heart rate, sleeping and eating. Within the brainstem are mechanisms for reflexive actions, all things we tend to do more or less unconsciously. The cerebellum, on the other hand, plays a major role in motor control, the part of our brain that controls our muscles and limbs. These are some of the oldest part of our brains, and in most vertebrates, the nerves of the inner ear directly connect to the brainstem and cerebellum, which can produce some interesting responses (Butler and Hodos 2005, 197). It gets a lot more complicated in humans, but the basic results are similar. Don't worry; we'll explore the auditory pathway from the ear to the brain in much greater detail in Chapter 7.

Sound stimulates the brainstem and then our muscles directly (Davis et al. 1982, 791). That's a hugely important point. A sudden loud sound bypasses all of our analytical circuits, and immediately triggers a reflexive muscle reaction. Makes good sense, doesn't it? A sudden loud sound shouldn't just go to the parts of the brain that analyze things, because sometimes you have to react without thinking. Rock falling—yikes! At that basic level, we can't afford to think about sound; we just react. Fortunately, the transmission from ear to muscles happens very fast, within about 14–40 milliseconds in humans (Parham and Willott 1990, 831), way before we have a chance to stop and think about it. This type of reaction is called the startle response or startle reflex. To demonstrate this phenomenon in my lectures, I will typically just randomly shout out sometime in my lecture at the top of my lungs, "HEY!" Everybody jumps of course—works every time! The downside is that it can be a bit hard to get back to the lecture because everyone is so, well, startled!

Startle response doesn't have a lot to do with what an animal consciously thinks. As far as we know, tetrapods didn't spend a lot of time consciously thinking about things anyway, not having evolved much of that part of their brain. Startle response happens without conscious effort; it's reflexive. Francis Crick, co-discoverer of DNA's structure, postulated that the reason our hearing would evolve with this "bypass" mechanism is strictly "fight or flight." In primitive worlds, stopping to think could cost you your life! In our modern minds, we most likely are simply "startled," hence the name for the phenomenon, the "startle" response (Crick 1994; Levitin 2007, 183). In our modern brains, we typically react physically, and then our thinking brain takes over and lets us know that we are not in any real danger. Primitive creatures don't have much of a thinking brain; they just react.

Related to the startle response is another effect called *habituation*. Habituation means if I just go HEY! HEY! HEY! HEY! . . ., you very quickly don't jump anymore because you've gotten used to the sound. Habituation is a condition in which we subconsciously learn to ignore sounds that persist and don't change. Even the simplest organisms experience habituation (Wood 1988). Basically, habituation occurs because the more you stimulate auditory neurons, the less they respond (Jourdain 1997, 54). They don't need to; the brain already knows the sound is there and it's not changing. Primitive animals needed to separate threatening sounds from all of the other constant sounds around them. Habituation accomplishes this, allowing animals to ignore sounds that don't change (like crickets at night) from sounds that do change (like the twig snapped by an approaching predator).

Without habituation and startle, there would probably be no horror movies. If you introduce the underscore in the appropriate place, and it doesn't draw too much attention to itself, then the audience will forget it's there. Then when the creature jumps out of the closet, we startle the audience with a very loud sonic punctuation. I mean, who among us has never used a sustained droning tone to habituate an audience, and followed up with a good startle effect?!! These really are the oldest tricks in the book—hundreds of millions of years old!

Of course, there would be no point in introducing underscore unless we had a purpose for it beyond making the audience forget it's there. To understand more about what we can do with habituation, we'll have to explore another amazing evolutionary development that occurred during the Cambrian Explosion.

When fish first wandered out of the water and onto dry land, they faced a new problem: how to breathe on dry land! To venture out on land, they needed organs that would allow them to directly breathe air: lungs. They also needed to develop a mechanism that would prevent water from entering those newly evolved lungs when they went back into the water. Lungfish evolved about 380 million years ago with just such a mechanism (Allen, Midgley and Allen 2002, 54–55).

A very simple sphincter-type muscle prevented water from entering the lungs. That muscle could also vibrate and produce sound when the lungfish exhaled (Fitch 2010, 222–224). Of course, this didn't necessarily mean that they immediately started singing Wagnerian operas. Imagine the sound you get when you pull the

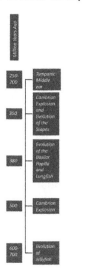

Figure 2.12 Hearing and vocal evolution timeline.

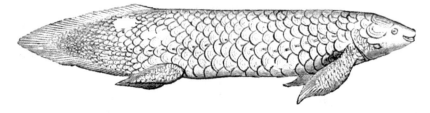

Figure 2.13 Australian lungfish.

Credit: From Günther, Albert. 1888. *Guide to the Galleries of Reptiles and Fishes in the Department of Zoology of the British Museum (Natural History)*. London: Taylor and Francis 98.

opening of an air-filled balloon tight, and allow air to squeak through as the opening vibrates against itself. Not the best form of vocalizing, but without some sort of sphincter-type muscle that would evolve into the larynx, there would never be a *Hello Dolly!* or *Hamilton*.

Perhaps as a consequence of wandering out onto land, perhaps as an enhancement that enabled wandering out onto land, tetrapods found themselves with a most unusual ability: the ability to communicate with each other by manipulating sound waves in time. Such an ability to communicate with one's own kind would be a very favorable evolutionary adaptation! Imagine an early tetrapod bleating out into the distance: "Anybody out there?" Now another tetrapod, who had also wandered out onto dry land, takes a quick look around, but does not readily see the first tetrapod. Streaming photons are like that. They reflect off trees and fauna that hide what is behind, whereas sound waves travel right through or bend around. Sound waves can be hard to stop! So, the second tetrapod hears the sound wave vibration and uses the somewhat limited ability provided by its two ears to localize to the direction of the sound: "Over here!" it calls back. To which the first tetrapod croaks "Where?" "Here!" calls the second. This goes on for quite some time until one of the tetrapods uses its superior visual acuity to identify the other. And then they get a hotel room and make beautiful music together, if you know what I mean.

Calling out in a lovesick lament must surely have been one of the earliest examples of animals communicating with each other. Mating is pretty important in survival of the fittest. Expressing anger was probably another. Tetrapods expressed emotion? Yes, yet another of the evolutionary miracles of the Cambrian explosion was the development of the *amygdala*.

The amygdala is the part of our brain responsible for processing emotions, making decisions about them, and storing and retrieving them in our emotional memory. It is a key part of a larger system, called the *limbic system* (see Figure 5.9). The limbic system is involved in emotions and memory, perhaps the two most important brain functions we encounter in sound design and music composition, so we'll be revisiting this area a lot throughout the book. In humans, the nerves from the auditory system connect directly to the amygdala through the brainstem and the thalamus (the primitive part of our brain responsible for routing signals from our senses). The amygdala has been around since the tetrapods. This means that we are entirely capable of emotionally reacting to an auditory stimulus without ever even consciously thinking about it (Robson 2011; Di Marino, Etienne and Niddam 2016, 91–95)!

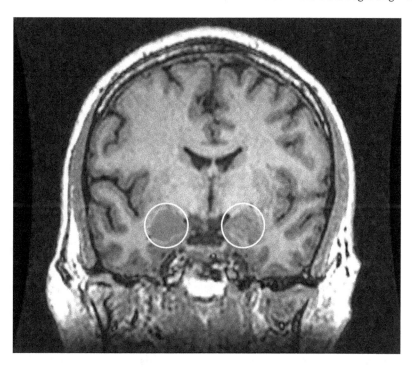

Figure 2.14 MRI coronal view of the amygdala in the human brain.

Credit: Amber Rieder, Jenna Traynor, Geoffrey B Hall.

The amygdala, two small almond-shaped groups of nuclei right next to the brainstem and cerebellum, have a profound significance for us in theatre. Darwin was perhaps the first to propose that even the most primitive creatures were capable of feeling and expressing emotion (Darwin 1904, 106). We can surmise, of course, that like everything else about these prehistoric creatures, the range of emotions and expressions must have been decidedly limited. Anyone who has sat in a traffic jam and attempted to communicate with the car in front using just their horn probably understands the dilemma of our primitive lungfish. Nevertheless, we can see in some of these creatures an ability to manipulate pitch, amplitude and time to express emotion. Even in the most primitive creatures on earth, we witness the manipulation of elements we associate with music: pitch, amplitude and duration. This is significant because these elements are not evidence of the use of symbols like we use in language. They are evidence of the use of musical elements that we use to express emotions and incite them in others, existing predominantly in the temporal domain.

Think about how we use the amygdala to process emotions and emotional memory in theatre. First, we play music, which stimulates the amygdala directly, contributing to the rising of an emotion in the listener. Then we create a "theme" out of that music and reuse it when we want to recall emotions. We play the music again in another section of the play, perhaps as a variation, and all of a sudden, we take people emotionally back to where they were the last time they heard the music. The audience associates, consciously or not, what was now happening with what happened before. This is much more than telling the audience, "Oh yeah, remember that?" We want the audience to recall and re-experience the emotions again, and attach them to the new scene to possibly create an even more complex emotional response based on both what happened in the current scene and how it relates to a specific musical memory. This is a hugely important technique in theatre, and its basis lies in our old friend, the amygdala, which has been around since the tetrapods. We'll explore it more in Chapter 10.

Now consider the power that we humans have when we combine habituation and startle with the ability to incite emotions and to effect recollections of them with the amygdala. Underscoring suddenly has a purpose. Now instead of simply habituating the audience in the horror movie, we can both habituate them, and simultaneously make them feel very uneasy before we smack them with that startle effect. And the next time the monster appears, we can repeat the habituating underscore to quickly transport the audience back emotionally to the last time it happened—and that, as they will emotionally recall, was not good!

We must be careful when and where we introduce underscoring, because it will initially not habituate and will draw attention to itself. I've had many directors ask me to just "sneak it in under the dialogue," but I find all too often, this just means that the change in sound distracts different audience members at different points in the action; we relinquish control over how we stimulate the audience. We typically start an underscore in its own acting beat, for example, during a pause between spoken lines. We will also work very hard to localize the underscore to where the eyes are already focused: the dramatic scene. If we localize to another space, above the proscenium, or on the side of the proscenium, for example, our audience will momentarily reflexively focus their attention to source of the sound. It's a reflex that's very hard to stop, and it's one of the reasons why a lot of underscoring is so distracting before it ever really gets a chance to work in a scene.

Once we've established the underscore, we work hard to immediately habituate our audience by carefully controlling the amount of variation in the music that could draw attention to itself. We tend to use droning sounds and musical keyboard "pads" in our underscores because they evolve slowly and don't call attention to themselves, and yet, still have powerful abilities to stimulate emotions. As a matter of fact, they work so well that we'll discuss them more in Chapter 8. We are careful about how we move underscore sound around in space, because spatial changes draw attention. When we add a new stimulus to the habituated sound we run the risk of *dishabituating* (yes that really is a word, it simply means to add a sound to or change a habituated sound in a way that causes the original sound to be consciously heard again!). We're careful about using melody in underscoring because it really has a tendency to draw attention to itself. I'll often advise students that they must consider the actors' vocalizations as being the main melodies they are orchestrating. Don't fight actors' melodies with your own melodies; habituate under them. If you can do that successfully, you open up a whole world for yourself in terms of manipulating the audience's emotions, first in the simple emotional stimulus you provide with the underscoring, and then in your ability to recall strong prior emotions by attaching new actions to them in scenes. All of this without the audience becoming too consciously aware of how or when it is being done, thanks to habituation. Harold Burris-Meyer, one of the pioneering fathers of modern theatre sound, was fond of saying, "you can shut your eyes, but the sound comes out to get you!"

In a larger sense, we must realize that habituation and startle are somewhat extreme examples of our ability to subtly use sound to manipulate the audience's focus in time, in the same way we might use lighting to manipulate the audience's focus in space. One of the characteristics of habituation is that as the stimulus gets weaker, the onset of habituation comes quicker and is more pronounced. A very loud continuous sound such as a fire alarm will probably produce no habituation at all. A very soft continuous sound like a well-designed ventilation system might never be noticed in the first place (Rankin et al. 2009, 137). In between are wonderful opportunities to manipulate the attention and focus of the audience, subtly drawing their attention to important lines or stage business by introducing small changes in the scoring. A chord change may barely be noticed and habituate quickly, but dramatically change the focus on the stage, or even bring the audience back if they have somehow drifted away. When we consider habituation and startle in this manner, we start to understand the dramatic possibilities we have available to us through careful manipulation of the dynamics of sound scores.

Eyes and Ears, Space and Time

It should not be lost on us that both habituation and startle are phenomenon that primarily happen in the time domain, as does inciting an emotion. Where the startle sound occurs in space won't have as much effect on creating a startle response as when the sound happens. Where the sound and effect happen is a secondary effect—still very important to potential prey once they've been alerted that there may be a problem, but the typical response at that point will be that the potential prey will look around to identify the direction of the disturbance, a primary response for the eyes. As we continue to move up the evolutionary ladder, we will continue to see the differentiation of hearing as primarily a temporal sense and secondarily a spatial sense. Evolution has brilliantly complemented hearing with vision, which is primarily a spatial sense and secondarily a temporal one.

Even in my earliest lectures, I began to understand that the eyes were the dominant sense when perceiving space, and sound the dominant sense when perceiving time. The eyes perceive mass through reflected light in space, the ears perceived mass through changes of air pressure in time. The eyes perceive time as a series of three-dimensional (spatial) images; the ears perceive space as a series of sequential (temporal) pressure variations. When the eyes perceive the reflection of an object, the position of the object in space correlates to a position on the retina of the eye (Jourdain 1997, 20). The ear perceives the position of an object as a temporal difference between the arrival of the sound at the two ears, or delay (typically measured in milliseconds) between the direct sound and the reflected sound in a space.

We see this complementary nature of sight and sound even in our ability to perceive the location of an object. It takes two eyes to perceive depth with some degree of accuracy, because the brain must interpret the slight variations in spatial position of the object on the two retinas. It only takes one ear, because a single ear can judge the closeness of a source by the difference in level between the direct sound coming from the source and the level of the indirect sound of the room (the part of the sound that takes longer to decay, such as the reverb in a cathedral). Conversely, it takes two ears to more accurately locate the direction of a source in the horizontal plane due to temporal differences of the arriving sound at each ear; it only takes one eye to do that because spatial positioning occurs on the retina.

We know about this eye-ear complement intuitively, too. We can take a photo and freeze a moment in time, and then study its spatial characteristics. We cannot freeze a moment of sound in time and examine its spatial characteristics by listening to that moment. We can focus on one video display in a sports bar, because we can focus on one particular stream of photons emanating from different displays in different spaces simultaneously. But if the bartender turns up the volume for every video display, we will have a very hard time understanding just one of the sound sources because the sound sources are all occurring at the same time, and our ears perceive all the simultaneous sounds at once.

We use spatial terms like length, width and depth to describe visual art. But we use temporal terms such as tempo, meter, rhythm, phrasing and duration to describe sound art. Scientists routinely specify light in wave*lengths*, but sound in cycles per *second*. When we want to measure objects we see, we use a tape measure. When we want to measure objects we hear, we use a stopwatch. Consider the old saying, "a picture is worth a thousand words." Yes, but how long does it take to say a thousand words?

The bottom line? The eyes have it when perceiving space. But when it comes to having a keen perception of time, as we shall see throughout this book, the ears excel.

Not exclusively, just dominantly. Obviously, the eyes can perceive temporal relationships, and the ear, spatial relationships. As we have seen throughout this chapter, sound and light function in a complementary fashion, providing a more complete apprehension of four of the dimensions of our universe than either can provide by itself. As we saw in the first part of this chapter, sound and light share many similar properties. It should not surprise us, then, that the eyes and ears evolved to perceive light and sound in many similar ways.

Consider the two types of images offered by John Booth Davies in 1978 (Davies 1978, 104). One is called *takete*, the other *uloomu*. Can you match the correct name with the correct picture? I've done this test with students and with international attendees at my lectures for almost 40 years. Overwhelmingly, participants will call the left one "uloomu" and the right one "takete." It appears

Figure 2.15 Uloomu versus takete.

Credit: Data from Davies, John Booth. 1978. *The Psychology of Music*. Stanford, CA: Stanford University Press 104. Adapted by Richard K. Thomas.

that there is, indeed, a correlation between what the eyes perceive in space and what the ears perceive in time.

This correlation between eyes and ears should come as no surprise. We witnessed a similar correlation between light and sound waves earlier in this chapter, and we should expect that our eyes and ears would evolve to favor perception of light and sound respectively. The eyes perceive color using photoreceptor cells, rods and cones, while the ear perceives color using hair cells on the basilar membrane (although color is localized along specific parts of the basilar membrane, and the color sensing cones of the eye are more or less distributed across the retina).

Both the rods and cones and the basilar membrane can be fatigued by overstimulation, resulting in a temporary inability to perceive overstimulated frequencies. We call the combination of all frequencies "white light" visually and "white noise" audibly. When colors don't go together, we either say they "clash" visually or are "dissonant" sonically. We know that the human brain has an "integration constant" of about 50 milliseconds: delay a reflection of a sound slower than about 50 milliseconds and we'll start to hear an echo in space; slow down the frame rate of the film projector lower than 20 frames per second (i.e., delay the next picture by more than 1/20th of a second, or 50 milliseconds) and we start seeing separate images in time.

Technology often prevented artists from exploring the temporal promises of visual art, but advances in the twentieth century found artists increasingly exploring time in the visual arts. A significant example is Tharon Musser, the famous lighting designer, who became known for her ability to treat light like a "living entity" by moving "light and stage picture in synchronized rhythm with the dialogue of the performance" (Unruh 2006, 59). In other words, she started treating light like music. At the same time, the invention of film finally made the possibility of moving pictures in time a reality, and stage scenery, which had remained relatively static for most of the history of theatre, began to experiment with time in the form of moving projections. In Chapter 4 we'll explore this emergence of the musicality of light in more detail, as we wrestle with the very definition of music.

While the visual designers in theatre work to develop methods of manipulating time that are as facile as manipulating space, we find a similar complementary problem with sound: manipulating space as effortlessly as we manipulate time. The obvious solution to getting the sound to correctly orient to a specific location has always been to simply put a loudspeaker there. But what about trying to recreate the acoustic signature of the space in which the sound originated? Until the late twentieth century, it was impossible to even conceive. Tomlinson Holman famously suggested that it would take about a million loudspeakers to fully reproduce the sound of one space in another (Holman 2001). Modern spatial imaging systems have found ways to reduce that number using similar tricks to those employed in 3D film, but like 3D, they are still tricks. We haven't yet, either for time in visual art or space in sonic art, been able to fully create four dimensions uninhibited by corporeal limitations.

But is a medium that is perfectly fluid in all four dimensions necessary? As we journey through the rest of this book, we will wrestle with the very nature of theatre itself. That struggle hinges on the nature of time. In Einstein's famous equation, $E = mc^2$, we see a definitive statement about the relationship of space and time to mass and energy: c is the ratio of distance (space) to time. Since we now confidently suggest that sight is weighted toward space and sound toward time, we can begin to more seriously consider sound's strong suit: time. As we continue to explore our evolutionary journey in the next chapter, we'll uncover some extraordinary discoveries related to our understanding of time that have had a profound influence on the medium we know that is theatre.

Ten Questions

1. What is the incredibly significant difference between light and sound that has tremendous implications for this book?
2. Describe the fundamental difference between electromagnetic waves and mechanical waves.
3. Light waves are ideally suited to reveal mass _____ in while sound waves are ideally suited to reveal mass in _____?
4. What was the most significant development during the Cambrian Explosion that would change the course of evolution?
5. What is the startle response?
6. What is habituation?
7. What is the amygdala and why is it important?
8. Give an example of how we could use the brainstem, the cerebellum and the amygdala in a sound score for theatre.
9. What are three lessons habituation teaches us about creating effective underscoring?
10. Provide three examples that light also has a temporal component and three examples that sound also has a spatial component.

Things to Share

1. Find a partner. One partner wears a blindfold; the other partner wears earplugs. Make a note about what time it is. Now go out and explore your environment. Make mental notes of the spatial and temporal aspects of what you discover. How do you describe the information your senses are providing you? When you think 15 minutes have elapsed, stop, record the actual time and length of your exploration and then your observations. Now, switch places so that whoever had earplugs now has a blindfold and whoever had a blindfold now has earplugs. Repeat the process. What did you discover about your perception of the passage of time?
2. Find a movie that has won an Academy Award for sound. Pick a movie that you love and wouldn't mind seeing again. Now get hold of the movie (perhaps buy it, because you can use it for other projects in this class, rent it from Netflix, or even check it out from your local library). Watch it with an eye toward habituation and startle, the use of dynamics to create an emotional response in the listener. If you can find some big startle effects, fine. Make a note of the time in the movie where the effect occurs so we can cue it up in class and you can share it with us. But also, feel free to consider subtler uses of habituation and dishabituation, as we discussed in this chapter. Pay careful attention to how the sound artists manipulate changes in the dynamics of the sound score to manipulate emotions in the listener. Be prepared to describe for us how you think the sound team is manipulating us. Bring at least two examples with you in case someone uses your first example.

Notes

1 Although this assertion·is constantly being challenged with new scientific inquiries.
2 Assuming all of that information is transmitted without significant loss in the medium. This is more likely to happen for sound when the source is close to the receiver. Light travels farther without significant distortion; sound is closer to human touch, requiring the source to be closer to the receiver in order to transmit without significant distortion.
3 This is on planet earth, where we'll confine most of our investigation! Once we consider light traveling from distant stars, scientists also use time to measure light in the form of light *years*—a further indication of the complementary relationship between light and sound. More on this complementary relationship later in this chapter.
4 As a side note, this particular effect is called the Haas or Precedence Effect, and we use it all the time in theatre. For example, consider a sound that travels directly from a source to the listener, and a reflection that arrives at the listener a certain amount of time later. According to Ahnert and Steffen, "the ear always localizes first the signal of the source from which the sound waves first arrive" (1999, 53). For humans, when one sound arrives less than about 30–50 milliseconds later, the listener will perceive the spatial location of the sound to be the earlier arriving one. What's even more amazing is that the second sound can actually be almost twice as loud, as the earlier sound (that is, greater than about 10 dB), and we will still localize to the earlier arriving sound. In pop festivals, we delay the sound from the remote loudspeakers covering the rear of the audience to the main loudspeakers on stage so that the sound from the stage arrives first. In theatre, we delay the sound from speakers under the front lip of the stage, the proscenium and balcony loudspeakers to loudspeakers buried on stage, or to the human voices on the stage, to keep the sound score localized to the dramatic action. Curiously, I have found that this technique works well even when the loudspeakers buried on the stage are small: as long as we delay the larger loudspeakers elsewhere in the theatre back to the smaller stage loudspeakers, we tend to localize to the stage. One of the most distracting things a sound designer can do is to localize the sound outside of the dramatic space; we are just naturally trained to focus our attention in the direction of the sound. Of course, we will habituate to this, but every time the habituation breaks down, we will be distracted from the dramatic action on the stage. I can't tell you how many sound designers have perfectly good cues cut from shows because the director was not aware that the reason the cue distracted was localization, not some other characteristic of the sound.

Bibliography

Ahnert, Wolfgang, and Frank Steffen. 1999. *Sound Reinforcement Engineering Fundamentals and Practice*. London: E&FN Spon.

Allen, Gerald R., Stephen Hamar Midgley, and Mark Allen. 2002. *Field Guide to Freshwater Fishes of Australia*. Collingwood, VIC: W. A. Perth.

Angier, Natalie. 2011. "So Much More Than Plasma and Poison." *New York Times* June 6: D1.

Burris-Meyer, Harold. 1959. *Sound in the Theatre*. New York: Radio Magazines.

Butler, Anne B., and William Hodos. 2005. *Comparative Vertebrate Neuroanatomy: Evolution and Adaptation*. 2nd Edition. Hoboken, NJ: Wiley-Interscience.

Clack, J. A. 1994. "Earliest Known Tetrapod Braincase and the Evolution of the Stapes and Fenestra Ovalis." *Nature* 369 (2): 392–394.

Collison, David. 1976. *Stage Sound*. New York: Drama Book Specialists.

Crick, Francis. 1994. *The Astonishing Hypothesis*. New York: Scribner/Maxwell Macmillan.

Darwin, Charles. 1904. *The Expression of the Emotions in Man and Animals*. London: John Murry, Albemarle Steet.

Davies, John Booth. 1978. *The Psychology of Music*. Stanford, CA: Stanford University Press.

Davis, Michael, David S. Gendelman, Marc D. Tischler, and Phillip M. Gendelman. 1982. "A Primary Acoustic Startle Circuit: Lesion and Stimulation Studies." *Society of Neuroscience* 2 (6): 791–805.

Di Marino, Vincent, Yves Etienne, and Maurice Niddam. 2016. *The Amygdaloid Nuclear Complex*. New York: Springer.

DOSITS. 2016. "How Do Fish Hear?" Accessed January 28, 2013. www.dosits.org/animals/soundreception/fishhear/.

Fitch, W. Tecumseh. 2010. *The Evolution of Language*. London: Cambridge University Press.

Fritzsch, B., and K. W. Beisel. 2001. "Evolution of the Nervous System." *Brain Research Bulletin* 55 (6): 711–721.

Holman, Tomlinson. 2001. "Future History." *Surround Professional*, March–April: 58.

Ibn-Ahmad al-Bīrūnī, Muhammad. 1879. *The Chronology of Ancient Nations: An English Version of the Arabic Text of the Athâr-ul-Bâkiya of Albîrûnî, Or "Vestiges of the Past."* London: William H. Allen.

Jourdain, Robert. 1997. *Music, the Brain and Ectasy*. New York: William Morrow.

Landau. 2001. Accessed May 7, 2001. http://Landau1.phys.Virginia.EDU/classes/109/lectures/spec_rel.html.

Levitin, Daniel J. 2007. *This Is Your Brain On Music*. New York: Penguin Group/Plume.

Manley, Gerald A., and Christine Köppl. 1998. "Phylogenetic Development of the Cochlea and Its Innervation." *Current Opinion in Neurobiology* 8 (4): 468–474.

Martindale, Mark Q., and Jonathan Q. Henry. 1998. "The Development of Radial and Biradial Symmetry: The Evolution of Bilaterality." *American Zoologist* 38 (4): 672–684.

Merker, Bjorn H., Guy S. Madison, and Patricia Eckerdal. 2009. "On the Role and Origin of Isochrony in Human Rhythmic Entrainment." *Cortex* 45 (1): 4–17.

New Scientist. 2011. "A Brief History of the Brain." September 21. Accessed January 31, 2016. www.newscientist.com/article/mg21128311-800-a-brief-history-of-the-brain/.

Parham, Kourosh, and James F. Willott. 1990. "Effects of Inferior Colliculus Lesions on the Acoustic Startle Response." *Behavioral Neuroscience* 104 (6): 831–840.

Parker, Andrew R. 2011. "On the Origin of Optics." *Optics & Laser Technology* 43 (2): 323–329.

Popper, Arthur N., Christopher Platt, and Peggy L. Edds. 1992. "Evolution of the Vertebrate Inner Ear: An Overview of Ideas." In *The Evolutionary Biology of Hearing*, edited by Douglas B. Webster, Richard R. Fay, and Arthur N. Popper. New York: Springer-Verlag.

Rankin, Catharine H., Thomas Abrams, Robert J. Barry, Seem Bhatnagar, David F. Clayton, John Colombo, Gianluca Coppola, et al. 2009. "Habituation Revisited: An Updated and Revised Description of the Behavioral Characteristics of Habituation." *Neurobiology of Learning and Memory* 92 (2): 135–138.

Robson, David. 2011. "A Brief History of the Brain." September 24. Accessed January 29, 2015. www.newscientist.com/article/mg21128311-800-a-brief-history-of-the-brain/.

Thomas, Richard. 2010. "The Sounds of Time." In *Sound: A Reader in Theatre Practice*, edited by Ross Brown, 177–187. London: Palgrave Macmillan.

Tremaine, Howard M. 1969. *Audio Cyclopedia*. 2nd Edition. Indianapolis: Howard Sams.

Unruh, Delbert. 2006. *The Designs of Tharon Musser*. Syracuse, NY: Broadway Press.

Wood, David C. 1988. "Habituation in Stentor: Produced by Mechanoreceptor Channel Modification." *Journal of Neuroscience* 8 (7): 2254–2258.

CHAPTER 3

THE GREAT MYSTERY OF TIME

Introduction: Babbling in Babelsberg

In acknowledging that sound is primarily a temporal form of perception, we suddenly find ourselves needing to broach the question, "What is time, anyway?" For most of the history of civilization we were content to consider that time was simply what we measured using seconds, minutes, hours, days, and years. That all changed when Einstein blew up our conventional understanding of the nature of time with his special theory of relativity. Einstein's theory coincided with the Modernists, theatrical practitioners who experimented with the experience of time in the theatre. Could there be a relationship between the relativity of time and the theatrical experience? If so, how do we exploit it? This chapter will hope to answer the former question; the rest of the book the latter question.

In 2001 I was invited to lecture at the prestigious Babelsberg Film Studio in Babelsberg, Germany. At the time, we were just beginning to make the case that sound was an essential art form in theatre internationally, having made great progress in the United States, especially through organizations like the United States Institute for Theatre Technology (USITT). We had just started the Sound Working Group in the International Organization of Scenographers, Theatre Architects and Technicians (OISTAT) the year before to advance the understanding that theatre sound was really an art form and not just a technological discipline. Imagine that!

I embarked on a campaign to find "sound designers" in OISTAT's member countries all over the world, and everywhere I went, I ran into the same reaction: "Sound design? We don't have that here!" I would have to follow up with: "Well, do you have any composers who work in theatre?" That would ring a bell, and it would not be long before they would introduce me to prominent composers in their theatres. It was through this approach that I met some of the most amazing "sound designers" in the world—Vladimir Franz in the Czech Republic, Heiner Goebbels in Germany, Yossi Marchaim in Israel, and Igor Drevalev in Russia, among many more. Although many referred to themselves as composers, they immediately recognized the common objective that we all shared—providing the aural soundscape for the theatrical experience—and were often thrilled to meet someone else that shared their passion for providing sound scores for theatre. I distinctly remember being introduced to the great composer, Philip Glass. He asked me "What do you do?" I told him, "I'm a sound designer." He smiled and replied, "So am I."

In Babelsberg, I was asked to address the question, "Scenography: Close Bounded with Sound and Light Design?" Originally, the term "scenography" was largely used to describe a more holistic approach to the spatial design of a theatrical performance that included both scenery and costumes. The term comes from the Greek *skēnographia*, which means the "painting of scenery" (Merriam-Webster Online Dictionary 2015). The legendary scenographer Josef Svoboda certainly helped to popularize both the use of the term and the approach. Almost simultaneous to my lecture in Berlin, my friend Pamela Howard proposed this definition: "It is the seamless synthesis of space, text, research, art, actors, directors and spectators that contributes to an original creation" (Howard 2001, 16). Pamela's reflection of the need to consider visual design in a much more holistic approach to theatre-making was very much on my mind when I was preparing my lecture for Babelsberg. I wanted my lecture to suggest that our understanding of scenography should naturally include the consideration of time, and if we were going to consider time, we would naturally need to consider its primary ally, sound.

Sound as scenography proved to be a very controversial proposal internationally. There was a fair number of member nations whose delegates thought that sound was a technical element of theatre, not an artistic element, and if included at all, belonged in the Technology Commission, not the Scenography Commission of OISTAT. I had been through this before in the United States, however. In 1984, I was invited by United Scenic Artists (USA) Local 350 to discuss inclusion of sound designers in the union (Thomas 1987). The discussion was heated and volatile, climaxing with a well-known scene designer arguing that sound should not be included in the union because "I paint scenery," to which I replied, "I paint aural scenery." At the time, it made no difference. Sound was perceived as a threat to the bottom line of visual designers. If sound were welcomed as a full member of the team, a fixed financial pie would have to be divided four ways, not three.

Fortunately for us, there was also quite a sizeable group that understood the artistic importance of theatre sound in OISTAT, and my invitation coincided with OISTAT's Scenography Commission meetings in Berlin. This provided me an opportunity to engage in this discussion not only with the students, faculty and artists at the Babelsberg Film Studio, but also with the dubious element of the Scenography Commission. The subject "Scenography, Close Bounded with Sound and Light Design?" gave me the perfect opportunity to explore the similarities and differences between visual and sonic art.

The stakes were high, and I wanted to develop a more compelling argument about the relationship of sound to the experience of theatre. As I mentioned in Chapter 2, I had been using Einstein's theory of relativity in my classes at Purdue to explain the relationship between space and time for many years. Since Einstein was German, I figured my German audience would appreciate my paying homage to their great theoretical physicist. There was only one problem: I still didn't know very much about relativity.

As my interest was more aesthetic than mathematical, I went to Stephen Hawking's outstanding but very non-technical book, *A Brief History of Time*, and eventually developed arguments about the role that sound plays in controlling the perception of time in theatre (Hawking 1988). The conclusions embellished upon in this book started with the kernel of those arguments that radically altered my fundamental understanding of the nature of theatre itself, an understanding that starts with exploring the unique nature of time, and how it is that we as humans came to have an awareness of it.

We start with the evolution of mammals, a higher order of animal with a larger brain that developed a conscious awareness that primitive tetrapods did not possess. Consciousness in mammalian evolution seems to have coincided with a prototypical development important to theatre: the evolution of dreaming. Dreams reveal inconsistencies in our perception of time that lead us into the discussion of the nature of time and its relation to theatre that I first presented at Babelsberg.

Incidentally, the lecture at Babelsberg went well. Mihai Nadin, the eminent scholar and researcher in such diverse fields as electrical engineering, aesthetics, semiotics and computing came by to listen to my lecture. Afterward, he took the time to carefully read my paper, and then invited me to his hotel to discuss it (Thomas 2001). Long story short, he expressed great enthusiasm for the ideas in the paper and encouraged me to continue to explore the subject. A lot of that exploration wound up in this book. Without Dr. Nadin's encouragement, I very likely would not have continued to develop these ideas, and I owe a measure of gratitude to him for encouraging me to do so.

The Mammalian Invasion

The tetrapod brain was largely reflexive. It reacted to its environment instinctively and didn't spend a whole lot of time thinking about things. Tetrapods couldn't

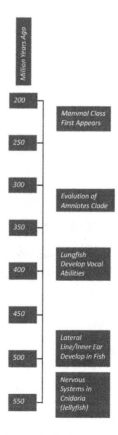

Figure 3.1 Timeline from Cambrian explosion to mammals.

consciously "think"; they only possessed a very simple brain that included the basal ganglia (see Figure 5.17), which helped them to control movement, and a few other organs like our old friend the amygdala, the seat of emotional memory (New Scientist 2011). Keep in mind that all of this evolution is highly controversial as to exactly what happened when. The particulars are not so critical in this case, however. What we really need to know is that sometime about 300–350 million years ago, a new, larger brain evolved in some early tetrapods, a clade known as *amniotes*, from which birds and reptiles would also evolve ("clade" just means animals that evolved from a common ancestor). While birds are noted for their eloquent singing abilities, just a few of them have learned how to synchronize to a beat, the phenomenon referred to in Chapter 2 as entrainment, and made famous by the YouTube viral sensation Snowball (Patel et al. 2009). The third distinguished member of the amniote clade, the class of animals known as *mammals*, evolved about 250 million years ago during the rise of the dinosaurs at the beginning of the Jurassic period (Kielan-Jaworowska and Cifelli 2004, 1–2).

Mammals are distinct from reptiles and birds because they possess a more sophisticated *neocortex* or "new brain."

There are six layers of tissues in the neocortex, compared to the four or fewer layers in the cerebra of birds and reptiles—a lot more room for a lot more connections.

The neocortex in mammals would eventually evolve to contain four main lobes: the *frontal* lobe, which is involved in decision making; the *parietal* lobe, which integrates sensory information from different parts of the body; the *occipital* lobe, the visual processing center of the brain; and the *temporal* lobe, which is all about time, as its name implies. The temporal lobe processes everything from the primary temporal perceptions of sound in the auditory cortex to the processing of time past: memory.

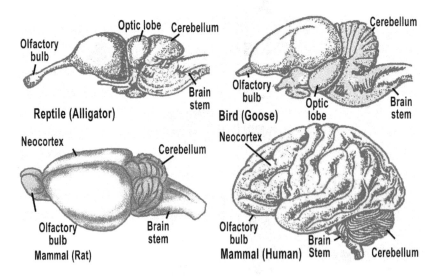

Figure 3.2 The neocortex in mammals.

Credit: Richard Granger, Adapted by Richard K. Thomas.

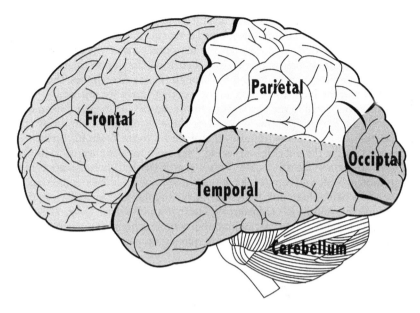

Figure 3.3 The lobes of the human brain.

Credit: From Gray, Henry. *Anatomy of the Human Body*. Lea and Febiger 1918, Figure 728. Adapted by Richard K. Thomas.

Figure 3.4 The earliest mammals were nocturnal and shrew-like, such as this restoration of a 160-million-year-old eutherian called a *Juramaia sinensis*.

Credit: Drawing by Nobumichi Tamura.

Those pesky dinosaurs would cause all sorts of problems for early mammals, so they hid during the day and snuck around at night. The vast majority were shrew to mouse size.

Most of the mammals snacked on insects, unlike the dinosaurs who were large to extremely large and snacked on, well, little mammals, among other things (USGS 2001). But mammals were most likely warm-blooded, and this allowed them to forage nocturnally, and in places where their cold-blooded predators could not (Kielan-Jaworowska and Cifelli 2004, 4–6). Even today, almost half of mammalian species are nocturnal. Over time, their bodies would adapt to favor their nighttime activities.

Remembering that eyes are not so useful in the dark, it should come as no surprise that these early mammals developed a hearing mechanism keenly evolved to perceiving space, albeit still through the temporal lens of the ear. Slowly but surely, a couple more bones migrated from their lower jaw up to their ears, eventually connecting the tympani (eardrum) through two of those bones, the malleus (or hammer) and the incus (or anvil), to the existing stapes (or stirrup).

The stapes connected to the basilar membrane we met in Chapter 2 in an organ we now call the *cochlea*. In this way, all of those mechanical vibrations could finally be transduced to nerve impulses that went on to the brain for further processing—sort of like the old children's song, "the leg bone's connected to the knee bone" and so forth ("Dem Bones"). This was a huge deal, because none of the other amniotes, birds and reptiles, have this three-bone middle ear extravaganza. They are stuck with three jaw bones (dentary, angular and articular), and just the stapes in their middle ear (Masterton, Heffner and Ravizza 1969, 972–973).

These early mammals had spectacular ability to hear high frequencies with this new middle ear arrangement. The upper frequency hearing of mammals averages

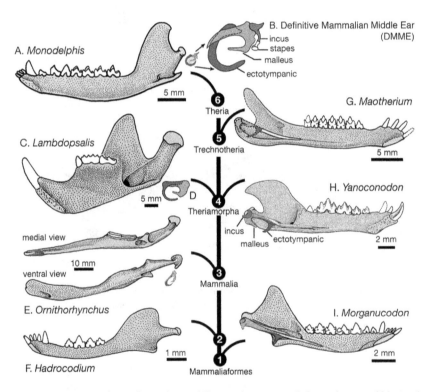

Figure 3.5 Diagram shows how the middle ear disconnected from the mandible in the period of evolution from mammals through the subclass from which humans evolved, Theria.

Credit: From: Ji, Qiang, Zhe-Xi Luo, Xingliao Zhang, and Chong-Xi Yuan, Li Xu. 2009. "Evolutionary Development of the Middle Ear in Mesozoic Therian Mammals." *Science* 326 (5950), October 9: 278–281. Reprinted with Permission from AAAS. Figure 3D adapted by permission from Macmillan Publishers Ltd: *Nature*. Meng, Jin, and André R. Wyss. 1995. "Monotreme Affinities and Low-Frequency Hearing Suggested by Multituberculate Ear." *Nature* 377 (6545) 141–144. Copyright 1995.

about 53 kHz! Curiously, humans and chimpanzees are the only mammals that don't routinely hear above 20 kHz. By comparison, birds seem to only be able to hear up to about 12 kHz, and, as we mentioned earlier, reptiles, a very poor 1 kHz.

Why would high frequency hearing be an evolutionary advantage? As we discussed in Chapter 2, animals with two ears determine location based on time differences between when the sound arrives at each ear and how loud the sound is at each ear. Since primitive mammalian heads were so small, it would be very hard for them to localize based on when, because the time-travel differences between the two ears were so small. But the higher the frequency, the easier it is for the head to absorb sound, creating intensity differences at each ear when a sound does not originate directly in front of or behind an animal. Small mammals could use intensity differences at each ear to localize sounds, but only at higher frequencies. Over time, many of these mammals even lost their ability to hear low frequencies—even below 1 kHz, a possible indication that hearing low frequencies was not as evolutionarily critical as localizing high frequencies for these nocturnal foragers.

Another useful advantage of this mammalian middle ear was its increased sensitivity to quiet sounds—20 dB or more above that of reptiles. Don't fret too much about this "dB" thing. Just know that most humans consider a change of 10 dB to be about twice as loud, or twice as sensitive, so 20 dB would be roughly four times more sensitive. That 20 dB difference would really give these early mammals an advantage in sensing predators and finding prey.

Hearing was not the most important sense to these early mammals, however. The sense of smell, developed in a sense organ called the *olfactory bulb* (see Figure 3.2), dominated early mammalian brains, not sight or sound. In contrast, the four different color sensing cone cells in the primitive mammalian eye were somewhat useless in seeing at night. And so, 150–200 million years ago, most mammals seem to have lost two of the four cone cells (Davies, Collin and Hunt, 3137). Curiously during this period, the nose and the ears may have become more important in sensing the spatial characteristics of a primitive mammal's environment than eyes.

As time went on, these primarily nocturnal mammals also developed a much more sophisticated neocortex. It included specialized areas that improved their sense of touch, sight and vision. Most importantly, the continuously evolving neocortex developed areas for such conscious activities as decision making. One such area was the auditory cortex, which developed connections to the basilar membrane, and allowed mammals to consciously perceive sounds and make decisions about how to act upon them (Molnar et al. 2014, 128).

The six layers of the human neocortex we mentioned earlier consist of what we call "gray matter": six layers of neurons compared to the single layer cortex of reptiles.

This gray matter is folded up in the human brain to allow more of it to fit in our brains! This is the part we most familiarly see when we look at pictures of the brain. Underneath this "gray matter," there is "white matter": millions of filaments connecting vertical "columns" of neurons in the six layers to other parts of the brain (Jourdain 1997, 52). More layers allow much more sophisticated distribution of sensory information to other layers, and then to other parts of the brain. Here we see additional evidence of the brain using space to perceive time, as the frequencies that localized along the basilar membrane also localized along the primary cortex (remember that frequency is a measure of cycles per *second*).

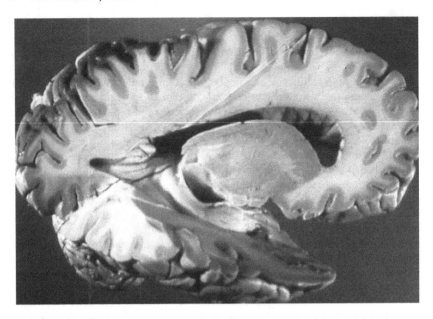

Figure 3.6 Dissected view of right half of brain shows gray matter and white matter.

This white matter also transmits information about when the sound happened, how loud it was (intensity) and how long it lasts (duration). This arrangement, unique to mammals, proved extremely useful, and perhaps contributed to an ever-enlarging brain (Rakic 2009). Over the next 100 million years, the size and number of areas in mammalian brains devoted to perception of sight and sound would continue to increase. Mammals would eventually develop brains ten times the size of reptiles the same size, and as mammalian brains grew in size relative to body weight, so did the number of neurons and their interconnections. This led to a much better ability to process sensory information, solve problems, and ultimately live a more complex and adaptive life (Northcutt 2002, 750).

The superiority of ears over eyes in the perception of space would be short-lived. A mass extinction event 66,038,000 years ago would wipe out the dinosaurs, and mammals would return to the sunlit world, eventually developing an additional cone cell type that allowed them to perceive the world in color (Renne et al. 2013, 684). Our ears would never lose their extraordinary ability to use time to perceive spatial positioning, and to this day provide us with a fascinating spatial perspective of the outside world. But the eyes once again emerged with a superior ability to perceive space in the mammalian environment. About that time, however, the unique mechanisms that early mammals developed to perceive temporal relationships would take an amazing turn toward providing us with a surprising understanding of the universe that would have major implications for sound designers and composers.

We Are Such Stuff as Dreams Are Made Of . . .

Sometime during this long evolution of mammals, or just before, an extraordinary phenomenon evolved that has tremendous implications for our story: the expanding neocortex provided new opportunities for anticipating problems and imagining solutions. According to some theories, one approach to problem solving was the development of a "threat simulation system," called *dreaming*. Dreaming allowed animals to test possible solutions (Revonsuo 2000, 877). Whether reptiles dream or not is debated, but highly doubted (Siegel 1998). Yet even Aristotle observed that horses, dogs, oxen, sheep and goats all dream. Researchers have measured and verified that rats, who are further up our evolutionary ladder, also dream (Goldman 2014). Rats diverged from our branch of the mammalian tree about 90 million years ago. We both evolved, however, in a special subdivision of mammals called *Placentalia*. The Placentalia subdivision means pretty much what you'd think it means: mothers who carry their fetuses in their uterus nourished by a placenta (Kaas 2011). We are pretty sure, then, that all "placental" mammals dream, as they have the same basic neural structures that are important to sleeping and dreaming (Bekoff 2012, 16).

Antti Revonsuo, a Finnish neuroscientist, defines dreaming as a "subjective experience during sleep, consisting of complex and organized images that show temporal progression." In other words, we subjectively experience space and *time* in dreams (Revonsuo 2000, 878). Dreams are important to us because they offer one of the most primeval possibilities of proto-theatre activity in animals. Nietzsche suggested an origin of theatre in dreams (Nietzsche 1872, 11; Jourdain 1997). Freud characterized dreams as *dramatizing* an idea, and spoke often about dreams and theatre as analogous in his book, *The Interpretation of Dreams* (Freud 1913, 23). Eli Rozik, in his book, *The Roots of Theatre*, also considers theatre and dreams to be analogous, one major difference being that theatre is "communicative" (Rozik 2002, 250). Dreams provide us an alternative, *subjective* way of experiencing time and space, in a similar manner to theatre, so it is important that we gain a better understanding of how we perceive space and time in dreams. Later we will find a potentially similar type of perception in theatre.

Dreaming works in an almost opposite way than the normal transmission of sound and light waves through the eyes and ears to the brain for processing. In dreaming, the brain itself generates images and sounds and sends those to the same parts of the brain for processing as would have occurred if they had been transmitted through the eyes and ears. We know this because we can now "look" at the brain during periods of sleep and wake with electroencephalography (EEG), which measures voltage fluctuations of neurons in the brain; positron emission tomography (PET), which uses X-rays to observe metabolic processes; and functional magnetic resonance imaging (fMRI), which measures brain activity associated with blood flow. In short, we now can tell fairly precisely, where spatially and when temporally, neurons fire in the brain. We can find a lot out about how the brain works that way. Once we know what each part of the brain does, we can explore which parts of the brain are doing something and what they are doing while we are dreaming. And it turns out neurons fire in many of the same places during dreams that they fire when we are awake, including our processing centers for sight and sound, the occipital lobe and the temporal lobe, respectively. In dreaming we really see, hear, touch, taste and smell (Nir and Tononi 2010, 89).

As twenty-first-century humans with allegedly superior brains, we recognize that our perceptions of unusual images in odd times and spaces are dreams.

Imagine, though, how a primeval rodent must have perceived dreams tens of millions of years ago. It would most likely perceive an extraordinary similarity to its waking world, because dreams are like that. Dreams present an experience very similar to the waking world, and dreamers feel like they are participating in that experience. For all practical purposes, the rodent's sight, sound, touch, taste and smell would all seemed to have been functioning normally. The rodent would have perceived the dream world to predominantly conform to its waking world, but would probably have felt much more emotionally stimulated—oh yes, our old friend the amygdala seems to often get quite hyperactive during dreaming, as do other older elements of a rodent's more highly evolved limbic system. As we introduced in Chapter 2, the limbic system consists of the part of the brain responsible for emotion, flight-or-flight behavior, memory and smell. It includes the hippocampus, which also stores and retrieves memories (see Figure 5.9). In short, as far as the rat was concerned, a dream *must* have been reality. Of course, there's no way to prove such a notion, but we do know that primitive human cultures considered dreams to be a form of reality (Lincoln 2003, 23, 27–30; Obringer 2016). It's hard not to imagine that primitive animals with even less cognitive ability to tell the difference between the dream world and the waking world would imagine a dream to be anything other than reality.

Another aspect of dreaming that seems like it would increase a primitive animal's perception of dreams as reality, is that most dreams are forgotten almost immediately upon waking. Curiously and conversely, we tend to forget a lot of facts about our waking world while we are dreaming, too. For example, we forget the simple fact that some of the characters we encounter in dreams are deceased. And yet, in our dreams we still accept the deceased characters as living without question. We accept activities that are impossible in the waking world, like flying, again, without question. It's not hard to imagine that for a primitive mind, what happened during a dream and while awake were just two realities, some characteristics of one forgotten as soon as the other replaced the first.

Even while accepting the dream world as real, there can be no doubt that time does not function in the same manner as it does in the waking world. In our dreams, we often suddenly change location spontaneously without question. Our perception of time in dreams can be quite different from that of our waking self. For many, time perception in dreaming can be exactly the same as in waking (Bolz 2009). For some, dream events seem to take longer than in real life (Erlacher and Schredl 2004; Erlacher et al. 2014). For others, time is much compressed, and many dreamers report lengthy dreams that pass in just a few minutes of waking time (Hancock 2010, 77). There is even some interesting evidence that, for some, time can run backward compared to events happening in our waking world! (Joseph 2012).

Our unique perception of time during sleep has been attributed to studies that show that the part of the brain (the *dorsolateral prefrontal cortex*; sort of behind the forehead, if you must know) responsible for the "temporal order of information retrieval" is relatively deactivated during REM[1] sleep and dreaming (Muzur, Pace and Hobson 2002, 477, 479). Meanwhile, other regions of our brain such as the hippocampus and our old friend, the amygdala, both keepers of memories, generate images in what can often be bizarre orders and timing. We seem to have no control over how time unfolds in a dream, because that area is not activated during REM sleep (Nir and Tononi 2010, 89).[2] It seems like the individual's perception of time, and not the common referencing to a waking clock in the laboratory, is more important in dreaming. In dreams associated with REM sleep then, our perception of time as we know it in waking life pretty much goes out the window. In a dream, unencumbered by our waking physical reality, our mind is free to construct its own passage of time, and this can be quite different from the passage of time in our waking world. And this perception of time occurs in what is typically a rather highly charged emotional environment—just like in music and theatre.

The Relativity of Time

A photon walks into a bar. The bartender takes one look at the photon and says, "you're new around these parts, aren't ya?" The photon says "yup," so the bartender asks him, "where ya from?" "I just got here from Gliese 832c," says the photon. "Gliese 832c?" says the bartender. "That's the closest planet to earth that might support life as we know it, but it's still 100,000 light years away. So I guess you're old enough to be in a bar. But I have to check your license anyway." So the photon hands its license to the bartender. The bartender takes one look at the photon's license and throws the photon out of the bar.

Figure 3.7 Zytglogge, the famous clock tower in Berne, Switzerland, that inspired Einstein's theory of relativity.

Credit: Photo by Sandstein.

Why?

Albert Einstein was working at the Berne, Switzerland, patent office in 1905 when he published his four papers that would forever change the way we think about time (Galison 2000, 368, 386). One of Einstein's famous "thought experiments" goes like this. Imagine that you are moving away from the clock tower in downtown Berne.

As you move away, the light must catch up with you. If you can move fast enough, the light will never catch up with you. Einstein proposed the speed at which the light would not catch up with you to be 186,300 miles per second. It is kind of the ultimate speed limit of the universe—nothing can travel faster than that speed. As we approach that speed, the clock would appear to slow down. If we were able to attain that speed, the clock would stop altogether.

Once we start thinking about space and time as waves whose information we receive via light and sound, Einstein's theory of relativity starts to tell us something even more interesting about time: it's not what we think it is!

To understand relativity, consider a man who throws a ball on a train (Nova Online 2000).

Another man stands on the side of the track watching. The speed of the ball varies with the speed of the train. Let's say the train is traveling at 30 miles per hour, and the man on the train is throwing the ball at 20 miles an hour. To the man on the ground, the ball is traveling at 50 miles an hour. To the man on the train, the ball is only traveling at 20 miles per hour. You argue, of course, that we all know the ball is really traveling at 50 miles per hour; the guy on the train is just mistaken. I beg to differ, because keep in mind that the earth spins at about 1,000 miles an hour around its center, and that we are rotating around the sun about 67,000 miles an hour, and our solar system is spinning around our galaxy at 490,000 miles per hour, so remind me again how fast is this ball moving? 558,050 miles per hour (Scientific American 1998)? It depends. Without a frame of reference, questions about motion and time are meaningless.

Now consider the same situation, but instead of throwing the ball, the man turns on a flashlight.

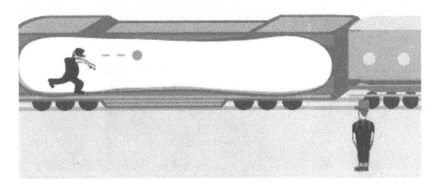

Figure 3.8 Man throwing ball on train.

Credit: From *Time Travel: Think Like Einstein.* www.pbs.org/wgbh/nova/time/think02.html © 2010–2017 WGBH Educational Foundation.

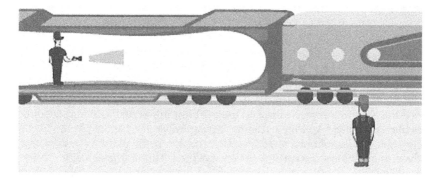

Figure 3.9 Man turning on flashlight on train.

Credit: From *Time Travel: Think Like Einstein*. www.pbs.org/wgbh/nova/time/think02.html
© 2010–2017 WGBH Educational Foundation.

Figure 3.10 The speed limit of the universe.

No matter how fast the train travels, light from the flashlight still travels at 186,300 miles per second. To the guy on the train, light is traveling at 186,300 miles per second. To the guy on the ground, light is traveling at 186,300 miles per second. Anywhere you measure from any point in the universe, the light is traveling at 186,300 miles per second. It doesn't make a difference whether you compare it to anyone else; it's still traveling at 186,300 miles per second. The speed of light is a constant. When we say speed of light, c isn't just the speed of light; c is the maximum speed of everything; consider it to be the speed limit of the universe.

Nothing goes faster! Light just happens to go that fast because it is transmitted by the massless photon.

Einstein observed that two different observers moving relative to each other, each measuring the speed of the same blob of light relative to himself, will both get c, even if the relative motion is in the same direction as the motion of the blob of light. If velocity is equal to the distance in time ($v = d/t$), and both the distance the light travels and the velocity of the light are the same for both observers, then time must be different for both observers! Time must be different! Einstein's theory of relativity doesn't say, "no, it's the same time, they are just perceiving it differently"; Einstein's theory says that time itself is different for both observers. This is a monumental concept.

Imagine that you are able to get on a rocket ship that can travel really, really fast—close to the speed of light. You blast off from earth, and you travel out into the universe close to the speed of light. Then you return to earth. Surprise! Everyone has aged considerably, but for you, time has proceeded normally. Your children now appear to be much older than you! Even their grandchildren might look older than you, depending on how fast you traveled and how long you were gone!

So why did the bartender throw the photon out of the bar? The bartender threw the photon out of the bar because the photon's license said that the photon was born that day. From the bartender's perspective, it took the photon 100,000 light years for the photon to reach the earth. From the photon's perspective, it arrived at the same instant it left Gliese 832c.[3] This is the same as Einstein's "thought experiment": if the photon looked back at a clock on Gliese 832c, the clock would not change because the photon was traveling at the speed of light!

Understanding the relativity of time helps us to understand our perception of time in dreams, especially when it doesn't conform to the way our clocks keep time in our waking world. In dreams, we no longer share the same frame of reference (e.g., an atomic clock that everyone mutually agrees is the current time). In our dreams, the mind creates its own frame of reference; it decides what our internal clock will be, mostly determined by the rate and order of images and memories it sends to our occipital and temporal lobes. And that time can be quite different from our waking clocks. Even in waking life we know this to be true. Everyone experiences time differently. One student gets involved in one of my lectures and the whole hour seems to pass by quickly. Another student (OK, realistically, more than one) finds my lecture to be nothing but a big bore, and time passes interminably slow, or they fall asleep, so I throw an eraser at them (not really). Theoretical physicist Sean Carroll suggested in his address at the 2011 International Conference on the nature of time that the time measured by extremely accurate clocks in our waking world isn't "as important as the time measured by our internal rhythms and the accumulation of memories" (Carroll 2011). That's relativity.

In our dreams, we experience a "reality" quite different than our waking world, complete with its own definition of how time passes and operates, and we do not question it. We gain a little bit of the same experience when we set our DVR to record the ball game to watch later. Well past the actual event, we watch the game, and before too long, we start getting into the game. We celebrate a great play, we get anxious about what will happen next, we root for our team as if they were playing in the present moment, all of this as if the game was occurring in the present, not in the past. At some point, the conscious part of our waking brain suddenly realizes that we have left the present waking moment, and have been experiencing as real the past time frame of the game.

In a similar way, we experience the same shift in our perception of reality when we are transported by a well-made theatre production. When we become immersed in theatre, our experience is very "dreamlike" because we experience the world and actions of the play as a present reality, our emotions are typically much stronger than in our average daily world, we don't exercise control over the story even though we feel as if we are an active participant (through the cathartic experience of identifying with the protagonist, which we will take up later in the book, especially Chapters 10 and 12). We also lose conscious awareness of how time is passing in the "waking world" outside of the dramatic context of the play, and time frames of reference can shift effortlessly, moving both forward and back in time, without our disengaging from the scene. In short, we experience the

sensation of "being there" in the dramatic moment of the play. It is this fundamental sense of "being there" that makes theatre such a special form of human
perception.

Our theatre experience isn't totally immersive like it is in typical dreams either,
though. Rather, it is more like a dream condition known as "lucid dreaming," in
which the dreamer becomes aware of the fact that they are dreaming.[4] One of the
interesting properties of experiencing live theatre is that we can simultaneously be
immersed and present in the dramatic world, experiencing the dream world of the
performers, and yet still retain a waking consciousness that allows us to consider
what that dream world means to us (or any other distractions, for that matter!).

I remember the first time I ever saw a live play. It was in my senior year in
high school. My private Catholic school had shut down after my junior year,
and I was forced to transfer to a much larger public school for my senior year,
L'Anse Creuse High School in Mount Clemens, Michigan. I had never seen a live
play before. One day our English teacher, Ms. McCarthy, who also served as the
school's drama teacher, took our class down to the gym to watch a dress rehearsal
of an upcoming play, an old chestnut called *The Curious Savage*. I was clearly not
expecting my life to be forever changed that day, but it was. Sometime during the
performance, I got involved, transported, and I suddenly started experiencing the
world of the play as if I was in that world. This shocked my waking mind when
I realized what was happening. These were my friends from English class; I recognized them! But there they were onstage, pretending to be other people, and I was
believing their performance to the point that I stopped experiencing the time of
the waking world of English class, and started experiencing the time of these five
crazy residents in a sanatorium called The Cloisters (the setting of *The Curious
Savage*). I had already been awarded a math scholarship to attend Michigan State
University, but my experience with *The Curious Savage* was so profound that
I decided then and there to change my major to theatre. I've never looked back.
Theatre can do that to a person.

Back at my 2001 lecture in Babelsberg, Mihai Nadin commented on my
thoughts about the relationship between Einstein's theory of relativity and the
nature of our experience of time in theatre. "It's true," he said. I was never able
to find out from him exactly what he meant by that. Was the time we thought
passed in a play, time passed in our lives? Was it time passed without the dis-
advantage of our corporeal bodies aging because we had disengaged from the
corporeal world? Indeed, the experience of the drama was now part of our memory, and that memory certainly included our experience of how long the story
lasted—which is typically much different from how long the play lasted in waking time. At first, I thought he must have meant what he said metaphorically, but
as time has gone on, I've become more and more convinced that the relativity of
time to the individual in our perception of theatre is very real. Einstein hinted
at this very much one day when he told his secretary how to explain relativity
to reporters and laypersons: "An hour sitting with a pretty girl on a park bench
passes like a minute, but a minute sitting on a hot stove seems like an hour"
(Calaprice 2005, 247).

In other words, something happens in experiencing a play that fundamentally alters our perception of the external world, that makes us believe that this
altered world is unfolding before our very eyes and ears. It is a world of exag-
gerated emotions in which time does not conform to our waking world, and
these two features somehow seem to be related to our being transported into this
dream world in the first place. We have already seen that the primary way that

we receive information about the world around us is through electromagnetic waves traveling in space, and mechanical waves traveling through mass. We have witnessed the evolution of eyes and ears in our human lineage right up through mammals to perceive those electromagnetic and mechanical waves, respectively. We have followed the evolution of the human brain to allow us to consciously process those waves in ever more perceptive ways. One of the mechanisms of the conscious brain for imagining our world is dreaming, and we now see that the brain itself can generate images that we perceive in a very similar way to how we perceive electromagnetic and mechanical waves from the outside world. Imagination and its close friend dreaming have led us to understand how our experience of the external world is fundamentally altered by our perception of time, which presents a unique experience to each of us because we now know that time itself is unique to each individual. Now, if there was just some way that we could manipulate our perception of time and emotional state to transport us into these dreamlike worlds of the theatre. . . .

Ten Questions

1. What characteristic of early mammals caused them to develop a much more sophisticated middle ear?
2. How do most mammals differ from humans in their ability to sense frequency and loudness?
3. What does the neocortex allow mammals to do that reptiles can't do?
4. What happened to cause the early mammal eyes to regain color vision and once again to achieve superiority over the ears in the perception of space?
5. How does dreaming differ from waking, in regards to seeing and hearing in mammals? How does it differ?
6. Give four reasons why a primitive mammalian rodent would perceive its dream world as reality.
7. Why is "time so out of joint" in many dreams?
8. How is it that time is relative to each individual?
9. Why is it that an atomic clock might not be a very good indicator of the passage of time for an individual, and what does this have to do with theatre and dreams?
10. Name five ways in which our perception of time in theatre resembles our perception of time in dreams.

Things to Share

1. Start a dream diary for a week, and keep it on your nightstand where you can readily access it after you dream. If possible, record as many details as you can remember of your dreams immediately after you wake from each dream (you will typically find that you have your dreams early in the morning during REM sleep, and most people have between about three and five dreams each night). If it is not possible to record them immediately upon waking, record them first thing in the morning (if you do this, you will find that you forget most of them). Pay special attention to how you perceive space and time in your dreams. Did your location change at all during the dream? Did you have features of two or more separate locations merged together into a single location? Was

time continuous in your dream, or were there gaps? Did different time periods co-exist in your dream; for example, did elements from your childhood combine with elements from your adult life? Did the dream appear to take the same, more or less time than the length of your dream in waking time (this is easier to judge if you have already awakened, and then fallen back to sleep)? Tell us about the most significant discoveries you made in your dreams, and provide examples about the unique way time and space works. If possible, draw a parallel to how time and space work in a scene in a play or movie you have seen. For the really ambitious and curious, develop the ability to lucid dream so you can manipulate time and space to your own liking, and develop your own ability to tell incredible stories (many websites have a wealth of information about how to develop this ability).

2. Find a movie that has won an Academy Award for sound. Pick a movie that you love and wouldn't mind seeing again. Now get hold of the movie (perhaps buy it, because you can use it for other projects in this class, or rent it, or even check it out from your local library). Watch it with an eye toward sound color, the particular combination of frequencies unfolding in time that create the unique timbre of each sound. Find what you consider to be an amazing sound. Tell us about what you find so amazing about it, and whether you think the sounds would be better received by the lateral line of fish (very low frequencies below 200 Hz, bass), reptiles (middle frequencies between 200 Hz and about 1,000 Hz, midrange), or mammals (high frequencies above 1,000 Hz). Explain how you think the sound affects us emotionally. Bring at least two examples with you in case someone uses your first example.

3. Find a movie that has won an Academy Award for sound. Pick a movie that you love and wouldn't mind seeing again. Now get hold of the movie (perhaps buy it, because you can use it for other projects in this class, or rent it, or even check it out from your local library). Watch it with an eye toward sound localization, the particular spatial characteristics of sound and music. Find what you consider to be an amazing use of space. Tell us about what you find so amazing about it, and whether you think the space is being used to localize the sound, or to further "immerse" us in the scene by recreating a specific acoustic environment. Explain how you think the sound affects us emotionally. Bring at least two examples with you in case someone uses your first example.

Notes

1 Rapid eye movement, a phase of sleep characterized by rapid eye movement and long associated with vivid dreaming.

2 We should note that studying the phenomenon of human perception of time in dreams appears to be a pretty hard thing to do, which may explain why there is so little hard research, and why that research is so inconclusive. Nevertheless, there is a wealth of anecdotal evidence out there about how our perception of time in dreams does not conform to our waking time references, and virtually all of my students and my own experience confirm a very different perception of time in dreams than in waking life. See the references in these last two paragraphs for a small sampling of examples.

3 Keep in mind that we aren't taking into account the effect of gravity on time, which is a whole other problem! We are also being silly, of course, because the act of the

bartender "seeing" the photon would involve his eye absorbing the photon, unless they could get the whole conversation/license check thing out of the way very very quickly!

4 Experienced lucid dreamers even develop the ability to control their dreams, a condition much more akin to playing a video game, in which the player becomes the protagonist of the game.

Bibliography

Bekoff, Marc. 2012. "Do Animals Dream? Science Shows of Course They Do, Rats Too." December 4. Accessed February 10, 2016. www.psychologytoday.com/blog/animal-emotions/201212/do-animals-dream-science-shows-course-they-do-rats-too.

Bolz, Barbara. 2009. "How Time Passes in Dreams." September 9. Accessed February 11, 2016. http://indianapublicmedia.org/amomentofscience/time-passes-dreams/.

Calaprice, Alice. 2005. *The New Quotable Einstein*. Princeton, NJ: Princeton University Press.

Carroll, Sean. 2011. "Ten Things Everyone Should Know About Time." September 1. Accessed February 15, 2016. http://blogs.discovermagazine.com/cosmicvariance/2011/09/01/ten-things-everyone-should-know-about-time/#.VsI99cdTLct.

Davies, Wayne I. L., Shaun P. Collin, and David Hunt. 2012. "Molecular Ecology and Adaptation of Visual Photopigments in Craniates." *Molecular Biology* Vol. 21, 3121-3158.

Erlacher, Daniel, Melanie Schädlich, Tadas Stumbrys, and Michael Schredl. 2014. "Time for Actions in Lucid Dreams: Effects of Task Modality, Length, and Complexity." *Frontiers in Psychology* 4: 1–12.

Erlacher, Daniel, and Michael Schredl. 2004. "Time Required for Motor Activity in Lucid Dreams." *Perceptual and Motor Skills* 99 (3 suppl): 1239–1242.

Freud, Sigmund. 1913. *The Interpretation of Dreams*. New York: Palgrave Macmillan.

Galison, Peter. 2000. "Einstein's Clocks: The Place of Time." *University of Chicago Press* 26 (2): 355–389.

Goldman, Jason G. 2014. "What Do Animals Dream About." April 25. Accessed February 10, 2016. www.bbc.com/future/story/20140425-what-do-animals-dream-about.

Hancock, Peter A. 2010. "The Battle for Time in the Brain." In *Time: Limits and Constraints*, edited by Jo Alyson Parker, Paul A. Harris, and Christian Steineck, 76–87. Pacific Grove, CA: International Society of the Study of Time.

Hawking, Stephen. 1988. *A Brief History of Time*. New York: Bantam Books.

Howard, Pamela. 2001. "What Is Scenography? or What's in a Name." *Theatre Design and Technology* (United States Institute for Theatre Technology) 37 (3): 13–16.

Joseph, Rhawn. 2012. "Dreaming and Dream Sleep." Accessed February 15, 2016. http://brainmind.com/Dreaming.html.

Jourdain, Robert. 1997. *Music, the Brain and Ectasy*. New York: William Morrow.

Kaas, Jon H. 2011. "Reconstructing the Areal Organization of the Neocortex of the First Mammals." *Brain, Behavior and Evolution* 78 (1): 7–21.

Kielan-Jaworowska, Zofia, and Richard L. Cifelli. 2004. *Mammals from the Age of Dinosaurs*. New York: Columbia University Press.

Lincoln, Jackson Steward. 2003. *The Dream in Native American and Other Primitive Cultures*. Mineola, NY: Dover.

Masterton, Bruce, Henry Heffner, and Richard Ravizza. 1969. "The Evolution of Human Hearing." *The Journal of the Acoustic Society of America* 45 (4): 966–985.

Merriam-Webster Online Dictionary. 2015. "Scenography." Accessed February 2, 2016. www.merriam-webster.com/dictionary/scenography.

Molnar, Zoltá, Jon H. Kaas, Juan A. de Carlos, Robert F. Hevner, Ed Lein, and Pavel Nemec. 2014. "Evolution and Development of the Mammalian Cerebral Cortex." *Brain, Behavior and Evolution* 83 (2): 126–139.

Muzur, Amir, Edward F. Pace, and J. Allan Hobson. 2002. "The Prefrontal Cortex in Sleep." *Trends in Cognitive Science* 6 (1): 475–481.

New Scientist. 2011. "A Brief History of the Brain." September 21. Accessed April 12, 2016. www.newscientist.com/article/mg21128311-800-a-brief-history-of-the-brain/.

Nietzsche, Friedrich. 1872. *The Birth of Tragedy Out of the Spirit of Music.* Translated by Ian Johnston. Leipzig: Verlag Von E. W. Fritzsch.

Nir, Yuval, and Giulio Tononi. 2010. "Dreaming and the Brain: From Phenomenology to Neurophysiology." *Trends in Cognitive Science* 14 (2): 88–100.

Northcutt, Glenn R. 2002. "Understanding Vertebrate Brain Evolution." *Integrative and Comparative Biology* 42 (4): 743–756.

Nova Online. 2000. "Think Like Einstein." November. Accessed February 15, 2016. www.pbs.org/wgbh/nova/time/think.html.

Obringer, Lee Ann. 2016. "How Dreams Work." Accessed February 10, 2016. http://science.howstuffworks.com/life/inside-the-mind/human-brain/dream3.htm/printable.

Patel, Aniruddh D., John R. Iverson, Micah R. Bregman, and Irena Schulz. 2009. "Experimental Evidence for Synchronization to a Musical Beat in a Nonhuman Animal." *Current Biology* 19 (10): 827–830.

Rakic, Pasko. 2009. "Evolution of the Neocortex: A Perspective From Developmental Biology." *Neuroscience* 10 (10): 724–735.

Renne, Paul R., Alan L. Deino, Frederik J. Hilgen, Klaudia F. Kuiper, Darren F. Mark, William S. Mitchell III, Leah E. Morgan, Roland Mundil, and Jan Smit. 2013. "Time Scales of Critical Events Around the Cretaceous-Paleogene Boundary." *Science* 339 (6120): 684–687.

Revonsuo, Antti. 2000. "The Reinterpretation of Dreams: An Evolutionary Hypothesis of the Function of Dreaming." *Behavioral and Brain Sciences* 23 (6): 877–901.

Rozik, Eli. 2002. *The Roots of Theatre.* Iowa City: University of Iowa Press.

Scientific American. 1998. "How Fast Is the Earth Moving." October 26. Accessed February 15, 2016. www.scientificamerican.com/article/how-fast-is-the-earth-mov/.

Siegel, Jerome M. 1998. "The Evolution of REM Sleep." In *Handbook of Behavioral State Control*, edited by Ralph Lydic and Helen A. Baghdoyan, 7.7–7.8. Boca Raton: CRC Press.

Thomas, Richard. 1987. "The Need for Union Representation for Theatre Sound Designers." Richmond Sound Design Ltd. January. Accessed February 2, 2016. www.richmondsounddesign.com/docs/need-for-union-representation-fall-1987-small.pdf.

———. 2001. "Dramatic Space and Time." May 9. Accessed February 2, 2016. www.richmondsounddesign.com/docs/dramatic-space.doc.

USGS. 2001. "What Did Dinosaurs Eat?" May 17. Accessed February 6, 2016. http://pubs.usgs.gov/gip/dinosaurs/food.html.

PART II

MUSIC = TIME MANIPULATED

CHAPTER 4

WHAT IS MUSIC?

Introduction: What's in a Name?

It is the essential uniqueness of human experience, our perception of time in particular, that makes our insistence on defining the word "aesthetic" as "how we perceive the world through our senses" so critical. Each of us perceives the world differently, first because of the uniqueness of our eyes and ears, but more importantly, because of how our brains process the information provided by those senses. And while there is a lot to be said for playwright José Rivera's description of theatre as "collective dreaming," we must acknowledge that only the stimulus is the same for each audience member[1] (Svich 2013, 47). What happens inside each person's brain is undeniably unique and different. Later in the book we will discuss how we combine the "collective dreaming" experience of theatre with our own experience to create a unique perception, unlike that of any other audience member.

It makes less sense, then, to evaluate a work of art as good or bad for anyone other than one's self. Whether we are singing along with a crowd of 100,000 people in Chicago's Grant Park to Coldplay or huddling together in a small community theatre laughing at a Neil Simon comedy, each one of us experiences something different. For some of us, the experience may be profoundly moving; others may wonder how quickly they can hit the exit. But we humans are social beings, and we crave shared experiences even if we know that we'll never experience an art work in exactly the same way as another audience member. The best we can hope for as artists, then, is that we provide an experience that a large enough group of people find meaningful or fulfilling in some way. Unless we are creating just for ourselves, we will probably want to avoid creating an experience to which no one relates.

So how do we create such an experience? How do we ensure that our audience will contain enough individual members, each having a sufficiently positive experience to justify our creating the art work in the first place? In the last chapter, we cited Rozik's assertion that the difference between dreams and theatre is that theatre is "communicative." That turns out to be a tricky description. To communicate means to convey information, to reveal something using "signs" (Merriam-Webster Online Dictionary, 2015). Such communication is certainly a major part, and for many, the point of the theatre experience. However, communication is a very different experience than suddenly finding yourself immersed in the dreamlike world of a play. Sure, your conscious brain can consider the ideas of the play as a spectator. But there is another part of your brain that becomes so immersed in the story that you feel that the events happening in the play are actually happening to you.

And that's the part of the play on which we are going to focus in this book: the parts involved in immersing and transporting the audience that include manipulating emotions and temporal perception. It will be hard to describe this as "communicating"; to use that word invites confusion with the words, images and ideas used in communication. As the noted neurologist Oliver Sacks was fond of saying, "music doesn't have any special meaning; it depends on what it's attached to" (Sacks 2009). Of course, we prefer to think about it the other way around. This book is about music, and the things we attach to it. Rather than describe music as a communication, we will use terms like "incite," "arouse" or "immerse." We will often accomplish such arousals and immersions through largely un*conscious* processes, not through the communication of ideas (although certainly not exclusively). The experience of music in theatre, we will discover, carries communication. It is not the communication in itself.

This may be a hard concept for many to understand. Hopefully this concept will become much clearer as one moves through this book. Many will argue that music is itself a communication, depending on one's definition of communication. Certainly, elements of performing, transmitting and listening to audible music may possess elements of communication. For example, we listen to a performer, and immediately recognize that the performer is playing a guitar. If we are musically trained, we might recognize that they are playing a C major chord. However, these elements of communication are not what we are primarily interested in when we experience music in theatre as an audience member. We are more interested in how music affects our "soul" (whatever that is). In this book, we need to separate the communicative elements of performing and analyzing music from the more immersive experience we have when we use music to transport us into the world of the play.

We must agree from the very beginning, then, that how we define and use the term "music" will be very specific to our purposes in this book. There are enough definitions of music floating around in the world to make your dentures float. Creating one to help you specifically understand what we mean when we use the term in this book should not cause problems for anyone who speaks the English language. Most words have several meanings—Merriam-Webster lists five just for the word "music."[2] We are all quite familiar with using the definition of a term most appropriate to a particular discussion. In this book, then, any time we use the term "music" from here on, we will mean the definition we develop in this chapter, and we'll just agree not to argue about it, because we know that music can have many, many definitions. After you finish reading this book, when you go out and you talk about music elsewhere, I don't have any intention of forcing this definition on you. The only reason we need to have this definition is so we can have a conversation in this book and all be sure we know exactly what we mean when we use the shortcut word "music." Of course, you are welcome to wander through the rest of your life using the definition I'll lay out in this chapter. It would be an honor to have you absorb it as part of your aesthetic.

We'll start with Edgar Varèse's definition of music as organized sound. We'll add on to that Rodriguez's insistence that music is a temporal art (big surprise, eh?). We'll separate the unique power of music to stimulate us from the ideas that words and images communicate. Then we'll add an interesting twist that you might not have seen coming: music is also a visual art. Finally, we'll break music down into its component parts—energy, time and space—so that we can more carefully understand what music is and is not. If we make it through all that OK, we'll be ready to propose a definition of music. If we can all agree that this definition is what we'll use throughout the rest of this book, we'll be ready to begin to explore our main thesis: that music is the chariot that carries ideas into the deepest part of our mortal coil.

Music Is Organized Sound

So let's define the term "music," because quite frankly, everybody has a different idea of what music is—my parents in particular. I know because they were always yelling at me, "you call that music?" That's my whole life.

Edgard Varèse was an early twentieth-century French composer. He was among the first to explore electronic music and move away from composition that employed traditional musical instruments. He famously proposed a very simple definition of music: "organized sound" (Varèse and Wen-Chung 1966, 18). This definition is good, because it allows for *non-traditional* sonic stimuli (e.g., synthesis, ambient sound, *musique concrète*). It is liberating; it frees up the imagination to think about composition in whole new ways, and begins to suggest a bridge between the terms "music composition" and "sound design." It's a bridge that I have crossed many times. So many times, in fact, that I have ceased considering the two terms, composition and design, to be functionally different. If you are truly interested in this discussion, compare the definitions provided by Encarta at the end of this chapter![3]

In 1976, I proposed a similar definition of theatre sound design as simply the "organization of the aural experience of the audience" (Thomas 1980, 3). I proposed this definition in order to challenge my colleagues and students to consider sound in theatre as a holistic experience. This definition makes it clear that everything an audience hears when they come to the theatre is a part of the sound design. This, of course, includes the music, sound effects and sound reinforcement system. But it also includes the actor's voices, the hum and noise of the air conditioning system, and even the audience' noises, both desired and undesired. Sound design, I suggested, was a very broad term; composers and sound effects technicians were sound designers, as were directors, playwrights, actors, acousticians, architects and audience members—especially those who coughed during the quiet parts.

Scene designers were sound designers, too, as they had a lot to do with how the sound transmitted from the stage to the audience. Unfortunately, they also often contributed to the cacophony of *unorganized* sound as the scenery rattled and rumbled unintentionally on its journey through space. Equally unfortunate were lighting designers who often added to the unorganized din, first with static lighting fixtures that just rattled and buzzed, but then with moving light fixtures that whirred and hissed and clacked and swiveled.

Lest anyone think that I'm overreacting here, let me convey a quick story about an experience I had at the 2002 London Sound Colloquium hosted by my friends Greg Fisher and Ross Brown. They had invited the gathered guests to a final preview of *Bombay Dreams* at a prominent West End theatre. I found myself seated next to a very prominent British sound designer. The curtain went up, the moving lights exploded in their signature sonic clatter, and that sound designer sitting next to me exploded in a most unexpected clatter of his own. He jumped seething into the aisle ranting about how moving lights were destroying theatre and I thought for a moment he was leaning toward violence. Understandably. When you increase the noise floor, you distract the audience, and you also decrease the amount of room between the actors' vocals and the noise floor where the composer's music needs to fit. As far as he was concerned, the unorganized sound was ruining the organized sound.

At any rate, I became quite fond of challenging students in my sound design classes to explain the difference to me between the word design and the words compose and composition, especially if music was "organized sound."

> "Well, music composition has notes and instruments."
> "What about *musique concrète?*"
> "OK, sound design is meant to support something else like a play."
> "Tell that to Danny Elfman."
> "Well music starts from nothing and sound design uses things that are already in existence."
> "So, you build the instruments before you play them then?"
> "Composition has less of a reference than design."
> "Maybe, maybe not. Depends on what's attached to either."

And so it goes on and on. I'm not just being cranky here. I have simply found in my life, in my aesthetic, that I can use the terms interchangeably, and I always mean they are synonyms for each other, they mean the same thing. It will be a lot easier, then, when I talk to you in this book, that no matter which term I use, you will know that I also mean the other. For me, design and composition are synonyms, they're the same thing; design and composition are nouns, and design and compose are verbs.

Oh, and by the way, I should note that my parent's complaints about my tastes in music were often related to artists such as Frank Zappa playing "Help I'm a Rock." Zappa, as it turns out, was perhaps Edgar Varèse's biggest fan. I guess I'll stick to the standard answer I always gave to my parents: "Yes, I do call that music!"

Narrowing Our Definition of Music

Another oft-cited definition of music, and one that you may guess is near and dear to my heart, is composer Robert Xavier Rodriguez's 1995 assertion that "Music consists of sound organized in time, intended for, or perceived as, aesthetic experience" (Dowling 2005, 470; Rodriguez 2016). Near and dear, first because it identifies music as a *time* art.

Michael Thaut summarizes this unique quality of music even more emphatically:

> One of the most important characteristics of music—also when compared with other art forms—is its strictly temporal character. Music unfolds only in time, and the physical basis of music is based on the time patterns of physical vibrations transduced in our hearing apparatus into electrochemical information that passes through the neural relays of the auditory system to reach the brain. (. . .) Music communicates critical time dimensions into our perceptual processes.
>
> (2005, p. 34)

Rodriguez's definition is also significant because it acknowledges the uniqueness of our perception of music as aesthetic experience, although Rodriguez most likely refers to the more modern definition of aesthetics, which concerns itself with "the nature of beauty, art and taste" as Merriam-Webster puts it (Merriam-Webster 2017). In Varèse's definition, a conversation in a grocery store could be considered "organized sound." Rodriguez helps clarify that music is somehow a separate temporal experience specifically related to art. While we certainly risk getting bogged down in an endless discussion of "What is art?," it does seem like it's a good idea to confine our definition to artistic endeavors, rather than any old organization of sound at all.

Both Rodriguez and Varèse's definitions have another problem that fundamentally undermines a key concept about the nature of music. Both definitions allow the inclusion of the language used in poetry. Neither separates the musical elements of poetry, such as rhythm and dynamics, from the ideas communicated by the words in poetry. Curiously, this is exactly how Plato defined music in his *Republic*, which we will come back to in Chapter 12 (*Republic*, p. II). For now, we should just content ourselves that Plato came out of a world in which his predecessors considered *mousike* to pretty much include all *time* arts, including history and astronomy, literally the arts inspired by the Muses. Aristotle, on the other hand, made a distinction between music and *song*, that is words with music (*Poetics*, Section I Part VI)—just like we will do in this book.

Why do we need to make such a distinction? Because an important part of this definition, of our whole approach, is understanding the key differences between word/images[4] and music. Music is largely devoid of semantic meanings, but has this magnificent power to incite emotions and manipulate our perception of time. Later we will discover evolutionary and biological evidence that will also support teasing out these differences between word/images and music. In order to understand those differences and how they impact our perception of music and theatre, we must define our terms in a manner that clearly identifies these differences.

Fortunately, there is another neuroscientist, Ian Cross, who conveniently defines music with just such a distinction: "Musics can be defined as those temporally patterned human activities, individual and social, that involve the production and perception of sound and *have no evident and immediate efficacy or fixed consensual reference*" (2003, 47). Now that's really getting us somewhere. First of all, Cross also confines his definition to temporal activities, which is hugely important. Music is about time, about the organization of time. But Cross really gets to the heart of the matter when he says "no . . . fixed consensual reference." Music exists on its own; it doesn't refer to anything else. It's not a semiotic kind of language full of meaning; there are no signs or symbols inherent in music. It is what is. Others have tried to attach ideas to music. For example, the Romantics tried to create music that told stories, but, of course, they were horribly unsuccessful at it, because everybody has a different story going on inside their minds when they listen to such music. At best, program music such as Berlioz's *Symphonie Fantastique* only communicates specific meanings because Berlioz attached written "program" notes to the music, thus telling the audience in referential words the images the music should have put into their heads all by itself (Berlioz 2002).

Language is really good at communicating ideas. Look at all the books there are that communicate ideas, some of them even brilliant ideas. Images are also really good at communicating ideas; even a simple stream of emojis can communicate a lot. Music contains no such references. Music consists of completely non-referential elements such as pitch, tempo, rhythm and loudness. When you hear a certain tone, you don't go "oh Cleveland."

That isn't to say that sound is not capable of generating images; a dog bark pretty much sounds like a dog barking! Sound does have some ability to refer to things in the real world; it just winds up being very poor at it. Many sounds are hard to distinguish from other sounds. "Is that rain or bacon frying?" Many sounds are hard to identify at all. "What's that squeaking sound?"

Language is really good at communicating ideas, and images—pictures, as we said before, are worth a thousand words. It doesn't make a difference whether a word is printed or spoken. The printed word "elevator" doesn't look like an elevator, and the phonemically pronounced word "elevator" doesn't sound like an elevator. It's just a symbol, but we all agree when we see that word or hear that sound, we mean an elevator.

It is these word/images that refer to things in our external world that we want to isolate out of our definition of music. Music, as Stravinsky famously said, "is powerless to express anything at all. . . . Music is the sole domain in which man realizes the present" (Stravinsky 1936, 53–54). Music doesn't simply tell us about emotions; it incites them, creates them in the present moment, first in the musician, and then, hopefully in the audience member. We'll start to get to "how" in the next chapter.

To help illustrate this point, consider again the sentence, "I'm going to the store" from Chapter 1. Language communicates the referential idea that I, Rick Thomas, am going to a place where merchandise is offered for retail sales to customers. But what about the musical elements of that sentence? Just looking at those five words on the printed page, there doesn't seem to be a whole lot of music there. The words on the page do not communicate how I *feel emotionally* about going to the store. That's the job of music. Even if you put your hand over your mouth when you say the words so that you can't understand them, you'll still hear the elements of music, loud and clear.

Music Is Visual as Well as Audible

We've just seen that sound can have referential meaning, for example, a train whistle that signals its approach readily refers to something we recognize in the real world. Play a train whistle sound and ask just about anybody what that is, and they will tell you "a train" (unless they've not had experience with the referent, of course!). Not all sound is music, and some sound can serve a dual purpose of both being referential and musical.

It should not surprise us then, that visual art also has a musical component. It's clearly not all referential. One reason this should not surprise us is that we've already discussed the eyes' perception of time as a secondary ability, next to space. As a secondary ability, we won't necessarily expect visual music to have the same capability as sound. Audible music has features not shared by either language or visual communication. For example, Thaut points out that audible music has the properties of being both sequential and simultaneous (Thaut 2005, 1–3). Audible and visual music are both sequential, meaning that their events unfold linearly in time, but audible music is also simultaneous, meaning that we can perceive multiple sounds simultaneously and individually, and within some psychoacoustic limitations, can focus our mind to concentrate on one sound while another occurs simultaneously. Without this feature, we would not be able to experience the piano, bass, drums and guitar of a jazz band simultaneously. We wouldn't even be able to experience the harmonies created by the simultaneous melodic lines in a Bach fugue.

In visual color, when we combine colors, we perceive a new color, not the individual colors. In order to perceive individual properties, we need to move our eyes sequentially from a space where one color exists to a space in which the other color exists. Language, as Thaut reminds us, is also "monophonic," in that we can only concentrate on one conversation at a time, just as we only see one thing at a time (2005, 1–3). That "monophonic" quality is great for communicating ideas, and word/images, but it's the simultaneity of music that really is so special and unique about the experience of music.

Thaut also observes that since our eyes move as we engage a static art work, such as a painting or a sculpture, there is an implied musical sense of time based on how our eyes move to perceive the art work. How much Michelangelo directs the movement of our eyes when we view the ceiling of the Sistine Chapel is debatable; certainly he would not be able to control when and where we start looking, how fast and in what direction we move our eyes once we start looking, when and where we stop, and so forth. So there is a discontinuity between the visual art creator and the visual art perceiver in such static works. Still, since there is a temporal component in experiencing visual art, visual artists often consciously use rhythm, for example, by regularly repeating elements of art to create the sense of movement (Delahunt 2014).

The discontinuity of rhythm between the visual artist and the viewer becomes something of a non-issue once visual art itself starts moving. Moving pictures have been around since the 1830s (Encyclopedia Britannica 2016). The ability to move static art images in time certainly unleashed a new era in art that further muddied the fine line between dream reality and waking reality. Indeed, legend has it that the addition of the time component to static images apparently caused a riot at a cinema in Paris in 1895 when the short movie *Arrival at a Train Station* premiered. Space puts us in the world, but time makes it real. The frightened audience members purportedly thought the train was going to come crashing right through the screen, and ran from their seats in terror (Gunning 2002). The advent of the talkies in *The Jazz Singer* in 1927 completed the illusion, providing filmmakers with a startling ability to transport audience members to strange new worlds while simultaneously controlling their perception of time.

The advent of the film editor suddenly brought the concept of music firmly into the visual realm. Walter Murch, one of the most respected and admired film editors in the history of cinema, compared the development of audible music with the potential for further development of visual music. Murch considered the cinema technique of his day to be roughly where Western music was before the advent of written musical notation. He credited the advent of musical notation to facilitating the tremendous advances in music before the eleventh century, when music was strictly an oral tradition. Murch wondered whether there would ever be such a thing as "cinematic notation" that would allow and instigate the sort of sophistication in visual music to develop that did in audible music (Murch 2002, 50–51).

That transformation may have taken place without the benefit of a visual music notation system with the advent of music videos on stations such as MTV, Music Television. MTV launched on August 1, 1981, in New York City with the Buggles's prophetic hit, "Video Killed the Radio Star" (CNN.com 2006). Almost instantaneously, MTV popularized visual editing to the beat, bypassing the need for Murch's cinematic notation by directly conforming the visual music to the soundtrack. The musicality of editing in music videos had a profound effect on everything else in cinema, especially advertising. It dramatically advanced our ability to perceive visual music, in which the content of the actual images often becomes secondary to the hypnotic editing that produces real musical sensations of tempo, rhythm and dynamics.

Closely correlated with the visual music of MTV editing was the rise of the ability to control lighting systems that could also synchronize with a musical beat. Throughout its early life, theatre lighting design focused predominantly on revealing space, although as we noted in Chapter 1, visionary designers such as Tharon Musser were keenly aware early on of the tremendous potential for light to revel in time. But it was the advent of concert lighting in the 1960s in such venues as Bill Graham's Fillmore Theatre shows in San Francisco, Bill McManus's designs at the Electric Factory in Philadelphia, and the Joshua Light Show at the Fillmore East in New York that really began to fully explore light as music; all found a way to transform audible music directly into visual music (Moody 2010, 5–6). Lighting designers who wanted to "play the console to the music" drove the development of more and more sophisticated consoles in the 1980s that were capable of greater synchronization with the musical beat (Moody 2010, 112–113). Sophisticated lighting as visual music emerged as a staple of concerts at the end of the twentieth century and led directly to the emergence of another major market for video music, concert projections. Today the visual music involved in just about any major concert rivals that of the audible music itself in complexity and sophistication, especially in highly specialized forms such as electronic dance music, or EDM.

MTV and concert lighting certainly had a pronounced impact on me. After spending many years wondering exactly how to infuse both audible and visual music into legitimate theatre, I started undertaking experiments in the early 1990s, starting with developing my first punk rock musical, *Awakening*. *Awakening* started a lifelong exploration into what I call "the gray area between concert and stage, music and play." In our 2000 production of *The Creature*, I specifically explored treating each scene like an MTV music video, disrupting the traditional dramatic continuity in favor of a more musical experience. In 2011's *Ad Infinitum*,[3] we finally abandoned the theatrical convention of a seated audience, which sacrificed a more contemplative seated experience in favor of the extraordinary stimulation of a standing audience encouraged to move with the music. We took the concept one step further in 2015's *Choices*, in which we abandoned the premise of a theatre altogether, in favor of setting our story in an EDM club in a style we called thEDMatre. Each successive experience led me to a greater understanding of the immense power of music to take control of the human body, typically unconsciously, without an audience's awareness. In short, my experiments in this "gray area" have convinced me more and more of the importance of dance in theatre, not just dance on the part of the performers, but as an experience in which the audience also participates.

This idea that music involves physical movement just as much as it does sound is not some new discovery that I've just made, however. Ethnomusicologist John Blacking pointed out that music appears to have involved movement for the greater part of human history (1995, 241). Daniel Levitin amplifies that idea, arguing that "One striking find is that in every society of which we're aware, music and dance are inseparable" (2007, 247). Every society! Later in this book we will examine the biological and neurological underpinnings of the essential connection between music and dance, music and physical movement. But for now, we should simply appreciate that the phenomenon we are attempting to define in this chapter, music, is one that cannot be limited simply to organized sound that we hear. Music is a much more deeply ingrained element of the human experience, one that we may experience with our ears or our eyes, or neither, as we may summon it up from deep within ourselves.

The Elements of Design

Thus far, we have widened our definition of music to include any sound we can possibly imagine, and then widened that to include not only sounds, but visual stimuli as well. We've also narrowed, first insisting that our sound and visuals need to be *organized*, and not just randomly occurring, *as art*, not for other purposes. We are looking for stimuli that unfold in *time*, and specifically do not reference to anything in our waking world like language and many visual images do. Lastly, we need to consider the constituent components of music, its elements that help us determine the answer to that age-old question my parents were so fond of asking: "You call that music?"

We started this book by observing that two of the only ways we have of perceiving our external world were through mechanical and electromagnetic waves. We followed the evolution of mammals to witness the development of ears to perceive mechanical waves and eyes to perceive electromagnetic waves. We argued that the ears are really good at perceiving time because of the nature of mechanical waves, and that the eyes are really good at perceiving space because of the nature of electromagnetic waves, although both eyes and ears were quite capable of perceiving that at which the other sense primarily excelled. We then discovered that the mammalian brain took an interesting twist in evolution when it developed not just the ability to perceive sight and sound, space and time, but to generate its own version of reality in a phenomenon we call dreams, and that the brain does this so well that, while under the influence of wakefulness or dreams, we are hard-pressed to remember that the other world even exists. We then went looking for a way to manipulate our brains in these two states, waking and dreaming, and all the states in between, one of which we call theatre. We discovered a great potential candidate in music. But the simple reality remains that the only way we can use music to control perception is by manipulating some form of mass in time and space. More importantly, we need to control our perception of mass, which comes to us in the form of energy either generated directly by the mass, or reflected off the mass. In other words, we should look for the elements of music in the energy characteristics we observe or create and in how they function in our perception of time and space.

Let's also not forget that this perspective traces back to my dubious beginnings teaching the sound part of a visual design class. But at the end of the day, it all turned out great, because we now discover in seeking our definition of music that the terms we need to use to describe the elements of music must readily apply to both visual and sonic stimuli![5] In our "formal analysis" of visual design in the class, we considered five components of a visual art object: color, mass (shape and form), texture, line and space (The J. Paul Getty Museum 2011). Van Phillips, who originated the class, had the keen intuition to add rhythm to these five. I then uncovered the auditory correlates of these visual elements, and I've been exploring them with my students for almost 40 years now. I've changed my approach a bit over the many years since that very first class, but only because we use words to describe things, and words are at best imprecise pointers at what theatre theoretician Eli Rozik calls "real doings." The elements themselves, thankfully, haven't changed much, even though others will call them by different names, describe them differently, and organize them in different ways.

Energy Characteristics

When we refer to "energy characteristics," we refer to either the wave energy that a mass generates, or the energy that is reflected off a mass. One way that the eyes and ears perceive these waves is color. Color is relatively easy to compare, since we refer to our perception of frequency by both the eyes and ears as *color*. In visual art, we tend to consider the hue (the dominant wavelength), and saturation or chroma (brilliance or intensity of a color, how pure the color is or how much it is mixed with other colors). In sonic art, we describe color in terms of pitch (the dominant frequency) and timbre (the combination of frequencies peculiar to a sound, similar to saturation).

In our original scenography class, we used the term mass, but that term has recently become standardized to *shape*, which is how we perceive objects in two dimensions, and *form*, which is how we perceive objects in three dimensions. Nevertheless, for simplicity's sake, we'll tend to continue to use the term "mass" in this book when we generically mean both shape and form in either the auditory

Element	Auditory	Visual
Energy	Color, Frequency, Pitch, Timbre	Color, Wavelength, Hue, Saturation
	Mass, Shape, Envelope, Dynamics, Volume, Loudness	Mass, Shape, Form, Volume, Value
Time	Rhythm, Beat, Pulse, Tempo, Meter, Phrasing, Duration	Rhythm, Beat, Pulse, Tempo, Meter, Phrasing, Duration
Space	Left/Right (x), Up/Down (y), Near/Far (z), Localization, Reflections, Reverberation	Left/Right (x), Up/Down (y), Near/Far (z), Direction, Boundaries
Energy in Time and Space	Texture	Texture
	Line, Melody	Line

Figure 4.1 Comparison of some common auditory and visual design elements.

or visual domain. Both visual and auditory objects have "shapes," although in sound we refer to the shape of a sound in terms of how it unfolds in time: its *envelope*. Envelope includes our perception of how a sound starts (its attack), how it initially decays (decay), its characteristics if the sound persists (sustain) and the way the sound ends (release). Together these are known as a sound's "ADSR" (attack, decay, sustain and release). Both visually and audibly, shape outlines the external boundaries of an object: the former in space, the latter in time.

The third dimension introduced by *form* also reveals the "volume" of a visual shape. Of course, we use exactly the same term, "volume," in sound, referring to the apparent loudness of a particular sound source. The greater the volume, the bigger the visual object or sound. One also finds a correlate in the visual design term *value*, in which the lightness or darkness of an object can be compared to the loudness of a sound, with silence correlating to absolute darkness. In both cases, volume and value, we are considering the apparent mass and size of an energy object, and it is this correlation that helps us sort out big sounds and big visual objects from small ones. Volume simply refers to the size of the sound or visual object itself, while value refers to the intensity of the reflection off the object. Since sound is a mechanical wave originated by the sound object, both terms sort of coalesce into the single term we use to describe this property, *loudness*, or its correlate when we manipulate loudness in time, *dynamics*.

Temporal Characteristics

In both visual and audible art, we use the term *rhythm* to describe how we organize art objects in time. Rhythm curiously uses a similar vocabulary in both visual and sound, particularly dance. Its primary components are beat, pulse, the part we tap our foot to, tempo, or the speed of flow of beats, meter, or how we organize beats in recurring ways, and phrasing, the unique patterns we create with individual objects, and how we group them. Finally, we also characterize sound and movement by how long it lasts, its duration. We'll spend quite a bit more time talking about these most precious elements of music in the next chapters.

Spatial Characteristics

Space describes the area that encloses the visual or sound object, and includes the visual or sound object itself. Negative space is the area outside the object, and positive space is the space occupied by the object itself. Visual space has two main qualities, direction (left/right or x, up/down or y, front/back, or z) and boundaries. We audibly perceive direction through *localization*, our ability to evaluate the direction of a sound object through temporal analysis. We audibly perceive boundaries as reflections and reverberations, again temporal characteristics our brain processes and analyzes.

Complex Elements that Combine Energy in Time and Space

Texture is an interesting element in that it has slightly different meanings depending on whether you consider it in its visual or auditory sense. This may stem from the simple fact that the word itself derives from the tactile sensation we get when we actually touch and feel an object. Technically, Webster's defines "texture" as something composed of closely interwoven elements, and that is precisely what our understanding of the use of the word in sound and visual art have in common

(Merriam-Webster Online Dictionary 2015). In visual art, texture can be implied in two dimensions by use of color, line, and shading of a color's value. In music, texture is also created by combining colors (timbres) and melodic lines in various amounts (analogous to shading). The main difference between how one typically considers visual texture and auditory texture, then, is that visual texture typically applies to a single visual object, or a part of a visual object (e.g., the weave of a fabric), while auditory texture often describes how multiple auditory objects work together in a composition (e.g., the orchestration of elements).

The Importance of These Elements of Music

I've discovered both in actual practice and in hosting multiple directors and visual designers in my sound classes over many years, that artists appreciate having a common vocabulary in which to engage in meaningful conversation about developing the music for a play—both audible and visual. Learning to understand the nuance of these design elements when used in either visual or auditory composition helps create a more effective way to talk about the music of a play without inhibiting the discussion about the meaning or intellectual communication of the play. It creates a bridge between the world of the sound designer/composer, who primarily creates non-referential elements of the theatre experience, and the visual artists, who often find themselves emphasizing referential elements of the theatre experience, especially considering the propensity of the American theatre toward realism. More than anything, it helps a director more effectively articulate what they are imagining. As one director put it:

> This course has deeply enhanced my capacity for examining and articulating the importance of musicality in my directing work. I have long known it was a priority, but I didn't have the vocabulary to address it with actors or designers. . . . I no longer feel shy or weird about expressing my intuitions about sound and musicality because I now have knowledge that validates them.
>
> (Anonymous 2015)

In proposing a definition of the word music for this book, understand that we are proposing a practical, pragmatic approach to the creation of music in theatre. It would be pointless for us to persevere through this entire book and arrive at a meaningful aesthetic regarding its role in theatre, only to find that it has no practical use in our artistic endeavors. With that in mind, and with a great amount of cautious enthusiasm, let's finally move on to proposing our definition of music.

A Proposed Definition of Music

We have established five criteria for defining music as we intend to use the term in this book. First, we must understand music to be a temporal endeavor; music is all about the organization of its elements in time. Second, we acknowledge that music is one of the forms of art. Third, we must carefully separate the referential qualities of words and images used in communicating ideas from the non-referential qualities of music used in creating emotion in an audience and in manipulating perception of time and space. Fourth, we must embrace that music is an endeavor in both auditory *and* visual art. Fifth, we identify that the elements we use to create music are energy characteristics such as color and mass (which includes elements such as envelope and shape, form and dynamics, volume, loudness, and value), that we manipulate in time and space creating lines and textures.

For the purposes of this book, then, when I use the term "music," I will mean:

A completely non-referential art form, separate from the referential communication of language and images, that emphasizes the manipulation of time over space through the organization and manipulation of the elements of energy in time and space.

Examples include instrumental music, the speech melody and prosodics of spoken language in poetry, the melody of song, and aspects of the temporal elements of visual art forms such as dance, film and theatre.

Ten Questions

1. If theatre is "collective dreaming," which part of that experience will we focus on in this book?
2. What are the two main differences between Varèse's definition of music and Rodriguez's? Why are they important?
3. What is the difference between the verbs "design" and "compose"?
4. What distinction does Cross's definition of music make that Rodriguez's and Varèse's definitions do not make? Why is this important?
5. What are two advantages that audible music has over static visual music, for example, the music associated with a painting?
6. What are two possible ways suggested by Walter Murch and the advent of music videos respectively that suggest the possibility of a transformation taking place in visual music and lighting?
7. What is arguably the most obvious example of a visual art form that is predominantly musical in nature? What physical characteristic of music ties audible music to visual music in this art form?
8. List six elements of music as they correlate to both auditory and visual music, and any associated names with the primary element.
9. What are three benefits to developing a common language to discuss the music of a play that helps directors and designers communicate?
10. What are five very important things to remember any time we use the term "music" in this book?

Things to Share

1. Let's get a feel for the power of referential sound. Go out with your audio recorder, and record a one-minute sound story—60 seconds, please, no more, no less! The catch is that you cannot use any words! What do we mean by story? Well a story should have a beginning, middle and end, as Aristotle pointed out. Keep the story simple, but definitely concentrate on communicating the story to your target audience, our class. We will play your story back for the class, and the rules of the game are that you cannot speak while we are listening or discussing your story. As a class, we'll attempt to tell you your story, as specifically as possible, just like if it contained other referential language such as words or visual images.

The more precisely you can communicate the facts of your story, the more successful we'll consider your sound story to be!

2. Now that you have a pretty good understanding of the element of color, it's time to explore its ability to stir emotions in your audience. Go out and find five colors, one for each of the following emotions: love, anger, fear, joy, sadness. Look for short sounds, 2–3 seconds long, whose pitch (or lack thereof) and timbre most incite one of these emotions in you. Most important: since we want to explore music, and not referential sounds, please work very hard to avoid any sounds with a referential communication, for example, kissing sounds to communicate love, baby laughing to communicate joy, a man sobbing to communicate sadness and so forth. Find sounds that the audience will not associate with "real doings."

We will play your five sounds back for the class, and the class will have to suggest which colors most incited which emotions in them. We'll poll the class to see which sounds they associated with each emotion, and then we'll ask you for the order you intended. We'll then tabulate the percentage of emotions you were able to correctly incite in each audience member, and discuss the results.

Notes

1 And, of course, we can't even argue that well, as we all perceive the play from a different physical position, and that implies both a different spatial and temporal stimulus.
2 In case you're wondering, we'll be building a definition somewhat like Merriam-Webster's 1a: "the science or art of ordering tones or sounds in succession, in combination, and in temporal relationships to produce a composition having unity and continuity."
3 Definitions for "design," "compose," and "composition":

design: v

1. vti to work out or create the form or structure of something
2. vti to plan and make something in a skillful or artistic way
3. vt to intend something for a particular purpose
4. vt to contrive, devise, or plan something

n.

1. the way in which something is planned and made
2. a drawing or other graphical representation of something that shows how it is to be made
3. a pattern or shape, sometimes repeated, used for decoration
4. the process and techniques of designing things
5. a plan or scheme for something
6. something that is planned or intended

compose: v

1. vt to make something by combining together
2. vt to put things together to form a whole
3. vt to arrange things in order to achieve an effect

4. vti to create something, especially a piece of music or writing
5. vt to make somebody become calm
6. vt to settle a quarrel or dispute (archaic)
7. vti to set type in preparation for printing

composition: n

1. the way in which something is made, especially in terms of its different parts
2. the way in which the parts of something are arranged, especially the elements in a visual image
3. the act or process of combining things to form a whole, or of creating something such as a piece of music or writing
4. something created as a work of art, especially a piece of music
5. a short piece of writing, especially a school exercise
6. a thing created by combining separate parts
7. a settlement whereby creditors agree to accept partial payment of debts by a bankrupt party, typically in return for a consideration such as immediate payment of a lesser amount
8. the formation of compound words from separate words
9. the setting of type in preparation for printing

Encarta® World English Dictionary © 1999 Microsoft Corporation. All rights reserved. Developed for Microsoft by Bloomsbury Publishing Plc.

4 Word/images simply refers to the fact that both words and images can and typically do have referents in the real world. The word car and an image of a car both "refer" to a car in the real world. A flute playing C sharp has little reference in the real world.

5 We'll save smell, taste and touch for another lifetime, although it is worth pointing out that babies in the first six months of their lives don't differentiate between the senses. According to Levitin, "Babies may see number five as red, taste cheddar cheeses in D-flat, and smell roses in triangles" (2007, 128). A similar condition called synesthesia exists in adults, in which one sensory organ (e.g., sight) perceives stimulus from another organ (e.g., sound).

Bibliography

Anonymous. 2015. THTR 363 Course Evaluations West Lafayette, IN, December 10.

Aristotle. 350 BCE "Poetics." The Internet Classics Archive. Accessed July 10, 2009. http://classics.mit.edu//Aristotle/poetics.html.

Berlioz, H. 2002. "Berlioz Music Scores: Texts and Documents, Symphonie Fantastique." August 2. Accessed February 23, 2016. www.hberlioz.com/Scores/fantas.htm.

Blacking, J. 1995. *Music, Culture and Experience*. London: University of Chicago Press.

CNN.com. 2006. "MTV Won't Say How Old It Is (But It's 25)." August 1. Accessed February 24, 2016. https://web.archive.org/web/20060811230032/www.cnn.com/2006/SHOWBIZ/Music/08/01/mtv.at.25.ap/index.html.

Cross, I. 2003. "Music, cognition, culture, and evolution." In *The Cognitive Neuroscience of Music*, edited by I. Peretz and Robert J. Zatorre. Oxford: Oxford University Press.

Delahunt, M. 2014. "ArtLex on Rhythm." March 14. Accessed February 24, 2016. www.artlex.com/ArtLex/r/rhythm.html.

Dowling, W. J. 2005. "Chapter fifteen: Perception of music." In *Handbook of Sensation and Perception*, edited by E. B. Goldstein, 470–494. Oxford: Blackwell.

Encyclopedia Britannica. 2016. "History of the Motion Picture." January 15. Accessed February 23, 2016. www.britannica.com/art/history-of-the-motion-picture.

Gunning, T. 2002. "Early Cinema and the Avant-Garde." March 8–13. Accessed February 23, 2016. www.sixpackfilm.com/archive/veranstaltung/festivals/earlycinema/symposion/symposion_gunning.html.

The J. Paul Getty Museum. 2011. "Elements of Art." Accessed February 26, 2016. www.getty.edu/education/teachers/building_lessons/formal_analysis.html.

Levitin, D. J. 2007. *This Is Your Brain On Music*. New York: Penguin Group/Plume.

Merriam-Webster Online Dictionary. 2015. "Scenography." Accessed February 2, 2016. www.merriam-webster.com/dictionary/scenography.

Merriam-Webster Online Dictionary. 2017. "Aesthetic." Accessed October 13, 2017. www.merriam-webster.com/dictionary/aesthetic#h2.

Moody, D. J. 2010. *Concert Lighting Techniques, Art and Business*. 3rd Edition. Burlington, MA: Focal Press.

Murch, W. 2002. *The Conversations*. New York: Alfred A. Knopf, a division of Random House, Inc.

Plato. 360 BCE. "Republic." The Internet Classics Archive. Accessed August 4, 2009. http://classics.mit.edu/Plato/republic.html.

Rodriguez, D. R. 2016. "Music and Human Experience." February 24. http://dox.utdallas.edu/syl17048.

Sacks, O. 2009. The Daily Show (J. Stewart, Interviewer) Comedy Central, June 29.

Stravinsky, I. 1936. *Igor Stravinsky an Autobiography*. New York: Simon and Schuster.

Svich, C. 2013. *The Breath of Theatre*. Raleigh, NC: lulu.com.

Thaut, M. H. 2005. *Rhythm, Music, and the Brain*. New York: Routledge Taylor & Francis Group.

Thomas, R. K. 1980. "A Beginning Course in Theatrical Sound Design." West Lafayette, IN: Unpublished Master's Thesis.

Varèse, E., and Wen-Chung, C. 1966. "The Liberation of Sound." *Perspective of New Music* 5 (1): 11–19.

_____

CHAPTER 5

PRIMATE NUMBERS

Introduction: Who's on First?

In Chapter 2 we examined two energy forms that reveal much of our world to us, electromagnetic waves and mechanical waves, and then we discovered how eyes and ears evolved an ability to perceive this world. Along the way, we discovered that not only did our ears evolve to perceive mechanical waves in the form of sound, but that they had a peculiar ability to apprehend time and directly connected to the emotional centers of our brains. In Chapter 3 we examined that unique relationship of our ears to our perception of time, and then discovered that time itself was something of a moving target. Time is not absolute as we often believe, but relative to each individual. We proposed then, that by manipulating sound we would be able to manipulate both a person's emotional state and their perception of time; in short, we would be able to manipulate their conscious experience and transport them into other worlds.

In Chapter 4 we described music as a tool we use to manipulate a person's perception of time, and along the way, incite, arouse and immerse rather than communicate. We set out to define music more precisely when we use the term in this book. We now continue our journey through time, and begin to look for early signs of the emergence of music, language and theatre in mammals. In music, we will be looking for clues that will lead us to the creation of an experience that is artistic, temporal and non-referential, and probably involves both sound and sight. We are still many millions of years before such an experience can legitimately be identified as an attempt at art. Still, in the next couple of chapters, we will find surprising signs in the evolution of mammals, primates, and early humans that just such an evolution took place—a "proto-music" that would fundamentally implicate music in the development of language and theatre.

And, oh, by the way, you may not have noticed, but we have slowly been narrowing our scope of inquiry to our human ancestors. Until slugs start writing symphonies or zebras start performing monologues, this seems like a logical choice. Our approach follows what is known in biology circles as *taxonomic classification*.

We started with the *kingdom* of Animals, and followed the evolution of our particular *phylum*, that is, Chordate, and its *subphylum*, Vertebrata, or vertebrates, animals with a spinal column. We mentioned our *superclass*, Tetrapods, when they exited the water and started roaming the earth, and out of that lineage, witnessed the evolution of our own *class*, Mammalia, or *mammals*. Mammals are

Life	
Kingdom	Animals
Phylum	Chordate
Subphylum	Vertebrata
Superclass	Tetrapods
Class	Mammals
Order	Primates
Family	Hominidae
Genus	*Homo*
Species	*Homo sapiens*

Figure 5.1 Our human taxonomic classification.

animals that have a three-boned middle ear, among other unique characteristics. In this chapter, we will continue to climb the branches of our "Tree of Life," as Darwin called it. We'll discover how our *order*, Primates, further contributed to the evolution of music, language, and the peculiar ability some animals developed to learn the behavior of others called *mimesis*. We'll continue to drill down through our *family* of Hominidae, whose members are called the Great Apes, to our *genus, Homo*. We'll explore the precursors to music, language and mimesis, and the earliest evidence of ritual that would ultimately lead to the beginnings of theatre (Darwin 2008).

But before we do, we need to talk for a moment about the many possible ways that evolution may have unfolded. It would be nice if we could simply pronounce one as correct, and follow that one, but at present there simply is not enough evidence to justify that. In fact, there is a strong likelihood that there will never be enough evidence to justify a unified theory of evolution. The fossilized bones and other evidence left behind by our ancestors can only tell us so much. Fortunately, just about every theory leads us to the same conclusion: that music, language and mimesis evolved intermingled. Each phenomenon was intimately involved in the other, and it would have been very hard for one to have evolved without the other. We are, as it turns out, the sum of ourselves, and that remains the whole point of this book: we cannot hope to achieve the best sound designs and compositions for theatre unless we view music as a foundational and holistic part of our theatre experience.

In proceeding in this manner, we will once again run into the common problem: biologists, anthropologists, neuroscientists and others often disagree about the specifics of the evolution of our species. There are those who argue that language either came before music or developed independently of it. I'll call that the "linguist" approach. It includes Derek Bickerton, who argues that language is based on the ability of Hominins (our human ancestors) to develop symbols, which evolved at a much later date into more complex thoughts using syntax and grammar (Bickerton 1990). This group also includes Steven Pinker, who argues that language is instinctual. Pinker goes on to famously suggest that music is not an evolutionary phenomenon at all, simply "auditory cheesecake," a bonus that came along with language (Pinker 1997, 524). There are those who argue that language developed from essentially music-like expressions of emotion, especially Darwin (Darwin 1871, 241). There are those who argue that music and language both evolved simultaneously, perhaps out of a common ancestral stage that was neither musical nor linguistic, a "holistic" "musilanguage." This group includes Steven Brown (Brown 2000), Allison Wray (Wray 1998) and Steven Mithen (Mithen 2006). Finally, neuroanthropologist Merlin Donald proposes that imitation, or its more sophisticated form, mimesis, must necessarily come first in the cognitive evolution of humans (Donald 1993a). And, of course, there are variants on all of these. While acknowledging substantial differences for *their* purposes, I don't see these arguments as being contradictory for *our* purpose: tracing the fundamental role that music plays in the development of what Oscar Brockett calls the *autonomous* theatre (Brockett 1992, 7).

One would think that there would be more research into the origins of theatre that included its anthropological, biological and neurological origins, but the theories about the origins of theatre tend to focus more on the history of the autonomous theatre, especially Western theatre, the theatre since the Greeks. Since we are interested in how the autonomous theatre developed out of music, how theatre is a *type* of music, we'll actually end our journey with the first autonomous theatre in Greece. After all, there hasn't been much evolution-wise that has changed in the blink of a 2,500-year eye. Fortunately, there are a lot of clues in these evolutionary theories that help us to understand the close and rather intermingled evolution of language, music and mimesis, the primary components of theatre.

Not surprisingly, a lot of the differences of opinion depend quite a bit on how one defines the words "music," "language" and "mimesis." We just made such a distinction between music and language in Chapter 4. Hopefully, distinctions such as this will help us not wander too deep into those controversies. There is little controversy about whether language is considered an evolutionary adaptation. David Huron and many others also favor the thinking that music is also an evolutionary adaptation selected to favor survival of the species (Huron 2006, 59). That point of view has perhaps been more definitively supported in the 2015 discovery of specific regions of the brain dedicated to music (Norman-Haignerem, Kanwisher and McDermott 2015). Merlin Donald's contention that mimesis is an evolutionary adaptation found its neurological evidence in 1992, when a group of Italian researchers discovered the existence of the so-called mirror neuron, perhaps the genetic basis for mimesis (di Pellegrino et al. 1992). We'll explore all of these discoveries as we move forward in our evolutionary journey.

But rather than spend our precious time debating "who's on first?,"[1] I'll try to continue on our path of discovering important developments in the evolution of our species. And when we do wander into areas where we are following one researcher's thesis over another, I'll always try to make sure that the research in question is cited. I'll inevitably make no one happy. As Merlin Donald, put it: "Evolution is generally kludge-prone and messy, and deals with terrifying degrees of complexity" (Donald 1993b, 782). But hopefully it will give you a rich set of possibilities to consider. Hopefully it might even influence your aesthetic.

Our journey continues in this chapter as we consider the communicable signs, the music-like expressions, and the emerging imitation in early primates. First, we'll explore signs, what many suggest are the prototypes of language. Next, we'll consider the extraordinary evolutionary step our ancestors took as they learned to walk on two legs, an important milestone in our full acquirement of musical rhythm. Finally, we'll discover a neurological basis for imitation, and consider early manifestations of *mimesis*, the ability to imitate, rehearse and perform the actions of another. In all three developments, we'll see the influence of the other two.

Music, Language and Theatre: The Really Early Years

We started this journey 14 billion years ago, and we now find ourselves down to the last 60 million years. And yet it's hard to imagine a time frame of 60 million years, especially when our recorded history is measured in thousands of years. There is a great tendency to mentally imagine things happening much, much

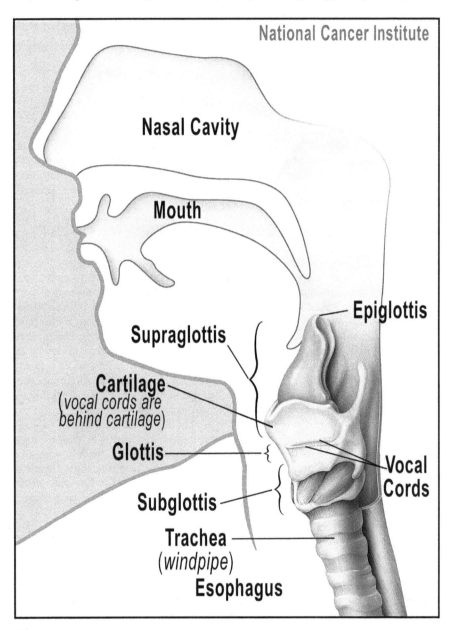

Figure 5.2 The larynx and nearby structures.

Credit: From the National Cancer Institute, Alan Hoofring, Illustrator.

faster than they did. So, when we suggest that about 60 million years ago, our order, primates, first appeared, it's important to never lose sight that our margin of error can often be much larger than the recorded history of human civilization!

Primates fully developed about 50–55 million years ago, about 10–15 million years after the extinction of the dinosaurs. By this time most members of the mammalian species had developed much more sophisticated vocal tracts that allowed them to produce a wider range of sound colors.

These must have had an evolutionary advantage, as some of these primates grew larger to about the size of a dog, developed larger brains, mainly lived in trees, and tended to be vegetarians (O'Neil 2012). Many mammals that evolved

Figure 5.3 An Old World monkey: mandrill.

Credit: Curioso/Shutterstock.com. Adapted by Richard K. Thomas.

later did not confine their emotional expressions to vocalizations. Deer, rabbits, elephant shrews and skunks, all exhibit a behavior called "foot-drumming," in which they stomp their feet repeatedly when they encounter a predator or are alarmed (Randall 2001, 1143). The only distant mammal that has showed a capacity for entrainment, the ability to synchronize to a beat, however, is a sea lion named Ronan (Goldman 2013). Hard to say whether there is an entrainment gene lurking somewhere in our distant past, or whether it is an adaptation that has evolved independently from us humans. Part emotion, part sign. At this early proto-stage, it is hard to tell proto-music and proto-language apart.

Matt Rossano describes ritual as an attention-getting, sequenced pattern of behavior governed by rules and formality, and meant to convey meaning (2010, 82; 2011, 42). Ritual involves participants *performing* sequences that do not vary and that the other participants do not create, but instead follow (Smuts and Watanabe 1990, 168). For example, there is the approach ritual of deer, elk and moose, in which the approaching male acts like he's a calf approaching his prospective mate to nurse, so as not to scare her off (Rossano 2010, 83). This does not surprise me. I have witnessed a fair number of approach rituals by the male species myself in the bars and clubs of college campuses.

Old World monkeys diverged from our line of descent about 30 million years ago[2] (Cambridge Encyclopedia of Human Evolution 1992; Nature 2011, 530). They are an important resource about we humans because we both diverged from the same ancestral line. There are two additional traits that we discover in both humans and Old World monkeys that provide clues about music, language and mimesis. The first we'll talk about is how they express themselves in color and rhythm, both as a primitive form of communication (proto-language), and as a method of expressing emotion (proto-music). The second trait we humans have in common with Old World monkeys is the evolution of imitation, essential to playmaking.

Old World monkeys also exhibit drumming activities in captivity. Of course, even in our more closely related cousins, we need to understand that we are not talking about rock star performances here.

When researchers Remedios and Kayser say that macaque monkeys drum, they mean three things: first, there is a periodic repetition of individual beats; second, these drumming outbursts are short (e.g., they last an average of 1.5 seconds); and third, they are created on "artificial sources," such as shaken branches or thumped-on logs, so they sound decidedly different than vocalizations. Not exactly Top 40 hit material, but it's a start when we consider how our inherent sense of rhythm evolved. Researchers often talk about this drumming in terms of expressing emotion (proto-music) or communicating information (a "proto-language," which is usually accompanied by the "proto-music" of drumming: rhythm, color, etc.). Remedios and Kayser have demonstrated that macaque monkey drumming does activate our old friend, the amygdala, as good an indication there is that drumming is an expression of emotion (2009, 18010–18014).

Research on one species of Old World monkey, the vervet, helps us understand the nature and extent of primitive vocal expression as communication. These monkeys developed distinctly different calls based on the type of predator spotted, so that they could communicate whether the threat was from above (e.g., an eagle), below (e.g., a python), or across (e.g., a leopard), and take appropriate evasive action, such as climbing a tree or hiding in a bush. For example, if the monkeys were on the ground, a leopard call might send them scurrying up trees (Seyfarth, Cheney and Marler 1980). Since the calls themselves indicate specific referents (signs), this type of signaling may represent very early evolutionary evidence of communication using vocalization.

At the same time, it would be hard to argue that the calls themselves did not have a proto-musical component. Imagine the monkey calmly standing by going, "dude, there's a leopard about to pounce on one of us." Not likely. Instead, expect a little startle effect, with the monkey barking loudly, perhaps at the top of his or her lungs (Mithen 2006, 108). Such calls would have had distinctive color, rhythm, mass and line characteristics that quickly and effectively changed the ambient emotional environment from calm to mega-tense. Those vocalizations would be accompanied by appropriate physical gestures, perhaps themselves prototypical of music's visual expression, dance. Darwin famously noted great similarity between monkey facial expressions and humans (Darwin 1871, 133–147). The referential information contained in the vocalization and physicalization certainly would have helped identify the source of the problem and outline a course

Figure 5.4 Macaque monkey.

Credit: Iakov Filimonov/Shutterstock.com. Adapted by Richard K. Thomas.

Figure 5.5 Vervet monkey.

Credit: Eric Isselee/Shutterstock.com. Adapted by Richard K. Thomas.

of action. But the musical aspects would have incited a sense of urgency that would be hard to ignore. The only component it lacked that would qualify it as music would be its artistic function, which, hopefully, was somewhat suppressed at that critical moment. Neurologist Steven Brown describes a signal of this sort as a "referential emotive vocalization" (Brown 2000, 291).

Almost simultaneously in the big picture of evolution, other Old World monkeys including geladas and baboons have been observed in what some anthropologists argue are primitive *ritual* behaviors.

Geladas developed elaborate social rituals for greeting, departing, grooming and warning each other that involve elaborate singing—modifications of melodic line, rhythm, mass and so forth (Mithen 2006, 109–110).

Baboons greet each other by performing the ritual of scrotum grasping. Yes, it means exactly what you think—male baboons rendering themselves extremely vulnerable while greeting each other.

Living in an environment in which baboons are routinely hostile toward each other, this manner of greeting far surpasses our human ritual of shaking hands,

Figure 5.6 Gelada.

Credit: Khort Esther Tatiana/Shutterstock.com. Adapted by Richard K. Thomas.

if for no other reason than the obvious potential danger involved (Smuts and Watanabe 1990, 152). Noteworthy is that the scrotum grasping is preceded by lip smacking and other visual gestures to indicate friendly intentions, introducing a proto-musical component into the ritual (Rossano 2013, 96).

Is there a biological basis for such behaviors? It turns out that there may be. In 1992, a group of researchers published startling research that documented the existence of a mirror neuron system in macaque monkeys. While initially controversial, this research seems to be gaining considerable acceptance in the mainstream of science.[3] Mirror neurons fire when an action is performed, which is typical for a neuron. But they also fire when an individual *observes* the same action performed (di Pellegrino et al. 1992). In research experiments, a monkey grasped a cup, and watched a cup being grasped, in both cases firing mirror neurons in their brains. It did not make a difference whether the monkey grasped the cup itself, or watched someone else grasp a cup; whether it was a human or a monkey grasping the cup, whether it was a cup or another object, or how far away the cup was from the monkey. In all cases, the mirror neuron fired. However, if someone just *mimed* grasping the cup, the neurons would not fire. Mirror neurons appear to be almost exclusively referential, at least in these studies.

Figure 5.7 Baboon.

Credit: Susan Schmitz/Shutterstock.com. Adapted by Richard K. Thomas.

The discovery of mirror neurons led to a number of fanciful speculations that really got the subject off to a bad start, leading two of the researchers that discovered mirror neurons, Rizzollatti and Carighero, to remind us that there are two main hypotheses regarding the function of mirror neurons that we must keep in mind. The first is that mirror neurons are an important but not sole part of a primate's ability to imitate another's action. There is a lot more going on in the brain when animals, including us, imitate. For example, the mirror neurons have to be programmed or re-programmed in order to function (2004, 172). Catmur, Walsh and Heyes conducted a series of experiments in 2007 that showed that mirror neurons develop through *sensorimotor*[4] learning, sort of a demonstration of a potential underlying mechanism to "monkey see, monkey do" (Catmur, Walsh and Heyes, 2007). The second hypothesis is that mirror neurons serve as the basis for one primate's *understanding* of another's actions (Rizzollati et al. 2004, 172). Mirror neurons do not directly cause imitation, but may provide a key evolutionary adaptation that would allow animals to learn to imitate (Arbib 2013, 118). Of course, it takes a lot more than evolving mirror neurons to make great theatre.

In a 2009 journal article, Marco Iacoboni extended this concept of the relationship between imitation, mirror neurons and understanding to the subject of empathy. Keep in mind that empathy is the ability or tendency to feel what another person is feeling. This differs from sympathy, which is simply the ability to understand what another is feeling, but not to actually feel the same emotion oneself. Iacoboni first observed that authors such as "de Montaigne (1575), Adam Smith

(1579), Nietzsche (1881) and Wittgenstein (1980)—have often associated imitation with the ability to empathize and understand other minds" (2009, 654). He describes a "low road" to imitation that "leads to imitation in a direct fashion, such that the perceiver acts the gestures, postures, facial expressions, and speech perceived in other people." But he goes on to suggest a "high road leads to complex and rather subtle forms of imitation, as shown by a number of experiments that lead to stereotype activation or trait activation" (2009, 657). The "high road" experiments often led to automatic responses of which the participants were not consciously aware. Iacoboni describes experiments specifically tailored to investigating our ability to empathize, that is to feel what someone else is feeling, and imitation. In short, he found that "through imitation and mimicry, we are able to feel what other people feel" (2009, 659). Iacoboni further described experiments that suggested that "the large-scale network composed of mirror neuron areas, insula, and the limbic system (see Figure 5.9) likely provides a simulation-based form of empathy" (665). These of course, are the same areas we have discovered (and will continue to discover!) that music plays an important and often unconscious role in stimulating. Here in a nutshell, we find a neurological and sociological basis for the fundamental processes involved in both music and acting. In later chapters, we will return to this phenomenon, as it has everything to do with the powerful combination of music and mimesis in theatre.

But what about sound and mirror neurons? Can imitating and representing real sounds effect real communication using mirror neurons? In 2002, Evelyne Kholer led a group who investigated whether a monkey's mirror neurons would

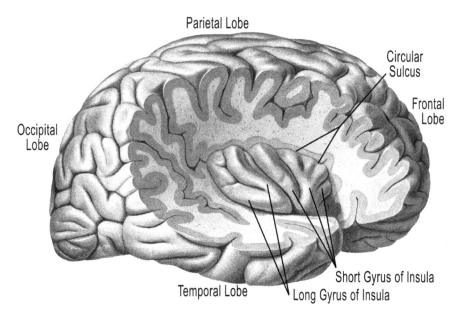

Figure 5.8 The insular cortex is tucked deep within the brain, in between the temporal, parietal and frontal lobes. It has a lot to do with emotions, so we expect that it has a lot to do with music! See Koelsch (2014, 171).

Credit: Sobotta, Johannes. 1909. *Textbook and Atlas of Human Anatomy*, edited with additions by McMurrich, J. Volume III. Philadelphia and London, W. B. Saunders. Figure 633, Page 147. Adapted by Richard K. Thomas.

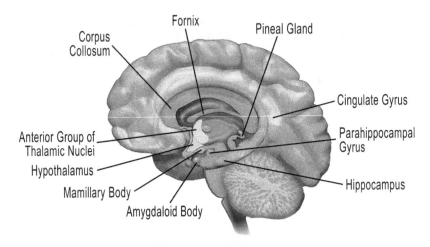

Figure 5.9 The limbic system consists of our old friend, the amygdala, and other structures such as the hippocampus that have a lot to do with both memory and emotions. We'll continue to explore it in later chapters.

Credit: Blausen.com staff. 2014. "Medical Gallery of Blausen Medical 2014." *WikiJournal of Medicine* 1 (2). doi:10.15347/wjm/2014.010. ISSN 2002–4436. CC-BY-3.0. https://creativecom mons.org/licenses/by/3.0/deed.en. Adapted by Richard K. Thomas.

fire to the sound of an action all by itself, with no visual reinforcement. In cases where monkeys were familiar with the sound of the action, 13% of the mirror neurons fired even when the visual stimulus was not present. These have been named *audiovisual neurons* (Kohler et al. 2002). Based on this, the researchers propose that mirror neurons may also be implicated in the development of spoken language as we will investigate in the next chapter.

Consider the relatively low percentage of audiovisual mirror neurons that fired relative to all of the mirror neurons in the brain.[5] We've already observed in the last chapter that sound performs rather poorly at "referring" to "real doings." Perhaps, we may find a neurological basis for this in mirror neurons. But it's not an entirely visually dominated referential world, either. In the study, there were a few instances where the sound alone stimulated the mirror neurons but the visual stimulus without the sound did not. For example, the cracking of peanuts stimulated the monkey's audiovisual mirror neurons, but watching someone crack peanuts without hearing the sound did not (Kohler et al. 2002, 847). Some sounds, what I refer to as *iconic* sounds (sounds that everyone immediately recognizes), carry tremendous referential power. But they tend to be few and far between.

When mirror neurons fire to sounds, meaning becomes attached to elements we describe as proto-music, that is, the color, rhythm, mass, line and so forth of the gesture or sound. These imitative actions, their sounds and finally the names we give them in language seem to be thoroughly intertwined when considered in this manner. It's hard to even imagine the gestures, music and meaning becoming dissociated from each other, but in modern theatre practice, this is a rather common occurrence.

An old Purdue University production of *The Matchmaker* required one of my students to create a horse-drawn carriage to pull up offstage. This "effect" was somewhat doomed from the get-go by a number of factors:

1. There was no visual gesture (i.e., a real carriage pulling up onstage) to help identify the sound.
2. The sound of a carriage moving is not necessarily iconic; it could (and did) sound like a lot of other things.
3. The carriage pulls up backstage, and that's what we hear, a carriage pulling up in the acoustic of the backstage area, not "outdoors" of this "home" as we are led to believe, (the imitation is inherently not very good).
4. The sound did not fit into the "music" of the existing scene.

Our poor student sound designer found himself facing what everyone considered to be a simple task ("Just pull the sound out of your sound effects library") and being the target of reviews like "sounds like a bunch of wood falling." The solution, of course, would be to attach the sound to a visual gesture, or to referential dialogue ("here comes the carriage!") that accomplishes the same task. But it is often impossible to do; the carriage is offstage and not visible, the playwright didn't write the necessary referential dialogue. In these cases, we really, really want the sound to do that referential signaling, just like our monkey friends hearing peanuts being cracked! My friend Joe Pino calls this sort of sound the "offstage one act," and suggests that he typically recommends truncating such scenes to be as short as possible (Pino 2017). A sound designer caught in the crosshairs of this compromise should first look to more *iconic* sounds (in this case, for example, lead with a horse whinny). Whether the horse whinnying triggered everyone's audiovisual mirror neurons as they imagined a carriage arriving offstage is anyone's guess, but this research certainly helps us to better understand how important it is to approach referential, imitative sound in a play carefully.

Even if we find the perfect iconic horse-drawn carriage sound to use in the scene, our effect may still distract rather than pull us deeper into the scene. The vervet monkey did not stand idly by, nonchalantly signaling the approaching leopard. The vervet monkey call would have been filled with an emotion appropriate to the scene. The fundamental problem related to using sounds from sound effects libraries is that the sound effects were not recorded with the underlying music of the scene in mind. Sticking sound effects on top of the music of a scene is no more useful than putting a party hat on the scrambling vervet monkey. Most of the great sound designers I have ever known disdain using sound effects libraries. They prefer to create each sound through imagining the music of the moment of the scene in which the sound must exist. In other words, they attempt to treat the sound *effect* as a piece of music, whose instruments are iconic sounds, with each sound orchestrated into the fabric of the scene. In the case of our carriage arriving, a punctuation was required in the rhythmic timing of the actors and the scene, not a long, sustained sound. The music of the carriage needed to not only be matched to the business of the horse, the driver and the carriage itself, but to the music of the scene playing out on the stage in which the audience was hopefully fully engaged. We will talk more about this particular problem in the next chapter when we discuss the concept of entrainment in more detail.

Apes diverged from the same branch of our ancestral tree as monkeys. Gibbons, or "lesser apes" next split off from this branch about 18–20 million years ago[6] (Nature 2011).

Gibbons are members of the *lesser* apes family, the next major branch of our taxonomic classification system. They are physically smaller than the family from which we humans descended, the *great* apes. Gibbons are particularly known for their beautiful haunting songs in which they produce relatively pure tones in stunning melodies to mate monogamously or to mark their territory. Hiroki Koda and others in Japan discovered that gibbons manipulated their singing voice in the same manner as human opera singers: they "tune" their vocal tract to the fundamental frequency, which amplifies their call considerably, allowing them to be heard from over a mile away[7] (2012, 347). This ability of gibbons to manipulate their vocal tracts to produce a wide variety of vocalizations is somewhat unique (musical or linguistic?) in apes. Many apes have obviously not developed vocal abilities to produce such auditory delights. At the same time, gibbons are not known for drumming. But seriously, if you had a voice like that, would you play percussion?

Orangutans, one of the family of great apes that includes us humans, diverged from our human ancestral line about 12–16 million years ago.[8]

They don't drum at all, as far as we know, but are said to be great learners, able to learn over 30 unique signs.

Figure 5.10 Gibbon.

Credit: Tanawat Ariya/Shutterstock.com. Adapted by Richard K. Thomas.

Figure 5.11 Orangutan.

Credit: Odua Images/Shutterstock.com. Adapted by Richard K. Thomas.

Gorillas diverged next, about 6–8 million years ago, although more recent evidence puts the split as early as 8–19 million years ago[9] (Nature 2011, 530; Langergraber et al. 2012). They can also learn signs, and like other primates engage in a form of group singing when enjoying certain foods (Shapiro 1982). Notably, they are also avid drummers who like to drum out beats on their chests.

In all of these primates we witness something of a common feature: the animals' vocalizations indicate and change with the animal's emotional state. Sometimes the animal is also communicating or attempting to communicate something quite referential, but not necessarily. When they do communicate, they communicate *holistically*, meaning that they vocalize complete communications that cannot be broken down into syntactical constructions of individual words (Wray 1998, 50–51). Also worth noting and central to our definition of music, expression in apes is multimodal, meaning that it involves gesture and sounds, proto-music and proto-dance. The ape may attach a communication to the qualities we have come to associate with proto-music, but those qualities may also exist simply for their own sake, for example, when gorillas sing while eating certain foods. Lea Leinonen's research on macaque monkeys showed that even humans can successfully identify their emotional states of fear, aggression, dominance and neutrality, suggesting that we tend to share the same vocalization (i.e., elements of music) patterns (Leinonen et al. 1991). Macaques also tend to *lateralize*[10] musical elements such as color, rhythm and mass in the right brain, and referential qualities in the left brain, as we'll later discover in humans. So, we are also seeing neurological support that these proto-musical elements are distinct from their proto-language elements, suggesting that, even in the "proto" stage, it is relatively easy for music to exist without language, but rather difficult for any kind of language to exist without music (Hauser 1999, 98). In fact, we won't see an ability for language to exist independently of music until written language makes its first appearance. We see in all these early primates, then, a rather ubiquitous property of music: it can exist just fine on its own for the purposes of expressing emotion, or it can have referential meanings attached to it that not only communicate ideas, but also incite in the listener emotions similar to the those generated by animal vocalizations and gestures (Hauser 1999, 77–79).

Our closest kin chimpanzees diverged about 4.5–6 million years ago, although, again, new evidences suggest the split may have occurred much earlier, about 7–8 million years ago[11] (Nature 2011; Langergraber et al. 2012). Chimpanzees also produce food-associated calls and can learn as many as 250 symbols, taking

Figure 5.12 Gorilla.

Credit: Aaron Amat/Shutterstock.com. Adapted by Richard K. Thomas.

Figure 5.13 Chimpanzee.

Credit: Aaron Amat/Shutterstock.com. Adapted by Richard K. Thomas.

important evolutionary steps along the way to the emergence of fully developed music, language and imitation in the human species (Luef, Breuer and Pika 2016, 1; Nature 2011; Mithen 2006, 105).

Chimpanzee learning and social behaviors are so divergent and extensive that researchers legitimately refer to them as "cultures." We have to be careful as we proceed to separate culturally acquired behaviors from evolutionary adaptations, which can be controversial. These behaviors include tool usage, grooming and courtship rituals. The important characteristics of culture are that it is "transmitted repeatedly through social or observational learning," and that the behaviors exist throughout the community. Separating culture from evolution becomes very important when we think about the communal nature of both music and theatre and our developing sense of rhythm as a social cohesive (Whiten et al. 1999, 682–683; King 2015, 393).

Chimpanzees and their close relatives, bonobos like to drum on resonant objects like tree trunks, and will come back often for a repeat performance when they find one whose sound they like (Center for Academic Research & Training in Anthropogeny 2015). Chimpanzees customarily drum and perform ritual "rain

Figure 5.14 Bonobo.

Credit: Sergey Uryadnikov/Shutterstock.com. Adapted by Richard K. Thomas.

dances" when it starts to rain, further evidence of an intermingling of music, language and mimesis in our distant past.

   None of this noise making is particularly synchronized or coordinated in time, however. In Chapter 2, we discovered a number of creatures with an odd ability to synchronize some particular rhythmic activity with each other in a phenomenon called entrainment. But its occurrence in our line of descent, seems somewhat random, and really didn't appear until much, much later in our evolution. In our own near lineage, we do find what might be called true rhythmic behaviors in bonobos, who exhibit a form of beacon effect called *staccato hoot*, in which males all bark together in unison to amplify their signal. In both humans and bonobos, the middle range in which human synchrony (entrainment to a beat) is possible is about 2 Hz, or 120 beats per minute. Both humans and bonobos may also have been able to use human movement—akin to bipedalism, but moving in place, as in a dance—to learn to increase the precision of their beat synchronization. Perhaps these commonalities provide an indication that our ability to entrain to beats derived from a common ancestor (Merker, Madison and Eckerdal 2009, 6–7).

Figure 5.15 Sahelanthropus tchadensis.
Credit: Copyright John Gurche.

Bipedal Primates

After splitting off from chimpanzees, our own ancestors did something quite stunning and remarkable: they stood on two legs and walked upright. Not just some of the time, as some members of our great ape family did, but habitually, a characteristic rare among mammals. Bipedalism evolved somewhere between 6 and 7 million years ago with evidence provided by a closely related genus, *Sahelanthropus*.

Genus is the next major narrowing of our taxonomic classifications after family. *Sahelanthropus* had a chimpanzee size brain, but the *foramen magnum*, the hole in its skull where the spinal cord enters the cranium, was at the bottom of the skull, as in humans, rather than in the rear, as in other apes (Brunet 2002, 2005).

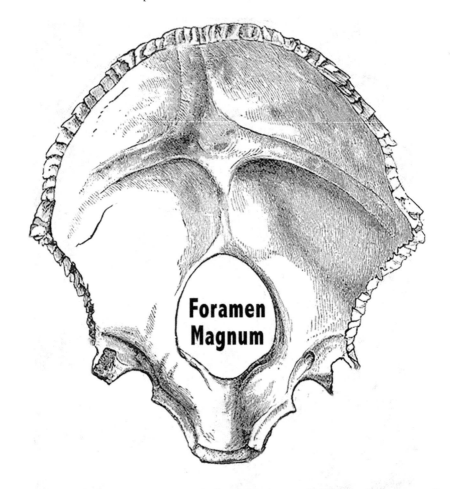

Figure 5.16 The foramen magnum, at the base of the human skull, allows humans to walk upright.

Credit: Gray, Henry. 1918. *Anatomy of the Human Body*. Lea and Febiger. Plate 130. Adapted by Richard K. Thomas.

This led anthropologists to conclude that *Sahelanthropus* was the first member of the Hominini tribe to walk upright. Such a restructuring of the skull would also have effected changes to the vocal tract, beginning a long pattern of evolution that would eventually see the larynx descend further down the throat (Mithen 2006, 129).

Cognitive scientist Philip Lieberman proposed that the evolution of human walking provides evidence of an evolving *basal ganglia*. The basal ganglia consist of groups of neurons that sit at the base of the *cerebral cortex* (the outer layers of the brain) indicating that the basal ganglia are a very primitive and old part of our brain. They are associated with controlling voluntary motor functions, learning and emotion.

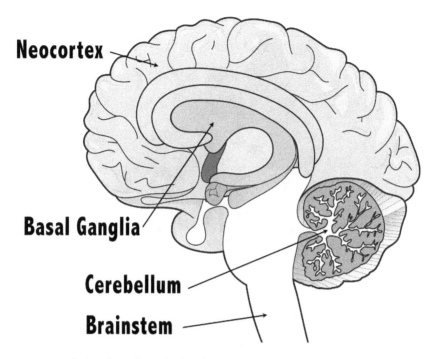

Figure 5.17 The basal ganglia and related structures.
Credit: Blamb/Shutterstock.com. Adapted by Richard K. Thomas.

The basal ganglia work in conjunction with the cerebellum, the oldest part of our brain, and our new brain, the *neocortex*, to "play a critical role in motor control, motor learning and cognition." Both walking and speech require the basal ganglia to work as a " 'sequencing engine' that can reiterate motor commands stored as motor pattern generators in other parts of the brain," putting together sequences of instructions into meaningful actions. Lieberman suggests that walking was perhaps the "starting point" for the evolution of human speech, language and cognition (Lieberman 2007, 47–52).

Steven Mithen argues that the basal ganglia are also the starting point for our superb sense of rhythm, as rhythm is essential to walking on two legs (Mithen 2006, 150). There is a direct relationship between music and walking in the basal ganglia: rhythm. The basal ganglia must jump into action anytime an internal beat must be generated, and this includes both walking and playing music with a beat. Chimpanzees and apes are bipedal for short amounts of time, but their ability to generate and maintain a beat is not ubiquitous or customary in nature, and very difficult for them to acquire in captivity. In *Sahelanthropus* and their descendants over the next few million years, we see a possible origin that connects the act of walking and our ability to generate and maintain a beat in musical rhythm.

About 4 million years ago, another genus, *Australopithecus*, emerged, and it has a very popular representative in Lucy, a 3.2-million-year-old skeleton, who captured the imagination of the world when she was first discovered in 1974 (Institute of Human Origins 2014; Martin 2015, 38; Falk 1999, 211).

Figure 5.18 Australopithecus reconstruction.

Credit: Nicolas Primola/Shutterstock.com. Adapted by Richard K. Thomas.

And while Lucy may have walked, Steven Mithen points out that she was not the first to run and jump, as it would take another million and a half years before bipedalism would develop to the full capabilities humans enjoy today (Mithen 2006, 139–144).

Bipedalism did allow Australopithecines to wander out of the forests and onto the savannahs. Mithen argues that this new habitat pressured Australopithecines to develop a more sophisticated and wider range of calls than apes or monkeys. They developed an ability to alert the presence of a group of predators or found food that would best be shared in an expanding social environment. Musically, Mithen suggests that Australopithecines developed the ability to modulate the mass (volume) of their calls to signal without alerting predators ("Shhh . . . there's a lion over there!"), and much more musically expressive rhythms and lines (melodies) than their gelada ancestors. But Mithen also tells of one archaeological find, a child swooped away from its mother by an eagle, that perhaps elicited the most musical vocal expression of all: the lament of a mother over a lost child (2006, 132). Neuroanthropologist Dean Falk concludes that these early ancestors used vocalization especially to express emotions. Falk based his analysis on chimpanzee social and vocalization habits, as well as their vocal tracts and cerebral cortices, emphasizing the more music-like purpose of their vocalizations over the referential (Falk 1999, 211). Mithen summarizes the communications of these early Hominins[12] as "Hmmmm:" Holistic (meaning that each vocalization comprised a complete thought rather than a part of a thought such as a word), multimodal (typically involving vocalization and gesturing), manipulative (a command or a request rather than an abstract thought) and musical (involving manipulations of melodic line, mass, rhythm, etc.) (2006, 138).

About three and a half million years ago, early Hominins[13] roamed eastern and southern Africa, and developed a very primitive ability to make rudimentary stone tools.

These tools are called Oldowan, after the lake in Tanzania where they were first discovered. They were basically chopping tools used for, among other things, cutting the flesh off of slaughtered animals (Mithen 2006, 125). What makes these tools so special is that it took a certain amount of sophistication to make them; in order to get their sharp edges, they had to be fashioned by striking one stone against another in a certain way to get a sharp edge, and to flake off other bits of stone that could be used for other "tool" purposes.

Merlin Donald sees in this tool-making process one of the first clues to developing human cognition. Donald thinks that Australopithecines might have been the first to break two mental barriers: first, the ability to voluntarily recall memories, and second, the ability to express knowledge in some sort of action, even, as he says "in simple pantomime"[14] (Donald 1993b, 35). The ability to voluntarily recall memories would allow the Australopithecine to voluntarily recall a technique that worked in creating a tool, to demonstrate that technique to another,

Figure 5.19 An Oldowan tool from Lomekwi, Kenya, dated to 3.3 million years old. According to author Erella Hovers, "The scars on the stone's surface indicate that it was used as a core from which flakes were produced."

Credit: Reprinted by permission from Macmillan Publishers Ltd: Nature. Hovers, Erella. "Archaeology: Tools Go Back in Time," *Nature 521*, 294–295. doi:10.1038/521294a, copyright 2015.

Millions of Years Ago	Important Characteristics
2.5	Fully human bipedal capabilities such as running and jumping
3.5	Oldowan tools
4	*Australopithecus* (Lucy); much more sophisticated vocal communication system
4.5–8	*Homo* genus and chimpanzees diverge; *Homo* walks upright; fully descended larynx
6–19	Gorillas diverge
12–16	Orangutans diverge
18–20	Lesser apes diverge
30	Old World monkeys develop capable of using vocal signs to communicate, drumming activities, proto-singing, and rituals; evidence of mirror neurons
50	Primates fully developed; much more sophisticated vocal tracts capable of producing a wide range of sound colors; many members exhibit drumming techniques
~250	Early mammals exhibiting primitive ritual behavior

Figure 5.20 Timeline from primates to *Homo*.

for the other Australopithecine to imitate it, and then to rehearse the learned technique until perfected (Donald 2012, 740–741). What a significant advantage this would have provided Australopithecines over other animals! Donald calls this ability *mimesis,* and expressly understands it to be the same basis for our much later cultural forms that include theatre and dance (Donald 1993a, 153).

Nevertheless, despite having improved on earlier hominid ability to develop and use tools, Australopithecines were not considered to be all that smart. Their brain size was only slightly larger than chimpanzees, weighing in at around 400–500 cubic centimeters (Mithen 2006, 123). While Donald suggested that the roots of mimesis lay in Australopithecines, he nevertheless concluded that "they did not leave any evidence suggesting major cognitive evolution" (Donald 1993b, 738). The next major chapter of cognitive development would be evidenced in a genus much closer to us anatomically and functionally, *Homo*. We'll explore them, and their contributions to music, language, and theatre in the next chapter.

Ten Questions

1. Trace the taxonomic classification of our human ancestors from kingdom through genus.
2. What two types of rhythmic behaviors do we witness in early mammals, and which animals exhibit them?
3. Name two significant traits we find in both humans and Old World monkeys.
4. Define ritual and give a mammalian example.
5. What is uniquely different about mirror neurons from other neurons?
6. What do the basal ganglia and the foramen magnum have to do with *Sahelanthropus*?

7. What is the biggest difference between chimpanzee and human drumming, and to what evolutionary development do some researchers ascribe that difference?

8. What in the world do mirror neurons have to do with choosing iconic sounds in theatre sound design?

9. The elements of color, mass, rhythm and line have been observed to be used in two ways by apes. What are they?

10. Why does Merlin Donald think that the ability of Australopithecines to make tools is so important?

Things to Share

1. In the last chapter, you explored manipulating color to incite various emotions in your audience. Since Australopithecines became more proficient in manipulating the mass (volume, shape, dynamics) of their vocalizations, we'll also explore manipulating intensity to stir emotions in your audience. To do this, we'll want to hold color constant, and let it have as little influence as possible on our audience. In this game, you get to use one breath, in which you may vocalize the "Shhhhhhhhh" sound for as long as you care in order to elicit each of the following emotions in your audience: love, anger, fear, joy, sadness (i.e., one breath per emotion!). Be careful not to manipulate the color of the sound by changing the formants in your throat, etc. Instead just manipulate the loudness of the sound to create five samples, one for each emotion. Record these five sounds as five different audio files, and label them "Take 1, Take 2," etc.

   We will play your five sounds back for the class, and the class will have to suggest which examples most incited which emotions in them. We'll poll the class to discover which sounds they associated with each emotion, and then we'll ask you for the order you intended. We'll then tabulate the percentage of emotions you were able to correctly incite in each audience member, and discuss the results.

2. Having explored the wonderful world of color, now it's time for you to explore color in composition. Compose or design a 1:00–1:30 piece that does not use a well-defined tempo, but instead, focuses on the interplay of a plethora of sonic colors. Work to stimulate a strong emotional response in your audience without using referential, iconic sounds— or at least without using them to reference their original source! (Feel free to manipulate and mangle well known sounds to create emotional responses, however.) Use original sounds that you have gone out and recorded yourself. Shun the sound effects libraries! Avoid traditional musical instruments such as guitar or piano! Find new sounds in the real world; long, sustained sounds, quick transient sounds, and everything in between. Sample those sounds and then manipulate and twist them into something entirely new! Orchestrate many sounds into your piece rather than just a few. Play and experiment!

Notes

1 For our younger readers, "Who's on First?" is a famous vaudeville routine performed by the comedy duo of Abbott and Costello in the 1940s. It's readily available for viewing on the internet.

2 The branch that includes both monkeys and apes is called a *Parvorder*, and the classification is *Catarrhini*. You will notice that I'm putting a lot of these more minor taxonomic classifications in footnotes, as they can get quite confusing, and I'm absolutely certain that anyone can become a great composer and sound designer without having mastered them. Still they are informative and interesting, so I don't want to leave them out.

3 For example, see the feature on the popular PBS series, *NOVA* (2005).

4 Quite literally the combination of sensory systems and motor systems in the brain.

5 In the particular area of the brain observed, F5 of the premotor cortex. See Figure 6.9.

6 In our taxonomy, apes belong to the superfamily Hominoidae, that also includes humans.

7 There are many videos on YouTube of gibbons singing. Look for ones in their native lands of Laos or Cambodia, where the natural acoustics of the forests add immensely to the beauty of their songs.

8 The technical name for this family is Hominidae—not to be confused with our superfamily Hominoidae!

9 In the subfamily Homininae—is this getting complicated or what? Fortunately, you don't really need to know all this in order to be a great composer for theatre! But it does help to follow the evolutionary chain that helps us understand how we came to be so musical.

10 Just a fancy way of saying "left brain" or "right brain."

11 In the tribe Hominini.

12 Hominins are a subtribe of Hominidae, that only include our human ancestors, not the other great apes.

13 We say Hominin here, because there isn't general agreement on whether Australopithecines or early *Homo* created these tools, and they are both Hominins.

14 Note that Donald first proposed these characteristics in *Homo erectus* in 1993, but updated to include some rudimentary form of it in the earlier Australopithecines due to their ability to make tools. See Donald (2012, p. 30).

Bibliography

Arbib, Michael, A. 2013. "Précis of How the Brain Got Language: The Mirror System Hypothesis." *Language and Cognition* 5 (2): 107–131.

Bickerton, Derek. 1990. *Language and Species*. Chicago: Chicago University Press.

Brockett, Oscar G., and Franklin J. Hildy. 1992. *History of Theatre*. Boston: Allyn and Bacon.

Brown, Steven. 2000. "The 'Musilanguage' model of music evolution." In *The Origins of Music*, edited by Nils L. Wallin, Björn Merker, and Steven Brown, 271–300. Cambridge, MA: MIT Press.

Brunet, Michel, and others. 1992. "Cambridge Encyclopedia of Human Evolution." In *Evolution of Old World Monkeys*, edited by J. S. Jones, R. D. Martin, D. Pilbeam and Sarah Bunney, 217–222. Cambridge: Cambridge University Press.

———. 2002. "A New Hominid From the Upper Miocene of Chad, Central Africa." *Nature* 418 (6894): 145–151.

———. 2005. "New Material of the Earliest Hominid From the Upper Miocene of Chad." *Nature* 434: 752–755.

Catmur, Caroline, Vincent Walsh, and Cecilia Heyes. 2007. "Sensorimotor Learning Configures the Human Mirror System." *Current Biology* 17: 1527-1531.

Center for Academic Research & Training in Anthropogeny. 2015. "Drumming." Accessed March 9, 2016. https://carta.anthropogeny.org/moca/topics/drumming.

Darwin, Charles. 1871. *The Descent of Man.* London: John Murray.

———. 2008. "The Origin of the Species." August. Accessed March 7, 2016. http://darwin-online.org.uk/content/frameset?itemID=F373&viewtype=text&pageseq=133.

di Pellegrino, G., L. Fadiga, L. Fogassi, V. Gallese, and G. Rizzolatti. 1992. "Understanding Motor Events: A Neurophysiological Study." *Experimental Brain Research* 91 (1): 176–180.

Donald, Merlin. 1993a. "Human Cognitive Evolution." *Social Research* 60 (1): 143–170.

———. 1993b. "Précis of Origins of the Modern Mind." *Behavioral and Brain Sciences* 16 (4): 737–791.

———. 2012. "Northrop Frye and Theories of Human Nature." *University of Toronto Quarterly* 81 (1): 29–36.

Falk, Dean. 1999. "Hominid Brain Evolution and the Origins of Music." In *The Origins of Music,* edited by Nils L. Wallin, Bjorn Merker, and Steven Brown. Cambridge, MA: MIT Press.

Goldman, Jason G. 2013. "Ronan the Sea Lion Dances to the Backstreet Boys. So What?" April 4. Accessed March 14, 2016. http://blogs.scientificamerican.com/thoughtful-animal/ronan-the-sea-lion-dances-to-the-backstreet-boys-so-what/.

Hauser, Marc D. 1999. "The Sound and the Fury: Primate Vocalizations as Reflections of Emotion and Thought." In *The Origins of Music,* edited by Nils L. Wallin, Björn Merker, and Steven Brown, 77–102. Cambridge, MA: MIT Press.

Huron, David. 2006. "Is Music an Evolutionary Adaptation?" *Annals of the New York Academy of Sciences* 930: 43–61. doi:10.1111/j.1749-6632.2001.tb05724.x

Iacoboni, Marco. 2009. "Imitation, Empathy, and Mirror Neurons." *Annual Review of Psychology* 60: 653–670.

Institute of Human Origins. 2014. "Lucy's Story." Accessed March 8, 2016. https://iho.asu.edu/about/lucys-story.

King, Glenn E. 2015. *Primate Behavior and Human Origins.* London: Routledge.

Koda, Hiroki, Takesha Nishimura, Isao T. Tokuda, Chisako Oyakawa, Toshikuni Nihonmatsu, and Nobuo Masataka. 2012. "Soprano Singing in Gibbons." *American Journal of Physical Anthropology* 149 (3): 347–355.

Koelsch, Stefan. 2014. "Brain Correlates of Music-Evoked Emotions." *Nature Reviews Neuroscience* 15 (3): 170–180.

Kohler, Evelyne, Christian Keysers, M. Allessandra Umiltà, Leonardo Fogassi, Vittorio Gallese, and Giacomo Rizzolatti. 2002. "Hearing Sounds, Understanding Actions: Action Representation in Mirror Neurons." *Science* 297 (5582): 846–848.

Langergraber, Kevin E., Kay Prufer, Carolyn Rowney, Christophe Boesch, Catherine Crockford, Katie Fawcett, Eiji Inoue, and others. 2012. "Generation Times in Wild Chimpanzees and Gorillas Suggest Earlier Divergence Times in Great Ape and Human Evolution." *Proceedings of the National Academy of Sciences* 109 (39): 15716–15721.

Leinonen, Lea, Ilkka Linnankoski, Maija-Liisa Laakso, and Reijo Aulanko. 1991. "Vocal Communication Between Species: Man and Macaque." *Language & Communication* 11 (4): 241–262.

Lieberman, Philip. 2007. "The Evolution of Human Speech, Its Anatomical and Neural Bases." *Current Anthropology* 48 (1): 39–66.

Locke, Devin P., et al. 2011. "Comparative and Demographic Analysis of Orangutan Genomes." *Nature.* January 26. Accessed March 8, 2016. www.nature.com/nature/journal/v469/n7331/full/nature09687.html.

Luef, Eva Maria, Thomas Breuer, and Simone Pika. 2016. "Food-Associated Calling in Gorillas (Gorilla g. gorilla) in the Wild." *PLOS ONE* 11 (2): 16.

Martin, Robert D. 2015. "Primate Evolution." In *Basics in Human Evolution*, edited by Michael P. Muehlenbein, 31–41. San Diego: Elsevier.

Merker, Bjorn H., Guy S. Madison, and Patricia Eckerdal. 2009. "On the Role and Origin of Isochrony in Human Rhythmic Entrainment." *Cortex* 45 (1): 4–17.

Mithen, Steven. 2006. *The Singing Neanderthals*. Cambridge, MA: Harvard University Press.

Norman-Haignerem, Sam, Nancy G. Kanwisher, and Josh H. McDermott. 2015. "Distinct Cortical Pathways for Music and Speech Revealed by Hypothesis-Free Voxel Decomposition." *Neuron* 88 (6): 1281–1296.

O'Neil, Dennis. 2012. "The First Primates." Accessed March 7, 2016. http://anthro.palomar.edu/earlyprimates/early_2.htm.

Pinker, Steven. 1997. *How the Mind Works*. New York: Norton.

Pino, Joe, interview by Rick Thomas. 2017. *Personal Interview*, April 21.

Randall, Jan A. 2001. "Evolution and Function of Drumming as Communication in Mammals." *American Zoologist* 41 (5): 1143–1156.

Remedios, Ryan, Nikos K. Logothetis, and Christoph Kayser. 2009. "Monkey Drumming Reveals Common Networks for Perceiving Vocal and Nonvocal Communication Sounds." *Proceedings of the National Academy of Sciences of the United States of America* 106 (42): 18010–18015.

Rizzolatti, Giacomo, and Laila Craighero. 2004. "The Mirror-Neuron System." *Annual Review of Neuroscience* 27: 169–192.

Rossano, Matthew J. 2010. *Supernatural Selection: How Religion Evolved*. New York: Oxford University Press.

———. 2011. "Setting Our Own Terms: How We Used Ritual to Become Human." In *Neuroscience, Consciousness and Spirituality*, edited by Harald Walach, Stefan Schmidt, and Wayne B. Jonas. New York: Springer.

———. 2013. *Mortal Rituals*. New York: Columbia University Press.

Seyfarth, Robert M., Dorothy L. Cheney, and Peter Marler. 1980. "Monkey Responses to Three Different Alarm Calls: Evidence of Predator Classification and Semantic Communication." *Science* 210 (4471): 801–803.

Shapiro, Gary L. 1982. "Sign Acquisition in a Home-Reared/Free-Ranging Orangutan: Comparisons With Other Singing Apes." *American Journal of Primatology* 3: 121–129.

Smuts, Barbara B., and John M. Watanabe. 1990. "Social Relationships and Ritualized Greetings in Adult Male Baboons (Papio Cynocephalus Anubis)." *International Journal of Primatology* 11 (2): 147–172.

Whiten, A., J. Goodall, W. C. McGrew, T. Nishida, V. Reynolds, Y. Sugiyama, C.E.G. Tutin, R. W. Wrangham, and C. Boesch. 1999. "Cultures in Chimpanzees." *Nature* 399: 682–685.

Wray, Allison. 1998. "Protolanguage as a Holistic System for Social Interaction." *Language and Communication* 18 (1): 47-67.

PART III

SONG = MUSIC + IDEA

CHAPTER 6

CAMPFIRE SONGS
Rhythm and Entrainment

Introduction: Welcome *Homo*

In the spring of 1990, the chair of our department, Jim O'Connor, gradually became more aware that my interest in theatre was not simply in the mechanisms of sound, but much more holistically, in the nature of theatre itself. For whatever reason, he nurtured this in me, and asked me to develop an introductory course in theatre for our majors. At the time, our majors took a large lecture, intro to theatre class along with non-majors, and Jim wanted to create an experience for them that was special and immersive, one that would take the impulses that had drawn them into theatre in the first place, and turn on the light bulb, so to speak. We wanted to awaken them to the magic of theatre—not just to the magic, but to the critical importance of exploring and understanding the world around us through theatre. In some ways, we wanted to do for them what now seems very much like the critical evolutionary "moment" when humans diverged from our ape ancestors—if something that took millions of years can be described as a "moment." For our ancestors, the light bulb that got turned on was the dawning of human cognition. It caused anthropologists to assign a very specific genus to those that have such cognition to separate them from those that don't: *Homo*.

I wanted to do so many things in that class, and I wanted to do them quickly. But first things first, I wanted the students to experience the joy of storytelling, something that I think is just naturally a part of the core fabric of not just theatre, but our humanity. I wanted to help them begin to think about theatre as much larger and more important than simple diversion, entertainment. At the same time, I wanted to help them develop a social bond with each other, similar to the ones I knew they had developed in high school, one that would unite them as a tribe on our campus, that would protect them from the inevitable attacks of their older peers, their non-theatre loving campus peers, their teachers and professors, even me. I wanted to help them form a group identity that would ensure their survival. In the syllabus, I wrote:

> Coming to a large University for the first time and undertaking a drastic change in lifestyle, learning and commitment is a process filled with conflicting emotions—excitement/nervousness, freedom/responsibility, curiosity/insecurity, etc. Choosing a theatre major tends to compound the challenge of this experience

because the commitment of the artist to the understanding of these human experiences is so great. As [Purdue professor] Rich Rand puts it, "Artists dwell on the same island as everyone else, but live closer to the volcano. They sometimes pay a mortal price for the discoveries they have made." This course exists to help you confront these challenges.

After you have completed this course, you should recognize the significance of your relationship to Purdue Theatre. You should develop bonds with your classmates that will endure forever. You will begin to understand your own unique relationship to theatre and why it is essential for you to give theatre and life your most whole-hearted effort. You will continue down the path of life-long learning and experience, and, hopefully, learn to enjoy the many twists, forks and crossroads that make the journey worthwhile.

(Thomas 1990)

I had done a lot of work with our local parks and recreation department, and I contacted an old friend there and arranged for us to go out to one of the parks, well past closing and into the dead of night. There we built a campfire, and I asked each student to prepare and tell a story around it. We did all the ritual things one does at camp fires: cooked s'mores, told our stories—some even acted them out, reminisced about what it was that drew us into theatre, and shared who we were in a much more intimate setting than a college classroom. In short, we bonded, and created connections with each other that let each other know that they were safe in our group. An attack on one would be perceived as an attack on the many. This experience would change our relationship to each other when we returned to the classroom. It was only years later that I would realize that I had subconsciously attempted to simulate the social experience our *Homo* ancestors must have first had a couple of million years earlier, and probably for pretty much the same reasons.

Social experiences play a huge role in the evolution of humans. Language, music and theatre all help to develop group cooperation, coordination and cohesion, even in their most primitive manifestations. Neuroanthropologist Steven Brown argues that "the straightforward evolutionary implication is that human musical capacity evolved because groups of musical hominids out-survived groups of nonmusical hominids due to a host of factors related to group-level cooperation and coordination" (Brown 2000, 296–297). Mithen furthers the arguments Thaut made in Chapter 4 about the unique simultaneity of music by applying it to advances in social development. In Mithen's opinion, being able to perform multiple elements of music simultaneously enables group coordination—as does being able to synchronize them to a beat, a phenomenon we'll explore more in this chapter (Mithen 2006, vii, 115). We saw the early vestiges of these in the ape and monkey calls of Chapter 4 that were also primarily social. They contained proto-elements of language, music and theatre in signaling, vocalization/physicalization, and imitation, respectively. We survived because we developed an even more sophisticated ability to share experiences, and learn from them. We should expect to see these abilities evolve and flourish in our species as our story unfolds, then, and we do.

In this chapter, we'll explore the evolution of our species in the context of the social pressures facing early *Homo*. We'll consider how those proto-elements of language, music and theatre—signs/symbols, vocalization/physicalization and mimesis—continued to evolve. We'll start with early *Homo*, and the evolution of an area of the brain known as Broca's area that activates for both language and physical gesture. We'll then consider *Homo erectus*, a much more sophisticated ancestor implicated in the harnessing of fire, and consider how this development may have led to an early lexicon and an expanding mimetic ability. We'll consider how the evolving ability of *Homo erectus* to run—not walk—helped them to evolve a very sophisticated timing system useful in developing rhythm in music. We'll consider how the development of that timing system may have given us an ability to manipulate the perception of time by others using the phenomenon of entrainment. We'll provide some examples of how we typically use pulse and entrainment in creating sound scores for theatre. Finally, we'll speculate on how these proto-elements of color, rhythm, mass, line and texture, words and gestures, and mimesis must have combined together to produce prehistoric rituals that would bind music and communication together in an emerging art form we would later call theatre.

One Giant Leap for Mankind

Early Homo

The earliest *Homo* species, *Homo habilis*, appeared about 2.4 million years ago in eastern and southern Africa (Smithsonian Museum of Natural History 2016).

Originally nicknamed "handyman" because of evidence found for their use of tools, later excavations found tool usage well before the known existence of *Homo habilis*. There have been a number of controversies over the years as to whether *habilis* should be categorized with *Homo* or with *Australopithecus* since they were so similar (Schwartz and Tattersall 2015). This matter has still not been resolved today, but fortunately, does not have much to do with the nature of theatre as a type of music. It simply reminds us that evolution is slow, unfailingly intertwined, and somewhat continuous.

Of greater interest to us is a related species, *Homo rudolfensis*, which existed about the same time as *Homo habilis*, but had a much larger cranium size, about

Thousands of Years Ago	Important Characteristics
1890–143	*Homo erectus*, 900 cc cranium, body shape closer to ours, more sophisticated tools, habitually walked upright, much greater social cohesion, used fire
1900–1400	*Homo ergaster*, 800 cc cranium, tall, slender and relatively hairless, barrel shaped chest, protruding nose
1900–1800	*Homo rudolfensis*, 700 cc cranium, evidence of Broca's area
2400–1400	*Homo habilis*, "Handyman," 500–600 cc cranium, known for use of tools

Figure 6.1 Timeline of major early *Homo* species.

Figure 6.2 Homo habilis.
Credit: Linda Bucklin/Shutterstock.com.

Figure 6.3 Homo rudolfensis.
Credit: Copyright John Gurche.

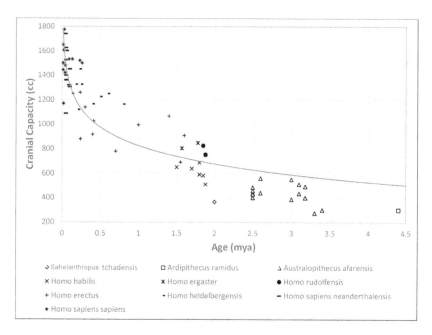

Figure 6.4 Selected Hominin cranial capacity.

Credit: Data from Schoenemann, P. Thomas. 2013. "Hominid Brain Evolution." In *A Companion to Paleoanthropology*, 142–151, edited by Begun, David R. Chichester. West Sussex: Wiley Blackwell. Chart by Richard K. Thomas.

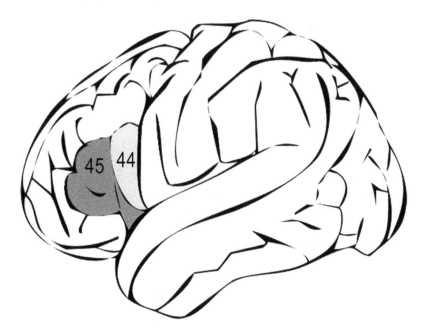

Figure 6.5 Broca's area, near the left temple, consists of two areas first identified and numbered by German anatomist Korbinian Brodmann, numbers 44 and 45.

Credit: Fatemeh Geranmayeh, Sonia L. E. Brownsett, Richard J. S. Wise. 2014. "Task-Induced Brain Activity in Aphasic Stroke Patients: What Is Driving Recovery?" *Brain* 137 (10): 2632–2648. doi:10.1093/brain/awu163. CC-BY-3.0. https://creativecommons.org/licenses/by/3.0/deed.en. Adapted by Richard K. Thomas.

Figure 6.6 Homo ergaster.
Credit: Visual&Written SL / Alamy Stock Photo.

700 cubic centimeters, compared with about 500–600 cubic centimeters for *Homo habilis*.

Neuroanthropologist Dean Falk examined one particular *Homo rudolfensis* fossil, and spotted what appeared to be evidence of an area known as "Broca's area," near our left temple, which activates in both speech and movement.

There are plenty of doubters on this view too, but evidence of a homologous area to Broca's have already been found in chimpanzees, and appear to clearly show up in the next *Homo* evolution, *Homo ergaster*.

Whether or not Broca's area clearly developed in *Homo rudolfensis*, or even whether *Homo habilis* belongs to the *Homo* genus, does not make such a difference for us. What makes a difference to us is that we see in these fossil remains some continuity between our cousins, chimpanzees, and the beginnings of some differences that suggest an evolving capacity for social communication.

Homo erectus

Homo ergaster roamed Africa about 1.9 million years ago, and provides us with evidence of another major leap forward in human evolution. They were tall and slender, perhaps relatively hairless, which would help improve body cooling through sweating, and had barrel-shaped chests that would provide additional muscular control over vocalizations. They also had a more human-like nose that projected outward compared to the flat nose of their predecessors. This nose provided additional resonant possibilities that could help produce a wider array of consonants and other musical expressions (Australian Museum 2015). The earliest specimen, Turkana Boy, shows a Broca's area more clearly, possibly indicating a more advanced speech capability, better gesturing abilities, or both (Holloway, Broadfield and Yuan 2004, 139).

How language evolved during this period is also a matter of some controversy, but the divergent views all show continuity to our central thesis. Derek Bickerton argues that language consisted of two stages, the first occurring during *Homo erectus*, and largely consisted of just words, a developing lexicon, which we have seen somewhat characterized in the old Tarzan movies as "me Tarzan, you Jane." He considers full mimesis to be a "spin-off" of language development (Donald 1993b, 749–750). At the same time, Bickerton recognizes that language itself must have begun as "a free-for-all, catch-as-catch-can mode that utilized sounds, signs, pantomime, and any other available mechanism that would carry intention and meaning" (Bickerton 2005, 514). Merlin Donald agrees that there may have been a "protolinguistic" stage of essentially "grammarless" speech, but argues that it would have come much later after an earlier mimetic stage (Donald 1993a, 157). Both agree, of course, that the pressure for social interaction drove the development of language.

There also seems to be little disagreement that humans would have used *onomatopoeia*, that is, imitations of naturally occurring sounds, to refer back to the origin of a sound source. Aarre Laakso uses the example of "grrr" as a vocalization one might use to invoke an angry dog: a vocalization that is part proto-musical (emotional) and part proto-language (referential). Laakso argues that once the use of this sound became prominent in a group, it might start to lose its immediate referent, the dog, and start to become a common symbol, for example, for anger, taking on a life of its own (Donald 1993b, 765). Mithen was so confident that some forms of imitation of animal sounds became the basis for early words and ideas that he proposed expanding "Hmmmm" to "Hmmmmm"—Holistic, manipulative, multimodal, musical and mimetic (Mithen 2006, 169–172).

Some paleoanthropologists include *Homo ergaster* as an early specimen in the species *Homo erectus*. *Homo erectus* lasted almost 2 million years, outliving our own species by nine times.

Homo ergaster migrated out of Africa into Asia, and possibly Europe. They had body shapes quite like ours, a much larger brain up to 800 cubic centimeters (Smithsonian Museum of Natural History 2016), and appear to be the first Hominin to use fire. Bickerton suggests that human lexicon development would have to have been in place in order to deal with the nuances of talking about fire. Bickerton also argues that in order to use fire productively, humans would have to have been able to refer to it symbolically, that is, use a word for it uncoupled from the emotion of a signaling call such as would be the case in the vervet monkey alarms[1] (Bickerton, Language and Species 1990, 140–141).

Homo erectus also distinguished itself by manufacturing more sophisticated tools such as hand axes and cleavers, known as the Acheulean stone tool industry.

Arbib, one of the discovers of mirror neurons, argues that the mimesis that began with Australopithecines must have seen a period of transition from simple imitation with limited grammar to a complex imitation that included the

Figure 6.7 Homo erectus.
Credit: Linda Bucklin/Shutterstock.com.

Figure 6.8 Two sides of an Acheulean stone tool.
Credit: Locutus Borg.

"conscious use of pantomime with a reliance on increasingly rich memory structures capable of holding hierarchical plans for both praxis and communication" (Arbib 2013, 130–131). Merlin Donald also suggests that the development of mimetic skills in *Homo erectus* would have affected many areas of their social life, including "group bonding and loyalty, a much-increased capacity for social coordination, which was probably necessary for a culture capable of moving a seasonal base camp or pursuing a long hunt" (Donald 1993b, 741).

Homo erectus (and *Homo ergaster*) were the first species that habitually walked upright, and the first that could run long distances. It is possible that *Homo erectus* were able to hunt in groups because they had acquired the ability to run long distances and work in social groups using coordinated vocalizations. By working in groups, they could tire and eventually kill their prey, although this theory also has its critics (Kaplan et al. 2000, 178–181; O'Connell et al. 2002). What appears to be clear regardless of whether humans were running after prey or running for other reasons, is that *Homo erectus* had achieved full bipedal form, characteristically stood upright, and, unlike their Australopithecine peers and ancestors, were capable of running long distances (Bramble and Lieberman 2004). This ability would have tremendous implications for the evolution of music.

Running, Tempo, Pulse, Tactus and Entrainment

Matz Larsson is one researcher who hypothesizes that bipedal locomotion has a lot to do with the evolution of our rhythmic and musical abilities. He proposes that a main difference between early humans such as *Homo erectus* and our ape ancestors lies in their more modern human gait, which is characteristically more pendulum-like, a feature much closer to the steady beat required in rhythm. This gait included oscillatory movement of not just the legs, but also the arms and the head, and is typically about 120 steps a minute when walking and as much as 170 steps per minute when running. Larsson pays special attention to the sound we make when walking, having measured the sound of walking on sand and gravel as about 38 to 62 dB above the threshold of hearing. Walking or running also sends a shock wave up the body that arrives at the brain about 10 milliseconds later, a sound you can easily verify for yourself by walking or running with earplugs inserted. Walking and running are also coupled to breathing rate in all vertebrates, and you may have noticed that you run best when your breathing is synchronized in what is called a phase-locked pattern, for example breathing in on step 1, breathing out on steps 2, 3 and 4. Other patterns runners use are 3:1, 2:1, 5:2 and 3:2, with 2:1 considered the most common (Larsson 2013, 2–5). Furthermore, Nomura, Takei, and Yanagida, a group of researchers from Japan, have demonstrated that when our heart beats close to our locomotor rhythm (running steps), our heart beat will entrain to the running steps (Nomura, Takei and Yanagida 1998).

I distinctly remember the first time I ever encountered this characteristic of pacing in running. I was student teaching at East Lansing High School in Lansing, Michigan, and tasked with teaching the John Knowles classic novel, *A Separate Peace*, to 11th graders. To be honest, I don't remember much about the story except that the main character, Gene, "jostled" the limb and sent his best friend Finny falling to the river bank below with a thud. But one other thing stuck out and has stayed with me all these years. Later in the book, Gene, who like me, was not much of an athlete (as compared to Finny or my brothers), was jogging around a course Finny had set up, when he suddenly, and for the first time in his life, stopped feeling the exhaustive pain of running, and suddenly felt "magnifi-cent." After that, running was easy. Finny explained it to Gene quite simply: "You found your rhythm" (Knowles 1960, 111–112). Quite possibly, Gene had found a pace to which both his respiratory and heart rates could entrain, a resonant frequency that simply made running easier.

This happened to me in college, and served as a turning point in my relation-ship with athletic activity, which I have pretty steadfastly pursued ever since in one sport or another. Jogging is a particularly interesting pastime for me, as I have been immensely fascinated about what happens when I jog and listen to music. The first thing I notice is that even if I'm not paying attention, my steps will find a way to synchronize with the beat, the basic externally provided unit of time in the music. If the *tempo*, that is, the speed at which the external beats of the music passes, is close, somewhere between 130 and 150 beats per minute, I'll naturally gravitate to a one-step-per-beat rhythm. I naturally breathe in on one, and breathe out on 2, 3, and 4 during running, and in on 1 and 2, and out on 3 and 4 during heavy running.

Even more amazing, I will unconsciously find another pattern if the tempo of the music is not 130–150 beats per minute. Here is where the fabulous *hemiola* comes in handy. A hemiola is a musical phrase in which one rhythm is played on top of another. This could be as simple as three notes in the space of two beats, or two notes in the space of three beats. But it can also mean forcing something like two measures of triple meter against three measures of duple meter (OnMu-sic Dictionary 2013). When running while listening to slower tempo songs, for example in the 90–100 beats per minute range, I'll often take six steps in the time of four slower beats of music, i.e., two measures of triple steps against three mea-sures of two beats. In this way, every first and fourth step will always land on a downbeat (or if the meter is 4/4, on beats 1 and 3). At 110–120 beats per minute, I'll often synchronize five beats in the space of four steps, and at a slow 80 beats per minute (or a very fast 150–160 beats per minute), I'll even take seven steps per measure. What seems to be subconsciously important is that I land on the downbeat of each measure of the music I'm hearing. But my body really doesn't like it when it can't find a stepping/breathing pattern related to the music I'm listening to, and I'll tire more quickly—a more common problem in the tempos that are between my natural running pace. Better to not listen to music than to listen to music that doesn't sync well with my running! Fortunately, just about everything I listen to will find a way to synchronize to my running subconsciously, as I also have great flexibility in the size of my stride and how many steps per minute I take. For example, I can take short, quick steps, or long, big steps, or any combination in between, and still maintain a "running" tempo.[2] And all of this applies pretty much the same to walking while listening to music, which I'll also often do. And right on cue, we now find music streaming applications available that will find music to play that synchronize to your running tempo.

I, like so many others, find when I walk or jog to music, I'm suddenly ener-gized, and typically lose any sense of exhaustion. Like Gene, I feel like I could just run forever. Once I'm free of the pain and exhaustion of running, my mind is free to wander to any of a number of more referential explorations, which often leads to unexpected problem solving, dreamlike mental wandering, and emotional shifts, typically toward a very simple but undeniable sense of joy. Kind of like my dreams, but now in a situation where I can consciously create the condition using music. It turns out that there is a physiological connection between my music and my running, and it's called *entrainment*.

So far, we've focused on the process of making beats in the drumming of our hominid ancestors; we've not spent much time at all talking about how we experience beats. We introduced the concept of entrainment in Chapter 2, when we talked about how crabs, ants, frogs, crickets and fireflies all use it, and in Chapter 5 where we discussed entrainment in other mammals like Ronan, the sea lion, and, in our own lineage, in bonobos. This does present a bit of an evolutionary problem: entrainment seems to pop up across the animal kingdom, and yet not all that often. We must presume, then, that the fundamental characteristics of it are either hundreds of millions of years old, or happened accidentally along the way for each creature. But the type of entrainment found among the varying phyla of our distant relatives differs considerably from the human kind, because the human version does not always involve sound, has the flexibility of synchronizing not just to the beat, but to multiples and fractions of the beat, and can withstand the nuances of beats moved off their precise location, as happens in syncopation, and tempo accelerandos, and ritards (Patel et al. 2005). Tempo in music is itself rarely stable and fluctuates quite a bit compared to felt *pulse* or *tactus*, the names we give to the psychological perception of the periodic succession of beats (Thaut 2005, 9; Thompson 2014, 1097–1099). Quite frankly, human entrainment is just more sophisticated.

As I'm now writing this chapter, I've been especially conscious of examples of entrainment occurring in my day-to-day waking world. A couple of weekends ago, I went to a local jazz concert in a small venue in town where a lot of local musicians also gathered. As we watched the musicians play, and listened to their music, I started looking around for signs of entrainment, the biological process in which our motor reactions are modified by exposure to external rhythms. The signs were everywhere. Surprisingly, the signs of entrainment manifested themselves in myriad ways. Just about everyone moved to the beat, but they didn't all move in exactly the same way. A significant number of people simply tapped their feet to the music. Some tapped their toes to the primary pulse, others doubled down and tapped twice to each pulse. A few only tapped once every other beat. One of my musician friends tapped on the first, third and fourth beat of each measure, creating her own "silent" contribution to the music. Then there were the head boppers. Some nodded front to back, some side to side. They were augmented by the finger tappers. Some tapped on their tables, some on their laps, some flammed their taps from baby finger to index finger. Some combined these; some got their whole body involved in a sort of seated dance. The effect of the band's music on the audience was multimodal. The auditory beats somehow found a way to create corresponding motor reactions in a wide variety of ways in the audience. It would have been interesting to shut off the music and close-mike every single person's movement and play it back together. Why? Because it would have all been pretty much in sync musically.

What's even more astounding about this phenomenon is that most of the audience members were unlikely to have been aware that they were physically moving to the beat. I know this because I've played music in my classes, and watched students react. Then I stopped the music and specifically asked them if they were aware of their physical movements. Some were, but the vast majority didn't even realize they were doing it. That's entrainment, and it is one of the most important techniques we use to manipulate a person's perception of time and, together with other elements of music, their emotions and moods.

Neuroscientist Michael Thaut discovered that our biological reaction to external rhythms is not what we always thought it was. We used to model rhythm and rhythmic formations as clocks, pulse counters or stopwatches. Now we understand that pulses from external music fundamentally entrain oscillatory circuits in our brains. Our brain encodes the neural firing rates of the auditory system and projects those rates on to other resonant brain tissue (Thaut 2005, 6–7). In other words, an external audible pulse is the tempo of our music; it modifies key circuits in our brains to oscillate at the rate of the external tempo. We don't simply imitate the external auditory pulses, we *become* them. That same direct connection we talked about in our primitive brain limbic system and cerebellum that made us jump at a startle event in Chapter 2, allows external rhythms to unconsciously manipulate us physically. We change. And it happens subconsciously—Harold Burris-Meyer's "You can shut your eyes, but the sound comes out to get you" is at it again! You can fight it with your conscious frontal lobe, but the moment you stop, it will creep back in again. Without even thinking, we start moving rhythmically in response to the external pulses of the music. That's different than imitation, where we make a conscious effort to say "alright, I go like this, and you do the same." This is entrainment, and it's a major function of music, and one that distinguishes music from the referential functions of language and images. We don't tap our feet to conversation. And it seems to be an area in which our auditory systems excel over our visual systems in perception of time; it's much harder for us to consciously synchronize to a visual pulse than an auditory one (Patel et al. 2005, 226; Thaut 2015, 256).

We as humans have evolved quite sophisticated abilities to create, manipulate and synchronize to beats. Our most fundamental sense of this is called pulse or tactus, the level of beats to which entrained humans typically tap their feet (Roholt 2014, 86). Tempo, then, refers to how the music is played in beats per minute, whereas tactus refers to how music is experienced. Tactus is an interval, period-based process expressed as the duration of each pulse (Thaut 2005, 8). For example, if we tap our feet 120 times per minute, then we would perceive two pulses per second, one every half a second, a 500 millisecond pulse. Humans seem to be able to perceive pulse intervals between 200 and 2,000 msec (30–300 beats per minute) (Grahn and Brett 2007, 894). However, humans tend to perceive tempos outside the region of 60–150 bpm as multiples or subdivisions of tempos in the 60–150 bpm range (Thaut 2005, 9).

Not all music is based on beats, of course. For example, a lot of ambient music consists of long flowing tones without a well-defined beat. We call this *unmeasured* music, as opposed to music with a well-defined tactus, which we call *measured* music. Measured music can be further subdivided into steady pulse and mutable pulse varieties. Most folk, dance and pop music typically has a steady pulse, whereas classical music often has a very changeable pulse that includes rubatos, ritards and accelerandos (Merker, Madison and Eckerdal 2009, 8).

Our perception of pulse, and how we react to it is fairly complicated. To begin with, it makes a difference whether we are consciously attempting to synchronize with a beat; for example, if we are attempting to play a piece of music along with someone, rather than simply listening to and enjoying music.

Simply listening to music activates brain circuits that automatically entrain to pulses. This is the part where we start tapping our toes without ever consciously thinking about hearing the beat. These automatic timing circuits are the ones we often try to tap into as playmakers; the ones where we can affect our audience without them having to pay attention to what we are doing musically. In scoring, we often want our audience to concentrate on referential images and language, and *not* to pay any attention at all to the music. The auditory system provides input to what are called the motor areas of the brain in the frontal and parietal lobes, roughly at the top center of our brain.

Without much help from our conscious brain, neural networks within a broad area of structures that include these motor centers, the spinal cord, the basal ganglia, and the cerebellum, match the timing of the audible pulses and send them down our spine to the various parts of our body physically creating the same beats, for example, by tapping our feet (Thaut 2015, 257). Researchers expect that our sensorimotor system (combination of auditory and motor systems) gets involved by simply copying the interval between pulses and then repeating them. However, this process only seems to work with small differences, temporal errors much less than the amount of time between the two most recent pulses, a process called phase correction[3] (Repp and Keller 2004, 500). Generally speaking, as long as the tempo doesn't change too drastically, our motor circuits correct our motor reactions to coincide to whatever the length of time was between the last two beats. We are constantly adjusting to the beat without even knowing it! Of course, we can cognitively control this also, but generally speaking, most humans can move to a tempo without consciously even thinking about it.

If things start to get too far off, or we decide we want to participate in a different way, such as tapping our hand instead of tapping our foot, our cognitively controlled timing circuits get involved in a process called period correction, which may average the duration of multiple pulses to find the new tactus. These circuits require conscious involvement from other parts of our frontal and parietal lobes associated with our memory and attention. Playing music and synchronizing our beat to another musician requires the use of both automatic timing circuits and

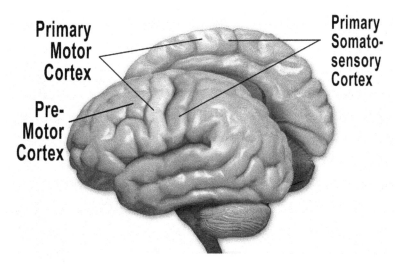

Figure 6.9 The motor centers of the brain. Note the highlighted area to the left, the primary motor cortex located at the rear of the frontal lobe, works together with the area to the right, the primary somatosensory cortex located at the front of the parietal lobe, to control movements.

Credit: "http://Blausen.com" Blausen.com staff 2014. "Medical gallery of Blausen Medical 2014". *WikiJournal of Medicine* 1 (2). doi:10.15347/wjm/2014.010. ISSN 2002–4436. CC-BY-3.0 (https://creativecommons.org/licenses/by/3.0/deed.en). Adapted by Richard K. Thomas.

cognitively controlled timing circuits. In practice researchers imagine that there is a "close and frequent" interaction between automatic and cognitively controlled timing systems (Merker, Madison and Eckerdal 2009, 11; Repp and Keller 2004, 501).

Tempo, Pacing, Tactus, Entrainment and Theatre Composition

When we create underscoring, we want the audience to focus on the referential language, images and action of the scene rather than on the music. However, when there's a show-stopping "song and dance" number in a musical, or even a simple song in a Shakespearean play, we will often want the audience to focus on the musical aspects of the play as well. So, it helps to know when we want to stimulate our automatic timing circuits (for example, by using a steady tempo), and when we want to draw conscious attention to the music (for example, by inserting substantial tempo changes). It does help to know that phase correction using our automatic timing circuits is very hard to suppress, which means we habituate to it quickly, and, as long as we don't start monkeying with the tempo too much, it will quickly return to its automatic, unconscious function (Repp and Keller 2004, 517–518).

One of the most common requirements in which sound typically carries the music of a theatre piece all by itself is scene change music. The term "scene change" seems to have been colloquially developed over a long period of time, but in actuality, the term can often be a misnomer, as the scene—the place where an incident occurs (Oxford Dictionaries 2016)—sometimes doesn't really change at all, for example, in a single unit set such as a drawing room comedy. What must change in virtually every case is time, and we use music to control our perception of time. So, in practice, I like to think of scene changes as *tactus* changes.

At the most fundamental and basic level, we are charged with changing the underlying pulse of the departing scene to that of the entering scene. To understand the difficulty in accomplishing this, we must first understand that the tactus of a given scene is quite mysteriously created by a combination of contributing musics.

First, there is the implied tactus created by the prosody of the actor's voices; the speech rhythms, melodies, dynamics and so forth that actors have carefully created over a long period of rehearsing, often referred to in theatre as *pacing*. Experienced sound designers, who spend a lot of time in rehearsals, know to expect certain changes in pacing as rehearsals progress into performances. At the first read-through, the pacing is often much faster than it will wind up being in performance. This is, of course, caused by the fact that the actors have not integrated the prosody of their speech with the music of their physical movements. Once they get in rehearsal, the actors start moving in time, creating a visual dance, that, for a while, slows down the pace—usually a bit too far, as the actors learn the distinct rhythms. This is not unlike how a piano player learning how to play a complicated section of music will first slow down to a speed they can play without mistakes. As the actors figure out their rhythms, their pacing will pick back up again until tech rehearsal, when the physical process of moving in and adapting to a new space will slow things back down again. Finally, during previews, the actors will tend to fully internalize the mimesis of the performance and the pace will stabilize, although the audience and other personal factors will still cause slight variances around the more stable pacing of the show. I remember the stage manager of *Tommy* on Broadway boasting that the pacing of the show was so stable (i.e., the music was performed to a "click" track) that the running time of each performance was within 30 seconds every evening! This is not typically the case, however, and experienced sound designers use specialized software and know-how to build cues and music to allow their sound scores to breathe musically within the slightly varying tempos of each performance.

Then there is the tactus created by the world inhabited by the actors; a world created by set, costume and light designers that may or may not correlate to the tactus implied by the script, and rehearsed by the actors. Phillip Silver eloquently addressed this issue in his 2003 address to the World Congress of OISTAT, in which he described the moving of a comedy from a theatre with a 9.5 meter proscenium to a 12.2 meter proscenium, a seemingly small change that required the actors to stretch out their physical timing—rhythms—to the larger space. That stretching of rhythms destroyed the comic timing the playwright had written into the smaller proscenium show (Silver 2003). On a more positive note, I designed sound for a production of Athol Fugard's *The Island* that played in a number of regional theatres for a couple of years, in which director/set designer Jim O'Connor constrained the set to a 10 foot by 10 foot square, thus forcing the actors' physical and vocal rhythms into the cramped confines needed to fully realize the abject despair of their imprisonment. The impact on the tactus of the actors was positively chilling, forcing short, chopped rhythms in a space with no room to move.

Once sound designers and composers understand the nature of all of the various rhythms, pacings and tempos interacting in a scene, they are in a good position to create "scene (or tactus!) change" music. First, they must have a fairly good sense of the tactus of both the composite outgoing and incoming scenes. Oftentimes they must deduce or predict this from just the printed words on the pages of a script. If they are lucky, they will get to participate in the rehearsal process themselves, and be able to develop firsthand a strong sense of the required tactus for the scene change.[4] More frequently, however, they must be prepared to "adapt" that tactus on the fly, especially when the tactus dictated by the arrival of a physical set and costumes during tech rehearsals also begins to integrate with the pacing developed by the actors.

To accomplish the tactus change, one of our most common techniques is to introduce a bit of music under the end of one scene, typically at the approximate tactus of the scene. If we nail the tactus correctly, then our introduction of music will habituate quickly, and the emotional quality of the music will incite a similar mood in our audience. At the scene change, then, we might abruptly change the tactus, drawing our audience's attention to it, which, of course, causes them to stop focusing on the outgoing scene. We establish a new tactus during the scene change, perhaps inducing a little bit of entrainment in the process, and then we finally introduce a new tactus for the incoming scene, hopefully creating a sense of the pulse in the audience appropriate for the actors' pacing at the commencement of the new scene.

But not always. There are perhaps an infinite number of variations on this process; if there weren't, the Tony Awards Committee would have been justified considering that sound design was not an art form worth including back in 2014.[5] Sometimes the creative team will want to introduce the tactus of the incoming scene during the outgoing scene, to begin to allow the rest of the music to impinge its emotional stimulation on the outgoing scene. Sometimes the team will do just the opposite: hold the tactus from the outgoing scene through the scene change and into the new scene, refusing to let go of the emotional qualities of the prior scene even as the incoming scene starts. And, of course, some times the team will introduce a thematic tactus, a pulse that they have used elsewhere in the play to subtly incite an audience recollection of a prior scene or event while still immersed in the current scene (more on this later, when we take up the subject of music's close relationship to memory). And, finally, they may choose no audible musical transition at all, preferring to allow the existing tactus of the outgoing scene to transition on its own to that of the incoming scene.

To multiply the possible options, consider that the creative team may make a conscious choice to contrast the current tactus of a scene with quite a different tactus. For example, a scene that ends in a major fight might be underscored with a piece of music with a very slow tempo, or a fight to the scene-ending death might be staged in slow motion while the music plays at a very fast tempo. The ability to contrast the referential content of a scene with the emotions and sense of time incited by the music creates an almost unlimited array of possibilities that can only be truly brought to life by a team that has the ability to imagine the possibilities.

In addition to understanding and designing around the existing pacing and tactus of outgoing and incoming scenes, we also need to manipulate our audience's perception of time, so that we become aware that a certain amount of time has passed between the outgoing and incoming scenes. To accomplish this, we turn to the more conscious method of entrainment employed in pulse manipulation, and period correction, in which we employ tactus changes large enough to attract our audience's attention. In its most simple form, we introduce a piece of music at the scene change that draws attention to itself. The audience soon entrains to the new music, forgetting what just happened in the outgoing scene. We end the scene change music and the next scene starts, establishing its own tactus. The duration of the scene change music, coupled with the shift in tactus that possibly includes its own entrainment, instills in the audience the sense that a certain amount of time has passed.

A long time ago producing radio dramas, I learned an old trick: how long the scene change music lasts helps the audience understand how much dramatic time passes between scenes. It's a very simple rule: if the next dramatic scene happens only a few moments later, do not have any scene change time at all. If the dramatic time is a few hours long, then have a relatively short scene change time. If the dramatic time was days, weeks or months long, create progressively longer scene changes, even consider adding a voiceover to help create the sense of time passing. In short, the longer the scene change time, the longer the dramatic time will appear to have passed. It's a simple and obvious rule, and one that complements Einstein's thoughts about the relativity and subjectivity of time quite well.

We don't tend to use this rule in theatre. In theatre, scene changes are largely determined by the decidedly undramatic amount of time it takes to change either the scenery or the costumes. It's somewhat understandable to have to extend the dramatically useful amount of scene change music if the scene change can't be performed in a short amount of time, but it has always been a bit baffling why we would shorten the scene change time if the scene change would not take as long as required dramatically.

A few years ago, I had the great pleasure to work with Janet Allen, artistic director of the Indianapolis Repertory Theatre, on a production of Ernest Thompson's American classic, *On Golden Pond*. Janet was understandably concerned because the single-set play required lengthy scene changes of both set and costumes due to the fact that each change took place at a considerably later point in dramatic time. For example, the set and costumes would have to change from spring to summer, even though the summer cottage setting did not fundamentally change. How would we fill the time? In our early conversations, Janet confided in me that she hates lengthy scene changes, because they allow the audience to disconnect from the play, and once disconnected, are very hard to get back. Instead, we talked about a way to *distract* the audience (my term), which is quite different from allowing them to disconnect. For our scene changes, we would use Carrie Newcomer music. Newcomer, a Grammy award-winning singer/songwriter, had been a long-time collaborator of mine (which I'm sure had a lot to do with why Janet hired me to design the sound in the first place!). Carrie writes provocative lyrics that poignantly resonate in themes such as those underlying *On Golden Pond*. Our strategy would be to distract the audience, getting them to focus on the thoughts and inspirations in Carrie's music, while the scene change unfolded in front of them visually for a bit of added distraction. There's nothing earth-shaking about this technique, but curiously, I had designed sound for close to 40 years without ever having a conversation with a director about how the technique actually works. In this case, the really important reason the technique works is because dramatic months pass in between the scenes, and providing these breaks helps the audience leave a scene and enter a new scene with a subjective sense that much more time has passed.

But at a subtler level, the scene change music itself created a rhythmic entrainment in the audience—it was literally long enough that you could see the physical evidence in the audience unconsciously moving in time to the music—the new tactus introduced to grab control of the audience's perception of time. Choosing the distracting music was a challenge, but not the hardest part. The most challenging part was figuring out how to blend the tactus of the departing scene into the distracting music, and then how to let go of the tactus of the distracting music in order to establish the tactus of the incoming scene. For example, in one scene we transitioned out of a moderate tempo Carrie Newcomer piece into an ambient tactus created by bullfrogs—themselves entrained at a very slow tempo—in order to bring the tactus of the incoming scene down to a much lower energy level, which in turn gave us a place to build a new rising action (increasing pulse) for the following scene. Embedded in all of this was a great need to create in the audience this sense of a substantial amount of time passing, but without letting them disconnect from the play in a way that would be very hard to get them back.

In tactus, and by extension to its physicalizing counterpart, entrainment, we witness another clue to the flexibility of time itself. Michael Thaut tells us that "Pulse rate defines, within given interval durations, how fast time, expressed through music, flows. . . . The primary element in music that creates the perception of time is rhythm" (Thaut 2005, 9, 15). Rhythm liberates us from the tyranny of a chronological clock; our brains and bodies are really not concerned with that in theatre anyway. While circadian rhythms, our biological entrainment to the cycle of night and day, have been a part of our core existence since the very earliest organisms, the division of that cycle into somewhat arbitrary periods of hours, minutes and seconds has little to do with our biological timing mechanisms (Scientific American 2007). Quite the contrary: in theatre, we may experience the passing of 24 hours, or even days, months or years, within the short chronological time of a couple of hours, just like many people report they do in dreams.

Entrainment suggests that our unique and subjective perception of time is more related to a diverse number of oscillatory circuits in our brain, especially the ones exterior pulses entrain to that cause motor movements in our bodies. Consider that we tap our foot the same number of times in 60 seconds at 60 bpm as we do in 30 seconds at 120 bpm. We are quite aware that it takes more time to tap 60 times in 60 seconds than it does to tap 60 times in 30 seconds. And yet, the same number of events take place in either case! Our perception of time is relative; time passes slower at slow tempos and faster with fast tempos, rather than being constant. Sometimes that's a good thing, and sometimes, not so good. Who among us has not witnessed a rehearsal in which the director begged the actors to "pick up the tempo"? Why? Because, at least for the director, and presumably for the audience, time seems to be passing incredibly slowly. Conversely, when the tempo is too fast for a scene, we disengage in a similar way: we don't fully transport into the world of the play; time is simply passing too fast for us to fully engage. But when the actors and musicians hit what I'll call the "resonant" tempo of a scene, that is, the ideal tempo, something magic happens: we no longer think about the passage of time, and enter that dreamlike state in which the world outside of the of the play ceases to exist and we are fully transported to the dramatic time and space of the performance.

We use tactus to transport our audience there in time. We use tactus to manipulate our audience's perception of time, knowing that our perception and our experience of time is unique to each individual, but ever determined to bring those individual perceptions more into a common one. Playwrights, directors, actors, designers—both visual and auditory—and composers all use tempo, pacing, pulse, tactus and entrainment, both knowingly and unknowingly, wittingly and unwittingly, to coax a common perception of time out of our audience. Since time is relative, we are keenly aware of how we are manipulating the pulse of our plays around what came before, and what comes next, for example, as part of the "rising action" of traditional linear plays. As we will see in later chapters, manipulating tactus is one of the ways in which we maintain arousal in our audience and hold their attention.

Our brains are keenly able to measure—anticipate—time via the individual length of pulses in external tempo/pacing and internal tactus. They physically respond to such pulses. When we develop the tactus of a play, we are working to pull our audience toward a common perception of time, oblivious to the ticking of the chronological clock outside of our dramatic experience. Rhythm is one of the most powerful tools we use to transport the audience from the external world of lobbies and house lights and our workaday problems to the more dreamlike world of the play. Referential visual images and language compel our audience to "suspend their disbelief," but participation in the tactus of the scene, which is almost always accompanied by a strong emotional reaction incited by the music of the play, carries those images and ideas into the heart and soul: Music as a Chariot.

When Music Meets Mimesis

Homo erectus migrated over a fairly large part of the world for almost 2 million years before finally dying out about 143,000 years ago. In order to migrate successfully, they must have developed tremendously in terms of their music, language and ritual abilities, and would have had to develop tremendous social abilities to hold their tribes together against the extraordinary pressures of both nature and predators. Imagine then, how all of this may have come together around a campfire somewhere in that distant past, a campfire not unlike the one we built to help my new theatre majors bond in our not so distant past. . . .

Presumably the tribe would gather around that campfire to cook the food they had gathered, hunted, scavenged or foraged. And while hanging out around that campfire, what do we imagine they did, just sit around and grunt? That hardly makes for a pleasant evening of entertainment; one imagines a much more socially active scenario. Daniel Levitin suggests that "singing around the ancient campfire might have been a way to stay awake, to ward off predators, and to develop social coordination and social cooperation within the group" (Levitin 2007, 183). Semiologist[6] Jean Molino proposed a common underlying phenomenon that would create extraordinary social cohesion around a campfire: rhythm. Molino imagined "a group of hominids would perform activities of collective imitation without language but accompanied by vocalizations and organized by rhythm: these would in fact be the first forms of the representation of scenes, that is, of narratives, leading to rite and to myth" (Molino 1999, 174). A very early linguist and feminist, Jane Harrison, found a clear link between just such an activity as this and theatre:

> When the men of a tribe return from a hunt, a journey, a battle, or any event that has caused them keen and pleasant emotion, they will often re-act their doings round the camp-fire at night to an attentive audience of women and young boys. The cause of this world-wide custom is no doubt in great part the desire to repeat a pleasant experience; the battle or the hunt will not be re-enacted unless it has been successful. Together with this must be reckoned a motive seldom absent from human endeavour, the desire for self-exhibition, self-enhancement. But in this re-enactment, we see at once, lies the germ of history and of commemorative ceremonial, and also, oddly enough, an impulse emotional in itself begets a process we think of as characteristically and exclusively intellectual, the process of abstraction.
>
> (Harrison 1913, 42)

An emotional impulse begets an intellectual process? Sounds like music carrying ideas to me. Imagine a group of *Homo erectus* gathering around a campfire to cook the evening meal. While waiting for the meal to cook, one of the leaders of the hunt, or maybe the "class clown," gets up and starts to imitate the hero leading the charge to take down the prey. And then something magical happens. . . .

Evidence for musical instruments is hard to come by and won't appear in the archaeological record for another hundred thousand years or more—maybe a lot more. But stones are easy to come by, and it wouldn't take much for a couple of members of the tribe to start pounding a couple together, egging our protagonist on to a rhythmic beat. Bones from prior kills would make even better percussion tools, despite the fact that they didn't have "Vic Firth" engraved on the side of them. They are hollow, more resonant, make a great sound when struck together, and raise the mystique of the hunt in a way that is not completely referential. Pretty soon everyone in the tribe is participating. Evolutionary psychologist Geoffrey Miller reminds us that music in tribal societies is almost always a group affair with everyone participating and no one simply sitting and listening (Miller 2000, 348). We can imagine everyone participating vocally too, imitating the sounds of the hunters, the sounds of the prey, perhaps they've even developed words and names for the prey, food, warriors and more and have learned to chant them in time to the beat. All of this emoting musically to a beautiful crescendo of socially connected cacophony.

And then it happens. The participants entrain to the beat, their bodies undulating to the external tempo of the pulsating beat. They transcend mimesis and *become* dancers, however simple, however primitive. They cease to be observers of the imagined hunt, and *become* participants. They enter the dreamlike state in which they quiet the parts of the prefrontal cortex that consciously remind them of their present surroundings. They indulge their more primitive cerebellum and limbic systems, thus creating internal mental images conjured by the imitations, and fueled by the entrainment that rhythmically and physically connects their bodies to the protagonist and the rest of the group. It is in that moment when they leave the scene around the campfire and enter the mise-en-scène[7] of their minds. They are no longer audience members watching a ritual unfold. They are no longer simply imitating. The *become* active participants in not just the ritual, but in the imaginary hunt itself. They have transported back in time to the hunt; they do not "relive" the hunt, they simply "live" it in the moment; for them it is actually happening, their perception of time controlled by the music and the entrainment. Some elements playing out in their dreamlike state coincide directly with the perception of everyone else in the group, creating a strong and impenetrable social bonding. But other elements are unique to each individual's experience and perspective, for example the visualization of the world in which this hunt took place. It is in this moment of music meeting mimesis that theatre is born. And music is the chariot that transports our ancient participants to this very real and yet very imaginary world.

Conclusion

In this chapter, we have traced the early evolution of our human ancestors, our genus *Homo*. In *Homo* we discovered evidence of evolving forms of music, language and theatre in the emotive expressions, in signs and an emerging lexicon, and in the mimesis of increasingly sophisticated rehearsals, re-creations and new creations; in the performances of imitative gestures and vocalizations. We paid special attention during this period to how the simultaneous evolution of the ability of humans to run—not walk—may have led to tempo, pace, pulse, tactus and human entrainment, the special ability to create a beat, and to synchronize that beat with others. We explored the unique connection between our auditory system and our motor system in entrainment, in which auditory pulses subconsciously cause physical movements in subjects. Without even thinking, we tap our toes to an external beat. Along the way, we've explored how these evolutionary traits manifest themselves even today in choices we make creating sound scores for theatre. In particular, we've explored how we use external tempos to manipulate our perception of time and pacing. Finally, we've hypothesized how the simultaneous evolution of music, language and mimesis may have manifested themselves around the campfire, how much more sophisticated ritual may have emerged, and how ritual bore the primal characteristics of theatre and dance, emerging art forms based in music, language and mimesis.

Ten Questions

1. Describe four early forms of the genus *Homo* and the major evolutionary developments of each that relate to music, language and theatre.
2. What is a major difference between Bickerton's evolutionary hypothesis for language development in *Homo erectus* and Donald's/Arbib's?
3. How does human entrainment differ from entrainment found in vertebrates such as frogs and fireflies?

4. How does tempo differ from the internal felt pulse?
5. Define rhythmic entrainment.
6. How is the multimodal nature of human entrainment different from that of our vertebrate ancestors?
7. How does entrainment demonstrate that our brain does not treat rhythm like a clock or a pulse counter?
8. Describe the differences between beat, pulse, tactus and tempo.
9. How does entrainment differ from imitation?
10. What are two different kinds of entrainment, and what are their characteristics that distinguish them from one another?

Things to Share

1. Download an app that allows you to tap out a beat and then tells you the tempo. Put together a playlist for a walk or run that includes music to which you think you might like to enjoy walking or jogging. Record the name of the song, artist, and beats per minute (bpm) of your playlist in the following spreadsheet. Put on a pair of closed ear headphones or earplugs. Don't pump any music through them yet. Just go out for a walk or a jog and pay attention to the tempo with which you typically like to walk or jog. Determine your natural walking or running tempo and make a note of that. Start your playlist, and go on your walk or run. Try not to pay attention to the relationship of your steps to the beat. Instead, consciously think about something else for a while. Eventually (say halfway through the song), let your attention turn to whether your body has unconsciously found a relationship between the beat in your music and your footsteps, and what that relationship is (one beat per step, three steps per two beats, etc.). Make mental notes about music that helped you run easier, and music that seemed to make running harder. When you finish your run, go back and make notes on the spreadsheet below about how many steps per beat you found yourself taking during each song, how many steps per breath you found yourself taking and any other notes. Which songs helped your run or walk, and which made it harder? What was the relationship between your steps per minute and your beats per minute? How did your breathing play into your comfort zone?

Name:			Location: Date and Time:		
Song	Artist	bpm	Step/beat pattern e.g., 1:1, 3:2, 4:3	Steps/Breath Pattern e.g., 1:1, 2:1, 3:1, 4:1, 3:2	Notes

2. Find a movie that has won an Academy Award for sound editing. Pick a movie that you love and wouldn't mind seeing again. Now get hold of the movie (perhaps buy it, because you can use it for other projects in this class, rent it from Netflix, or even check it out from your local library). Watch it with an ear toward a composer consciously using entrainment, and, if possible, manipulating the pulse in a tactus change. Make a note of the time in the movie where the entrainment or tactus change occurs so we can cue it up in class and you can share it with us. Pay careful attention to how the sound artists manipulate changes in the tempo of the sound score to manipulate the sense of time in the listener. Be prepared to describe for us how you think the sound team is manipulating us. Bring at least two examples with you in case someone uses your first example.

3. Having explored the wonderful world of mass (volume, shape, dynamics), now it's time for you to explore these concepts in composition. Compose or design a 1:00–1:30 piece that does not use a well-defined tempo, only uses one color such as a guitar or piano, and focuses on manipulation of the dynamics and volume of the moment. Find a place to introduce both a habituation and a startle moment. Play with crescendos and decrescendos. How close can you get to the noise floor of the listening environment, and how can you make the other extreme—the overloading of your meters—seem all the more loud because of how quiet your composition got? As always, play and experiment!

Notes

1 It is worth noting that, as of this writing, the earliest hard evidence we have of *Homo erectus* using fire is only 1 million years ago, leaving a gap of almost a million years between their arrival and their use of fire (Berma et al. 2012, E1215. Also, see James 1989).
2 Running being defined as a form of locomotion in which one of my feet is always in the air.
3 Phase in this case simply means the difference in time between where in time the next expected pulse should start, and where it actually starts, typically measured in degrees with 0° meaning no error and 360° meaning one whole pulse off.
4 If they are really lucky, they will be composing the music to a musical or opera, or other form in which the composed music dictates the tempo of the tactus change!
5 Fortunately, the Tony Committee came to their senses (literally!), and as of this writing in 2017, have reinstated the Tony Awards for Sound Design.
6 A semiologist is a person who studies semiotics (i.e., sign processes and meaningful communication).
7 A French term that literally means "putting on the stage." In modern theatre it typically refers to the composite visual images created and experienced in a play. Our point in this example, of course, is that the roots of theatre do not lie in the visual elements of the play; they are created in the minds of the audience by attaching ideas to music.

Bibliography

Arbib, Michael A. 2013. "Précis of How the Brain Got Language: The Mirror System Hypothesis." *Language and Cognition* 5 (2-3): 107–131.

Australian Museum. 2015. "Homo Ergaster." September 25. Accessed April 2, 2016. http://australianmuseum.net.au/homo-ergaster.

Berna, Francesco, Paul Goldberg, Liora Kolska Horwitz, James Brink, Sharon Holt, Marion Bamford, and Michael Chazan. "Microstratigraphic Evidence of in Situ Fire in the Acheulean Strata of Wonderwerk Cave, Northern Cape Province, South Africa." *Proceedings of the National Academy of Sciences of the United States of America* 109 (20): E1215-20.

Bickerton, Derek. 1990. *Language and Species*. Chicago: University of Chicago Press.

———. 2005. "Language Evolution: A Brief Guide for Linguists." *Science Direct* 117 (3): 510–526.

Bramble, Dennis M., and Daniel E. Lieberman. 2004. "Endurance Running and the Evolution of Homo." *Nature* 432 (7015): 345–352.

Brown, Steven. 2000. "The 'Musilanguage' Model of Music Evolution." In *The Origins of Music*, edited by Nils L. Wallin, Björn Merker, and Steven Brown, 271–300. Cambridge, MA: MIT Press.

Donald, Merlin. 1993a. "Human Cognitive Evolution." *Social Research* 60 (1): 143–170.

———. 1993b. "Précis of Origins of the Modern Mind." *Behavioral and Brain Sciences* 16 (4): 737–791.

Grahn, Jessica A., and Matthew Brett. 2007. "Rhythm and Beat Perception in Motor Areas of the Brain." *Journal of Cognitive Neuroscience* 19 (5): 893–906.

Harrison, Jane. 1913. *Ancient Art and Ritual*. New York: Henry Holt.

Holloway, Ralph L., Douglas C. Broadfield, and Michael S. Yuan. 2004. *The Human Fossil Record*. Vol. 3. Hoboken: John Wiley & Sons.

James, Steven R. 1989. "Hominid Use of Fire in the Lower and Middle Pleistocene: A Review of the Evidence." *Current Anthropolgy* 30 (1): 1-26.

Kaplan, Hillard, Kim Hill, Jane Lancaster, and A. Magdalena Hurtado. 2000. "A Theory of Human Life History Evolution: Diet, Intelligence, and Longevity." *Evolutionary Anthropology* 9 (4): 156–185.

Knowles, John. 1960. *A Separate Peace*. New York: Bantam.

Larsson, Matz. 2013. "Self-Generated Sounds of Locomotion and Ventilation and the Evolution of Human Rhythmic Abilities." *Animal Cognition* 17 (1): 1–14.

Levitin, Daniel J. 2007. *This Is Your Brain On Music*. New York: Penguin Group/ Plume.

Merker, Bjorn H., Guy S. Madison, and Patricia Eckerdal. 2009. "On the Role and Origin of Isochrony in Human Rhythmic Entrainment." *Cortex* 45 (1): 4–17.

Miller, Geoffrey. 2000. "Evolution of Human Music Through Sexual Selection." In *The Origins of Music*, edited by Nils L. Wallin, Björn Merker, and Steven Brown, 329–359. Cambridge, MA: MIT Press.

Mithen, Steven. 2006. *The Singing Neanderthals*. Cambridge, MA: Harvard University Press.

Molino, Jean. 1999. "Toward an Evolutionary Theory of Music and Language." In *The Origins of Music*, edited by Nils L. Wallin, Björn Merker, and Steven Brown, 165–176. Cambridge, MA: MIT Press.

Nomura, Kunihiko, Yoshiaki Takei, and Yasuyoshi Yanagida. 1998. "Analysing Entrainment of Cardiac and Locomotor Rhythms in Humans Using the Surrogate Data Technique." *IEEE Engineering in Medicine and Biology Magazine* 17 (6): 54–57.

O'Connell, J.F., K. Hawkes, K.D. Lupo, and N.G. Blurton Jones. 2002. "Male Strategies and Plio-Pleistocene Archaeology." *Journal of Human Evolution* 42 (6): 831–872.

OnMusic Dictionary. 2013. "Hemiola." February 14. Accessed March 11, 2016. http://dictionary.onmusic.org/terms/1697-hemiola_36.

Oxford Dictionaries. 2016. "Scene." Accessed April 2, 2016. www.oxforddictionaries. com/us/definition/american_english/scene.

Patel, Aniruddh D., John R. Iverson, Yanqing Chen, and Bruno H. Repp. 2005. "The Influence of Metricality and Modality on Synchronization With a Beat." *Experimental Brain Research* 163 (2): 226–238.

Repp, Bruno H., and Peter H. Keller. 2004. "Adaptation to Tempo Changes in Sensorimotor Synchronization: Effects of Intention, Attention, and Awareness." *Quarterly Journal of Experimental Psychology* 57 (3): 499–521.

Roholt, Tiger C. 2014. *Groove: A Phenomenology of Rhythmic Nuance*. New York: Bloomsbury.

Schwartz, Jeffrey H., and Ian Tattersall. 2015. "Defining the Genus Homo." *Science* 349 (6251): 931–932.

Scientific American. 2007. "Why Is a Minute Divided into 60 Seconds, an Hour into 60 Minutes, Yet There Are Only 24 Hours in a Day?" March 5. Accessed March 24, 2016. www.scientificamerican.com/article/experts-time-division-days-hours-minutes/.

Silver, Phil. 2003. *Communication of Space and Place—35 Years of PQ*. Prague, June 13. Unpublished.

Smithsonian Museum of Natural History. 2016. "Human Evolution Timeline Interactive." March 25. Accessed March 28, 2016. http://humanorigins.si.edu/evidence/human-evolution-timeline-interactive.

Thaut, Michael H. 2005. *Rhythm, Music, and the Brain*. New York: Routledge Taylor & Francis Group.

———. 2015. "The Discovery of Human Auditory-Motor Entrainment." In *Music, Neurology and Neuroscience: Evolution, the Musical Brain, Medical Conditions and Therapies*, edited by Eckart Altenmüller, Stanley Finger, and Françoise Boller, 253–266. Amsterdam: Elsevier.

Thomas, Richard K. 1990. "THTR 202 Fall 1990 Syllabus." West Lafayette, IN: Unpublished, August 16.

Thompson, William Forde, ed. 2014. *Music in the Social and Behavioral Sciences*. Vol. 1: Los Angeles: Sage.

CHAPTER 7

MUSIC AND LANGUAGE

Introduction: "All Theatre Starts with a Script"

In 1999, I was invited to participate in a Scenography Symposium at the OISTAT Scenography Commission meetings in Antwerp, Belgium. The symposium title was "Theatre and Design Today: Does the Scenographer Need to Become Director?" But before that subject could even get off the ground, Belgian director Marc Schillemans took me by surprise when he started his presentation by saying, "All theatre starts with a script." While I simultaneously recognized that most everybody in the room tacitly agreed with his assessment, I also knew that we had been traveling down two very different aesthetic paths.

Schillemans's assumption inevitably led me to the subject of my presentation at the Bregenz Opera the following year, and ultimately to many of the ideas in this book. In Bregenz, I developed a lecture that grew out of Adolphe Appia's famous proclamation that all theatre starts with music: "Out of Music (in the widest sense) springs the conception of the drama" (Appia 1962, 27). I have discussed Appia's thesis in detail in my 2001 *Theatre Design and Technology Journal* article, "The Function of the Soundscape" (Thomas 2001). Still, it is certainly interesting to consider how music—in its widest sense, as both Appia suggested, and we have defined—manifested itself in the evolution of humans, in the time arts, and, in my opinion, in the evolution of theatre itself. Whether music, language or mimesis came first may ultimately depend on how you define each, and of course, you can define theatre as an artistic endeavor that starts with a script, but there is a lot to be said for the intermingled role that emotive vocal expression, gesture and mimesis must have played in our earliest rituals.

While there is no consensus about when exactly music, speech and human ritual became fully developed, there does appear to be general consensus that they were pretty much firmly in place by about 40,000 to 60,000 years ago. In this chapter, we'll trace the period from about 700,000 years or so ago that led up to these monumental events. We'll try to get some idea of what must have happened biologically in order for us humans to take such a critical leap forward. Having arrived at an anatomically modern brain, we will next focus our attention on that. Since our brains are pretty much the same now as they were 200,000 years ago, we can finally examine how our brains process both music and language. We can consider which parts of the brain process common elements of both music and language, which parts process analogous parts of music and language in separate, but homologous[1] areas of the brain, and which parts of

Figure 7.1 Homo heidelbergensis.

Credit: Marcio Jose Bastos Silva/Shutterstock.com.

the brain process elements of music and language completely separately and differently from each other. We'll conclude by considering how music and language may function together to create a force potentially more powerful than either separately: *song*. Perhaps in a nod to both camps (Schillemans and Appia), I'll argue that all theatre doesn't start with a script, but with a *song*.

Brain Gains

About 700,000 years ago, a new *Homo* species appeared, *Homo heidelbergensis*, sometimes referred to as archaic *Homo sapiens* (Smithsonian Museum of Natural History 2016a).

They were the first early humans to migrate into Northern Europe, where they left evidence of an ability to build shelters and to hunt animals with wooden spears (Smithsonian Museum of Natural History 2016b). In 1997, archaeologists discovered a large number of similar bones from about 400,000 years ago at the bottom of a deep pit in the Sima de los Huesos cave at Atapuerca in Northern Spain.

Thousands of Years Ago	*Important Characteristics*
200–present	*Homo sapiens sapiens*, 1350 cc cranium, sole surviving species left in *Homo* genus
400–40	*Homo sapiens neanderthalensis*, 1500 cc cranium, first to wear clothing, may have had language
700–200	*Homo heidelbergensis*, 1250 cc cranium, migrated to Europe, built shelters and hunted animals with spears, first evidence of ritual, likely had the *Fox P2* gene
1890–143	*Homo erectus*, 900 cc cranium, body shape closer to ours, more sophisticated tools, habitually walked upright, much greater social cohesion, used fire
1900–1400	*Homo ergaster*, 860 cc cranium, tall, slender and relatively hairless, barrel shaped chest, protruding nose
1900–1800	*Homo rudolfensis*, 750–800 cc cranium, evidence of Broca's area
2400–1400	*Homo habilis*, 500–800 cc cranium, "Handyman," known for use of tools

Figure 7.2 Timeline of *Homo* genus.

Credit: Cranium sizes from https://australianmuseum.net.au.

They suspect that the pit was a burial pit, and even more significantly, they also found a quartz hand axe that may have been ceremonially dropped into the pit along with the deceased. If so, this would provide evidence of the earliest known instance of a human ritual (Tremlett 2003).

A burial site such as the one in Spain must have been a place of extreme emotional distress, as a possible loved one was getting buried there. The loss would certainly cause a lot of great emotion, and a group that had a strong sense of caring about each other—which we know they did in this period—the obvious and perhaps only way to express this would be through music. A Hallmark greeting card would, of course, have been out of the question, but emotional wailing droning over a simply kept rhythm? Very possibly at once *cathartic* and healing.

Catharsis. That's the first time we've used that word, but in Chapter 12 we will find that it plays an extremely important role in the relationship between music and theatre. It's a tricky word to precisely define, but for right now consider this definition from Oxford Dictionary: "a process of releasing, and thereby providing relief from strong emotions" (2016). Our earliest human ancestors may have already figured out that sometimes the only way to cope with extreme emotional situations is through music. Neuroscientist Ian Cross suggests that the collective expression and experience of emotion in musical catharsis would also reinforce "group" traits. Such traits would include the formation of coalitions, promotion of cooperation among group members, and the potential creation of hostility for those outside the group (especially the perpetrator of the deceased member's demise!). Music could reinforce the value of group ritual activities for survival, an important contributor to the emergence of human culture (Cross 2003, 50–51).

Beyond the implications for the evolution of music in a ritual-driven base, there is more evidence that *Homo heidelbergensis* had taken another leap forward in increased mental capacities. *Homo erectus* brains averaged about 1,050

Figure 7.3 Map of Atapuerca mountains, site of the "pit of bones."
Credit: Best-Backgrounds/Shutterstock.com.

cubic centimeters, whereas *Homo heidelbergensis* brains averaged about 1,250 cubic centimeters[2] (Australian Museum 2015). Larger brains allow for a more numerous and complex array of synaptic connections between the many different and evolving areas. As humans evolve, our neural wiring gets more complex, and that allows us to do more complicated and sophisticated things, like putting words together in sentences using syntax and grammar. Of course, this didn't happen overnight, but it certainly did *eventually*.

In recent years, we have been able to sequence the genomes of both modern humans and our recent Hominin ancestors. A group of researchers from the Max Planck Institute for Evolutionary Anthropology sequenced the genome of a direct descendant of *Homo heidelbergensis*, *Homo sapiens neanderthalensis*, in 2007.

They discovered that *Homo sapiens neanderthalensis* shared an important evolutionary difference with us that separates us from our primate ancestors: the *FoxP2* gene.

The *FoxP2* gene is a part of our DNA important in speech and language. Researchers discovered that the Neanderthals' *FoxP2* gene had undergone the same changes[3] as our direct *Homo sapiens* ancestors (Krause et al. 2007). This indicates that our common ancestor, *Homo heidelbergensis*, also contained this

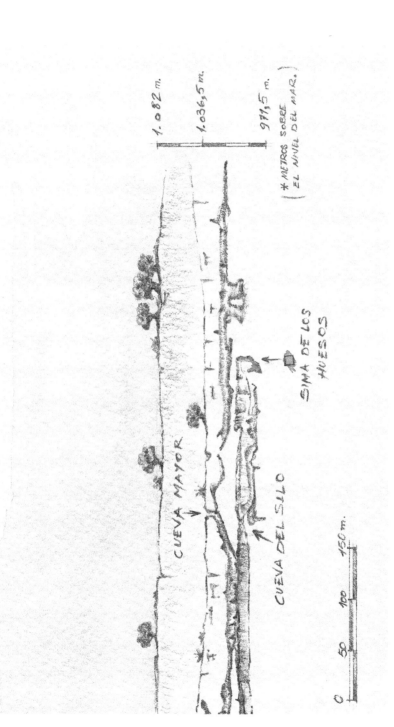

Figure 7.4 Map of the cave system at Atapuerca. Just to the right of center, notice the Sima de los Huesos ("Abyss of the Bones"). While it looks small in the picture, that vertical drop is about 43 feet straight down! No wonder excavators have uncovered any number of human and animal bones at the bottom.

Credit: Javier Trueba/Science Source, a Division of Photo Researchers, Inc.

Figure 7.5 Archaeologists excavate the "Abyss of the Bones" at Atapuerca.

Credit: Javier Trueba/Science Source, a Division of Photo Researchers, Inc.

Figure 7.6 Homo sapiens neanderthalensis.

Credit: © Elisabeth Daynes/LookatSciences.

evolutionary adaptation. Scientists discovered the *FoxP2* gene by noticing that mutations of the chromosome in human subjects impaired their ability to physically repeat words (and even non-words, among many other symptoms).[4] They concluded that the *FoxP2* gene appears to express itself in our ability to communicate using language, especially since the genetic adaptations that created the *FoxP2* gene occurred around the same time humans acquired language. Many researchers consider it much more than a coincidence that the *FoxP2* adaptation should so closely coincide with humans acquiring language, but as yet the proof that the *FoxP2* adaptation directly led to humans acquiring language is inconclusive (Preuss 2012; Lieberman 2007, 51–52).

Other anatomical changes that would make language possible may have occurred in the transition from *Homo heidelbergensis* to Neanderthals and modern humans 400,000 to 200,000 years ago. In Chapter 5 we discussed Phillip Lieberman's proposal that the face of early *Homo* flattening out and the human larynx beginning to descend to its current lower position were a consequence of our transition to walking upright, signaling the start of an almost 2-million-year journey to the evolution of fully formed language. When these transformations completed is still a matter of controversy, however. While the evolution of the brain, vocal tract, and oral chamber certainly seems to have allowed the possibility of language, there is no conclusive evidence for when language fully formed in humans, nor whether language evolved slowly or suddenly (Bickerton 2005, 515). As Frayer and Nicolay put it, "the paltry amount of actual evidence for language origins as recorded in fossils should be a little sobering to those willing to offer opinions about the origin of linguistic ability" (2007, 217). So, we won't.

Homo erectus may have started using words well over a million years ago, as Bickerton suggested (Donald 1993b, 749). Language may have gradually evolved from *Homo erectus* into fully formed languages such as Lieberman proposes (2007, 52). Words may have been a much later evolutionary development out of mimesis as Donald suggests (Donald 1993a, 157), or were parsed out of musically holistic phrases as Mithen and Wray have suggested (Wray 1998, 50). We may know the answer to this puzzling question someday. Fortunately, we don't need to know that answer to consider the implications of music and language developing in such a confusing, controversially intertwined way. It is important that we recognize that somewhere between *Homo erectus* and modern humans, fully formed languages evolved, and they are closely intertwined with music and mimesis. It's also important to know that this all pretty much happened sometime about 300,000–200,000 years ago when our most direct ancestors *Homo sapiens sapiens* emerged.[5]

So, yes, about 300,000–200,000 years ago, our own species, anatomically modern *Homo sapiens*, or *Homo sapiens sapiens*, emerged from archaic *Homo sapiens*. The redundancy is not a typo; it's used to separate us from our extinct cousins like *Homo sapiens idaltu*. And with this arrival comes a whole new method for observing ourselves. Not only do we have all of the other methods for examining our past—archaeology, genome sequencing, cognitive neuroscience and so forth—now we can simply examine our own brains. Our genomic sequence is 99.9% the same as our *Homo sapiens sapiens* ancestors, so we can be quite sure that what we discover about ourselves now corresponds pretty well to our past *Homo sapiens sapiens* selves (Smithsonian Museum of Natural History 2016b). For example, we know that our human brain size is huge compared to our ancestors, averaging 1,273 cubic centimeters for men and 1,131 for women

Figure 7.7 Homo sapiens sapiens.

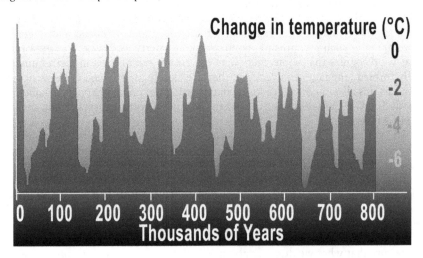

Figure 7.8 Graph shows ice ages, about 140,000 and 70,000 years ago.

(Allen, Damasio and Grabowski 2002, 347).[6] For all of our differences among races and cultures on this planet, we are remarkably the same. How could this happen?

About the same time that anatomically modern *Homo sapiens* appeared, earth experienced another mini-ice age and ice sheets descended from the North Pole, covering much of Europe and North America.

Ice ages suck moisture out of the atmosphere, and this mini-ice age resulted in a massive drought in Africa. The drought created a "bottleneck" of humanity in South Africa about 140,000 years ago: only four to six potential locations existed in Africa that contained a phenomenally small breeding population of about 600 individuals. Every human on earth evolved genetically from this small population (PBS 2011). Not just from this small population, but from one single ancestral mother, dubbed by the media as Mitochondrial Eve (Cann, Stoneking and Wilson 1987). Think about it. If our genetic code is the same as theirs, somebody must have been the first one to have it! And even though their brains were biologically developed, there are still many who argue that they had not fully developed language (Arbib 2013, 130; Bickerton 2005, 520).

About 70,000 years ago, another period of glaciation combined with a massive eruption of a super-volcano near Lake Toba on the island of Sumatra to create major climate pressures on these tribes (Marean 2015, 34). Our human ancestors were once again decimated, leaving less than 2,000 (Chesner et al. 1991; Wells 2007). The big difference this time was that humans were ready for it, having much more sophisticated tools and ability to work collectively in highly organized social groups, and perhaps more fully formed language capabilities. Small groups migrated up the coastline and out of Africa into Yemen (see the Map of Human Migration in Figure 8.4). They eventually crossed over into southeast Asia and Australia. And just about everybody agrees that by about 90,000–50,000 years ago, our ancestors, *Homo sapiens sapiens*, had fully acquired language and music.

Fantastic Voyage

Having now arrived at a point in time where everyone seems to agree that our human ancestors had acquired both language and music raises an interesting problem for us: if we aren't changing genetically, then how do we change over 50,000 years? Surely we're not that similar to our cave dwelling ancestors? It is true that we have entered into an era in which we witness few genetic changes—50,000 years is just too short a time to witness much evolutionary change caused by genetic mutations. Instead, we enter into a period of rapid change called Lamarckian evolution, named after the French biologist Jean-Baptiste Lamarck. Lamarck thought that we can pass on our acquired characteristics to our offspring, and on to their offspring, and so forth. Such a theory would allow humans to evolve much more rapidly than standard theories of evolution would appear to allow. Molino argues that cultural evolution seems "quite Lamarckian since information acquired at each generation can be transmitted in whole to the next generation." Of course, such an idea is not without its critics, but anthropologist Jean Molino makes a very good point when she suggests that "these differences do not in any way threaten the stability of the edifice" (the edifice being genetic evolution, of course) (Molino 1999, 166). In our particular case, it will become increasingly difficult to separate genetic traits that we inherited in our species from cultural traits acquired through the passing down of knowledge from generation to generation. With this murkiness in mind, we will continue to explore how the innate traits that first manifested themselves in vocal/physical expression of emotion, and signs (and now symbols) developed to become an art form we call theatre.

But first, in order to truly understand how we use music and language to manipulate our audiences in theatre, we must understand how we hear and process those sounds. So now would be a good time to stop and examine how the brain processes music and speech (the auditory form of language). Let's consider which parts of the brain music and speech share, and then, let's consider where they diverge.[7]

John Bracewell, a longtime professor at Ithaca College, may have been the first collegiate faculty in theatre sound in the United States. He was the first commissioner of the USITT Sound Commission, and the person I have to thank for dragging me in to do some of my first lectures and presentations in the organization. When I started working on my master's degree in 1977, I wrote to John, and got a copy of his 1971 master's thesis on theatre sound. I asked John how he started learning about sound in theatre. John told me that when he started working on his thesis, he met Harold Burris-Meyer, one of the earliest pioneers of theatre sound, and asked him, "what do I need to study to be a good sound designer?" And Harold Burris-Meyer responded, "well, you start with the ear. Because you really need to know how you hear." In other words, in order to have an aesthetic of sound design, you need to understand that particular sensory organism, and how it works. It's really hard to create something (a sound score) that manipulates something else (an audience member) unless you know how that something else works. In Harold Burris-Meyer's and John Bracewell's time, relatively little was really known about our auditory system, but the two of them helped pave the way for this book. Today, we know much more about how the brain works, and that knowledge provides clues about the nature of hearing that should influence how we think about creating sound scores.

So, fasten your seatbelts, refer to Figures 7. 9, 7.10, 7.11, and maybe even have a look back at Figures 5.9 and 5.17 when appropriate, as we take the fascinating journey of a sound from the outside world into the deepest regions of our brain. . . .

If you will recall from our first few chapters, all sound, whether naturally occurring, music, language or all of the above, enters our perceptual mechanism through the pinnae of our two ears.

The pinnae gather up sounds, and send them down the external auditory canal that resonates—amplifies—sounds between 2,000 and 4,000 Hz. Very handy when a predator steps on a twig behind you! The sound vibrates the tympani (eardrum), which in turn, vibrates the malleus (hammer), then the incus (anvil), then the stapes (stirrup), three bones you will remember that we acquired in our transition from water to land that helped our mammalian class match the impedance of air to the inner ear.

The stapes vibrates the oval window at the entrance to the cochlea, a spiral-shaped organ that contains the basilar membrane.

The basilar membrane vibrates in response to fluids in the cochlea that the oval window has set in motion. The basilar membrane sets into motion the hair cells along the membrane that are localized depending on the frequency of the incoming sound. High frequencies localize toward the near end and low frequencies toward the far end, kind of like the spectrum analyzers sound folks used to use to measure the auditory response of theatres. This division of "tones" according to their "place" on the basilar membrane is called a *tonotopic* organization. You

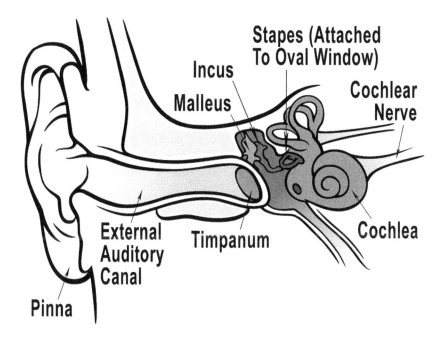

Figure 7.9 Overview of the human ear.

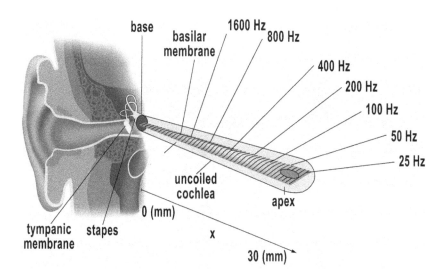

Figure 7.10 The basilar membrane uncoiled.

will be surprised as we go along at how far the human nervous system maintains this tonotopic organization up into the brain![8] The hair cells of the inner ear convert their mechanical vibrations into electrochemical pulses and send them along the auditory nerve to the brainstem. The neurons fire in digital-like pulses, either on or off, nothing in between. Which nerve fibers fire determines frequencies, how fast the pulses occur determines amplitude (Giraud and Poeppel 2012, 180).

A couple of milliseconds later, the sound travels through the *internal auditory canal*, an opening through the skull, and into the brainstem as part of the *eighth cranial nerve*,[9] known as the *vestibulocochlear nerve*.

This nerve has over 30,000 nerve fibers (Spoendlin and Schrott 1989). The first stop in the brainstem is the *cochlear nucleus*, which is at the juncture of the *medulla oblongata* and the *pons*.

In the cochlear nucleus, the data from the eighth cranial nerve contacts neurons that each form a parallel circuit and perform their own analysis on the data. For example, one circuit preserves the timing of auditory events (simple information about when the sound arrives), while another circuit is sensitive to how we identify sound (Rubio 2010). The medulla oblongata is a part of the *hindbrain*, the gateway to the lower part of the body, along with the *pons* and *cerebellum*. The medulla oblongata is the lowest part of the brain that sits on top of the spinal cord, and has a lot to do with the involuntary control of muscles like breathing, heart rate and blood pressure. Music, as it turns out, can have a great effect upon the brainstem, and we'll investigate that in Chapter 9. The pons goes in the other directions—up, toward the rest of the brain and laterally to the cerebellum,

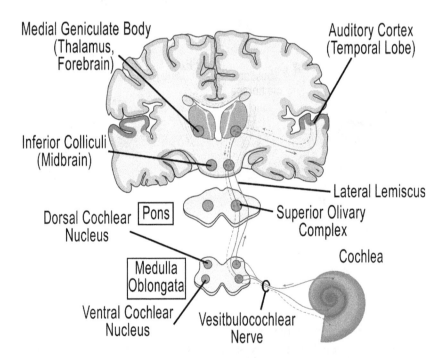

Figure 7.11 The auditory pathway from cochlea to auditory cortex.

Credit: Blamb/Shutterstock.com. Adapted by Richard K. Thomas.

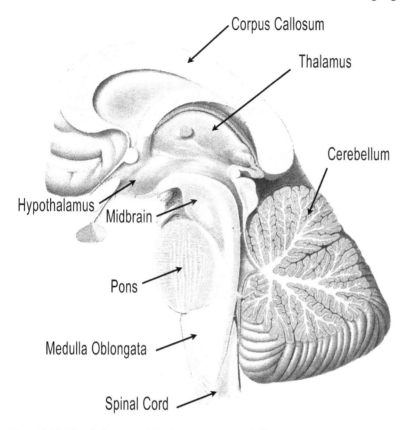

Figure 7.12 The thalamus, midbrain, pons and medulla.

Credit: Sobotta, Johannes. 1909. *Textbook and Atlas of Human Anatomy*. Edited with additions by McMurrich, J. Volume III. Philadelphia and London, W.B. Saunders Company. Figure 648, Page 156. Adapted by Richard K. Thomas.

especially important in hearing and speaking. The pons sits below the part of the brainstem called the midbrain.

Inside the pons is the *superior olivary complex*, a group of nuclei that is thought to determine localization in the horizontal plane, by comparing the time arrival and intensity difference between the auditory stimulus from each ear (Kandel, Schwartz and Jessell 2000, 591–624). From here, sound travels to the *lateral lemiscus*, a group of nerve fibers whose function is not understood, but is sensitive to timing and amplitude changes. The sound continues up to the *inferior colliculi* in the *midbrain*, where all of the various components that have become separated along the various pathways become integrated before continuing on to the brain itself. The inferior colliculi are also involved in a type of habituation that inhibits startle response (Parham and Willott 1990).

Next, the sound leaves the brainstem and enters the *thalamus* in the forebrain, the area of our brain that sits on top of the midbrain, and pretty much connects to every other part of the brain (see Figure 7.12). The thalamus acts as the main distribution system of the auditory signal to different parts of the brain, having been compared to the bouncer in a nightclub, deciding who to let in and who to kick out (Leonard 2006). It connects to the hippocampus, the seat of memory, and the basal ganglia that we met in Chapter 5 (see Figure 5.9 for the hippocampus, and 5.17 for the basal ganglia). The basal ganglia sequences patterns from other parts of the brain and sends them back to the thalamus for routing to our motor circuits when we walk or run (Lieberman 2007, 47–52). It is also active during rhythmic entrainment, although its function is not clearly understood. The thalamus also connects directly to the cerebellum, and there is a complex relationship related to entrainment we discussed in the last chapter involving the thalamus and cerebellum (Thaut 2005, 48–51). But most significantly, the auditory signal next goes from a part of the thalamus called the *medial geniculate nucleus* to the *auditory cortex* in the temporal lobe of our neocortex, or "new brain."

At this point, you should either be yelling "jackpot!" or "my mind is fried and I need a break." Hopefully the former. And if so, keep in mind as we progress to the auditory cortex that the frequencies that were so carefully separated along the basilar membrane in the cochlea of our ears, still remain separated in the thousands of nerve fibers entering the auditory cortex.

Up until this point, the brain has more or less treated incoming sound the same, whether it is a dog bark, a symbolic word, or a strain of music. Once it enters the auditory cortex, however, we start to see a noticeable split between how the brain deals with speech and auditory music. And this is where things really start to get interesting.

Inside the temporal lobes are the auditory cortices (yup, there are two, one on each side of the brain, left and right). Each auditory cortex is divided into two areas: the primary auditory cortex (also called the core), and the secondary auditory cortex (also called the belt and the parabelt; the belt being the section closest to the core, and the parabelt being adjacent to the belt).[10]

As we discussed, the auditory system maintains the frequency discrimination created by the basilar membrane in the cochlea of the ear all the way through to the core of the auditory cortex, where the signal lands in an area of the primary auditory cortex called Heschl's gyrus. The primary auditory cortices process the individual frequencies and pass them on to the secondary auditory cortices for more processing, although these areas seem to discriminate frequency more broadly than the primary auditory cortices (Giraud and Poeppel 2012, 169).

The primary cortex also follows external tempos and radiates a brainwave, called M100, which increases in intensity (i.e., the number of neurons simultaneously firing) as tempo changes. Small tempo changes produce small increases in the M100 brainwave; larger tempo increases produce larger increases. Presumably these brainwave firings are projected onto our motor structures (especially through the thalamus) in order to synchronize things like foot tapping, but it is not well understood yet how and where this happens. Equally murky is the strong likelihood that since we already know that the cochlea connects directly with other parts of the brain such as the basal ganglia and cerebellum, parallel timing networks might also be working simultaneously to synchronize tempos. These networks might also activate differently depending on whether we are consciously or unconsciously synchronizing to an external tempo (Thaut 2005, 45–49).

One of the first things that the auditory cortex does is to attempt to separate incoming sounds into *sound objects*. Sound objects are how our brain separates one sound from another. They are similar to our description of color, in that they consist of the spectral characteristics of a sound (the particular frequencies of the sound) as they unfold in time (which we have described as the ADSR—attack,

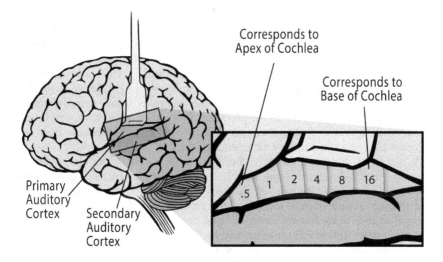

Figure 7.13 The primary and secondary auditory cortex (belt and parabelt) show the tonotopic relation to frequency first derived in the basilar membrane (see Figure 7.10).

Credit: Chittka, L., and A. Brockmann. 2005. "Perception Space—The Final Frontier." *PLOS Biology* 3(4): e137. Accessed July 20, 2017. https://doi.org/10.1371/journal.pbio.0030137. CC-BY-2.5. https://creativecommons.org/licenses/by/2.5/deed.en. Adapted by Richard K. Thomas.

decay, sustain and release). Parsing incoming sounds into sound objects is a hugely important task—otherwise we would not be able to tell the difference between the lion roar and the background noise, between the lovely cello part and the violins. It turns out that the first task of the auditory cortex is to segregate sounds in the core. Research suggests that parsing sounds into sound objects is likely to happen in the auditory cortex even before perception of timbre and spatial characteristics (Griffiths, Micheyl and Overath 2012, 203).

Before we move on, let's consider another point of view regarding how humans process and segregate incoming sound. Michel Chion is one of the most highly regarded writers on the subject of the aesthetics of sound in the cinema. He has proposed a great way for categorizing sound objects that will be useful to us as well. Chion describes three types of listening in his book *Audio-Vision*. The first type corresponds to identifying the source of sound objects, which he calls causal listening. It is the type of listening that answers the question, "What was that sound?" We listen to determine the cause of the sound. The close correlation between causal listening and sound objects, is perhaps a result of our evolutionary heritage. One of the first things we would want to know when we hear an unusual sound is, "What was that?" And to know "that," we have to be able to segregate that sound from the many others that are always occurring simultaneously. We have already discussed the rather limited use that this type of listening has for us as theatre composers and sound designers. Chion recognizes a similar problem, describing causal listening as "the most easily influenced and deceptive mode of listening" (1990, 26).

Chion's second type of listening is semantic. This is the sound of language, speech. In speech, we derive meaning not from the cause of the sound, but from the aural symbols used to represent words in language. Chion's third type of sound is the sound itself, which, in and of itself, has no reference to the outside world whatsoever. Chion refers to this type of listening as reduced (1990, 25–34). Chion's reduced listening bears a strong resemblance to our definition of music. Both are concerned with the inherent characteristics of a sound rather than what caused them or any particular referential meaning we might derive from them. In Chion's last two types of listening, we find a parallel to our categorization of speech and music. How the brain processes these are critically important to us as sound designers and composers, as they provide clues about how they work together to create the auditory experience of theatre.

It turns out that the secondary auditory cortex is one of the first places that processes music differently from speech. In 2015, a group of researchers at MIT discovered that, while the primary auditory cortex seemed to process both words and musical sound objects the same, the secondary auditory cortex processed musical sounds more toward its front[11] and back[12] areas adjacent to the primary auditory cortex and words more toward its side[13] (Norman-Haignere, Kanwisher and McDermott 2015, 1285). This doesn't sound like much, except that it provides clear evidence for the very first time that there is a part of the brain dedicated to processing music. Music could not then just be a fringe benefit of speech, "auditory cheesecake"; it must have evolved as its own adaptation to some sort of condition in the world. Biologically, we have now discovered genetic evidence for music, language and imitation: music and speech in the unique processing of the auditory cortex, and imitation, in the mirror neuron.

So what is the big difference between music and speech that our brain uses to analyze each? Robert Zatorre proposed that understanding speech requires very fine temporal resolution—we need to be able to differentiate between consonants that are all sequencing very quick. In music, however, we need very fine spectral resolution—an ability to very precisely tell the difference between different pitches. Zatorre noted that the different parts of the brain seemed to have evolved to discern these differences: some parts favoring fine temporal resolution, and other parts favoring fine frequency resolution. Zatorre noticed a similarity between this behavior and that of all linear systems:[14] temporal and spectral resolutions are inversely related; the more you have of one, the less you get of the other (Zatorre 2003, 241–242). Can it be that some parts of the brain favored fine spectral resolution and others fine temporal resolution?

When I first heard Zatorre's hypothesis, a light bulb went off: "wait a minute, this sounds very much like the tradeoff sound designers experience when they use typical FFT[15] audio measuring systems!" In an FFT-based audio measurement system such as SmaartLive, we see exactly the same trade-off: using a longer sample time provides greater spectral resolution (you can see a larger region of frequencies at once), but you can't examine what they are doing very quickly; the response feels "sluggish." On the other hand, if you use shorter sample times, you can tell a lot better what is happening at each instant, but can't see as large of a range of frequencies (Henderson 2016). Fortunately, the manufacturers of the SmaartLive systems have figured out some pretty nifty ways around these limitations in practical use, but you probably never imagined your brain working just like your audio analyzer!

The MIT researchers found much more of this temporal/spectral discrimination within each side of the secondary temporal cortex, but other researchers, including Zatorre, found significant speech and music differences lateralized between the left side and the right side of the auditory cortex and the brain in general (Norman-Haignere, Kanwisher and McDermott, 1287). We have perhaps all heard the well-known cliché that our left brain is logical and our right brain is creative. Unfortunately, the brain is far too complex for such a simplistic idea to hold up under close scrutiny. But the division that Zatorre and others identify precisely matches the way we have categorized and defined language and music—semantic and reduced listening in Chion's parlance. For example, Giraud and Poeppel found that the right auditory cortex played a more essential role in coding pitch information that we use to identify a person's voice, and in prosody, the "music" of speech, whereas the left hemisphere is better at processing shorter sounds like consonants, which are critical to our understanding of words.

To understand this difference, try to read this sentence:

Th qck brwn fx jmpd vr th lzy dg.

Now compare it to this sentence:

E i o o ue oe e a o.

In the first sentence, only the consonants of the sentence "The quick brown fox jumped over the lazy dog" were included. In the second, only the vowels. Giraud and Poeppel's measurements suggest that the left auditory cortex is better at processing the fast-changing signals like consonants, while the slower but wider frequency discriminating right auditory cortex is better at processing vowels (Giraud and Poeppel 2012, 231, 242). Consonants provide much of the meaning of words, vowels provide much of the music. Robert Zatorre and Dean Falk approached the auditory cortex from the vantage point of music, and came to similar conclusions: the right hemisphere of the auditory cortex is better at perceiving fine variations in pitch and the linear sequencing of notes in melody (line), while the left auditory cortex works better with rhythm, since it is the side that seems to favor fine temporal discrimination (Zattore and Zarate 2012, 265–268; Falk 1999, 202–204).

We've done a pretty good job, so far, of figuring out what's going on as our brain processes sound from the ear to the auditory cortex, but beyond that, things start to get a bit trickier. The auditory cortex sends signals out to just about every other part of the cerebrum, and receives signals back. The auditory cortex sends signals back to the thalamus and out to the cerebellum, forebrain, midbrain and all the way back to the ear itself. There are four times more auditory projections going from the auditory cortex to the thalamus than coming from the thalamus! (King and Schnupp 2007, R239). That's a lot of processing to decipher! But neuroscientists do seem to be slowly gaining a better understanding of the fundamental ways in which the auditory cortex interacts with the rest of the brain when processing speech and music.

Steven Brown suggests considering the brain's role in processing speech and music in three ways: first, the processes that speech and music share, second, those that operate in parallel (typically in a left brain, speech, right brain, music, manner), and finally those that are distinctively different for either activity. We've already seen examples of shared activity in the brainstem, hindbrain, midbrain, basal ganglia, cerebellum, thalamus and auditory cortex. In Brown's second category, parallel processing, we have seen that there are homologous areas between the left auditory cortex and the right auditory cortex that parallel each other when analyzing speech and music. It turns out that much of the cerebral cortex seems to process speech in its high temporal resolution left lobe and music in its high spectral resolution right lobe. For example, Broca's area in the left frontal lobe helps us understand sentence structure, and it's homologue on the right side helps us make sense of melodies[16] (Brown, Martinez and Parsons 2006, 2800). Both frontal lobes check in with our hippocampus and memory centers to see if we've ever experienced that structure or pattern before, or to see if we attach any sort of meaning to what we've heard (Levitin 2007, 130). So there are notable brain activities that process in a parallel manner for speech and music, and often operate in a left brain-speech and a right brain-music sort of fashion.

There are distinctly different areas of the brain that process music but not language, and language but not music. The processes we've described related to the direct connection between the cochlea and the cerebellum in startle and habituation have no correlates in language (Levitin 2007, 61). At the same time, there are distinct areas of the brain that process language meaning that have no correlates in music. Steven Brown identifies several specific areas in the parietal,[17] temporal[18] and frontal[19] cortices that have no known parallel processes for music. Perhaps this is because, as Brown suggests, "the informational content of music (i.e., its 'semantics') is still ill-defined." More useful to our approach, as Oliver Sacks put it in Chapter 4, is that "music doesn't have any special meaning; it depends on what it's attached to" (Sacks 2009). Or, as we prefer to think, what is attached to it.

It is perhaps because music has no inherent meaning that it can stimulate its audiences across cultural boundaries. Claude Lévi-Strauss famously said that music is "the only language with the contradictory attributes of being at once intelligible and untranslatable" (Lévi-Strauss 1969, 18). The noted cognitive neuroscientist Aniruddh Patel explains that although we can translate between words in any two languages, we can't translate a Beethoven chamber work into a Javanese gamelan work (Patel 2008, 300–301). At the same time, one culture is quite able to quickly adapt and derive meaning from the music of another culture without any translation. For most of us, we would gain almost nothing reading a play by Aristophanes in Greek. It would literally be "all Greek to me!" However, we could probably derive quite a bit of understanding of the play by listening to a performance of the play in Greek. Even though we do not understand the Greek language, we could certainly find ourselves immersed in the emotional journey of the play simply by experiencing the prosody of the spoken word. Having traveled to many foreign countries and been invited to experience theatre performed in the native tongue, I can attest this is true—and the more music, the greater my comprehension of the mimesis.

Finally, we should note that rhythm does not neatly fit into Steven Brown's neurological framework of shared, parallel and distinctly different areas of auditory processing. Thaut says, "rhythm processing is a widely distributed bilateral function and not lateralized hemispherically" (2005, 53), suggesting that we cannot simply think about rhythm as a neurological process that is added on top of our more fundamental brain processes. As an example, consider what happens to the brain as the external auditory tempo changes. When the tempo is constant the brain's response is limited to the areas you would pretty much expect: auditory and motor cortices as well as subcortical regions. Start changing the tempo and the frontal lobe gets increasingly involved: first middle front, then the front sides, and then the back sides, spreading out from the center as it were as the tempo changes vary (2005, 48–49). While this is going on, keep in mind that the cerebellum is also activating in very complex ways, the more complex the rhythm, the more activation patterns in the cerebellum, for example, in the running example of Chapter 5 when running in a hemiola pattern (2005, 51).

Rather, rhythm is a core process of the brain that underlies many, if not most, brain functions. Daniel Mauro has observed this core relationship between fundamental properties of music and basic neurological temporal functions of the brain. He suggests that "three facets of brain processing (frequency, synchrony and temporal pattern), are reflected in three essential properties of rhythm (tempo, meter, phrasing)," respectively (2006, 164). A diverse array of neurological networks are responsible for each of these in virtually every part of the brain, and how we organize and use them largely depends on how our culture, language and musical traditions developed. We don't have dedicated rhythm processing centers, because rhythm is so fundamental to everything we do. That's why we are so lucky as sound designers and composers to be blessed with a tool that gives us access at such a primal level to human conscious and unconscious processes. Since rhythm evolved in the animal kingdom in such a fundamental way, we need to think about it as a foundation on which other brain processes build; as Thaut says, "rhythm must be viewed as a biological fact, not just as a cultural phenomenon" (2005, 57).

Conclusion: Song = Music + Idea

Thus far, we can see a relationship between language and music that complements each other in extraordinary and cognitively complete ways. This relationship facilitates human communication and creates shared experiences in ways far beyond the strengths of either separately. On the one hand lies language, which we use to communicate referential and extremely complex meaning according to semiotic rules and structures. On the other hand, we have music, which we use to incite a wide array of complex emotions and to manipulate our sense of time. When we combine the two, as we typically do in theatre, we create songs; songs that traverse a continuum from the more traditionally considered songs characterized by lyrics with melody, through verse (lyrics with prosody), through prose (speech with prosody). In theatre, any of these forms may be accompanied by instrumental music, which creates a hierarchical level of song (melody or speech with accompaniment) that sound designers and composers cannot afford to ignore.

Many researchers separate instrumental "music" from the speech "music" of spoken language in their investigations, preferring to draw the line between "music" and "speech." They then note many similarities between the music and speech, such as pitch, rhythm, contour and so forth! We have found that it is more helpful to make the distinction between speech language, which refers to the meaning of speech, and speech music, which carries the meaning of speech, and includes tonal color, prosody and so forth, and fundamentally aligns with instrumental music in its elementary components of color and dynamics operating in space and time (e.g., rhythm, line and texture). There are far fewer similarities when we divide our perceptions in this manner! In this chapter, we have observed that the brain seems to process how we listen and respond to speech music and instrumental music in much the same way, adding additional support to our thesis about how we evolved hearing to perceive the fundamental nature of the mechanical waves we call sound. Music works quite differently than language. Language activates far fewer parts of the brain than music. Music activates a large part of the brain, and the most primitive parts of our brain. Language functions tend to be localized in a relatively constrained and lateralized neural network (Thaut 2005, 2). Even in a different modality such as American Sign Language (visual vs. auditory), language relies on many of the same left hemisphere brain areas as spoken language (Patel 2008, 364).

As composers and sound designers for theatre, it helps tremendously to understand that composing instrumental music orchestrates the spoken word in much the same way it does melody, with greater constraints typically being placed on melody due to the use of a fixed pitch system. In either case, the instrumental music is carefully arranged to support the lead melody or prosody of the spoken lyric or prose. Once we fully separate the semiotic functions of speech from the musical, we can develop fundamental properties of music that carry the complex meanings of language and incite in the listener an appropriate emotional reaction to the communication. Some will argue that the musical elements provide language with meaning. I tend to think that music carries the meaning of language, because on its own, the music has very little meaning in the traditional sense of the word. The term "communication" implies cognitive processes that we often typically attempt to avoid when we compose sound scores for theatre. Instead we work to create shared states of mood and emotion, to which we attach meaningful language. Because we are interested in fully studying the fundamental role that music plays in theatre, we need to keep music and language separate. This method of categorization allows us to group similar auditory perceptions as color, shape, rhythm, dynamics, line and so forth into a category shared with visual art, suitable for further inquiry, and leaves the referential aspects of language such as semiotics and phonemes to others. In other words, Music as a Chariot.

It may be true, then, that "all plays start with a script," if that is how you choose to define theatre. However, it seems to me that if we ignore millions of years of evolution that consistently point to the theatre experience evolving out of a unique combination of music, language and mimesis, we might simultaneously undermine much of our theatrical endeavors in the twenty-first century. Rather, I think that a more appropriate approach to developing a work of theatre might be to consider that every play starts with a song which must be brought to life through mimesis.

In this chapter, we have seen our species evolve from primitive humans through to our fully formed modern anatomical state, *Homo sapiens sapiens*. We explored how this modern brain hears sound, how it converts sound from mechanical waves into neural firings, and then how the brain processes those neural firings. Simultaneous with this evolution, we witnessed the distinct evolution of language and music, a curious and distinct feature of these modern brains not shared with any other species. We saw many similarities in how the brain processes language and music, and some important differences. We then separated music and language according to these biological differences, noting that considering them in this manner is of the utmost value to the theatre composer and sound designer because it creates a hierarchy that we must not ignore.

In the next chapters, we'll further consider the developing elements of music as humans discovered more sophisticated means of expressing themselves. Concepts of consonance and dissonance became much more critical when we started dividing the frequency spectrum into discreet pitches. We'll take a closer look at how consonance and dissonance also entrain neurological circuits, adding to our argument that music, and its offspring, theatre, are fundamentally immersive and experiential in nature, like dreams. And, of course, we'll examine how these biological underpinnings are important to us as composers and designers.

Ten Questions

1. What was the significance of the quartz hand axe discovered in the Sima de los Huesos cave at Atapuerca in Northern Spain? Why?
2. Name two significant differences between *Homo heidelbergensis* that separate them from *Homo erectus*.
3. How does *Homo sapiens sapiens* differ from *Homo sapiens*, and why does that difference allow us to study them by studying our own anatomy?
4. Why is it so important for composers and sound designers to understand how human hearing works?
5. In remarkably few words, identify ten components of the human ear and describe what each does.
6. In remarkably few words, identify ten components of the human hearing system between the output of the cochlea and the auditory cortex and describe what each does.
7. Describe two things the primary auditory cortex (core) does.
8. What are Michel Chion's three types of listening, and where and how do they manifest themselves in the auditory cortex?
9. How does the human brain function like an FFT-based audio analysis system, and what does this have to do with processing human speech and music?
10. Briefly describe the shared, parallel and different ways the brain uses to process speech and music and explain why rhythm does not neatly fall into any of these categories.

Things to Share

1. Now that you have a pretty good understanding of the element of rhythm, it's time to explore its ability to stir emotions in your audience. Imagine five rhythms, one for each of the following emotions: love, anger, fear, joy, sadness. Using the eraser end of a pencil, tap out these short rhythms and record them. Record these into five separate takes as audio files. Keep your takes short, less than about five seconds.

   We will play your five recordings back for the class, and the class will have to suggest which rhythms most incited which emotions in them. We'll poll the class to see which tracks they associated with each emotion, and then we'll ask you for the order you intended. We'll then tabulate the percentage of emotions you were able to correctly incite in each audience member, and discuss the results.

2. Find a short poem that you are particularly fond of and track how you imagine the prosody of the poem should be performed melodically. Use a horizontal line to track your base pitch (what researchers call F0), and then notate opposite the actual text where you think the melody goes up, and where the melody goes down, and by how much. See the example below. Prepare your entire poem for presentation, and then "sing" the

poem to the class, using your graph as a guide to your performance, grossly exaggerating the pitch variation you would normally use to help us perceive them better. Make copies of your poem to share with the class so we can follow along!

To be or not to be, that is the question.

Notes

1 Having the same relation, relative position, or structure, in the brain.
2 See Figure 6.4 for a comparison of Hominidae brain sizes.
3 Technically the changes are two amino acid substitutions.
4 See the references at the end of this paragraph regarding the KE family, who did indeed inherit such a mutation involving the *FoxP2* gene that affected half the family members. Those afflicted had difficulty constructing grammatical sentences, often speaking in very simple speech.
5 Just when you thought it was safe to make a statement about the age of *Homo sapiens* (conventionally placed at about 200,000 years ago), new research shows that we may be much older than originally thought: 300,000 years or so. See Hublin et al. (2017). This helps to demonstrate that evolutionary biology, like so many of our sciences, is always a work in progress, and that it can be very hard to narrow down some of these conclusions definitively. As is typical for us, however, these nuances do not upset the applecart of our central premise.
6 I've left the discrepancy in between this reference and the Australian Museum reference of Figure 7.2 as a healthy reminder that there it can sometimes be hard to find precise agreement among researchers!
7 With great apologies, we are going to increasingly focus on auditory sound and music. We'll leave it to other enterprising theatre artists to trace the journey for visual language and music!
8 Remember when we said in Chapter 2 that "sound reveals time by defining it relative to space"?
9 One of 12 or 13, depending on who you talk to!
10 Some researchers still divide the cortex into two areas, the primary auditory cortex (the core), and the secondary auditory cortex (the belt and the parabelt).
11 The planum polare.
12 The left planum temporale only.
13 The superior temporal gyrus.
14 A linear system is simply a system in which what you get out is directly proportional to what you put in. A graph showing input versus output will always be a straight line (hence "linear"). The brain, of course, is wildly non-linear, but Zatorre noticed a connection in this particular instance.
15 Fast Fourier Transform, a mathematical equation that transforms a signal from the time domain to the frequency domain and back again. This allows one to look at the same signal displayed as either frequency or time along the horizontal axis, with amplitude in the vertical axis.

16 Brodmann Area 44.
17 Left inferior parietal cortex, including an area known as Wernicke's area, critical to understanding the meaning of words (Brodmann Areas 39 and 40).
18 Left middle and inferior temporal gyrus (Brodmann Areas 20 and 21).
19 Inferior frontal gyrus (Brodmann Area 47).

Bibliography

Allen, John S., Hanna Damasio, and Thomas J. Grabowski. 2002. "Normal Neuroanatomical Variation in the Human Brain: An MRI-Volumetric Study." *American Journal of Physical Anthropology* 118 (4): 341–358.

Appia, Adolphe. 1962. *Music and the Art of Theatre.* Coral Gables, FL: University of Miami Press.

Arbib, Michael A. 2013. "Précis of How the Brain Got Language: The Mirror System Hypothesis." *Language and Cognition* 5 (2–3): 107–131.

Australian Museum. 2015. "Homo Erectus/Homo Heidelbergensis." September 25. Accessed April 6, 2016. http://australianmuseum.net.au/homo-erectus; http://australianmuseum.net.au/homo-heidelbergensis.

Bickerton, Derek. 2005. "Language Evolution: A Brief Guide for Linguists." *Science Direct* 117 (3): 510–526.

Brown, Steven, Michael J. Martinez, and Lawrence M. Parsons. 2006. "Music and Language Side by Side in the Brain: A PET Study of the Generation of Melodies and Sentences." *European Journal of Neuroscience* 23 (10): 2791–2803.

Cann, Rebecca L., Mark Stoneking, and Allan Wilson. 1987. "Mitochondrial DNA and Human Evolution." *Nature* 325 (6099): 31–36.

Chesner, C.A., W.I. Rose, A. Deino, R. Drake, and J.A. Westgate. 1991. "Eruptive History of Earth's Largest Quaternary Caldera (Toba, Indonesia) Clarified." *Geology* 19 (3): 200–203.

Chion, Michel. 1990. *Audio-Vision.* New York: Columbia University Press.

Cross, Ian. 2003. "Music, Cognition, Culture, and Evolution." In *The Cognitive Neuroscience of Music*, edited by Isabell Peretz, and Robert Zatorre. Oxford: Oxford University Press.

Donald, Merlin. 1993a. "Human Cognitive Evolution." *Social Research* 60 (1): 143–170.

———. 1993b. "Précis of Origins of the Modern Mind." *Behavioral and Brain Sciences* 16 (4): 737–791.

Falk, Dean. 1999. "Hominid Brain Evolution and the Origins of Music." In *The Origins of Music*, edited by Nils L. Wallin, Björn Merker, and Steven Brown, 197–216. Cambridge, MA: MIT Press.

Frayer, David W., and Chris Nicolay. 2000. "Fossil Evidence for the Origin of Speech Sounds." In *The Origins of Music*, edited by Nils L. Wallion, Björn Merker, and Steven Brown, 217–234. Cambridge, MA: MIT Press.

Giraud, Anne-Lise, and David Poeppel. 2012. "Speech Perception From a Neurophysiological Perspective." In *The Human Auditory Cortex*, edited by David Poeppel, Tobias Overath, Arthur N. Popper, and Richard R. Fay, 225–260. New York: Springer.

Griffiths, Timothy D., Christophe Micheyl, and Tobias Overath. 2012. "Auditory Object Analysis." In *The Human Auditory Cortex*, edited by David Poeppel, Tobias Overath, Arthur N. Popper, and Richard R. Fay, 199–224. New York: Springer.

Henderson, Paul D. 2016. "The Fundamentals of FFT-Based Audio Measurements in SmaartLive®." Rational Acoustics. Accessed April 20, 2016. www.rationalacoustics.com/files/FFT_Fundamentals.pdf.

156   Song = Music + Idea

Hublin, Jean-Jacques, Abdelouahed Ben-Ncer, Shara Bailey, Sarah E. Freidline, Simon Neubauer, Matthew M Skinner, Inga Bergmann, et al. 2017. "New Fossils from Jebel Irhoud, Morocco and the Pan-African Origin of Homo Sapiens." *Nature* 546 (7657): 289–292.

Kandel, Eric R., James H. Schwartz, and Thomas M. Jessell. 2000. *Principles of Neuroscience*. New York: McGraw-Hill.

King, Andrew J., and Jan W.H. Schnupp. 2007. "The Auditory Cortex." *Current Biology* 17 (7): R236–239.

Krause, Johannes, Carles Lalueza-Fox, Ludovic Orlando, Hernán A. Burbano, Jean-Jacques Hublin, Catherine Hänni, Javier Fortea, et al. 2007. "The Derived FOXP2 Variant of Modern Humans Was Shared with Neandertals." *Current Biology* 17: 1908–1912.

Leonard, Abigail W. 2006. "Your Brain Boots Up Like a Computer." August 17. Accessed April 10, 2016. www.livescience.com/980-brain-boots-computer.html.

Lévi-Strauss, C. 1969. *The Raw and the Cooked: Introduction to a Science of Mythology*. Translated by J. Weightman and D. Weightman. New York: Harper and Row.

Levitin, Daniel J. 2007. *This Is Your Brain on Music*. New York: Penguin Group/Plume.

Lieberman, Philip. 2007. "The Evolution of Human Speech, Its Anatomical and Neural Bases." *Current Anthropology* 48 (1): 39–66.

Marean, Curtis, W. 2015. "The Most Invasive Species of All." *Scientific American*, August: 32–39.

Mauro, Daniel. 2006. "The Rhythmic Brain." *The Fifth International Conference of the Cognitive Sciences*. Vancouver.

Molino, Jean. 1999. "Toward an Evolutionary Theory of Music and Language." In *The Origins of Music*, edited by Nils L. Wallin, Bjorn Merker, and Steven Brown, 165–176. Cambridge, MA: MIT Press.

Norman-Haignere, Sam, Nancy G. Kanwisher, and Josh H. McDermott. 2015. "Distinct Cortical Pathways for Music and Speech Revealed by Hypothesis-Free Voxel Decomposition." *Neuron* 88 (6): 1281–1296.

Oxford Dictionaries. 2016. "Scene." Accessed April 2, 2016. www.oxforddictionaries.com/us/definition/american_english/scene.

Parham, Kourosh, and James F. Willott. 1990. "Effects of Inferior Colliculus Lesions on the Acoustic Startle Response." *Behavioral Neuroscience* 104 (6): 831–840.

Patel, Aniruddh D. 2008. *Music Language and the Brain*. New York: Oxford University Press.

PBS. 2011. "Becoming Human Part 3." August 31. Accessed April 8, 2016. www.pbs.org/wgbh/nova/evolution/becoming-human.html#becoming-human-part-3.

Preuss, Todd M. 2012. "Human Brain Evolution: From Gene Discovery to Phenotype Discovery." *Proceedings of the National Academy of Sciences* 109: 10709–10716.

Rubio, Maria E. 2010. "The Cochlear Nucleus." June. Accessed April 24, 2016. http://neurobiologyhearing.uchc.edu/Course_Content_Library/Cochlear_nucleus/Rubio-cochlear%20nucleus%201.pdf.

Sacks, Oliver, interview by John Stewart. 2009. *The Daily Show*. Comedy Central. June 29.

Smithsonian Museum of Natural History. 2016a. "Homo Heidelbergensis." June 9. Accessed June 14, 2016. http://humanorigins.si.edu/evidence/human-fossils/species/homo heidelbergensis.

———. 2016b. "Human Evolution Timeline Interactive." March 25. Accessed March 28, 2016. http://humanorigins.si.edu/evidence/human-evolution-timeline-interactive.

Spoendlin, H., and A. Schrott. 1989. "Analysis of the Human Auditory Nerve." *Hearing Research* 43 (1): 25–38.

Thaut, Michael H. 2005. *Rhythm, Music, and the Brain.* New York: Routledge Taylor & Francis Group.

Thomas, Richard K. 2001. "The Function of the Soundscape." *Theatre Design & Technology* 37 (1): 18–26.

Tremlett, Giles. 2003. "Excalibur, the Rock that May Mark a New Dawn for Man: Palaeontologists Claim 350,000-Year-Old Find in Spanish Cave Pushes Back Boundary of Early Human Evolution." *Guardian (London)* January 9: 3.

Wells, Spencer. 2007. "Out of Africa." *Vanity Fair* July: 110.

Wray, Allison. 1998. "Protolanguage as a Holistic System for Social Interaction." *Language and Communication.* 18 (1): 47-67

Zatorre, Robert. 2003. "Neural Specializations for Tonal Processing." In *The Cognitive Neuroscience of Music*, edited by Isabelle Peretz and Robert Zatorre. Oxford: Oxford University Press.

Zattore, Robert J., and Jean Mary Zarate. 2012. "Cortical Processing of Music." In *The Human Auditory Cortex*, edited by David Poeppel, Tobias Overath, Arthur N. Popper, and Richard R. Fay, 261–294. New York: Springer.

CHAPTER 8

CONSONANCE AND DISSONANCE
The Evolution of Line

Introduction: The Roots of Who We Become

I got my first guitar for Christmas when I was five or six years old—a Roy Rogers children's toy. A couple of years later, it was deemed that my older brother Tom would take lessons at Willis Music, the local music store on Gratiot Avenue a couple of miles from my house. My parents bought him a Gibson ES-120T Thinline Fully Hollow Body Electric Archtop. It was the cheapest electric guitar that Gibson made, but to me it seemed like it must have cost a million dollars. I became infatuated with it, and snuck in to my brother's room whenever he wasn't around to play it. Eventually, he lost interest in guitar playing, and I became more brash in my playing it, eventually claiming some kind of ownership, a point that remains in dispute to this day. I have proven the old adage, however, that "possession is nine-tenths of the law."

In high school I joined our church folk group—folk music became permissible and popular in church almost simultaneously with my shift from altar boy to musician. Folk music is all about melody, and I was an avid song writer, having written a whole collection of songs in junior high. Years later I would go back to my church for a wedding and found one of my old songs still in the church hymnal. I can remember the tune to this day, even though it's one of those tunes one really wishes they could forget (see my discussion about "banal" hooks in Chapter 10). This background, however, gave me an affinity for melody, and would contribute enormously to my early career as a sound designer until I discovered that a gift for memorable tunes isn't always a desired commodity in theatre composition.

In 1977, my first year as a graduate student, I used some Fripp and Eno music in a sound score for Sam Shepard's *Cowboys #2*, a sound score that would eventually find its way to my first professional production at the Perry Street Theatre in New York that same year. A pharmacy student experienced the production, and was shocked to find out that someone else at Purdue University knew who Fripp and Eno were. He contacted our chair at the time, Dr. Dale Miller, and Dr. Miller put him in touch with me. That's how I met my first business partner, Brad Garton, who went on to become director of the Computer Music Center at Columbia University, and a marvelous composer in his own right. Brad and I decided to work on a production of Shakespeare's *The Tempest* at Purdue together, a major endeavor that would require an almost continuous sound score. Brad was a godsend, quite frankly because he had a boatload of gear, including a Teac 3340 four track reel-to reel tape recorder and a Micro Moog synthesizer, and I was a poor kid from Detroit who had spent his entire salary from the previous summer's work at the Black Hills Playhouse in Custer, South Dakota to buy a Teac 2300 two track reel-to-reel. Even better, he knew how to use his equipment. What became immediately obvious was that I had a really nice affinity for melody and Brad was a genius at orchestration. We complemented each other really, really well. The show was a big hit, and Dr. Miller used the sound track to demonstrate the power of music in theatre in his Theatre Appreciation classes for many years.

Brad and I started our business together, Zounds Productions. We would operate quite successfully for five years, when Brad decided to study computer music at Princeton University with the legendary computer music composer, Paul Lansky. It was at that moment that I realized that Brad had a huge advantage over me in orchestration: he had studied classical piano as a child, and that taught him how to manage multiple simultaneous ideas in both his mind and his fingers. You can do that with guitar, but in a much more limited way. I started studying classical piano with Caryl Matthews at the ripe old age of 30, and continued for another 20 years. This would be too late to become a concert pianist, of course; our brains and muscles are just not plastic enough anymore at that age. But studying classical piano changed my life and taught me an incredible amount about orchestrating music. There is a reason why students in music schools are required to study piano in addition to their primary instrument. To this day, I recommend that students who want to become serious composers for theatre study classical piano; not so much for performance, but to learn how to think contrapuntally, and to study how other great composers have done so.

Around the same time I worked with Brad, I read a book about modern composition that said that, in the twentieth century, all composition was really a matter of managing consonance and dissonance. So while I was studying all the "rules" of voice leading and chord progressions and so forth, I was also experimenting with simply letting my ear be my guide, and manipulating tension and release using varying amounts of consonance and dissonance. It would be many years before I would be able to let go of melody enough to simply explore inciting emotion and creating/releasing tension through consonance and dissonance. Eventually I learned that theatre sound scoring is fundamentally about managing consonance and dissonance. We manage consonance and dissonance both vertically through simultaneously sounded notes (chords) and horizontally through sequences of notes (line/melody). The combination of these two practices is harmony, and every composer *and* sound designer needs to understand as much as they possibly can about how consonance and dissonance work in both visual music and audible music if they want to learn to manipulate them to carry the ideas of the play.

Most of us start to learn about consonance and dissonance by learning about Western music practice. This is fine and highly recommended, but it may also help to consider how consonance and dissonance came to be, and how our brain works in its most primitive way to perceive both, and how that, in turn, affects us emotionally. You don't have to be Rachmaninoff to create effective sound scores. But you do have to understand how to manipulate consonance and dissonance over time to create and release tension and to manipulate emotions.

In this chapter, we'll start by considering the next step in our evolutionary development, the near simultaneous development of language, visual-spatial arts, and music—not just proto-music, but music in the fullest sense of our original definition. For the first time, we'll find evidence of non-referential manipulations of time as a form of *art*. That evidence comes in the form of primitive flutes capable of playing discrete pitches, which naturally introduces the possibility of consonance and dissonance. We'll examine our modern brain to look for clues as to how the brain processes consonance and dissonance. Finally, we'll consider how we use consonance and dissonance in theatre to incite emotions in our audience while they are simultaneously immersing them in the dreamlike world of the play.

The Evolution of Line

When we last left our *Homo sapiens sapiens* ancestors, they were struggling with another mini ice age coupled with a giant volcanic eruption near Lake Toba on Sumatra in Indonesia 70,000 years ago. The eruption once again almost decimated the small human population. But this was a vastly improved iteration of *Homo sapiens sapiens*, one that had developed sophisticated tools, advanced language, and *art*. The emergence of art was most likely not a sudden discovery. Archaeologists have discovered other artifacts that may provide evidence of art created by *Homo erectus* as early as 300,000 years ago (Brahic 2014). But, starting around 100,000 years ago, archaeologists have discovered an increasing amount of evidence of the use of *ochre* (iron oxide that can be made into a pigment), bone, and charcoal in artistic applications. One very early and very significant example was found in a cave in Blombos, South Africa, dating back 75,000 years (Henshilwood et al. 2016).

Of course, like language, the evidence of the origins of fully developed music is often contested. Nevertheless, the Blombos cave provides uncontested evidence of human artistic endeavor, and there is general consensus that early humans had established a long tradition of geometrically engraving stones and other artistic activity by then (Henshilwood, d'Errico and Watts 2009).

During the next 40,000 years, humans developed the ability to draw pictures of themselves and the world around them. This was a monumental achievement, because for the first time, it allowed humans to record their stories outside of their memories. Merlin Donald calls it the third major cognitive breakthrough, after the mimesis of Australopithecines and *Homo erectus* and language development in *Homo sapiens* (Donald 1993a, 160; Donald 1993b, 35). Imagine the consequences of the slow movement from the biologically based, limited storage capacity of the human brain that expired with its human host, and the permanence of

Thousands of Years Ago	Important Characteristics
20–35	Flutes found in caves in Isturitz, France
35–42	Flutes discovered in caves in Hohle Fels and Geißenklösterle Germany
50–40	Human migration to Europe
70–60	Human migration to southern Asia and Australia
75	Human art in a cave in Blombos, South Africa
300	Earliest possible evidence of human art

Figure 8.1 Timeline of earliest human art.

cave paintings. Such cave paintings would ultimately develop into written languages that used symbols to communicate and preserved ideas among members of each tribe (d'Errico et al. 2003, 31–32).

Humans once again spread out from Africa at a lessening of one of the worst periods of the ice age that occurred about 70,000 to 60,000 years ago[1] (see Figure 7.8).

They first followed the coast through Yemen and into southern Asia, and then migrated into Australia at a time when sea levels were probably about 300 feet lower, creating a land bridge that allowed easier migration (National Geographic 2016). They were well-equipped to travel, having clearly developed much more sophisticated forms of language, music, ritual and visual art (among many other things). The development of language would have allowed them to pass their stories from one generation to another, thus beginning ancient "oral traditions" that would couple language and music in complementary ways essential to the

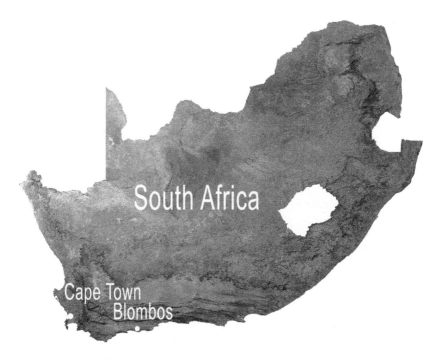

Figure 8.2 Map of Blombos cave.

Figure 8.3 Blombos cave engraved ochre.

Credit: Image courtesy of Professor Christopher Henshilwood.

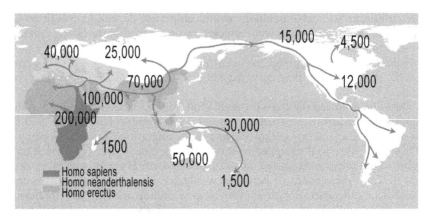

Figure 8.4 Map of human migrations shows periods when *Homo sapiens* migrated throughout the world.

Credit: Map re-drawn by Altaileopard, Urutseg, and NordNordWest at https://commons. wikimedia.org/wiki/File:Spreading_homo_sapiens_la.svg, with data from Göran Burenhult, *The First People*, Weltbild Verlag, 2000. ISBN 3-8289-0741-5. Accessed July 21, 2017. Adapted by Richard K. Thomas.

development of theatre, especially in ritual. The sculptures, engravings, and cave and rock paintings that became commonplace would become the basis for written language that would eventually supplant the oral tradition.

By about 50,000 to 40,000 years ago, the earth's climate had warmed sufficiently for humans to migrate to Europe (Higham et al. 2011; Benazzi et al. 2011). This particular migration pattern is important to us for two reasons. First, it's important because we are marching toward the establishment of the first autonomous theatre in ancient Greece, which is definitely in the direction of Europe from Africa. Second, the first hard evidence of human musical instruments was discovered in caves in Germany and France about 35,000 years ago. The German flutes were discovered in the Hohle Fels cave in southwestern Germany, and dated about 35,000 years ago (Conard, Malina and Münzel 2009), while flutes found in the nearby Geißenklösterle caves dated between 35,000 and 42,000 years ago (Higham et al. 2012).

The French flutes were discovered in a cave in Isturitz, France. They are estimated to be between 20,000 and 35,000 years old and are reasonably complete (d'Errico et al. 2003, 39). The flutes from the above archaeological sites are generally accepted as authentic musical instruments.[2] These flutes indicate a distinct change in the way humans made music, including a knowledge of discrete pitches and scales necessary for the creation of melodic lines, and even harmonies if two are played simultaneously.

Consider how the development of musical line corresponds to a certain degree with the development of visual line in art. At first glance it appears that visual line predates auditory line by tens of thousands of years or more. But this may not necessarily be the case. One of the archaeologists who discovered the German bone flutes, Nicholas J. Conard, suggested that the "finds demonstrate the presence of a *well-established* musical tradition at the time when modern humans

Figure 8.5 Map of Germany shows location of Hohle Fels and Geißenklösterle caves.
Credit: Best-Backgrounds/Shutterstock.com. Adapted by Richard K. Thomas.

colonized Europe" (Conard, Malina and Münzel 2009). It seems likely that the flutes weren't invented in the German caves, but were brought by the migrants who traveled and settled there. d'Errico and others have noted a distinct similarity between the German and the French flutes, even though they were separated "in time by hundreds or even thousands of years, making a common, much earlier origin 'increasingly possible'" (d'Errico et al. 2003, 45–46).

Consider also, the technical challenges of crafting a workable flute compared with picking up a burned stick and creating a charcoal drawing. We should also expect that the evolution of a sophisticated instrument like a flute came much later than more simple developments in music. Many potential primitive musical instruments consist of materials that decay over time (stretched animal skins over hollowed out logs for drum heads, for example). A flute could indicate the presence of an advanced musical mode of expression that developed between the time when *vocal* expression evolved from unfixed pitch (such as that of gibbons) and when fixed pitch mode instruments appeared (as reflected in the bone flutes). It's hard to imagine fixed pitch vocal music coming *after* the engineering of flutes, particularly, when, as we will see in later sections, the human brain

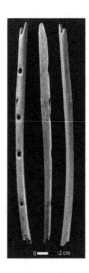

Figure 8.6 A bone flute from Hohle Fels.

Credit: Adapted by permission from Macmillan Publishers Ltd., *Nature*. Conard, N.J., M. Malina, and S.C. Münzel. "New Flutes Document the Earliest Musical Tradition in Southwestern Germany." *Nature* 460: 737–740. doi:10.1038/nature08169, copyright 2009.

had much earlier evolved predisposed to consonance and dissonance. In the final analysis, given the ongoing controversies as to what constitutes visual art and what constitutes music, the dates and evidence are murky enough to allow us to imagine that music and line, in both their visual and auditory manifestations, may have developed side by side as human cognitive abilities developed. In the big picture of evolution, both visual and auditory line appear at very similar points in time.

It is one thing to understand that music evolved alongside visual art in these prehistoric cultures. However, in this book we are even more interested in the answer to the questions, *how was music used, and for what purpose?* Caves in which both art objects and musical instruments were found, were often, if not typically, used as gathering places. The cave at Isturitz, for example, seems to have been used as a large gathering place in the spring and fall. Ian Morley cites additional studies suggesting that the acoustics of the caves themselves would have been "highly significant." You can hopefully imagine the reverberant possibilities of a flute played inside a cave of this sort (remembering that space is also an element of music), not to mention that of the human singing voice. Morley also describes a veritable orchestra of bones, beaters and rattles at another cave in Mezin, Ukraine, dating to about 20,000 years ago found in the same cave as piles of red and yellow ochre. By this time ochre was widely used symbolically throughout the ancient world, including in burials, cave and rock paintings and so forth (Henshilwood, d'Errico and Watts 2009, 28). Morley suggests these caves were used for large scale gatherings over a very extended period of time. He concludes that it would be hard to imagine that ritual did not play an important role in the gatherings of this culture, and that music would play an important role in the rituals: "The performance and perception of music can provide the perfect medium for *carrying* symbolic (including religious) associations because of its combination of *having no fixed meaning* [italics mine] . . . whilst having the potential to stimulate powerful emotional reactions" (Morley 2009, 170–171). Music as a Chariot.

In this period between 100,000 and 30,000 years ago, we witness the development of art, music and ritual on a scale unprecedented in any other species. While hard evidence is hard to come by due to the temporal nature of the events and practices, evidence does exist of art in burial sites dating back to 100,000 years ago. Henshilwood and others suggest that "elaborated burials . . . are considered to be the archaeological expression of symbolically mediated behaviors" (Henshilwood, d'Errico and Watts 2009, 27). Even the simple quartz dropped into the Sima de los Huesos cave at Atapuerca in Northern Spain (discussed in Chapter 7) suggests that humans were considering where they came from, and where they went after they died. It is hard to imagine a ritual that humans developed to assist in the transition from death to whatever came after that did not involve music. It seems much more than chance, that line (or its audible manifestation in melody) created possibilities for the social expression and experiencing of emotion unmatched in other species.

Consonance and Dissonance

Something as simple as holes in a pipe can mean quite a lot in human development. It provides concrete evidence of humans sequencing sounds by discrete pitch steps. Remember in Chapter 4 when we talked about the definition of music we marveled how music, unlike visual objects or language had the unique property of being sequential and simultaneous? With these pipes we now have evidence of an ability to produce discrete pitches both sequentially and simultaneously. Sequential production of notes on a single pipe produces an audible line (melody), with characteristics similar to the lines on the red ochre pieces uncovered in the cave at Blombos. Simultaneous production of notes (on different pipes) results in harmony. The foundation of harmony is not scales or modes as you might think. That's because scales and modes are culturally derived ways of dividing up pitches; they vary from country to country and culture to culture. What doesn't change wherever you go, and is as much a foundation of language and theatre as it is of music, is consonance and dissonance.

What Is Consonance and Dissonance?

The musical concept of consonance and dissonance appears to hold across all cultures and time periods. Roederer specifically indicates this in his book *The Physics and Psychophysics of Music*, "Tonal music of all cultures seems to indicate that the human auditory system possesses a sense for certain special frequency intervals—the octave, fifth, fourths, etc." (Roederer 2008, 170). This is important because in order for the phenomenon to be evolutionary, we should see it across all cultures, and it should have been that way for a long period of time. We should see evidence of it everywhere. And this is exactly what we find with consonance and dissonance. A wide variety of research has shown that cultures around the world perceive consonance and dissonance in similar ways. This applies, according to Tramo and others, "over a wide range of musical styles enjoyed by people throughout much of the industrialized world: contemporary pop and theatre (including rock, rhythm and blues, country and Latin-American), European music from the Baroque, Classical, and Romantic eras (1600–1900), children's songs, and many forms of ritualistic music (e.g., church songs, processionals, anthems, and holiday music)." Tramo's studies suggest that all of us have "common basic auditory mechanisms" for perceiving consonance and dissonance (Tramo et al. 2003, 128; Fritz et al. 2009). In this part of the chapter, we'll attempt to identify those mechanisms.

What exactly is consonance? According to Tramo, consonance means "harmonious, agreeable, and stable," while dissonance means "disagreeable, unpleasant, and in need of resolution" (2003, 128). Not everyone, including me, fully agrees that dissonance is a negative thing, and so I tend to simply think of consonance as eliciting a state of calm, rest and resolution, and dissonance eliciting a state of arousal. Consonance is determined by the simplicity of the ratio of two pitches (frequencies) x:y, where y is the lower of the two pitches. The simplest of these ratios is 1:1 (unison), followed by the octave (2:1), fifth (3:2), fourth (4:3), major third (5:4) and minor third (6:5). At the other extreme, dissonant intervals do not have simple numerical ratios, for example, minor seconds (16:15) and tritones (45:32), approximately including the augmented fourth or diminished fifth. Humans can tolerate about 0.9%–1.2% of error in determining pitches, however, which allows us to use the equal-tempered scale in Western music to compensate for problems caused by reducing intervals in an octave to simple numerical intervals (i.e., so-called Pythagorean tuning) (2003, 132). These constraints apply to frequencies from about 25 Hz to 5 kHz (2003, 130).

Subcortical Consonance and Dissonance Perception

As we've discussed before, the basilar membrane in the cochlea converts sound waves into neural pulses (see Figure 7.10). These pulses are separated along the basilar membrane by frequency. When they are separated, the neural pulses then fire at intervals consistent with the amount of time it takes to complete one cycle. A 480 Hz (cycles per second) tone would produce a neural spike along the particular neural fibers dedicated to that frequency every 1/480 seconds, or every 2.1 milliseconds (msec). The greater the amplitude of the sound wave, the greater the number of neural pulses firing at that time interval. Now if we simultaneously play a tone that is a musical fifth above that, at 720 Hz, the neural fibers dedicated to that frequency will also start firing every 1/720 Hz, or every 1.39 msec.

But here's where things start to get interesting. Every once in a while, an auditory stimulus will include both frequencies, and that will generate the corresponding neural pulses on their respective neural fibers at the same time. The first frequency triggers neural pulses at 2.1 and then 4.2 milliseconds; the second at 1.4, 2.8 and 4.2 milliseconds. They have a simple numerical ratio to each other that causes their pulses to coincide every two pulses for 480 Hz, and every three pulses for 720 Hz, a 3:2 frequency ratio that causes pulses to coincide every four msec.

Also note that there will be a series of simultaneous pulses then at 4.2 msec (240 Hz), 8.4 msec (120 Hz), 12.6 msec (80 Hz), and so forth, for as long as the stimulus lasts (although very quickly they fall outside the frequency range of audible hearing). This all happens in the cochlea, before the sound ever reaches the brain, but it turns out that the brain really likes these short interspike intervals, or ISI, as they are called.[3]

Now consider what happens for the musical interval of the fourth, having a basic frequency ratio of 4:3 such as 640 Hz and 480 Hz (see Figure 8.7). These tones will only fire simultaneously on every fourth cycle of 640 Hz (1/640 Hz = 1.56 msec; 4 × 1.56 msec = 6.3 msec), and every third cycle of 480 Hz (1/480 Hz = 2.1 msec; 3 × 2.1 msec = 6.3 msec). So they still fire at the same time every

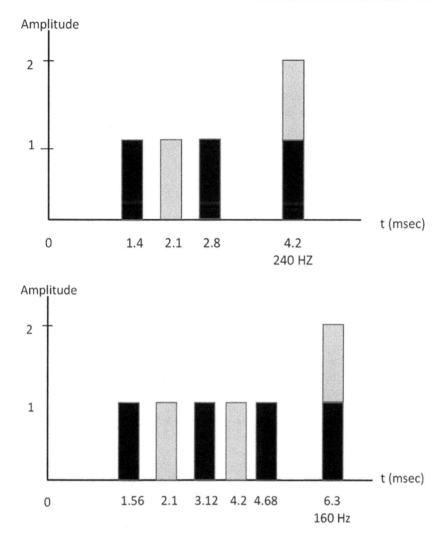

Figure 8.7 Top graph: neural periodicities of 480 Hz and 720 Hz (fifth) interval. Bottom graph: neural periodicities of 480 Hz and 640 Hz (fourth) interval.

6.3 msec (160 Hz), 12.6 msec (80 Hz), and so forth. The interspike intervals of the fourth take longer to repeat than the fifth, and humans subjectively perceive that to be less consonant. In musical terms when you have a simple numerical ratio of frequencies combining together, you will often perceive a frequency that is the difference between the two frequencies (in the preceding example 640 Hz – 480 Hz = 240 Hz)—even if the lower frequency (240 Hz) is not acoustically sounded! This is called the *missing fundamental*, a phenomenon particularly observed in the way frequencies are emitted by certain bells when struck. Now, we begin to see a neurological basis for it.

Finally, consider an interval that everyone perceives to be dissonant, the minor second, which has a frequency ratio of 16/15. We'll spare you the math, but imagine how long it takes before the first spike frequency repeats 16 times, while waiting for the second frequency to repeat 15 times in order to occur at the same time.[4] Much research has demonstrated that this periodicity is extremely important in consonance and dissonance perception (Stolzenburg 2015, 216).

In the preceding examples, we've mentioned such Western concepts as musical intervals of the fifth, the fourth and the second. We must remember, however, that we used these as convenient examples from a system with which most everyone is familiar. We could just as easily have used examples from other cultures (OK, it would have taken a bit more work). The biological phenomenon we are investigating is that there appears to be a continuum in all music and cultures from more consonant to more dissonant.

But periodicity is not the only factor the brain perceives relative to consonance and dissonance. Another factor that appears to contribute to the perception of dissonance is called "roughness." As early as 1862, Hermann Helmholtz first identified roughness as a function of the cochlea in his landmark book *On the Sensation of Tone* (Helmholtz 1877, 159–173). Roughness is caused by two frequencies that are very close together creating a variation of the loudness of the sound. If one note is tuned to 220 Hz and the other plays at 225 Hz, we will hear a rising and falling of the amplitude of the combined tone corresponding to the period of 5 Hz, or oscillating between loud and quiet every 200 msec (225 Hz – 220 Hz = 5 Hz, 1/5 Hz = 200 msec).

This is called a "beat" frequency. If the difference between the two frequencies is between 20 and 200 Hz, the resulting combination will sound "rough."[5] For small frequency differences, within the just noticeable difference threshold of about 1%, the pitch of the combined sound will now be perceived as a single frequency fluctuating in amplitude (getting louder and softer) (Tramo et al. 2003, 138).

Guitar players use beat frequencies to tune their guitars. As they bring the strings closer together in pitch, they can hear the pitch differences until at a certain point, they no longer hear pitch differences, just a single pitch varying in amplitude according to the beat frequency (i.e., the frequency difference that the two strings are out of tune). To tune the guitar, they simply try to slow the beat frequency until it stops altogether. At that point, the two strings are exactly in tune.

The periodicities of consonances and dissonances can also be detected in other parts of the neural pathway beyond the cochlea, however, in contrast to beat frequencies and roughness which appear to only be detected in the cochlea (Fritz et al. 2013, 3099–3104). Tramo and others wanted to see how these periodicities manifested themselves in other parts of the auditory system, so they measured over 100 auditory nerve fibers of our reasonably close mammalian cousins, cats.

Keep in mind that the human auditory nerve contains about 30,000 of these fibers, but Tramo's group measured just the auditory nerve fibers associated with the most consonant and dissonant intervals in cats (fifth, fourth, minor second and tritone). Their results indicate that if you integrate the measurements from the individual nerve fibers together, you will get the same periodicities as in the acoustic waveforms, including the subfrequencies generated (i.e., the missing fundamental). However, when Tramo's group measured dissonant intervals like the minor second and the tritone (diminished fifth) they found little or no correlation to the pitches in the acoustic intervals (Tramo et al. 2003, 136).

Fritz and others put two acoustic tones in separate ears so that the cochlea couldn't process the two frequencies simultaneously (Fritz et al. 2013). With the cochlea out of the way, they found that the inferior colliculi in the midbrain were also involved in the perception of consonance and dissonance (see Figures 7.10

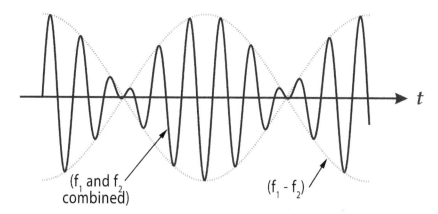

t

(f₁ and f₂ combined)

(f₁ - f₂)

Figure 8.8 A beat frequency. If two closely matched frequencies are combined with one another (f₁ and f₂ combined), as shown in the solid line, the overall amplitude envelope of the combined frequencies will follow the difference between the two frequencies (f₁ – f₂).

Credit: Hellwig, Ansgar. 2005. "Beating of Two Frequencies." Accessed June 20, 2017. https://commons.wikimedia.org/wiki/File:Beating_Frequency.svg. CC-BY-2.5. https://creativecommons.org/licenses/by/2.5/deed.en. Adapted by Richard K. Thomas.

and 7.11). Remember that the inferior colliculus is the area in the midbrain between the pons (lateral lemniscus) and the thalamus that integrates the two streams of auditory data from both ears.[6]

All of this research further supports the well-established conclusions that consonance and dissonance perception is biologically based, and probably not related to "musical training, long-term enculturation, (or) memory/cognitive capacity" (Fritz et al. 2013, 3100). Even in pitch and consonance perception, it's all about time. The consonance of two tones is the amount of periodicity (synchronization in time) that exists between tones, and according to Stolzenburg, it does not matter whether the tones occur simultaneously or sequentially.[7] Our brains determine consonance by determining periodic patterns of neuronal firings; the shorter the time between the repetitions of the periodic pattern, the more consonance we perceive (Stolzenburg 2015, 216–217).

There is one problem with many of these tests: they have been undertaken almost exclusively using dyads (two-note chords). Yet we also perceive triads and other sound structures as being more or less consonant. Stolzenburg proposed a mathematical solution that explained how the brainstem can still perceive periodic patterns even for three- and four-note chords, including for sequential notes in melody. Remember that the hair cells in the cochlea only have a finite amount of resolution, that is, they can only discriminate pitch to a certain degree, about 0.9%–1.2%. A typical person will not practically be able to tell the difference between a 991 Hz tone and a 1,000 Hz tone. Because the brain has this kind of "slop" in determining pitches, it is possible that the cochlea and brainstem work together to smooth our perception of intervals to the simplest numerical ratios possible within that ~1% range.[8] As it turns, out, when you have a little more room to work with like that, it's easier to find simple ratios (Stolzenburg 2015, 222).

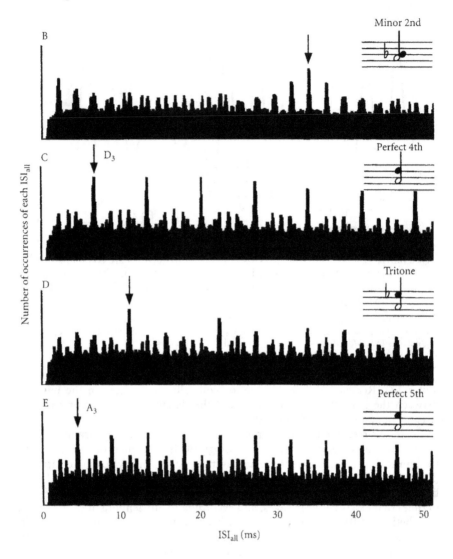

Figure 8.9 Tramo and others: nerve fiber measurements in cats. Notice how the more consonant the interval, the shorter the interspike intervals (ISI).

Credit: Tramo, M. J., P. A. Cariani, B. Delgutte and L. D. Braida. 2001. "Neurobiological Foundations for the Theory of Harmony in Western Tonal Music." *Annals of the New York Academy of Sciences* 930: 92–116. doi:10.1111/j.1749–6632.2001.tb05727.x.

Stolzenburg demonstrated that even when there are multiple pitches generated either simultaneously in chords or sequentially in melodies, there is still a relative periodicity that arises due to complex relationships between the tones that can be simplified not only on paper mathematically, but also by the human auditory system. How does this happen? Stolzenburg suggests that the brain does not need to perform the sort of complex mathematical manipulation he performs in his paper. Rather, our neural system may find the relatively simple numerical ratios

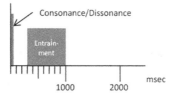

Figure 8.10 A comparison of consonant and dissonant entrainment.

available within the less than noticeable differences we humans can perceive. This occurs through synchronization with so-called oscillator neurons. Basically oscillator neurons are neurons in the brain that communicate with each other by firing at a set number of frequencies. According to Stolzenburg, "the external signal is synchronized with that of the oscillator neurons, which limits signal precision."

Does all this sound familiar? In case you haven't noticed, we seem to be describing consonance as a form of entrainment, very similar to entrainment in rhythm, but with much shorter time periods, and correspondingly much higher frequencies. Just such a model for neural entrainment has been proposed by Heffernan and Longtin. And while there are inherent problems in the model, "for simple integer ratios of stimulus frequencies . . . the oscillators entrain one another" (Heffernan and Longtin 2009, 104).

Such a conclusion argues once again for an understanding of music, and subsequently theatre (in as much as theatre can be shown to be a specific kind of music) as something much more than a cognitive process. Music and theatre involve a unique experience that functions at the subconscious level. Both harmonic periodicity and rhythmic entrainment are related to the temporal separation of neural spikes, and both seem to originate at very primitive levels of brain function.

Consonance and dissonance are such fundamentally perceived phenomena that we may consider them to be to line (melody) and texture (harmony) as pulse is to rhythm. They help to immerse us into the musical dreamlike world of theatre even without our consciously paying attention to them.

Cortical Consonance and Dissonance Perception

In the last section, we explored how much processing has been accomplished in the cochlea, the brainstem, and the midbrain even before the stimulus reaches the auditory cortex in our very human "new brain." This processing probably includes transducing the signal into discrete frequencies in the cochlea, and then determining the simplest numerical frequency ratios possible through entrainment of oscillatory neurons in the auditory nerve, including further processing in the inferior colliculus and other organs in the brainstem and the midbrain (Heffernan and Longtin 2009, 97). The connections that we have with our emotional reactions, however, require greater processing power at higher levels of the brain. At some point, our neocortex also gets involved, and it must communicate not only with the auditory pathway, but also with our more primitive limbic system, the parts of our brain responsible for emotions and memory (see Figure 5.9).

The auditory cortex first sorts out elements such as pitch and roughness within about 100 msec of the ear perceiving the sound (Koelsch and Siebel 2005,

578), with the right front of the auditory cortex activating for dissonance (Foo et al. 2016, 16). Experiments also show that people with lesions in the auditory cortex have difficulty perceiving consonance (Tramo et al. 2003, 144–146).

The extracted features next enter into the *echoic memory*, a short term holding space primarily in the auditory cortex that temporarily stores the sound (depending on who you talk to), in order for the dorsolateral prefrontal cortices to analyze it[9] (Sebri et al. 2004, 69; Alain, Woods and Knight 1998, 23). Echoic memory is the auditory form of sensory memory. Memory researcher Nelson Cowan defines sensory memory as "any memory that preserves the characteristics of a particular sensory modality: the way an item looks, sounds, feels, and so on" (Cowan 2015). As an example, the visual form of sensory memory, iconic memory is limited to about 200 msec.[10] We experience visual iconic memory when we watch children twirl sparklers; if they twirl them fast enough, we see the patterns sustain, as circles, loops and so forth. The auditory cortex holds information in its echoic memory for enough time so that it may confer with the rest of the brain and process the sound.

In a 1999 study, Blood and others demonstrated that different parts of the brain activate after the initial auditory processing depending on whether the stimulus is consonant or dissonant.

Dissonance activated the parahippocampal and medial part of the parietal cortex (both associated with memory). Consonance activated the orbitofrontal lobe (decision making), medial subcallosal cingulate (which plays a key role in processing emotions), and right frontal polar cortex (right behind our forehead, whose function is not well understood). The Blood group's research also supported the general thinking that the right hemisphere of the brain activated more for emotional processing of music, further demonstrating that the brain processes emotional responses to music separately from more perceptual process (In theatre, we often don't want the audience to be consciously aware of the sound score, we just

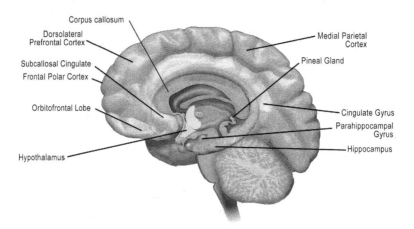

Figure 8.11 Section of the brain showing areas activated during consonance and dissonance perception.

Credit: "http://Blausen.com" Blausen.com staff. 2014. "Medical gallery of Blausen Medical 2014". *WikiJournal of Medicine* 1 (2). DOI:10.15347/wjm/2014.010. ISSN 2002–4436. CC-BY-3.0 (https://creativecommons.org/licenses/by/3.0/deed.en). Adapted by Richard K. Thomas.

want to use the score to incite an emotional reaction, so this is good news that perceptual emotional and perceptual responses can be separated.) (Blood et al. 1999).

A decade later in 2009, Dellacherie and many others were able to better identify the key cognitive processes in perceiving consonance and dissonance, and to document the order in which different parts of the brain processed both. Their work confirmed the early involvement of the auditory cortex we have already discussed, especially showing that dissonance is processed early in the right auditory cortex. About 500–1,000 msec later, the orbitofrontal cortex became activated as it analyzed the nature of the sounds. Finally, at a very late 1,200–1,400 msec, our old friend the amygdala activated, indicating a subconscious emotional reaction to the stimulus music. The researchers suspected that the late activation of the amygdala occurred because the test subjects' attention was consciously focused on a different task, and their perception of the emotional properties of the stimulus was subconscious (Dellacherie et al. 2009, 339).

Finally, a 2014 study by Omigie and others was able to look very closely at how signals flow between three areas: the auditory cortex, the orbitofrontal cortex and the amygdala. The subjects had been implanted with depth electrodes (planted deep within the brain) for presurgical evaluations for epilepsy. This provided an opportunity to study more precisely where and when interactions took place than normal electroencephalograph (EEG) measurements, which place electrodes on the scalp. The researchers confirmed the general results of Dellacherie and many others that came before, but this group was able to show that the amygdala actually modulates (or modifies) the processes of the orbitofrontal cortex and the auditory cortex, indicating that emotional responses and memory have a strong influence over our conscious perception of consonance and dissonance.

How the different parts of the brain, such as the auditory cortex, the amygdala, and the orbitofrontal lobes communicate with each other turns out to be quite important. Neural oscillations called brain waves fire between cortical areas to synchronize processes in different parts of the brain. Two particular frequency regions, the theta (4–8 Hz) and the alpha (8–13 Hz), were found to particularly activate in Omigie's tests. The theta band is noted for processing emotions. In their study, the auditory cortex activity peaked at 100 msec, and then the orbitofrontal and amygdala became increasingly activated between 200 and 600 msec, with the amygdala modulating (changing and influencing) both the orbitofrontal and the auditory cortices (Omigie et al. 2015, 4038–4039).

In plain and simple terms, Omigie and others found that it was our old friend the amygdala, the center of emotional reactions that was modulating the orbitofrontal lobe, the center of decision making, not the other way around: "the amygdala is a critical hub in the musical emotion processing network . . . one part of this role . . . might be to influence higher order areas which are involved in the evaluation of a stimulus' value" (2015, 4044). In theatre, we use consonance and dissonance as an emotional stimulant to modulate (change) what our audience is thinking about what they hear, because the researchers found that "the causal flow from the amygdala to the orbitofrontal cortex (was) greater than in the reverse direction." If the reverse direction were true, we would analyze the intervals, and use that information to tell us whether we felt happy, sad, aroused and so forth. In acting we call such a technique "indicating," when an actor indicates an emotion by first thinking about it, and then creating an action that points to the emotion, rather than truly feeling the emotion and inciting us to feel it, too. We almost always (never say never!) want to avoid indicating emotion with music. That's why I avoid describing music as a "communication." We work hard as composers and sound designers to incite emotion in our audience, not to tell them what emotions they should be feeling. Isn't it curious that our reaction to this can actually be measured in how the brain processes it?

Consonance and Dissonance in Theatre

Omigie and the work of others brings us to the fundamental relationship between consonance/dissonance and theatre. Let's start by breaking this relationship down into absurdly simple relationships: consonance = resolution; dissonance = conflict. Plays are about conflict, most typically a protagonist in conflict with an antagonist. The arc of a simple play is that the general situation at the beginning of the play is fairly resolved, and then something happens (the inciting incident) to create a conflict between the protagonist and the antagonist. The conflict builds throughout the play until the climax, where, one way or another, the conflict gets resolved. In its most simple form musically, plays go from consonance to dissonance to consonance again, taking the audience on an emotional journey to which we attach the fundamental ideas/story/meaning of the play. In real world plays that last for hours, such a simple scheme would be hard to sustain. So, in actuality, there is a lot of back and forth between consonance and dissonance in a play, and a lot of shades in the continua between them. As composers and sound designers, we don't necessarily track the conflicts tit for tat. We might have much more sophisticated and devious agendas for the emotional journey of our audience.

For example, in the opening scene of Arthur Kopit's *Indians* that I composed for Purdue University in 1992, we started out with a grand and very consonant circus theme that started impossibly slowly at a tempo of maybe 30 bpm, slowly revealing Buffalo Bill 70 feet away beyond the fire curtain and at the back of the paint shop in the old Loeb Theatre. Over the next minute and a half, we brought Buffalo Bill, tiny due to his distance from the audience, to life, slowly increasing the tempo as he moved from slow motion to live action toward downstage center, thus never giving up the triumphant consonance of the musical theme. By the time he got to the downstage of the theatre, at the final tempo of 130 bpm, he was much larger than life, much grander than humanly possible, and very, very subtly shallow and hollow, isolated in the spotlight with a creeping look of horror in his eyes. The music never made us feel that; quite the contrary, the music was boundlessly happy and triumphant. It was the contrast between the consonance of the music and director Jim O'Connor's brilliant visualization that created such a powerful feeling of uneasiness in the audience from the very opening of the show. And all with a very happy, consonant sound score. The sound score does not always need to fundamentally follow the emotional journey of the audience in order to fundamentally affect that journey. The great filmmaker Kurosawa suggested that techniques such as this actually increase the power of the medium:

> I changed my thinking about musical accompaniment from the time Hayaska Fumio began working with me as a composer of my film scores. Up until that time film music was nothing more than accompaniment—for a sad scene there was always sad music. This is the way most people use music, and it is ineffective. [Ebrahimian 87] . . .

Kurosawa ultimately came to the following perhaps not-so-surprising conclusion:

> Cinematic strength derives from the multiplier effect of sound and visual being brought together.
>
> (Kurosawa 1983, 107)

Line/Melody

As our discussion of the relationship between theatre and music develops, it is inevitable that our attention should turn to line. Stravinsky said, "I am beginning to think, in full agreement with the general public, that melody must keep its place at the summit of the hierarchy of elements that make up music . . . Melody is the most essential of these elements. . . . What survives every change of system is melody" (Stravinsky 1947, 41–43). The musical line is contained in melody by definition: Webster's states that line is "a succession of musical notes esp. considered in melodic phrases" (1963, 491). We are fortunate, as in the case of rhythm and color, to be sharing, from the beginning, a coincidental vocabulary with the visual artists.

Unfortunately, defining melody as "any succession of single tones" (Goetschius 1970, 64) is simply not adequate if we are to include the "mystique" of melody. Since the musical world is so sharply divided between whether a melody is achieved by intuition or by logical manipulation, a more concise definition is impossible. A better definition, first postulated by F. Busoni may, however, include a "list of ingredients":

> A row of repeated ascending and descending intervals which, organized and moving rhythmically, contains in itself a latent harmony and gives back a certain atmosphere of feeling; which can and does exist independent of text for expression and independent of accompanying voices for form, and in the performance of which the choice of pitch and of instruments exercises no change over its essence.
>
> (Holst 1966, 13)

The smallest element of the melodic line is the single tone. I have discussed these single tones individually in the section on color. It is important to make the distinction that melody is only concerned with the relative pitch of the perceived color, and exists completely independently from the timbre of the tone-producing device.

Western intervals divide the octave into a series of well-defined steps that proceed in neurologically well-defined ways. It fairly meticulously follows the brain's perception in terms of increasing complexity of ratios from consonance to dissonance: Perfect consonances include the unison (1:1), then the octave (2:1), then the fifth (3:2) and finally the fourth (4:3). Imperfect consonances come next, starting with the third (5:4), then the sixth (5:3), then the minor third (6:5), and finally the minor sixth (8:5). These progress to increasing dissonances: the second (9:8), the seventh (15:8), the minor second (16:15), the minor seventh (15:8) and finally, the tritone (45:32) (LoPrestor 2009, 146). It is interesting to note, however, that of the 1,500 possible pitches that can be distinguished by the average human at medium intensities, Western music uses only about 100 (Lundin 1967, 68). Seashore believed that the reason for this was that "our present half-tone step is as small a step as the average of an unselected population can hear with reasonable assurance, enjoy, and reproduce in the flow of melody and harmony in music." (Seashore 1967, 128).

It is equally important for us to not consider melody simply in terms of Western intervals. In some cultures, you can have 70 or more points marked off within an octave. In all cultures you still have the same basic relationship, moving on a scale from consonant to dissonant, from calm to arousing. The general physiological sensations produced in the brain work on all sound, not just traditional Western music intervals. The more that frequencies combine in simple numeric ratios, the greater the perceived emotional stability. Tension is introduced as fundamental frequencies combine that are close to each other, or generate harmonics that are close to one another, and loud enough to factor into the perceived timbre. A fricative consonant is more dissonant than the simpler harmonic structure of the vowel "ooh."

Modern composition and sound design provides us with endless opportunities to explore consonance and dissonance, either in the well-established culturally acquired forms of Western music, in the scales of other cultures, or more primitively, in simply exploring the range of pitch and harmonic relationships that we discover on the continuum between consonance and dissonance. We don't normally associate consonance and dissonance with naturally occurring sounds or human speech, but we should, because it's important in understanding how we combine music and speech in theatre. The screech of a crow is naturally more dissonant than the purer tones of a robin or a sparrow.

We must also consider prosody as a type of consonance and dissonance. A mother attempting to soothe her child will use more consonant tones with a simpler harmonic structure than the dissonant tonal structure of a person shrieking in anger at the checkout counter. We generally determine the gender and size of a person subjectively through our perception of the fundamental frequency of their voice. We determine vowels by the relative strengths of the first and second harmonics of vocalizations (Giraud and Poeppel 2012, 228–229). And of course, we humans can create all sort of inharmonic frequencies with our voices when we get agitated. Consonance and dissonance apply as much to the prosody of an actor's voice as they do to the music that orchestrates their speech melody.

Beyond the inherent consonance and dissonance of complex sounds, it is only when we associate these single tones together that line is formed, just as visual lines cannot be formed by a single point. In theatre, we have melodies and we have tunes. I learned this from Imogen Holst, who wrote a whole book about the latter, called *Tune*. Melodies don't exist well without their orchestrations; they fulfill and reveal themselves in their accompaniment. So we should talk about those more in the next section when we discuss harmony. Tunes, on the other hand, are self-contained; and after hearing one a few times, we can hum and sing a tune on its own without any accompaniment, and it still captures us. We refer to the part of the tune that deliciously sticks in our memory as a "hook." In popular music it's most often the chorus or a part of a chorus. Since hooks have a lot to do with memory, we'll talk much more about them in Chapter 10 when we talk about memory. For the time being, let me just attempt to put this little hook into your memory: tunes have been very important to me in composing for theatre, because of how easy it is to attach important ideas and meanings of the play to them that the audience can then carry out of the theatre.

Harmony

For me, creating melodies and then orchestrating them to score scenes is much more of a craft than finding a tune that metaphysically transcends "any succession of single tones." I learned this from Jack Smalley, or more properly from his book *Composing Music for Film* (Smalley 2005). Jack Smalley is a prolific composer of music for film and television. Unlike this author, Smalley is a man of few words, but he chooses them carefully and makes every one count. He wrote a short, amazingly concise book that provides a wealth of precise techniques for composing and orchestrating music for film. You have to order the book directly from Mr. Smalley, but it's well worth it, and I highly recommend it. The most important thing he taught me was how to craft a score, and not to worry about inspiration. Smalley starts from the development of a theme—not a tune, but the smallest group of notes you can form into an identifiable, useable shape, typically one, two or three measures long. One then develops this theme systematically into a complete movie score. As I've mentioned before, the opportunities to create and use a memorable tune in theatre are somewhat rare. The opportunities for crafting a cohesive sound score in theatre are almost endless.

Line (melody) usually plays a somewhat diminished role in theatre scoring due to the simple fact that the actors, playwright and director have already crafted the lead melodies using the prosody of dialogue. Our job as composers and sound designers then becomes to orchestrate those melodies, and there's plenty we can do with consonance and dissonance to incite emotions in our audience beyond melody, and—significantly differing from film—in our actors. In film the score happens after the actors have "left the building," so to speak. In theatre, the actors also experience the underscores we create, a point that theatre composers must never forget. It is a much more intimate experience composing music for live theatre, because we share the character with the actor in a much more concrete way. Get the scoring right and the actor will adore you. Mess it up and the actor may try to get you fired.

We don't necessarily need musical instruments to score the actor's prosody either. The room tone, or a silent recording of the ambience in a room (which is not really silent at all!), can be manipulated for consonance and dissonance over long periods of time. I used such a technique with the (synthesized) wind in the cave for Joel Fink's production of Edgar Allen Poe's *Cask of Amontillado* in Chicago; manipulating it from a relative consonance when Montressor and Fortunato first entered to a stronger dissonance as the scene turned ugly and Montressor walled up Fortunato in the niche of the wine cellar. I almost never let my ambiences just sit in a scene; I actually learned that trick from my old partner Brad Garton, who taught me that, in music synthesis, never let sustained tones sit unchanged. Always put some sort of subtle movement into them, otherwise, their constancy will draw attention to itself. And as long as we are putting some subtle movement in our sustained tones, why not take the opportunity to very, very subtly manipulate the emotional mood in the scene?

The most common compositional technique using traditional music instruments is the *pad*. We first met pads back in Chapter 2, which should be just as good an indication as any that they reach the most primitive parts of our brains. A pad is simply a sustained tone, chord, or complex texture that can be sustained for as long as one desires in a scene. Pads are insanely popular, and quite frankly, hopelessly overused, because they work so well. If you want to create tension in a horror scene what do you do? You take two violins and you put them a minor second apart, right? And then you just sustain that dissonance to habituate the audience in an endlessly tense suspension until whatever startle effect you need. Everybody knows it and everybody's done it, and the thing is, it works, without us thinking about it. I distinctly remember using it in a world premiere of Ross Maxwell's play *His Occupation*, and then mischievously watching the audience physically jump each night at the startle moment. We don't have to intellectually think, "oh my, here comes the monster jumping out of the closet!" You don't have to know anything about music in order for it to work. It is quite easy to manipulate emotions using pads; one simply has to migrate the tonal clusters from increasing consonance to increasing dissonance based on the simple numerical ratios discussed earlier. Along the way, a wide range of emotions can be achieved and important ideas attached without ever pulling focus from the lead melodies of the actors. More sophisticated composers, however, will put great effort into their pads, burying extremely subtle but powerful rhythms and textures within them that nevertheless appear at first listen unchanging and habituating.

It might not be going too far to suggest that most underscoring either starts with a pad, emphasizing consonance and dissonance, a pulse, emphasizing rhythm, or both. If one can capture the emotion in a scene with one or both of those simple tools, then the challenge is to simply not draw attention with all of the harmonic decorations one puts on top to develop emotional nuance (unless that's what needs to be done, of course). And, of course, to avoid the banal contrivances that also draw attention to themselves for their hokiness.

As we discussed in the chapter on pulse, consonance and dissonance can also be used to effect transitions between scenes; it can resolve a scene tending toward consonance, or leave it left unresolved tending toward dissonance. In the exposition of a play, everything on the surface may seem to be right between the main characters, but the underscoring tells us that there is a lot more going on just below the surface. Shakespeare provided just such an opportunity in the opening line of *Twelfth Night*: "If music be the food of love, play on," which is followed in a very few lines with the indication, "Enough; no more: 'Tis not so sweet now as it was before." In the horror scene example above, the monster gets killed in the end, and we expect the scene to resolve musically, but it doesn't. We immediately know there will be a sequel.

Conclusion: Consonance and Dissonance and Time

In this chapter, we traced the evolution of our human species to the discovery of the first undisputed musical instruments, which somewhat coincided with the discovery of visual art, and an emerging cognition of a world beyond the simple day to day living of our *Homo sapiens* ancestors, which perhaps raised the question, "Where does life come from, and where does it go when it ends here?" This led to an increased use of ritual to explore such questions, and we argue that ritual proceeds from a musical base that helps transport us into that other world. With music as a fully evolved human activity that now included the ability to create discrete pitches on primitive instruments such as bone flutes, we examined how the brain evolved to sort those pitches on a scale from consonant and calm to dissonant and aroused. We then examined how we can use those qualities to create sound scores for theatre.

Subtly throughout this chapter, however, we have returned to our discussion about how we perceive time, and how we use time to modulate the emotional states of our audience. Consonance and dissonance represent some of the shortest time spans we humans perceive in sonic stimuli. The time intervals we create in consonance are much shorter than they are in pulse and entrainment, which is the next major temporal region we use to manipulate the sense of time and emotional states of our audience.

We hold both of these in our echoic, sensory memory, a significant evolutionary development that allows us humans to consciously examine the immediate past when need be, perhaps referring to the amygdala to discover if there is anything in our emotional memory that triggers a strong emotional reaction to the auditory stimulus.

In the next chapter, we will turn our attention to the matter of attention itself—what grabs and holds our attention; how we arouse our audience, how we manipulate their conscious perception, and the rewards we provide them for going along on the journey. We will explore one of the first manifestations of music being put to an activity that bears a strong resemblance to theatre, ritual, and how we use music in ritual to grab hold of the conscious experience of an audience and transport them into the dreamlike worlds of our dramatic imagination.

Ten Questions

1. Name three human activities that developed 50,000 to 100,000 years ago that signaled a dawning consciousness in humans that would forever separate them from their ape ancestors.
2. What are Donald's three major cognitive breakthroughs, and why is the third one so important—so critically important—in advancing human cognition?
3. Provide four reasons why researchers think that flutes weren't invented in German caves, but were brought by those who settled in the area that contribute to a general conclusion that language, music, ritual and visual art all developed alongside each other.
4. Why do researchers think that musical instruments and visual art appear so often in prehistoric caves?
5. Why does the brain perceive the fifth to be consonant and the minor second to be dissonant?
6. What is roughness, where does it occur, and what is the sensation with which it is associated?
7. What does relative periodicity have to do with entrainment?
8. Describe three main areas of the brain that process consonance and dissonance for emotion, and describe the order in which they process sound stimuli.
9. How do consonance and dissonance specifically relate to the typical plot structure of a play?
10. Why is it so important to learn the craft of composition in theatre?

Interval	Example	Liked	Did Not Like
	1		
	2		
	3		
	4		
	5		
	6		
	7		
	8		
	9		
	10		
	11		
	12		

Trained Musician?

Figure 8.12 Student preferences for standard intervals.

Rank Order	More Consonant	Class Average
	Octave	
	Fifth	
	Fourth	
	Major Sixth	
	Major Third	
	Minor Third	
	Minor Sixth	
	Tritone	
	Major Second	
	Major Seventh	
	Minor Seventh	
	Minor Second	
	More Dissonant	

Figure 8.13 Cumulative student average perception of consonance and dissonance.

Things to Share

1. An in-class experiment: the instructor draws the names of each of the 12 intervals of the chromatic scale out of a hat, and plays each interval in succession, always using Middle C as the lowest tone. After the instructor plays each interval, students enter whether they liked the sound or didn't like the sound in the following spreadsheet.

    Student responses are tabulated (averaged) during a break, and then compared against the simple numeric ratios to find out how well the class correlated consonance and dissonance on a continuum with the expected results.

    See (LoPrestor 2009) for more information on this experiment.

2. Find a movie that has won an Academy Award for sound editing, or music composition. Pick a movie that you love and wouldn't mind seeing again. Now get hold of the movie (perhaps buy it, because you can use it for other projects in this class, rent it from Netflix, or even check it out from your local library). Watch it with an ear toward a composer consciously using consonance and dissonance, and especially examples in which they transition from one into another. Make a note of the time in the movie where the consonance and dissonance transition occurs so we can cue it up in class and you can share it with us. Pay careful attention to how the sound artists manipulate changes in the consonance and dissonance of the sound score to manipulate the sense of calm and arousal in the listener. Be prepared to describe for us how you think the sound team is manipulating us. Bring at least two examples with you in case someone uses your first example.

3. Having explored the wonderful world of rhythm (rhythm, beat, pulse, tempo, meter, phrasing, duration), now it's time for you to explore these concepts in composition. Compose or design a 1:00–1:30 piece that explores rhythm in all its glory: expressive or abrupt tempo changes, rhythmic nuance, multiple and perhaps even compound meters, a variety of approaches to phrasing your rhythms and many layers of durations—pads, whole, half, quarter, eighth and sixteenth notes, and so forth. If you don't consider yourself a composer, consider using samples and exploring a drum machine app of some sort. Stick to a relatively small color palette, so that your rhythm will predominate. As always, play and experiment, but still work to create a cohesive composition.

Notes

1   Technically, the "ice age" is a glacial period called the Würm that occurred between 115,000 and 11,700 years ago. It is part of a much larger ice age that dates back 2,588,000 years. See Clayton et al. (2006).

2   Note that earlier specimens have been discovered, one from the femur of a cave bear found in a cave in western Slovenia dated between 82,000 and 67,000 years ago. However, archaeologists dispute the authenticity of these earlier flutes (d'Errico et al. 1998).

3   For those of you with calculators blazing, thinking, "Hey, the numbers don't add up!" Relax. We've rounded, of course, but much more importantly, remember that the basilar membrane only discriminates frequencies that are greater than

0.9%–1.2% apart. Can you tell the difference between a 1,000 Hz tone and a 1,001 Hz tone? Probably not, at least most people can't. Human hearing is highly subjective, and it's always a good idea to know what our tolerances are before getting too wrapped up in endless digits beyond the decimal points.

4 31.2 msec (32 Hz) for a 480 Hz tone and the second above, 512 Hz, if you must know! And since you're reading this, also note that the next interspike interval would happen at 62.4 msec (16 Hz), below the threshold of human frequency perception, which might also help to explain why consonance is not perceived.

5 Assuming the difference frequencies do not share a simple numerical ratio with the stimulus frequencies. For example, a 100 Hz tone and a 150 Hz tone would not sound rough because the difference frequency, 50 Hz, suggests a simple 3:2 relationship between the 150 and 100 Hz tones.

6 The left pulvinar in the thalamus may also be responsible for helping an individual focus attention on the dissonances presented to the inferior colliculus.

7 Roughness, according to Tramo, can only occur in the vertical, or simultaneous dimension (Tramo et al. 2003, 143–144).

8 Note that Stolzenburg cites a different study which suggests that the "just noticeable difference" increases to about 3.6% at 100 Hz, and decreases to .7% at higher frequencies (Stolzenburg 2015, 222).

9 Echoic memory may store sound for as little as a few hundred milliseconds to three to four seconds, to as much as 30 seconds, also depending on who you talk to! See Cowan (1997, 27).

10 Cowan suggested that there was no difference between auditory and visual sensory memory: "The conclusion was that the persistence of sensory storage does not appear to differ among modalities" (1997, 27). More about this in Chapter 10 when we explore memory.

Bibliography

Alain, Claude, David L. Woods, and Robert T. Knight. 1998. "A Distributed Cortical Network for Auditory Sensory Memory in Humans." *Brain Research* 812 (1): 23–27.

Benazzi, Stefano, Katerina Douka, Cinzia Fornai, Catherine Bauer, Ottmar Kullmer, Jirí Svoboda, Ildikó Pap, et al. 2011. "Early Dispersal of Modern Humans in Europe and Implications for Neanderthal Behaviour." *Nature* 479 (7374): 525–529.

Blood, Anne J., Robert J. Zattorre, Patrick Bermudez, and Alan C. Evans. 1999. "Emotional Responses to Pleasant and Unpleasant Music Correlate With Activity in Paralimbic Brain Regions." *Nature Neuroscience* 2 (4): 382–387.

Brahic, Catherine. 2014. "Shell 'Art' Made 300,000 Years Before Humans Evolved." *New Scientist*, December 2014.

Carroll, Sean. 2011. "Ten Things Everyone Should Know About Time." September 1. Accessed February 15, 2016. http://blogs.discovermagazine.com/cosmicvariance/2011/09/01/ten-things-everyone-should-know-about-time/#.VsI99cdTLct.

Clayton, Lee, John W. Attig, David M. Mickelson, Mark D. Johnson, and Kent M. Syverson. 2006. "Glaciation of Wisconsin." *UW Extension*. Accessed 07 26, 2017. http://www.geology.wisc.edu/~davem/abstracts/06-1.pdf.

Conard, Nicholas J., Maria Malina, and Susanne C. Münzel. 2009. "New Flutes Document the Earliest Musical Tradition in Southwestern Germany." *Nature* 460 (7256): 737–740.

Cowan, Nelson. 2015. "Things We See, Hear, Feel or Somehow Sense." In *Mechanisms of Sensory Working Memory*, edited by Pierre Jolicoeur, Christine Lefebvre, and Julio Martinez-Trujillo, 5–22. New York: Academic Press/Elsevier.

D'Errico, Francesco, Christopher Henshilwood, Graeme Lawson, Marian Vanhaeren, Anne-Marie Tillier, Marie Soressi, Frédérique Bresson, et al. 2003. "Archaeological Evidence for the Emergence of Language, Symbolism, and Music—An Alternative Multidisciplinary Perspective." *Journal of World Prehistory* 17 (1): 1–70.

D'Errico, Francesco, Paola Villa, Ana C. Pinto Llona, and Rosa Ruiz Idarraga. 1998. "A Middle Palaeolithic Origin of Music? Using Cave-Bear Bone Accumulations to Assess the Divje Babe I Bone 'Flute'." *Antiquity* 72 (275): 65–79.

Dellacherie, Delphine, Micha Pfeuty, Dominique Hasboun, Julien Lefèvre, Laurent Hugueville, Denis P. Schwartz, Michel Baulac, Claude Adam, and Séverine Samson. 2009. "The Birth of Musical Emotion: A Depth Electrode Case Study in a Human Subject with Epilepsy." *Annals of the New York Acadmy of Sciences* 1169: 336–341.

Donald, Merlin. 1993a. "Human Cognitive Evolution." *Social Research* 60 (1): 143–170.

———. 1993b. "Précis of Origins of the Modern Mind." *Behavioral and Brain Sciences* 16 (4): 737–791.

Foo, Francine, David King-Stephens, Peter Weber, Kenneth Laxer, Josef Parvizi, and Robert T. Knight. 2016. "Differential Processing of Consonance and Dissonance Within the Human Superior Temporal Gyrus." *Frontiers in Human Neuroscience* 10: 1–12.

Fritz, Thomas, Sebastian Jentschke, Nathalie Gosselin, Daniela Sammler, Isabelle Peretz, Robert Turner, Angela D. Friederici, and Stefan Koelsch. 2009. "Universal Recognition of Three Basic Emotions in Music." *Current Biology* 19 (7): 573–576.

Fritz, Thomas Hans, Wiske Renders, Karsten Müller, Paul Schmude, Marc Leman, Robert Turner, and Amo Villringer. 2013. "Anatomical Differences in the Human Inferior Colliculus Relate to the Perceived Valence of Musical Consonance and Dissonance." *European Journal of Neuroscience* 38 (1): 3099–3105.

Giraud, Anne-Lise, and David Poeppel. 2012. "Speech Perception From a Neurophysiological Perspective." In *The Human Auditory Cortex*, edited by David Poeppel, Tobias Overath, Arthur N. Popper, and Richard R. Fay, 225–260. New York: Springer.

Goetschius, Percy. 1970. *The Structure of Music*. Westport, CT: Greenwood Press.

Heffernan, B., and A. Longtin. 2009. "Pulse-Coupled Neuron Models as Investigative Tools for Musical Consonance." *Journal of Neuroscience Methods* 183 (1): 95–106.

Helmholtz, Hermann L. F. 1877. *On the Sensations of Tone as a Physiological Basis for the Theory of Music*. 4th Edition. London: Longmans, Green.

Henshilwood, Christopher S., Francesco d'Errico, and Ian Watts. 2009. "Engraved Ochres From the Middle Stone Age Levels at Blombos Cave, South Africa." *Journal of Human Evolution* 57 (1): 27–47.

Henshilwood, Christopher S., Francesco d'Errico, Karen L. van Niekerk, Yvan Coquinot, Zenobia Jacobs, Stein-Erik Lauritzen, Michel Menu, and Renata García-Moreno. 2016. "A 100,000-Year-Old Ochre-Processing Workshop at Blombos Cave, South Africa." *Science* 334 (6053): 219–222.

Higham, Thomas, Laura Basell, Roger Jacobi, Rachel Wood, Christopher Bronk Ramsey, and Nicholas J. Conard. 2012. "Testing Models for the Beginnings of the Aurignacian and the Advent of Figurative Art and Music: The Radiocarbon Chronology of Geißenklösterle." *Journal of Human Evolution* 62 (6): 664–676.

Higham, Tom, Tim Compton, Chris Stringer, Roger Jacobi, Beth Shapiro, Erik Trinkaus, Barry Chandler, et al. 2011. "The Earliest Evidence for Anatomically Modern Humans in Northwestern Europe." *Nature* 479 (7374): 521–524.

Holst, Imogen. 1966. *Tune.* New York: October House.

Koelsch, Stefan, and Walter A. Siebel. 2005. "Towards a Neural Basis of Music Perception." *Trends in Cognitive Sciences* 9 (12): 578–584.

Kurosawa, Akira. 1983. *Something Like an Autobiography.* New York: Vintage Books Edition.

LoPrestor, Michael C. 2009. "Experimenting With Consonance and Dissonance." *Physics Education* 44 (2): 145–150.

Lundin, Robert W. 1967. *An Objective Psychology of Music.* Westport, CT: Ronald Press.

Morley, Ian. 2009. "Ritual and Music: Parallels and Practice, and the Palaeolithic." In *Becoming Human: Innovation in Prehistoric Material and Spirtual Cultures,* edited by Colin Renfrew and Ian Morley, 159–175. Cambridge: Cambridge University Press.

National Geographic. 2016. "The Human Journey: Migration Routes." Accessed May 2, 2016. https://genographic.nationalgeographic.com/human-journey/.

Omigie, Diana, Delphine Dellacherie, Dominique Hasboun, Nathalie George, Sylvain Clement, Michel Baulac, Claude Adam, and Severine Samson. 2015. "An Intracranial EEG Study of the Neural Dynamics of Musical Valence Processing." *Cerebral Cortex* 25 (11): 4038–4047.

Roederer, Juan G. 2008. *The Physics and Psychophysics of Music.* 4th Edition. New York: Springer Science+Business Media, LLC.

Seashore, Carl. 1967. *The Psychology of Music.* Mineola, NY: Dover.

Sebri, Merav, David A. Kareken, Mario Dzemidzic, Mark J. Lowe, and Robert D. Melara. 2004. "Neural Correlates of Auditory Sensory Memory and Automatic Change Detection." *NeuroImage* 21 (1): 69–74.

Smalley, Jack. 2005. *Composing Music for Film.* 3rd Edition. JackSmalley.com: JPS.

Stolzenburg, Frieder. 2015. "Harmony Perception by Periodicity Detection." *Journal of Mathematics and Music* 9 (3): 215–238.

Stravinsky, Igor. 1947. *Poetics of Music.* Translated by Arthur Knodel and Ingolf Dahl. New York: Vintage Books.

Tramo, Mark Jude, Peter A. Cariani, Bertrund Delgutte, and Louis D. Braida. 2003. "Neurobiology of Harmony Perception." In *The Cognitive Neuroscience of Music,* edited by Isabelle Peretz and Robert J. Zatorre, 128–151. Oxford: Oxford University Press.

Webster's Seventh New Collegiate Dictionary. 1963. Springfield, MA: G&C Merriam.

PART IV

THEATRE = SONG + MIMESIS

CHAPTER 9

RITUAL, AROUSAL, REWARD, ECSTASY

Introduction: From High Mass to Ecstasy

I grew up in a little town outside of Detroit, Michigan, called Chesterfield Township. When I was six years old, St. Louis parish opened its new church in neighboring Mount Clemens, and I followed my brothers to the parochial grade school there having no idea what to expect as I entered first grade. Perhaps anxious to make the most out of its beautiful new church, our school year started out with a High Mass in Latin. If it was their intention to clearly impress upon me that I was an insignificant pea in the face of the Almighty, they succeeded. Really succeeded. I can still remember my overwhelmed reaction to what seemed like the enormous sanctuary and nave, dimly lit, smoky and full of the sweet smell of incense. There were priests in colorful garments and students all organized in the pews according to grade. As peons go, I was first class. But most of all I remember the music. Over a thousand students sang the Catholic liturgy in Latin, with the most experienced up in the organ loft singing harmonies into the massively reverberant hall. High Mass was still in Latin in 1959, so I had no idea what they were all singing about. But I can still conjure up my overwhelming feelings of awe, reverence and wonder, the music carrying my soul to the heavens. I was pretty sure that I had come to God's house and God was right there watching me, and, hopefully, protecting me. The High Mass embodied ritual at its finest.

Sir James Frazer may have been the first person to suggest in his 1890 book, *The Golden Bough*, that the origins of theatre lay in the religious rituals of primitive humans (Frazer 1922). In the years that followed, that concept became widely accepted. The famous School of Cambridge, led by Jane Harrison, embraced the idea, and Harrison herself proposed a critical clarification of the theory, that theatre evolved out of primitive ritual *dance* (1951, 42). Remember that dance and music were inseparable in primitive cultures, and our definition considers dance to be a visual form of music. Looking back at one of the earliest experiences in my life, it is not hard for me to understand the extraordinary influence that that music, manifested in ritual, could have on a person's connection to the unknown.

But how did we humans get from the fairly simply organized rituals of our ape ancestors to the elaborate myths, stories and dramatic enactments of our human ancestors? Enactments that most agree led to the first fully autonomous Western theatre in ancient Greece? Prominent theatre theorist Richard Schechner traces modern theatre to ritual and *shamanism*:

> I think we will find that the new theater is very old, and that
> our localized urban avant-garde belongs next to worldwide,

rural-tribal tradition. . . . Among primitive peoples the creative
condition is identical with trances, dances, ecstasies; in short,
shamanism.

He continues, quoting Andreas Lommel: "Shamanism is 'a method, a psychic
technique' of which the 'fundamental characteristic . . . is ecstasy, interpreted
as the soul forsaking the body' " (1988, 40–41). I wouldn't quite describe my
Catholic Church experience as ecstasy, but I can certainly sense its origins in such
a practice. I can also recall numerous music and theatre experiences I've had that
I would describe as having delivered me into ecstasy.

In this chapter, we will pick up our story where we left off in Chapter 8, about
30,000 years ago. The period is called the "Upper Paleolithic Period," or the later
stages of the stone age, a time when we still made our tools from stone. This is
a period of tremendous explosion in human advancement, most notable for the
clear, unique, and unambiguous development of *human* consciousness. In the earlier chapters of this book, we described the energy and temporal characteristics
of sound. We considered startle and habituation in terms of mass/dynamics, and
entrainment in terms of rhythm. We saw how animal brains evolved to process
sounds and use them to communicate or express emotions. In the last couple of
chapters, we witnessed the earliest primates who *consciously* manipulated acoustic energy in time, starting with primitive drumming. Later humans expanded
their musical abilities, exploring consonance and dissonance through melodic
lines made possible by the *invention* of primitive bone flutes. As we continue our
journey, we'll see how humans started using these elements to create primitive
music that manipulated the conscious states of others. We create proto-theatre
activities in ritual by adding mimesis to this music, leading to our very simple
formula, theatre = song + mimesis. To understand how ritual works, we will look
deep inside human physiological and psychological systems. We'll discover how
music affects our mood, grabs our attention, and rewards us—especially in the
context of ritual and theatre. We'll conclude the chapter by exploring some of the
ways that I have come to understand these things, and have worked to incorporate them into my own personal aesthetic.

The Development of Ritual, Shamanism, and Altered States of Consciousness

Thirty thousand years ago, our *Homo sapiens sapiens* ancestors were expanding
their musical chops and developing much more sophisticated social systems. These
social systems inevitably led to sophisticated belief systems, including their expression through ritual. Matt Rossano, an evolutionary psychologist from Southeast-
ern Louisiana University, proposed four stages in the development of primitive
animal ritual into humanity's first fully formed religions. He argues that these
four stages provide evidence of ever-expanding human cognitive abilities (Rossano 2007). The first stage includes the animal rituals we explored in Chapter 5:
those of elk, deer, moose, gelados, baboons, chimpanzees and bonobos. Rossano
follows Merlin Donald, identifying the second stage as the emergence of mimetic
capabilities in *Homo erectus*. He suggests that *Homo erectus* "took control of
their rituals, and increasingly directed them toward the deliberate manipulation
of conscious experience" (2007, 95–96). In Rossano's third stage that flourished
during the Upper Paleolithic, humanity's first religion emerged: *shamanism*. We'll

investigate shamanism in this chapter. In the fourth stage, which we'll save for the next chapter, shamanism develops a much more sophisticated capacity for human narrative due to advances in memory: our ability to store and recall information. Human ability to pass narratives from generation to generation allowed the creation and preservation of religious myths and associated stories.

Keep in mind that there is, as always, controversy surrounding the evidence available in *pre*historic times. Prehistory, by its very nature, does not provide us with much direct evidence, because it is after all, *pre*history. Evolutionary biology, anthropology and archaeology tend to supply us with what limited evidence there is. The rest must be inferred and induced by studying similarities in our living *Homo sapiens* populations who appear to have changed the least. We are sometimes left to compare existing primitive tribes that have not undergone the same technological advancement as most of human civilization, comparing their traits and behaviors to the imagined ones of our ancestors. But remember, that we can now also analyze our own neurological systems because they are fundamentally the same as our *Homo sapiens sapiens* ancestors. Still, the lack of physical evidence is highly likely to make any conclusions we draw controversial and legitimately suspect. I wouldn't do it, however, if I hadn't found deep resonance in my own art and in decades of teaching and learning. Keep those caveats in mind as we move forward.

In the Upper Paleolithic, we find an abundance of evidence of expanding human cognitive abilities in cave art that suddenly appeared all over the inhabited world from Asia to Africa to Europe.

Anthropologist Michael Winkelman also finds clear evidence in the cave art for the emergence of shamanism in the Upper Paleolithic. He, like Rossano, traces its origins back to the rituals of our hominid ancestors. Winkleman particularly

Figure 9.1 Replica of an Upper Paleolithic cave drawing depicts a possible shaman in the cave art at Lascaux, France.

Credit: Arterra Picture Library/Alamy Stock Photo.

notes the fundamental role of "chanting, music, and group ritual activities based in mimetic capabilities" (Winkelman 2002, 78). Winkelman provides important support for the powerful combination of song and mimesis in proto-theatre activities.

While the term "shaman" derives from an ancient Siberian term and practice, there are elements of the practice that are common to many primitive cultures, indicating ancient origins. Rossano cites a commonly used definition that describes shamanism in terms of practices appearing across many cultures: a religion indicating "the attainment of altered states of consciousness for the purpose of interacting with the spirit world for the benefit of one's community. . . . in its incipient form, the adaptive benefit of shamanism would have been healing" (2007, 102). Winkelman proposes that similarities in shamanic practice across the globe "are a consequence of independent inventions, or derivations, from a common neuropsychology." Similarities include "visionary experience, soul journey, guardian spirit quest, healing practices, and self-transformation experiences such as death and rebirth" (Winkelman 2002, 72). Theatre theorist E. T. Kirby distinguished shamanistic ritual from other rituals such as "rites of passage" because shamanism depended on "the immediate and direct manifestation to the audience of supernatural presence, rather than its symbolization" (1975, 2). Shamanism meant *becoming* the supernatural presence, not simply imitating it. In other words, mimesis.

According to Winkelman, "The shamanistic ritual was typically an all-night ceremony attended by the entire community" (2002, 72). But there were also private and individual rituals that appeared to take place deep in the recesses of caves.

Many cave paintings have been found as far as a half-mile deep inside the caves. Now, if I were living in a cave, I wouldn't take up residence a half-mile deep in a cave! I'd stick close to the entrance where I could guard it, and get out quick if necessary. So, it seems quite likely to me and many others that these paintings deep within the caves indicate another type of ritual, more individual in nature.

Figure 9.2 Location of cave of Altamira.

Credit: Best-Backgrounds/Shutterstock.com. Adapted by Richard K. Thomas.

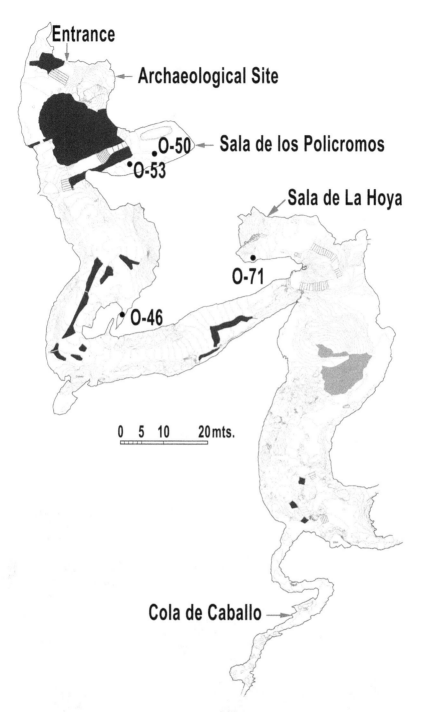

Figure 9.3 Altamira plan of cave, dates from 35,000 to 15,200 years ago. Note that the cave is over one-half mile long, and "figures are distributed throughout the cave, whilst being concentrated in . . . the Cola de Caballo or 'Horse's Tail', the final passage" (García-Diez et al., 4100).

Figure 9.4 Location of Cueva de las Manos (Cave of the Hands) in Patagonia, Argentina.

Credit: Best-Backgrounds/Shutterstock.com. Adapted by Richard K. Thomas.

Figure 9.5 Cave of the Hands in Patagonia, Argentina, although these handprints are from a later period, 13,000–9,500 years ago, they are an excellent example of children's handprints that appear in caves all over the world.

Credit: Eduardo Rivero/Shutterstock.com.

The handprints of children found on the walls of many caves across differing time periods and geographical locations all suggest coming-of-age ritual activities.

The cave art suggesting shamanism appeared at the height of the stone age at a time when primitive cultures developed an *anthropomorphic* worldview.

During the stone age, our human ancestors developed not just social knowledge about the mental states of others as our ape ancestors did, but conceptions of the unknowable—gods and spirits and non-human entities, especially animals. They imagined these entities to have human characteristics, and then inferred what those entities must have been thinking (Winkelman 2002, 75). This belief that every living thing and inanimate object was created or inhabited by a unique spirit that had human characteristics is called *anthropomorphism*.

Figure 9.6 The lion man ivory figurine is one of the oldest figurative carved sculptures in the world, dating back some 30,000 years, and is an outstanding example of an anthropomorphic figure.

Russian archaeologist Ekaterina Devlet adds:

> A common belief throughout Siberia is that in the mythical, time-
> less period 'before' the remembered time of human beings . . .
> there were no distinctions in form or essence between people,
> animals and birds. Shamans could cross these boundaries of time
> and space to change their essence and appearance.
>
> (Devlet 2001, 45)

Such a worldview was based on the anthropomorphic belief that every living thing and inanimate object was created or inhabited by a unique spirit that had human characteristics.

The combination of sound and mimesis held a very special place in this belief system. Marius Schneider detailed how primitive cultures placed a special value on sound in their anthropomorphic worldview. When a person successfully imitated the sound made by an animal or object, tribes believed that the actual animal or object's spirit inhabited that person. For primitive humans, sound was by far the most effective means of imitation. Primitive peoples can imitate the world around them with uncanny accuracy—and are even known to hold "nature concerts" in which each singer imitates a particular sound—wind, waves, animals and so forth. Masks, dance and other ornaments are not nearly as effective in primitive mimesis. For this reason, sound was considered to have a special connection to the spirit world; sound was *indestructible*, and carried the soul of the individual away upon death. Other humans could bring back the spirit of the deceased human, animal and so forth through imitation of the sound of that person, animal or object. Sound had a special connection to the spirit world that no other element possessed (Schneider 1955, 8–12).

Sound and music were arguably the most important tools used to immerse the shaman and community into altered states of consciousness. To understand an altered state of consciousness, one must first understand consciousness, and then develop an understanding of where an altered state of consciousness fits in the consciousness "continuum." Rossano considers consciousness in terms of an individual's overall level of awareness or arousal. Dreaming can involve consciousness just as much as waking does. Rossano describes one model of consciousness as a continuum "moving from wakeful, externally-directed, task-oriented consciousness to autistic, internally-directed, dreaming consciousness." This continuum might move as follows:

waking externally directed problem solving →
waking realistic fantasy, internally directed abstract problem solving →
daydreaming without the constrictions of reality →
hypnagogic[1] (states with vivid images and sounds teetering on sleep →
dreaming.

(Rossano, 2007, 91–92)

David Lewis-Williams is a South African scholar who also specializes in shamanism, and, in general, follows the same line of reasoning as Rossano and Winkelman. He describes the placement of altered states of consciousness in the continuum in this way:

Daily, all people move in and out of alert and introverted states; they also move through hypnagogic states into dreaming and eventual deep sleep. In addition, they have the capacity to move along an intensified spectrum through stages of altered consciousness into deep hallucinations.

(Winkelman 2002, 86)

Altered states of consciousness—to which theatre shares a close relationship—lie somewhere between dreams and our shared perceptions, which we often refer to as "reality."[2] Winkelman noted the fundamental similarity between the neurophysiological and cognitive functions of dreaming and shamanic altered states of consciousness. He suggested that shamanic altered states of consciousness were typically induced during nighttime rituals specifically to incorporate dream episodes. Rossano suggests that "the experience (of consciously induced altered states) share similarities with those of dreams, but are often more compelling and 'real' for the person involved" (Rossano 2007, 92). In the very roots of theatre, we see a close connection between shamanic ritual that involves entering into an altered state of consciousness, and dreaming.

Shamans used a variety of methods to enter altered states of consciousness (Winkelman 2002, 72). These could include sensory deprivation, like crawling through freezing waters a mile deep into a cave (!), but also simply closing the eyes and focusing on a mantra. Other methods include stressful or painful trials such as rites of initiation or isolation, fasting, and even ingestion of psychotropic substances (Rossano 2007, 93). But there is one thing that it appears that all shamanic rituals could not do without: music.

There is a tremendous amount of controversy and perhaps even conflicting explanations for the artifacts left behind by our stone age ancestors. But I have never encountered a single researcher who has suggested that music did not play a central role in the rituals of our human ancestors. Winkelman puts it very succinctly: "Music, singing and chanting are universal features of shamanic practice" (2002, 78). He describes a time in which shamans encountered the spirit world through song and dance. He notes, as many others have, the discovery of musical instruments including percussion instruments and bird flutes in cave sights and foot prints indicative of dancing (2002, 76). One of the first authorities on the origins of musical instruments, Curt Sachs, argued that the first musical instruments were created as an extension of the human need for rhythmic movement, dance:

Among the earliest instruments we find the *strung rattle*,[3] used . . . by Paleolithic hunters, as we know from excavations of prehistoric strata . . . made to stress dancing. . . . Gourd rattles are the essential implements of many shamanic rites.

(Sachs 1940, 26–27)

The rock art of Siberian shamans consists of numerous images of shamans with drums, leading Ekaterina Devlet to suggest that "the drum may be seen in Siberia as one of the essential shamanic attributes, of crucial assistance in attaining an altered state of consciousness." She goes on to describe how shamans used drums as a "mode of transportation for visits to other spheres of the universe," consistent with the anthropomorphic view of early human cultures (Devlet 2001).

The shamanic rituals closely tied music and dance as we observed in Daniel Levitin's assertion in Chapter 4: "One striking find is that in every society of which we're aware, music and dance are inseparable" (2007, 247). Music and dance seem to be a natural evolutionary development of rhythmic entrainment that emerged in our bipedal ancestors, as we explored in Chapter 6. Wallin and others argue that "musical expression tends to be inextricably linked to movement and gesture in the context of most group rituals. In musical rituals, gesture and vocalizing function as coordinated, mutually reinforcing processes at both the individual and group levels" (Wallin, Merker and Brown 1999, 9–10). It seems like it would be hard to argue convincingly that music and mimesis were not universally a part of the shaman's ritual journey into altered states of consciousness.

E. T. Kirby's examples of the influence of music on the shamans and their audiences are prevalent throughout his book, *Ur-Drama*. He considers extant tribes that presumably have not changed much over thousands of years, finding evidence in the primitive cultures from Asia, Africa, North America, South America and Oceana that trace back to 13,000 to 6,000 BCE. He provides a list of components of the shamanic ritual and their effect: "Dialogue, enactments, ventriloquism, incantations, music, dance, and song create a swirling stream of images drawn from a number of performance modes. The effect is literally hypnotic and hallucinatory" (1975, 1–5). Note the almost seamless connection between the music of the performer and the other musical sounds that accompany the performance. The components that Kirby describes in this instance are all temporally based and predominantly auditory and musical.

In the following recount of a passage by A. F. Anisimov, Kirby describes a typical example of a shaman ritual fundamentally driven by music. Just note how much musicality is discussed in this passage (I have italicized the musical references for emphasis):

> At this moment, the *song* ceased and the *sounds* of the *drum* were gradually *muffled*, becoming a *soft roll*. The listeners with bated breath awaited the appearance of the spirit. The ensuing *silence* was broken by a sharp blow on the *drum*, changing into a sort of *roll*. In the *silence* following this, the *voices* of the spirits could be clearly *heard*: the *snorting* of beasts, bird-*calls*, the *whirring* of wings, or others, according to the spirit appearing before the shaman at the moment. . . . The journey of the khargi [an animal spirit helper] to the other world is described in the shaman's *songs* in such fantastic form, so deftly accompanied by *motions*, imitations of spirit *voices*, comic and dramatic *dialogues*, wild *screams*, *snorts*, *noises*, and the like, that it startled and amazed even this far-from-superstitious onlooker.
>
> The *tempo* of the *song* became faster and faster, the shaman's *voice* more and more excited, the *drum sounded* ever more *thunderously*. The moment came when the *song* reached its highest *intensity* and feeling of anxiety. The *drum moaned*, dying out in *peals* and *rolls* in the swift, nervous hands of the shaman. One or two *deafening beats* were *heard* and the shaman leaped from his place. *Swaying* from side to side, *bending* in half a circle to the ground and smoothly *straightening* up again, the shaman let loose such *a torrent*

of sounds that it seemed everything *hummed*, beginning with the poles of the tent, and ending with the buttons on the clothing.

Screaming the last parting words to the spirits, the shaman went further and further into a state of ecstasy, and finally, throwing the *drum* into the hands of his assistant, seized with his hands the thong connected to the tent pole and began the shamanistic *dance*—a pantomime illustrating how the khargi, accompanied by the group of spirits, rushed on his dangerous journey fulfilling the shaman's commands . . . Under the hypnotic influence of the shamanistic ecstasy, those present often fell into a state of mystical hallucination, feeling themselves participants in the shaman's performance.

(1975, 5)

Feeling themselves *participants* in the shaman's performance. Not spectators, but participants. This is theatre, the experience of *being there*. Arguably not Broadway, not Shakespeare, perhaps not even must-see television, although I do think I might subscribe to that channel. At the end of the day, all one really needs for theatre is song—the combination of idea and music—and mimesis, the rehearsed imitation of the story transformed into immersive experience. Together, these two elements, song and mimesis, transport us—and our human ancestors—in ways that no other experience outside of music can.

Theatre = Song + Mimesis

The impact of the development of such a potent consciousness altering medium should not be underestimated. Indeed, Winkelman argues that

Shamanism's central role in image (visionary experience), chanting, and mimesis (ritual enactment), suggest that it must have had an essential role in the emergence of modern cognition.[4] Shamanic ideologies . . . constituted the basis for a major development in human cognition and helps explain the evolution of cognitively modern humans tens of thousands of years after the emergence of anatomically modern humans.

(2002, 84)

Theatre changed lives then, just as it does now. And music is a fundamental source that helps transport human consciousness to theatre's own worlds, to theatre's own special altered states of consciousness.

The Neuroscience of Arousal and Reward in the Altered States of Consciousness of Shamanism and Theatre

Introduction: Dreams, Altered States of Consciousness and Theatre

Dreams, altered states of consciousness and theatre all transport our minds to other worlds. In these worlds, we leave behind the physical reality of our bed, our cave, or our theatre, and imagine ourselves immersed in another realm, often times with ourselves the main character driving the action. What is the process by which this happens? Of course, it is quite complex, but let's try to explore some of its qualities in this and the next chapter. We'll start with the most basic cognitive responses necessary to the process: we first must become aroused, interested, engaged in the other world. Then, we must somehow synchronize our physiological responses appropriately to that world while immersing ourselves in the world of our imagination. If this happens successfully, we are transported out of our waking world and into the world of the dream, the spirit world, or the play. If this happens successfully, there is also a reward for us that will keep us coming back for more. In this section, we'll explore the processes by which we enter the altered states of dreams, rituals and theatre.

What does the shaman do that immerses the audience so completely in an altered state of consciousness that E. T. Kirby describes? We suggested that it was really quite simple: the shaman combined song (music and idea) with mimesis. Neurologically, I jokingly suggest that the formula becomes "altered states of consciousness = entrainment + mirror neurons," but just to jump-start already heated controversies. A better place to start is to remind ourselves about the similarities between the immersive experience of theatre and the nature of dreaming. In Chapter 3 we discussed the remarkable similarity that others have found between dreams and theatre.

In dreams, areas of our thinking brain, the frontal lobe (the dorsolateral prefrontal cortex, see Figure 8.11) responsible for guiding thought, action and emotion become almost inactive, and our limbic system (see Figure 5.9) runs wild, generating its own stories on its own time. Inasmuch as an altered state of consciousness lies closer in the consciousness continuum toward the dreaming end, we might expect similar neurological processes. However, instead of allowing the limbic system to generate all of its stories on its own, in theatre we input the basic framework of the stories through our sensory inputs, in our case, especially our ears. It would seem that the more we can input sensory information without overactivating the areas of the brain responsible for guiding thought, action and emotion, the more likely we will be to immerse our audience in the world of the play.

According to the neurologist, Jeffrey Avner, the first step in entering an altered state of consciousness is the reduction of self-awareness and reduced awareness of one's environment (Avner 2006, 331). In both altered states of consciousness and theatre, then, our job as composers and sound designers is not to reduce activation of the prefrontal cortex, but to take it over with our sensory input, to take the audience's minds out of the physical world of the theatre or the cave and focus them on the stories of the characters. The more we are able to do that, the more we are able to transport our audiences into the spirit worlds of the shaman or the imaginary worlds of the playwright. Visual support—scenery, costumes, and lights—can help quite a bit, but we must remember that in our earliest incarnations of theatre, the visual element was often removed or minimized (i.e., the darkness of the cave) and the focus was on the song and mimesis of the shaman. The staging was but a medium to our imagination.

And so, a primary difference between dreams, some forms of altered states of consciousness, and theatre, is that sleep creates the appropriate conditions for the perception of other worlds in dreams, whereas the shaman and the playmakers must *create* the appropriate conditions for altered states of consciousness and theatre. But how does one go about doing that? We start to do this by manipulating our audience's state of *arousal*.

The Basic Neuroscience of Arousal

Researchers used to think that the human brain operated on the basis of simple stimulus-response interactions. Neuroscientist Michael Thaut suggests the more current thinking that the "human brain is an arousal-seeking system" (2005, 23). According to Thaut, " 'Arousal' is a term referring to multiple processes in the nervous system relating states of heightened physiological activity" such as an increase in heart rate, blood pressure, hormone activity, muscle activation, or brain activities. Closely associated with arousal is *activation*, which refers to "behavior states associated with physiological arousal states" (2005, 20). To put things simply, we go to theatre and we listen to music to become aroused. I remember a conversation I had with Broadway producer Michael Jenkins when we were discussing how we assessed the way a theatre production was affecting the audience. We both agreed that we didn't watch the play. Instead, we watched the audience, because when you watch the audience, you can immediately tell their various states of arousal, from edge of their seat to fallen off to sleep. When our audience is aroused, we know that they are focused on the world of the play. They may even imagine themselves existing *in* that world, much the same way we become immersed in the world of our dreams.

As Thaut states, when we become aroused, we experience increased activity in a number of different systems. It all starts with the synapses between the neurons

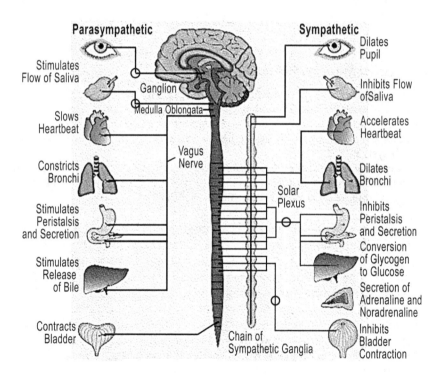

Figure 9.7 Overview of the autonomic nervous system.

Credit: Kimball's Biology Pages © John W. Kimball. 2016. Accessed July 21, 2017. www.biol-ogy-pages.info/P/PNS.html. CC-BY-3.0. https://creativecommons.org/licenses/by/3.0/deed.en. Adapted by Richard K. Thomas.

in our nervous system that contain chemical substances known as neurotransmitters. These chemicals transmit nerve pulses across the synapses between neurons (Thayer 1996, 91). One important system for us, the *autonomic nervous system*, predominantly uses the *cholinergic*[5] neurotransmitter *acetylcholine*.[6] The autonomic nervous system is the involuntary system (meaning we don't typically consciously control it) that controls physiological responses such as heart rate, blood pressure, respiratory rate, and most of the body's internal organs. There are two branches in the autonomic nervous system, the *sympathetic nervous system*, which predominates during emergency conditions, and is often described as the "fight or flight" system, and its opposite, the *parasympathetic nervous system*, which dominates during quiet, resting conditions (McCorry 2006, 3).

Another important chemical system is called the *aminergic*[7] system. It involves neurotransmitters that include *norepinephrine, dopamine* and *serotonin*. These neurotransmitters have many functions in the body, so we'll just concentrate on some of the ones important to this discussion. Norepinephrine and dopamine are similar in function; both are associated with activated states of arousal. Exercise and tension (stress) release norepinephrine in the brain and other parts of the body. The dopamine neurotransmitter is directly connected to rewards in the brain, and its release in particular parts of the brain may be responsible for many positive and pleasurable emotional states. Serotonin is another neurotransmitter that regulates mood. Increases of serotonin contribute to a positive mood. Serotonin activity does not change during tension like norepinephrine and dopamine do, so it is possible to remain in an elevated mood even when we are tense, a phenomenon we take great advantage of in theatre (Thayer 1996, 91–94).

The Effect of Music on Physiological Systems

As you will hopefully have suspected, music directly affects both cholinergic (autonomic nervous) and aminergic (norepinephrine, dopamine, serotonin) systems. As a matter of fact, there have been numerous studies in recent years to try to more specifically determine how music works to do that. Let's examine a few for each system.

It is clear now that music has pronounced effects on the autonomic nervous system that manifest themselves in changes to physiological systems such as heart respiratory rate. Mona Lisa Chanda and Daniel Levitin:

> Music modulates brainstem mediated measures, including heart rate, pulse, blood pressure, body temperature, skin conductance, and muscle tension. Stimulating music produces increases in cardiovascular measures, whereas relaxing music produces decreased patterns observed even in infants.
>
> (2013, 185)

Ian Cross suggests that interaction between music that is "fast, loud, broad in tessitura and bright in timbre" and music that is "low, soft, narrow in tessitura and dark in timbre . . . is likely to lead to the elicitation of complex and compound affective states, which will in turn shape the meanings that we abstract in the processes of listening"[8] (2010, 73).

Iwanaga and others cite many studies that have shown that sedative music, "which is characterized as melodious, delicate, harmonic, and romantic" (in this case Satie's *Gymnopedie No. 1*) helps to reduce anxiety and activates the parasympathetic nervous system, while "loud, dynamic, and rhythmic" music (Stravinsky's *Rite of Spring*) "elicits tension and excitement," and activates the sympathetic nervous system while decreasing parasympathetic activation (2005, 61–62). Iwanaga's group was also able to tie specific components of heart rate variability (a measure of variations in time between heartbeats) to sedative and excitative music, although repeated exposure to excitative music decreases its effects (2005, 65). It's important to know that we can manipulate cardiovascular response using music, but if we keep repeating the same excitative theme over and over, we'll reduce its effects, a form of habituation. Music and theatre must have their "downs" in order to have their "ups."

An important concept to understand, then, is that we use music to create both calm and tense, excited states. We don't tend to think of calming music as an activation state; rather we tend to think of it as our natural "resting" state. But in actuality, it is something we have to work with an audience to attain when we want it. Each audience member comes into the theatre affected by their own very different activation state. Some may be fired up because they got into an altercation with the cab driver on the way to the theatre; others may be exhausted from a long day's work. Our job as sound designers and composers is to take control of their activations states, and, in the process, pull them out of their world and into ours. We have to create the resting places, the low energy places in the play, just as much as the high-energy moments, not simply assume they are happening.

Ferreira and others aimed to investigate how long it took the autonomic nervous system to recover from stimuli provided by sedative (Pachelbel's *Canon*) and excitative music (in this case, heavy metal, noting that techno, hip hop and heavy metal have all been shown to cause physiological arousal) (2015). Once we lull the autonomic nervous system into a particular state of activation, how long does it take before the effect wears off? In their study, Ferreira and others found an increase in parasympathetic activation 10–15 minutes *after* the heavy metal music stopped playing (indicating a calming influence), and the reverse effect after the Pachelbel (indicating return to a more energized state) (2015, 113). It's interesting to note that the effects of music continue for quite some time after the music ceases, and that the body must activate the opposite system to that influenced by the music in order to bring the two systems back into balance. As theatre artists, then, we become aware when we introduce a certain style of music, that we are not just changing the moment of the music, but that the change will also have an effect in the scene that follows.

Ferreira and others also specifically tied the mechanism in cardiac autonomic responses to startle effect, in other words, to a sudden change in dynamics or mass (2015, 113). Startle effect causes a sudden rise in blood pressure and heart rate. The Ferreira group cites research that used levels of 110 dB to create startle effect, but other research suggests the threshold required may be as low as 80 dB (Ramirez-Moreno and Sewjnowski 2012, 169). My own experience suggests that the level required for startle depends greatly on the ambient level of noise in the room. For example, I have been quite startled in my bed at night when falling asleep in an extremely quiet environment when a modestly louder sound occurs, such as a creak or a tick in the house. All of this is important to us as theatre artists because it suggests that we have quite a bit of ability to modulate arousal using the dynamics of music in our productions regardless of the ideas and mimesis of the moment.

We already know about the ability of tempo in music to entrain motor movements in our audience from Chapters 5 and 6, the part where we play a tempo, and the audience unconsciously moves rhythmically to the music. Chanda and Levitin suggest that

> (Physiological) effects are largely mediated by tempo: slow music and musical pauses are associated with a decrease in heart rate, respiration and blood pressure, and faster music with increases in these parameters. This follows given that brainstem neurons tend to fire synchronously with tempo.
>
> (2013, 186)

It has been much harder to demonstrate exactly how synchronization between an external tempo and our physiological responses occurs, especially cardiovascular and respiratory systems, but it turns out that it might be worth our while to consider the possibilities.

A number of studies have found connections between physiological responses that depend on *how* we manipulate elements of music within relatively short time spans. In one of the earlier studies, Etzel and others found that subjects' respiratory systems became partly entrained to tempo and suggested that because of their testing procedures, it was "likely that the subjects unconsciously matched their breathing to dominant tempos" (2006, 66). What musical elements could cause the audience to synchronize their breathing with the tempo of the music?

It turns out that how we create musical *phrases* has a lot to do with cardiovascular response and human respiratory rates (the amount of time it takes for us to breathe in and out). Bernardi and others discovered that our respiratory rates "mirror" the "music profile, especially during crescendos," and that "music induces predictable physiological cardiovascular changes even in the absence of conscious reactions." In simple terms, music affects our respiratory and cardiovascular systems regardless of whether we pay conscious attention to it or not! Bernardi's team observed a similarity in several operas, particularly Verdi's, that contained musical phrases of about six per minute, or one every ten seconds. It turns out that six cycles per minute is the standard frequency of cyclic changes in blood pressure in all humans called the *Mayer Wave*. They discovered that "specific music phrases (frequently at a rhythm of six cycles/minute in famous arias by Verdi) can synchronize inherent cardiovascular rhythms, thus modulating cardiovascular control." This synchronization suggests the possibility that our cardiovascular system can be *entrained* to music, especially when we develop energy changes in long, slow, ten-second phrases (Bernardi et al. 2009, 3177).

Blood pressure tends to follow the music envelope; an increase in energy in the music tends to cause an increase in blood pressure, especially when the increase

Figure 9.8 Mayer wave entrainment compared to rhythm and consonance/dissonance.

occurs over a ten-second period. Regardless of whether we are listening or not, long, slow modulations in music, especially crescendos, have a direct and unconscious effect on cardiovascular response and respiratory rate. Bernardi's team discovered that this entrainment surprisingly occurred regardless of the emotional characteristics of the music (2009, 3178).

Laczika and others examined the so-called Mozart effect, a phenomenon in which listening to Mozart's music increases arousal, demonstrating that music and breathing appear to be "two weakly coupled oscillators," both in the way musicians synchronize their breathing patterns to each other, and in the way the audience synchronizes their breathing to Mozart's music (Laczika et al. 2013). Sato and others went in the opposite direction. They created a music playback system that synchronized the playback speed (tempo) to the respiratory rate of listeners. Despite not knowing that this was happening, listeners were more aroused by the synchronized than the non-synchronized playback (Sato et al. 2013).

In another study, Watanabe and others reported that an area of the medulla (see Figure 7.11) in the brainstem[9] responsible for regulating blood pressure responded to *both* musical tempo and respiratory rate. Significantly, they found that heart rate only increases when *both* respiratory rate *and* musical tempo increase, which may help to explain some discrepancies found in other studies[10] (2015).

So it may turn out that we can have our cake and eat it too. One way to increase arousal may be to modulate tempo and/or phrasing around typical respiratory/cardiovascular rates. I remember my friend and collaborator Carrie Newcomer talking to our director Robin McKee when we were doing our musical, *Betty's Diner*: "I tend to keep my tempos around the human heartbeat," Carrie said. Of course, I had worked with a lot of her music, and already knew that she tended to keep them slightly *faster* than the resting heartbeat, not in the normal range of 70–90 bpm, but just at the upper end of that, between 90 and 100 bpm, suggesting a subtle nudge toward arousal. Electronic dance music, or EDM tempos, however, typically range in the much faster, 120–160 bpm range. Why? Because the participants are typically dancing in some form, and that sort of movement generates this type of heart rate. When I work out, I can't help but notice the green area of recommended heart rate goes down as we get older, suggesting that we also might want to consider the age of our audience as we develop our tempo maps for our shows.

When we think about such a relationship in terms of an actor's tempo and phrasing, this research suggests that there is a sympathetic relationship between the actor's pacing and the playwright's/actor's phrasing. Could this relationship between tempo and phrasing have something to do with why sometimes the pacing seems to drag or the actors appear to be racing? Could it have something to do with why Shakespeare wrote in iambic pentameter? And how does the sound designer and composer work in conjunction with the actors and director to find the ideal resonance between tempo and phrasing? Interesting questions, most likely not with quantifiable answers—this is an art form after all! More likely these questions suggest an interesting relationship between phrasing, tempo and physiological response that theatre artists commonly exploit—whether they realize it or not!

All of these studies point to various types of involuntary entrainment mechanisms in our physiological systems that must have been around for millions of years—long before music since they are predominantly mediated by the ancient brainstem. It is worth noting, of course that all of these physiological responses can be modulated by "individual differences in personality and cognitive traits" (Chanda and Levitin 2013, 185). We should be more likely to choose our style of music based on what we think will arouse our audience rather than alienate them. Nevertheless, Chanda and Levitin suggest that our biological responses may be related to survival signals that have long existed in the animal kingdom: for example, the sympathetic activating alarm calls of some species versus the parasympathetic activating purring and cooing in maternal vocalizations (2013, 185–186). If our goal is to take our audience on a journey into another world, it seems like a great place to start would be inducing in our audience physiological responses appropriate for each moment in that world.

The Effect of Music on Psychological Systems

Throughout this book, we have repeatedly discussed the primary sensation of music rooted in the expression of emotion—music that incites similar emotions in others around us. In theatre, we typically do not use music to *represent* or *present* emotion. While anything is possible in theatre, almost always in my life *representing* or *presenting* emotions in theatre has been considered bad for the production.[11] Oliver Sacks beautifully described this phenomenon in his book *Musicophilia*: "Music . . . has a unique power to express inner states or feelings. Music can pierce the heart directly; it needs no mediation. One does not have to know anything about Dido and Aneas to be moved by her lament for him" (2007, 301). The purpose of the shamanist's journey was not to tell his followers about ecstasy, but to bring them into a state of ecstasy. Winkelman reminds us that "at the core of hunter-gatherer shamanism is a cultural universal—*entering* ecstasy" (italics mine) (2002, 95). If theatre is, indeed, a type of music, then we must accept first and foremost, that music carries the mediating aspects of theatre—elements of acting, sets, lighting, costumes, and sometimes, even sound—directly into the hearts and souls and imaginations of our audiences. It needs no mediation, as Sacks wonderfully suggested.

But there is a disconnect here. Was the pain of enduring the journey a mile deep through freezing water, and being deprived of food and sensory stimuli really compensated for by the ecstasy of the altered state of consciousness? Consider this in more modern terms: if the point of listening to music and going to theatre is all about the emotional experience, then why would we ever participate in any experience that wasn't solely a "happy" one? Have you ever thought about why people go see a play like *Hamlet*, or *King Lear*, or any of these plays that have horrible tragic endings? Why would anybody in their right mind derive pleasant satiation out of going to experience somebody's interminable, epic, catastrophic annihilation? Even in comedies people get shot and killed. Horrible things happen in our comedies. And yet we just flock to them and pay good money to see them! Have you ever asked yourself why is that? How can that possibly be? Are we just that bankrupt spiritually and emotionally? What could possibly be so good about feeling bad?

Once again, Oliver Sacks comments on this phenomenon: "there is, finally a deep and mysterious paradox here, for while such music makes one experience pain and grief more intensely, it brings solace and consolation at the same time" (2007, 301). Chanda and Levitin describe the phenomenon in this way: "Even opposite emotional valences (e.g., 'happy' or 'sad') can be experienced as pleasurable and listeners often report that the most moving music evokes two or more emotions at once" (2013, 180). What's involved in the neuroscience of the pleasure we derive from experiencing the full range of emotions in music and theatre?

In his popular book, *This Is Your Brain on Music*, Levitin discusses the fascinating journeys that sound takes through the nervous system and our brain when we listen to music. We've already discussed the fastest journey, the direct connection between our cochlea in our ear and our very ancient cerebellum, associated with startle effect and "fight or flight" reactions. In Chapter 5 we discussed the role of the basal ganglia and cerebellum (Figure 5.17) in processing rhythm after the transduced sound travels through the brainstem, midbrain and forebrain. In Chapters 7 and 8 we discussed the processing that occurs in the auditory cortex (Figure 7.13), and some of the processing that occurs in our frontal cortex (Figure 8.11) that allows us to analyze the sound and decide what to do about it.

But we haven't said much yet about another path that the auditory signal takes: through a network of regions called the *mesolimbic* system.

The mesolimbic system, literally, the middle part of the limbic system, is a particular pathway that starts out in the *ventral tegmental area* of the midbrain where dopamine is released.

Opioids (properly opioid peptides) are hormones that travel in the circulatory system and primarily serve to provide relief from pain, mimicking the effects of morphine on the body, among other functions (Chanda and Levitin 2013, 180). Levitin describes the mesolimbic system as "involved in arousal, pleasure, and the transmission of *opioids* and the production of dopamine, culminating in activation in the *nucleus accumbens*" (Levitin 2007, 191). The nucleus accumbens is part of the *ventral striatum* in the basal ganglia of the forebrain. Because of its

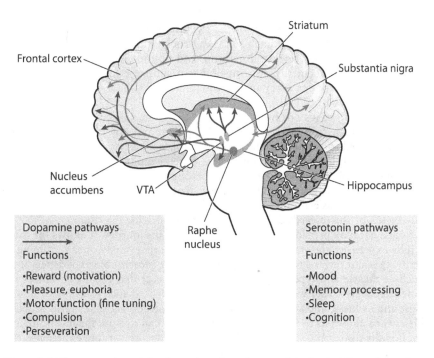

Figure 9.9 The serotonic and the dopaminergic pathways of the brain. The pathway from the ventral tegmental area (VTA) to the nucleus accumbens and striatum is the mesolimbic dopaminergic pathway.

Credit: Blamb/Shutterstock.com. Adapted by Richard K. Thomas.

208 *Theatre = Song + Mimesis*

role in providing this pleasure, the nucleus accumbens is known as the reward center of the brain (2007, 180).

In *The Neurochemistry of Music*, Chanda and Levitin update what we've learned and describe the arousal and reward process in more detail. It starts with developing an appetite for the reward, for example, when we get hungry, or, develop a craving for drugs. There are three parts to developing an appetite for a reward: learning about the reward, developing goal-directed behaviors to acquire the reward, and finally, anticipating getting the reward. The release of dopamine in the ventral tegmental area of the midbrain regulates these behaviors. The reward of anticipation is consumption, consuming the thing that brings us reward. When we consume the desired commodity, the ventral tegmental area releases the neurotransmitter dopamine that stimulates the nervous system and the hormone opioid peptides that travel through the circulatory system. Both interact in the nucleus accumbens, creating subjective feelings of pleasure by the binding of opioid peptides to receptors there.

Of course, I wouldn't have put you through all of this if it didn't have something to do with the effects of music. In their paper, Chanda and Levitin document a number of studies that show that music has the same neuroanatomical and neurochemical effect on listeners, and uses the same mesolimbic system to unleash dopamine and opioids in the brain[12] (2013, 180–183). Hopefully this will not surprise you. Consider the old expression, "wine, women and song," attributed to Martin Luther (Bartlett 1898, 811). Now consider the 1970s Ian Dury punk rock song, "Sex, Drugs and Rock and Roll," which morphed into a similarly famous quotation, "drugs, sex and rock and roll," in the latter part of the twentieth century. What do they have in common? Wine/drugs, women/sex, song/rock and roll? All three references describe activities that release dopamine and opioids in the brain. Isn't that amazing? At the end of the day, music has a similar effect on us that drugs and sex do. No wonder everyone on the planet must have it, needs it, wants it and can't live without it!

Fueled by music, it's not hard to imagine then that music in the ancient rituals of the shaman really did provide a dopamine- and opioid-induced reaction that contributed to the altered states of consciousness we describe as *ecstasy*. Of course, the spirit journeys deep into caves were also most likely wrapped up in emerging cosmologies, social needs of tribes, and fueled by sensory deprivation and more. But it seems clear that the ecstasy that Lommel, Kirby and Winkelman all describe above as central to the shamanists' ritual would have been fundamentally fueled by the rewards delivered by the music driving the ritual.

Sacks' paradox provides a reward at the end of the journey. It allows the mind to fully experience the emotions of the journey—be they happy or sad, calming or terrifying—and reward the journey with a positive pleasurable experience. Inasmuch as theatre is a type of music, we should expect that theatre produces the same effects also. And we all have certainly experienced such journeys of untold angst and sadness, and somehow emerge satiated. Knowing that music provides this reward allows us to attach ideas to music that can explore the most difficult, emotionally distressing subjects, and yet still provide a rewarding experience. We don't just go to theatre because we "should" go, or because it is "good for you." We go because no matter how tragic the story, the music of theatre rewards us with pleasurable sensations that mitigate the difficult, tragic, depressing elements we may encounter along the way.

One final story that might help us to understand Sacks' paradox. Don't forget that while all this dopamine and opioid production has been going on, the inner ear has been communicating with the basal ganglia, cerebellum, and motor areas of the brain, perhaps causing us to move in time to our internal pulse entrained to the external tempo. One often discussed phenomenon that occurs during particularly exciting passages of music, and by association, particularly exciting moments of theatre, is called *frisson*. Frisson is an intense emotional reaction to music and theatre that sends "shivers" down your spine. My friend Chris Wagner used to call them "weebyjibbers." Neurologist David Huron researched this and suggested that this reaction could be caused by an odd mix of fear and pleasure. The fear results immediately when we encounter something in music that is quite unpredictable, such as a rapidly large increase in loudness, an abrupt change in tempo or rhythm, or a broadening of frequencies due to an increase in sound sources. Such a change could induce a "startle effect" which travels quite quickly to the amygdala and cerebellum that trigger a motor reaction (shivers). Relatively shortly after that, the signal travels through our auditory cortex and gets processed by our frontal lobe, which indicates that the sound is indeed, not a threat, which causes a somewhat delayed pleasurable sensation (Lasky 2008). In this little microcosm, we see a sequence that is repeated often in music and theatre: immediate emotional reactions indicative of our total immersion in the moment, followed by a pleasant sensation when our conscious mind places the moment in its proper context.

But wait, there's more! According to J. Allan Hobson, a pioneer in dream research, the cholinergic system (acetylcholine releasing, as found in our autonomic sympathetic and parasympathetic systems) modulates or changes dreaming, while the aminergic system (involving the neurotransmitters norepinephrine, dopamine and serotonin) modulates our waking state (1994, 14). Rossano expands on Hobson's and Martindale's models that considers three factors in determining types of consciousness (2007, 91–92). The first is cognitive activation, activities that require focused attention and analytical processing. The second is neuromodulator mode, which determines whether the cholinergic or aminergic systems are more dominant in the brain. In waking focused consciousness, the two systems are highly active, but in balance with one another. As we tire during the day, the levels drop. At night while we sleep, however, the cholinergic activity increases back to our waking levels. However, aminergic activity remains low. Serotonin and norepinephrine levels, which are necessary to maintaining coherent thoughts remain low, and our dreams become much more fragmented and incoherent. The third factor in Hobson's model is whether the information being processed by the brain is originating from outside of the brain (in our senses) or inside the brain (e.g., in our limbic system and other areas, as in dreaming). See Figure 9.10 below for a summary of the possible combinations of factors in different types of consciousness, and some speculation on my part of how theatre might fit into this paradigm.

Rossano finds in these models support for his theory of a fourth stage to the three-stage model we discussed at the outset of this chapter. Recall Rossano's first three groups: (1) the general primate stage we explored in Chapter 5; (2) coordinated group mimesis such as proposed by Merlin Donald that we explored in Chapter 6; and (3) the emergence of shamanism out of group rituals as most likely the oldest form of religion. Rossano adds to these (4) the joining of human narrative capacity to ritual that ultimately would lead to songs and theatre.

Consciousness Level	Cognitive Activation (activities that require focused attention or analytical processing)	Neuromodulator Balance Cholinergic (acetylcholine)/ Aminergic (serotonin, norepinephrine, dopamine)	Internal or Externally Generated
wakeful problem solving	High	Both high and in balance	Externally
waking realistic fantasy (abstract problem solving)	High	Both high	Internal
daydreaming (constrictions of reality are released)	Reduced	Cholinergic greater/ aminergic weakens	Either
hypnagogic states (vivid images and sounds, near sleep)	Even more reduced	Both low	Internal
dreaming (REM states)	High	Cholinergic dominant (cholinergic high/ aminergic very low)	Internal
Altered states of consciousness	Moderate	Cholinergic dominant, but moderate aminergic (not incoherent like dreams)	Internal (sometimes external)
Theatre	Control with music	Control with music	Internal or external

Figure 9.10 Rossano, Martindale, Hobson model of human consciousness with Thomas speculations about the nature of theatre consciousness.

Credit: Data from Rossano, Matt J. 2007. "The Evolution of Conscious Experience: Ritual, Altered States and the Origins of Religion." In *New Developments in Consciousness Research*, edited by Vincent W. Fallio, 89–111. Hauppauge, NY: Nova 91–92.

Unfortunately, I know of no studies that have attempted to track the factors of Figure 9.10 in theatre audiences, because there are simply too many variables to control. That's the great joy of being a member of the production team! I suspect that the results of such a study would vary quite significantly depending on the nature and quality of each audience member's focus, arousal, and how "immersed" they happen to be in the scene (if you've ever been to a play, you know how the mind can wander!). But if we connect the dots of the discussion of this chapter we begin to see that we, as sound designers and composers, seem to have the ability to manipulate both cholinergic (through the autonomic nervous system) and aminergic states using music in theatre. If Rossano, Lewis-Williams and Winkelman are correct—that the level and balance of these two states contributes significantly to whether we are awake, asleep, or somewhere in between in an altered state of consciousness—then we should, as sound designers and composers, be able to use music to transport our audience into whatever state of consciousness we desire. We should be able to transport them equally well into the wide-awake and focused-on-the-scene consciousness Brecht seems to have preferred, or into a dream world of fantasy, imagination and free association associated with progressively more altered states of consciousness.

It is certainly interesting to speculate on the relationship between various levels of consciousness in the preceding model, and our own abilities to manipulate the audience using music in theatre. For example, I suspect that early in the performance the audience's cholinergic/aminergic levels would be high and in balance, as they arrive and anxiously anticipate the start of the play. They are wide awake and consciously focused. However, as our performance unfolds, I suspect that aminergic levels would moderate as a natural result of becoming habituated to a comfortable theatre. If the audience's cholinergic level were to also drop, they would probably fall asleep. In other words, if we don't use music to arouse the audience in some of the many ways we have described, they will probably doze off to sleep. All of us can attest to this happening in a performance. Hopefully, the structure of the play generates enough "fight or flight" moments to keep that from happening. We'll talk more about using musical structures to modulate their level of arousal later in this chapter.

A most interesting question is whether the information processed by the audience is internally or externally generated in the Model of Differing Consciousness Levels (Figure 9.10). In our earlier discussion, we suggested that this internal versus external generation of images is a factor controlled by the playwright and the production team. The production team exercises some control over how much of the information the *medium* of the performance gives the audience, versus how much each audience member has to construct themselves from their own experience. Still, there is a lot to be said for Rozik's thesis that the real world of the theatre lies within the "spontaneous image-making faculty of the human psyche" (2002, xi).

In exploring and comparing the nature of audience activation with those on the spreadsheet above, then, it seems that the theatre experience really does compare to a true altered state of consciousness when we are at our very best in realizing the production. And even nicer, it's an effect that we as sound designers and composers contribute to in a very fundamental way.

Cognitive Models for Music in Theatre
Robert Thayer's Model of Psychological Moods

Before this chapter, we pretty much confined our discussion of the effects of music on humans to emotions which Hess and Thibault describe as "relatively short-duration intentional states that entrain changes in motor behavior, physiological changes and cognitions" (2009, 120). But remember, back in Chapter 1, how I described an experience listening to Pink Floyd that did not just incite an emotional reaction, but changed my *mood*? Robert Thayer produced a useful theory in 1996 that also has applications to our theatre-making processes. He considers moods to be similar to emotions, but typically not as intense and lasting longer. There is some evidence that listening to pleasant music elevates mood-enhancing serotonin levels as opposed to listening to unpleasant music, which appears to lower serotonin levels, although more research on that subject is needed

	energetic	*tired*
calm	calm/energetic	calm/tired
tense	tense/energetic	tense/tired

Figure 9.11 Robert Thayer's four modes of mood.

Credit: Data from Thayer, Robert E. 1996. *The Origin of Everyday Moods*. New York: Oxford University Press, 5–6.

(Evers and Suhr 2000). Moods are generally positive or negative, and conscious (we are usually aware of them, as are others around us). Positive moods appear to be related to high energy levels, and negative moods appear to be related to high tension (Thayer 1996, 5–6).

Thayer, however, sees moods as an interactive product of the two states of energy and tension expressed as continua, between tired and energetic, and calm and tense. This produces four archetypal states: people feel best when they are in a calm and energetic mood, and worst when they are in a tired and tense mood.

We tend to be in a calm and tired mood just before we fall to sleep. Perhaps the most interesting mood of all for us in theatre, is the combination of tense and energetic. As we discussed in the section on the sympathetic nervous system, tension releases acetylcholine, which in turn releases the hormone adrenaline. However, our bodies can release adrenaline while we are in either a tired or energetic mood (Thayer 1996, 11–14).

If we consider my journey listening to side three of Pink Floyd's *Ummagumma*, it's easy to see that I began the journey in a very tense and tired state. But that first movement somehow transformed me with its rhythms, harmonies and dynamics from tired to energetic. The second movement piano solo calmed me down significantly, and the funky and dissonant third movement increased the tension again, but now in another more dreamlike world in which I was energetically engaged. It erupted into the quietude of the acoustic guitar and natural ambience of the fourth movement, and concluded with that whimsical group of small furry animals grooving with a pict. Tense/tired-calm/energetic-tense/energetic-calm/energetic-tense/energetic. No wonder I was transported and my mood changed! Notice how the music kept me engaged by continually manipulating my calm/tense states?

Consider then, how we use music in theatre to manipulate mood. To begin with, remember that the tools we use to create music are all related to manipulating energy in time and space: color, rhythm, mass/dynamics, line and texture. We create tension with dissonance, faster tempos, complex rhythms, sudden changes in mass, and louder sounds. We create calm through consonance, slower tempos, simple rhythms, habituation, and quieter sounds. We've just considered that if we don't activate our cholinergic systems, and our aminergic system is low, we'll probably fall asleep. We've also discovered that once activated, our cholinergic system will remain active for up to 15 minutes after we remove the stimulus. But if we continue the stimulus, the listener will habituate to it, and the music will lose its effect. This suggests a need for a structure in both music and theatre that alternates between tense and calm to maintain maximum arousal.

Having said this, you are probably saying to yourself, "well duh, we've known that since the dawn of theatre." Throughout most of the history of autonomous theatre, we have ascribed the ups and downs of the theatre experience as due to "rising actions" that lead to a climactic moment, rather than as fundamental characteristics of the music driving the story. In the late twentieth and early twenty-first centuries, however, it seems that we have finally become more aware of the freedom that treating theatre structure as developed out of musical structure rather than linear rising actions provides us. We are no longer bound to linear presentations of time; we are free to explore simultaneous lines of actions that weave in and out of themselves; we may dispense with traditional storytelling altogether. In short, recognizing the foundations of theatre in music opens the door to the postmodern theatre. We realize that what is really important in our theatre journeys is the continuous manipulation of tension and release, perhaps building toward a climactic moment that provides us with the pleasurable reward of simply having experienced the journey. Our stories don't need to be linear (of course they still can be), and they don't need to meticulously follow in cause and effect fashion; they just need to keep us aroused. In practice, you can find examples of failure to observe this simple principle in both linear and non-linear theatre every time audience members start dozing off during a performance.

The process of manipulating the emotions and moods of the theatre audience begins the moment they enter the performance space. One can certainly imagine that the reason the shamans' rituals took place in the deep dark recesses of caves was that the shamans wanted to make sure that everyone was in the right "mood" for the ritual-tense and energetic! Anthropologist Jean Clottes imagines that "the attitude of mind of Paleolithic people voluntarily going into what they thought was a supernatural realm—such a belief about the deep caves is widespread all over the world—must . . . have been quite favorable to inducing visions" (Winkelman 2002, 93). Getting an audience in a receptive mood is one of our most important functions before the performance begins, and we put a lot of effort in our theatres to accomplishing that. As sound designers and composers, we are often asked to "put the audience into an appropriate mood" from the moment they enter our theatre space. We call this period the "preshow." Essentially our aim is to affect mood without (typically) affecting focus or attention, because if we attract attention, then we have, for all practical purposes, simply started the play with the preshow, and that probably makes the first 30 minutes (or however long the preshow lasts) really boring.

We have little control over the mood of the audience when they enter. If our marketing team has done a great job, a large portion of them will hopefully enter the theatre in a calm but energetic mood, excitedly anticipating the performance. On the other hand, if the babysitter backed out at the last minute, and the check came late at dinner, and work was a bear and it's only Wednesday night and someone has to get up early in the morning . . . well, it's highly likely that some of our audience, despite the best efforts of our marketing team, will enter in a tired/tense mood. And our job is get them into a calm/energetic mood.

We start with comfortable seats and maybe even the option of an alcoholic beverage at the lobby bar. We give them a program to get their minds off of where they've been and focused on where they are now. And then we subtly work to increase their energy. There are as many ways to do this as there are sound designers and composers, and even in a preshow, one must be conscious of varying the tension to keep from lulling the audience asleep.

One other thing I'd like to mention that is not often thought about in theatre: curtain times and arousal. Has anyone ever wondered why most shows start at 7:30 or 8:00 p.m., and matinees start at 2:00 p.m.? Curiously these start times seem to play right into human circadian rhythms, one of the human body's key oscillators that is controlled by secretions of the hormone melatonin (derived from serotonin) in the pineal gland (see Figure 8.11). It turns out that we tend to reach our peak energy levels about seven hours after we wake, and again about 13 hours after we wake (Thayer 1996, 16–17). Of course, the effects vary widely for different people, and this is on average. But if we wake at 7:00 a.m., that suggests that we peak at 2:00 p.m., and then again at 8:00 p.m. We are most likely to be in calm/energetic moods at curtain time! Notice then, that both our cholinergic and aminergic activations will start to decrease as the play wears on, lulling us into either sleep or an altered state of consciousness, if we are able to activate cholinergic levels by increasing tension. If we composers and sound designers are doing our job well, it might just be that we can prevent sleep and incite altered states of consciousness—although, at the end of the day, there's not much we can do if our audience is dog-tired!

Berlyne's Theory of Arousal in Aesthetics and Psychobiology

Once the performance starts, we are faced with the somewhat daunting task of continuously maintaining arousal over a period of a couple of hours or more. We know now that we must cyclically increase tension, and that we will use the elements of music at our disposal to accomplish this. When the curtain goes up, however, we enter into a different realm, one in which we must work to focus the audience's attention to the matters at hand. Unlike the preshow, where we consciously worked to ensure that we did not command the audience's focus, now we must use our music continuously to direct the audience's attention. As anyone who has ever staged a theatre production knows, this is much easier said than done.

One of the more significant influences on my own personal aesthetic over the last ten years has been neuroscientist, Michael Thaut, who has done amazing research on rhythm. More importantly, he has focused his research on developing groundbreaking therapies that use music to treat such baffling diseases as Parkinson's disease. Thaut introduced me to D. E. Berlyne's theories in *Aesthetics and Psychobiology*, a book Thaut describes as generations ahead of its time (Thaut 2005, 19; Berlyne 1971). Berlyne's theories helped me understand important underlying mechanisms we use in music and theatre to focus the attention of our audience on our very temporal art forms. The ideas that I present below, then, are necessarily a combination of Berlyne's original work, and Thaut's connection of them to modern neuroscience.

Berlyne proposes two key dimensions in art that produce arousal: energy and structure. We have spent most of this book identifying how humans came to apprehend elements of energy in music, which Berlyne describes as (our terms follow in parenthesis) tempo (rhythm), intensity (mass), waveform (envelope), color (Berlyne also uses this word rather than timbre for its cross-modal applications [1971, 69]), and rate change (energy/time or dynamics). The brain processes energy changes in terms of excitement, intensity or stimulation. We have only recently begun to address questions of structure in this chapter, which Berlyne describes as melody (line), harmony (texture), rhythm and form. Structure and energy manipulation create expectations whose resolution (or lack thereof) leads to an emotional response. For example, Thaut suggests:

> A suspended fourth chord, an unexpected modulation to a new key, or a deceptive cadence may create a temporary violation of

musical predictions, which in turn leads to a heightened state of arousal to search for a meaningful resolution of the musical tension. This process of tension and release. . . (unfolds) in the continuous interplay between expectation and temporary suspense, tension and release, arousal and de-arousal, arsis and thesis, through the patterns of a well-crafted musical composition.

(2005, 5)

Thaut also notes that Berlyne's theories are driven by Gestalt perception, the psychological theory that the "whole" is a different entity than simply the sum of individual parts, a concept that it would be wise for us to not forget as we continue to investigate so many parts (2005, 21)!

The essence of Berlyne's theory is that we derive a pleasurable, positive aesthetic experience based on the complexity created by the energy and structure of the work. As energy and structure increase in complexity, arousal is increasingly activated. At some point, however, we reach a point of maximum acceptable complexity. If the energy and structures become more complex than this, we start to reject the work. We can plot this response as an "inverted U."

In theatre, there are three typical cycles involving activation that we distinguish by their length. The cycles themselves typically involve three actions. They start with some form of habituation, which is followed by an action that breaks the habituation and activates us, creating arousal. Once aroused we enter a stage of anticipation (suspense), in which we look for a resolution that may or may not come. The three larger activation cycles are the acting *beat*, the *scene*, and the entire play. All three of these cycles work simultaneously, increasing complexity as the play unfolds.

We refer to the shortest cycle as an acting beat, musically we often refer to this as a *cadence*. Acting beats are the smallest units of action that contain the entire process of habituation, activation, arousal, anticipation and resolution. Typically, we call the "beat" the slight pause caused by the minor moment of temporary suspension or resolution, before the next beat begins. Depending on their length, they find their foundations in the *periods* of music, a complete section of music

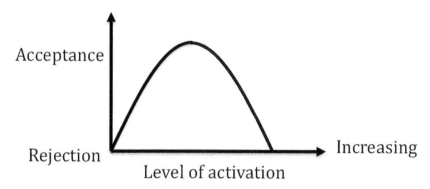

Figure 9.12 Berlyne's arousal model in aesthetics and psychology.

Credit: Data from Thayer, Robert E. 1996. *The Origin of Everyday Moods*. New York: Oxford University Press, 5–6.

that (typically) suspends or resolves in the form of a cadence. Keep in mind, however, that theatre is its own peculiar form of music, so it would be a mistake to attempt to impose another style such as the traditional antecedent/consequent requirements of classical music onto this period form.

In traditional storytelling, we start each scene with some sort of habituation, the so-called given circumstances for the scene. The scene is activated by something unexpected that disrupts the status quo. This creates arousal, for which we anticipate resolution, which the scene may or may not provide. This process is fundamentally a musical one, and, as orchestrators of each scene, we are charged with finding the "magic point" of activation that creates maximum arousal, acceptance and aesthetic pleasure. In many cases, the music (prosody) of the dialogue is all that is needed, in others, the composer and sound designer can increase arousal through additional orchestrations which increase the sonic complexity, and, presumably, the activation level of the scene (just ask any director of an action or adventure film). In some scenes, there is no dialogue whatsoever, and the musical orchestrations create the required sonic complexity to reach maximum arousal all by themselves. Scenes are specific types of musical movements that, even though they exist in the larger form of the play, can typically be performed on their own and provide an aesthetically pleasing sense of closure in and of themselves.

The largest structural form is the arc of the play itself. In typical linear types of plays, each scene builds and resolves itself, but increases the overall complexity of the story in a manageable way, so that each scene builds to a musical climax, typically the point of highest tension and arousal, and, as you can imagine, is often characterized by the fastest tempos, loudest dynamics, most dissonance. Even plays without linear storylines, however, seem to want to have an overall arc that slowly builds tension throughout the entire length of the performance—although there are, of course exceptions. Resolution follows the climax, and it is here where the structural form of the story differs most significantly from the musical form. The resolution in the story typically establishes a new order in the world that results from the way the climax resolved. The musical form—and this is often the case in the music of theatre also, typically recapitulates important themes from earlier in the play. The reason for this divergence has to do with memory—which we will explore in our next chapter.

Conclusion: Experiments in Ecstasy

We began this chapter by exploring the roots of theatre in ritual. We discovered in our Upper Paleolithic past much evidence of the emergence of ritual in *Homo sapiens* throughout the inhabited world. The emergence of the shaman, a religious leader who took on the character of animals and spirits, suggested an origin for the final piece of the theatre puzzle that separates traditional storytelling (song) from theatre: mimesis. In the shaman's ritual, we found an almost singular requirement: leading its participants into ecstasy. We found the primary technique of the shaman in entering altered states of consciousness, and investigated its relationship to other states of consciousness, and the neurological similarities between altered states of consciousness and theatre. We then looked into the neuroscience of the shaman's technique, looking for correlations between primitive rituals and modern theatre. We found those in the ability of music to create arousal as evidenced in the physiological stimulation of cardiovascular, respiratory and other systems, and in the psychological systems which provide rewards in the brain. We found a neurological connection between ecstasy and music. Finally, we looked at the most fundamental ways that we use music in theatre to create these epic journeys: to manipulate mood, stimulate arousal, and create the various musical structures in the play.

Over the years, as I've slowly come to fully understand the implications of the foundations of theatre in music, I've become more and more interested in exploring what I call the "gray area" between theatre and music, concert and play. About 20 years ago, I started asking questions about why young people don't go to the theatre; about the oft remarked "sea of white," the "gray-hairs" one encounters when you stand at the back of the theatre and scan the audience. So I began a journey collaborating with my punk rock–producing friend Mass Giorgini on our own punk rock musical, *Awakening*—15 years before Broadway co-opted the idea into its own hit, *Spring Awakening*. I discovered that young people would go to the theatre if the theatre offered something that appealed to them.

As time went on I found other groups of young people who were interested in exploring and exploding theatre form to target younger audiences.

In 2010, on a whim I headed to Chicago to see Green Day play live at the United Center. I had become enamored with their album, *American Idiot*, and actually consider it to be one of the best popular music albums since the Beatles. Mass had worked quite a bit with Green Day in their early careers, and he held them in the highest regard. I was psyched (calm and very energetic!). So, I went up early in the day, camped out all day to avoid getting stuck in the nose-bleeds of general admission land, and secured a place in the mosh pit within spitting distance of the stage. There's no other way I can describe that concert experience other than absolute ecstasy. And I mean that in the most literal sense of the word. I had a shared experience with the band and the crowd that night that was more intense than any I had ever experienced in theatre.

After the Green Day concert, I got together with a group of like-minded artists at Purdue and we created a new theatre experience based on gaming, *Ad Infinitum*.[3] One novel invention of the performance was that audience members could use their smartphones to create avatars on the screen as a part of the performance, an attempt to create an active performance that would draw and arouse young people and break down the proverbial fourth wall. In gaming, each audience member doesn't simply identify with the protagonist, they become their own protagonist. In the spring of 2011 we had a workshop performance at Purdue before we took the production to its eventual opening at the 2011 Prague Quadrennial. The audience entered and politely sat in their seats and the production began. As the performance began, people sat quietly and politely played the game, when suddenly two of our composers, Andy Muehlhausen and Ryan Hopper, started yelling at the screen. I was incensed! What were they doing? You don't talk out loud at plays! I went home and mulled it all over during a long and sleepless night, and realized that they were right. The wall that had been built between the audience and the play in the eighteenth century was killing the very fundamental purpose of our theatre: the ritual gathering of our community. We held a meeting the next day and decided that we would take the seats out, and re-imagine the performance as a loud participatory ritual experience in which the audience stood, and hopefully danced. We actively encouraged them to vocally participate in every moment of the performance. The difference in audience response was night and day, and we came close to providing that elusive experience of collective ecstasy.

As I had been studying the rituals and primitive cultures of early shamans, I became preoccupied with creating that ecstasy in a theatre audience. I wanted to do for theatre what Green Day and any number of other bands were already doing for song and music. I had already been to a number of EDM (electronic dance music) festivals, another place where the pursuit of ecstasy was a prime reason for attending. I decided to gather another group of like-minded artists together, this time in pursuit of a theatre piece grounded in EDM. I wanted to see if I could bring the audience during the climactic moments of the play to the same frenetic ecstatic moment I had found in so many of the music concerts I had been attending. Over the summer, I met with our projections designer, Kindari O'Connor, and we slowly developed a story, grounded in music, but still embracing the hallmarks of theatre in a cohesive story (although not at all linear).

We created the production and performed it for a couple of packed houses at Purdue in the spring of 2014. Again, we dispensed with seats, forcing the audience to stand—because it's really hard to dance sitting down, don't you know. It wasn't until I was editing down the video for eventual exhibition as part of the USITT National Exhibit in 2015 that I found the perfect evidence of ecstasy in the audience I was hoping for. Sure, we had managed to get the entire crowd jumping up and down, waving their hands in the air, and chanting along to the music in the climax. But as the music subsided and then faded away and the performers left the stage, the camera panned back exposing the audience reaction. Lots of exhausted audience members, and toward the back of the audience, hugging it out, were two guys, clearly overcome by the ecstasy of the moment.

You don't see that too often in theatre. Tony award–winning theatre, probably not; but an experience the audience will not forget can be all that you'll ever need to come back for your next production.

Figure 9.13 Crowd reaction to the 2014 Purdue production of *Choices*.

Credit: Still Image from Video by K. Henke Evans.

Ten Questions, Part I

1. What two basic activities does anthropologist Michael Winkelman attribute to shamanism that have important implications for the emergence of theatre?
2. What is anthropomorphism, and what is its relationship to sound in the worldview of our ancestors?
3. What is an altered state of consciousness, and what does music have to do with it?
4. How does an altered state of consciousness compare to dreaming? How does it differ?
5. What's the first step in entering an altered state of consciousness, and how do we accomplish it in theatre?
6. What is arousal, and what does it have to do with neurotransmitters?
7. Describe the basic characteristics of the cholinergic and aminergic neurotransmitter systems.
8. What is the relationship between stimulating and relaxing music and the autonomic nervous system? Name two things we must remember about using music to affect the autonomic nervous system.
9. What is the relationship between habituation and startle and the autonomic nervous system?
10. Describe the relationship between blood pressure, breathing, heart rate and music, especially phrasing.

Things to Share, Part I

1. Divide the class into groups of three to five members, about four groups per class. Each group goes online and researches techniques on how to enter an altered state of consciousness (endogenous drugs ONLY, please!). They develop and lead a short five- to seven-minute exercise in which they attempt to lead the audience into an altered state of consciousness using music as a core element. A representative from each group will lead the class in a five-minute discussion after the exercise to explore the experience of the participants.

Ten Questions Part II

1. What is the difference between expressing and inciting emotion and presenting and representing emotion?
2. Describe four distinct pathways that sound takes after being transduced into nerve impulses by the cochlea, and their purpose.
3. Describe the three parts to developing an appetite for a reward.
4. What is the reward for satiating appetite, and how does it work in terms of neurotransmitters and hormones?
5. What is Sacks' paradox, and how does it relate to theatre?
6. How does David Huron explain that frisson works?
7. Describe three factors in determining types of consciousness (e.g., dreaming versus awake), and explain the similarities between theatre and altered states of reality relative to the three factors.
8. Identify Thayer's four basic moods, relate them to theatre, and explain a fundamental structure used in both theatre and music to maintain maximum arousal.

9. Explain Berlyne's theory of arousal in aesthetics and psychoacoustics in terms relevant to music and theatre.
10. Describe the five elements of each arousal cycle in terms of the three major cycles we typically encounter in theatre productions, and how they relate to music.

Things to Share, Part II

1.   Divide the class into groups of three to five people, about four groups. Each group will work to create a two- to five-minute ritual/theatre experience grounded in music that will lead the audience into a moment of ecstasy. Feel free to embrace and explore as many of the techniques explored in this chapter as possible, from shamans to EDM, through creating a cycle of habituation, activation, arousal, anticipation and resolution, by combining storytelling with an original sound score, involving everyone in the class or allowing those outside of the group to participate as *audience* (literally meaning *to hear*) members; the possibilities are endless.

Notes

1 Hypnagogic is simply our state of mind just before we fall asleep.
2 Recall our discussion in Chapter 4 of José Rivera's description of theatre as "collective dreaming," another way to consider the shamanistic ritual.
3 Strung rattles are simply rattles hung from various parts of clothing to make audible the movements of different parts of the body, such as arms, legs, hips, etc.
4 I'm hoping that you have also noticed Winkleman's subtle reinforcement of one of the primary theses of this book: theatre = idea (image) + music (chanting) + mimesis. Winkleman takes this concept one step further by suggesting that it played a large role in the development of human cognitive abilities.
5 Choline is simply a water-soluble nutrient found in most animals. Acetylcholine is one type of choline.
6 Acetylcholine also triggers the release of the hormone adrenaline (also known as epinephrine) produced in the adrenal gland. Hormones are chemicals that travel through the circulatory system to control physiological response, in this case, the "fight or flight" mechanism of the sympathetic nervous system, explained below.
7 Another naturally occurring chemical derived from amino acids.
8 Cross uses different descriptions to describe similar things: he describes stimulating music as "fast, loud, broad in tessitura and bright in timbre" and relaxing music as "low, soft, narrow in tessitura and negatively valenced."
9 Rostral ventrolateral, if you must know.
10 Their tests showed, however, that the synchronization between respiratory rate and acoustic tempo does not need to be particularly tight in order to stimulate the cardiovascular system. In their tests, they kept respiratory rate steady at 80 cycles per minute, while varying the tempo of the external music from between 78, 80 and 82 beats per minute. In all cases, they showed an increase in heart rate (2015, 8).
11 See our discussion of "indicating" in the last chapter.
12 In Levitin's studies, activation of the ventral tegmental area also activated the hypothalamus, which is known to modulate our autonomic responses including heart rate and respiration. They also found significant interactions with the insula and orbitofrontal cortex, which are also involved in autonomic, somatic and emotional functions (2007, 181–182).

Bibliography

Avner, Jeffrey. 2006. "Altered States of Consciousness." *Pediatrics in Review* 27 (9): 331–338.

Bartlett, John. 1898. *Quotations*. Boston: Little, Brown.

Berlyne, D. E. 1971. *Aesthetics and Psychobiology*. New York: Appleton-Century-Crofts.

Bernardi, Luciano, Cesare Porta, Gaia Casucci, Rossela Balsamo, Nicolò F. Bernadi, Roberto Fogari, and Peter Sleight. 2009. "Dynamic Interactions Between Musical, Cardiovascular, and Cerebral Rhythms in Humans." 119 (25): *Circulation* 3171–3180.

Chanda, Mona Lisa, and Daniel J. Levitin. 2013. "The Neurochemistry of Music." *Trends in Cognitive Sciences* 17 (4): 179–193.

Cross, Ian. 2010. "Listening as Covert Performance." *Journal of the Royal Musical Association* 135 (S1): 67–77.

Devlet, Ekaterina. 2001. "Rock Art and the Material Culture of Siberian and Central Asian Shamanism," in *The Archaeology of Shamanism*, edited by N. Price, 43-54. London: Routledge.

Etzel, Joset A., Erica L. Johnsen, Julie Dickerson, Daniel Tranel, and Ralph Adolphs. 2006. "Cardiovascular and Respiratory Responses During Musical Mood Induction." *International Journal of Psychophysiology* 61 (1): 57–69.

Evers, Stefan, and Birgit Suhr. 2000. "Changes of the Neurotransmitter Serotonin but Not of Hormones During Short Time Music Perception." *European Archives of Psychiatry and Clinical Neuroscience* 250 (3): 144–147.

Ferreira, Lucas L., Luiz Carlos M. Vanderlei, Heraldo L. Guida, Luiz Carlos deAbreu, David M. Garner, Franciele M. Vanderlei, Celso Ferreira, and Vitor E. Valenti. 2015. "Response of Cardiac Autonomic Modulation After a Single Exposure to Musical Auditory Stimulation." *Noise & Health* 17 (75): 108–115.

Frazer, Sir James. 1922. "Internet Sacred Text Archive." Accessed June 7, 2016. www.hermetics.org/pdf/Sir_James_Frazer_-_The_Golden_Bough.pdf.

Harrison, Jane E. 1951. *Ancient Art and Ritual*. London: Oxford University Press.

Hess, Ursula, and Pascal Thibault. 2009. "Darwin and Emotion Expression." *American Psychologist* 64 (128): 120–128.

Hobson, J. Allan. 1994. *The Chemistry of Conscious States: How the Brain Changes Its Mind*. Boston: Little, Brown.

Iwanaga, Makota, Asami Kobayashi, and Chie Kawasaki. 2005. "Heart Rate Variability With Repetitive Exposure to Music." *Biological Psychology* 106 (42): 61–66.

Kirby, E. T. 1975. *Ur-Drama the Origins of Theatre*. New York: New York University Press.

Laczika, Klaus, Oliver P. Graber, Gerhard Tucek, Alfred Lohninger, Nikolas Flin, Gertraud Berka-Schmid, Eva K. Masel, and Christoph C. Zielinski. 2013. " 'Il Flauto Magico' Still Works: Mozart's Secret of Ventilation." *Multidisiplinary Respiratory Medicine* 8 (1): 23–31.

Lasky, Arielle. 2008. "Mystery Behind Music-Induced Shivers." Stanford Story Bank. May 28. Accessed August 4, 2009. http://storybank.stanford.edu/stories/mystery-behind-music-induced-shivers.

Levitin, Daniel J. 2007. *This Is Your Brain On Music*. New York: Penguin Group/Plume.

McCorry, Laurie Kelly. 2006. "Physiology of the Autonomic Nervous System." *American Journal of Pharmaceutical Education* 71 (4): 1–11.

Ramirez-Moreno, David Fernando, and Terrence Joseph Sewjnowski. 2012. "A Computational Model for the Modulation of the Prepulse Inhibition of the Acoustic Startle Reflex." *Biological Cybernetics* 106 (3): 169–176.

Rossano, Matt J. 2007. "The Evolution of Conscous Experience: Ritual, Altered States and the Origins of Religion." In *New Developments in Consciousness Research*, edited by Vincent W. Fallio, 89–111. Hauppauge, NY: Nova.

Rozik, Eli. 2002. *The Roots of Theatre.* Iowa City: University of Iowa Press.

Sachs, Curt. 1940. *The History of Musical Instruments.* New York: W. W. Norton.

Sacks, Oliver. 2007. *Musicophilia.* New York: Alfred A. Knopf.

Sato, Takashi G., Yutaka Kamamoto, Noboru Harada, and Takehiro Moriya. 2013. "A Playback System that Synchronizes the Musical Phrases With Listener's Respiration Phases." In *CHI '13 Extended Abstracts on Human Factors in Computing Systems*, 1035–1040. New York: ACM.

Schechner, Richard. 1988. *Performance Theory.* Revised and expanded edition. New York: Routledge.

Schneider, Marius. 1955. "Primitive Music." Vol. 1. In *New Oxford History of Music: Ancient Music*, edited by Egon Wellesz, 1–82. London: Oxford University Press.

Thaut, Michael H. 2005. *Rhythm, Music, and the Brain.* New York: Routledge Taylor & Francis Group.

Thayer, Robert E. 1996. *The Origin of Everyday Moods.* New York: Oxford University Press.

Wallin, Nils L., Björn Merker, and Steven Brown. 1999. "An Introduction to Evolutionary Musicology." In *The Origins of Music*, edited by Nils L. Wallin, Björn Merker, and Steven Brown, 3–24. Cambridge, MA: MIT Press.

Wattanabe, Ken, Yuuki Ooishi, and Makino Kashino. 2015. "Sympathetic Tone Induced by High Acoustic Tempo Requires Fast Respiration." *PLOS ONE* 10 (8): 1-14. doi:10.1371/journal.pone.0135589.

Winkelman, Michael. 2002. "Shamanism and Cognitive Evolution." *Cambridge Archaelogical Journal* 12 (1): 71–101.

CHAPTER 10

MUSIC, MIMESIS, MEMORY

Introduction: Traveling Backward in Time

When I first started designing sound at Michigan State University, I apparently raised enough of a ruckus that people wanted me to come to their classes and explain what I was doing. That, of course, would be difficult, because I really didn't have a clue. But I found an old tape in the sound closet that taught me a lot about how music works in the theatre. It contained recorded scenes from Elia Kazan's *Death of a Salesman*. More importantly, it featured Alex North's provocative score. The play opens with a haunting flute line underscoring Willy's return from one of his many trips. Immediately we make a connection between the haunting flute line and Willy. We already feel his pain, and the play has barely begun. There were several more examples on the tape where Willy Loman's theme underscored important moments, but the one that gave me my own bout of frisson was the last cue: Willy's wife Linda talking to the now deceased Willy at his grave. I can still *remember* what she said: "Forgive me Willy, but I can't cry." And then we hear that flute line, haunting as ever. "It just seems like you are away on one of your trips." I still get goosebumps thinking about how the music created the sense of Willy's presence in that scene.

I would develop my first lectures about theatre sound around the flute in that play. It drove me to explore the use of thematic music in my first original sound score for Paul Zindel's *The Effects of Gamma Rays on Man-in-the-Moon Marigolds*. For years, I would always look for ways to score the protagonist's journey, inciting emotions at moments in which I *knew* it was important that the audience *remember* a scene from earlier in the story, and *develop a strong emotional connection-identification* with the protagonist of the play. It would be many, many years before I would begin to understand what I was doing, and how it actually worked. But learning about the magnificent gift of memory to composers and sound designers may possibly be the biggest leap one can have in learning how to empower a show with music.

In Chapter 3 we explored the great mystery of time. We bumped into the "speed limit of the universe," 186,300 miles per second, and explored the phenomenon that as a traveler approached the speed of light, time begins to slow down, and at the speed of light, time stops completely. Science has borne out these theories, and demonstrated our ability to travel forward into the future. But we haven't been able to find a way to practically travel backward in time. Or have we?

From Einstein's famous thought experiments, we have learned that time itself is relative, subjective and unique to each individual.[1] Because time is unique to each individual, we experience an alternate reality in our dreams that doesn't conform to waking time. Another characteristic of our distinctly human subjective perception of time is that we routinely *relive* past experiences. We don't just remember them, we *re-experience* them in our "mind's eye" (and ear!). Memory researcher Endel Tulving first identified this unique human characteristic in 1972, eventually naming the phenomenon *mental time-travel*, or *autonoesis* (1972; 2002, 1). Our ability to mentally exist not just in the present moment, but to mentally travel back in time and relive past episodes of our lives is a distinct feature unique to human consciousness. You won't catch your dog pining for the good ol' days—he has a hard time knowing whether you left eight minutes or eight hours ago! And if that's not bizarre enough, consider that Tulving also thought that our ability to remember the past also provided us the opportunity to project ourselves into future scenarios, which could be helpful in determining the best course of action.

We left the concept of our subjective perception of time for many chapters; other animals have no concept of time other than the present, for them there is no "subjective." But in Chapter 9, we returned to our species, modern *Homo sapiens*. We once again considered our subjective perception of time in the altered states of consciousness of the shaman's rituals, and how we could use music to manipulate that. We noted the similarities to our subjective experience of time in dreaming—except that our limbic system provides the stimulus in dreams. External sounds and sights stimulate us in ritual and theatre. In Chapter 9, we focused on activation and arousal. In this chapter, we'll focus on the role that one facet of our subjective perception of time, memory, plays in human consciousness. In particular, we'll focus on our ability to manipulate memory through music in ritual and theatre.

In Chapter 4 we learned that perhaps the most powerful way to manipulate our perception of time is through music, which we have literally described as "time manipulated." In subsequent chapters, we have attempted to consistently bring the discussion around to this central theme: how we use music in theatre to manipulate human consciousness. Now, let's consider how we use the powerful trio of music, emotion and memory to manipulate the conscious "present" of our audience in ways that transport them from the physical trappings of the auditorium to the imagined worlds of our plays.

We'll begin, as always, by placing the development of our unique human memory capacity in the context of human evolution. We've already witnessed the last and "most recent" pieces of human genetic evolution fall into place in the last few chapters: anatomically modern human brains that first evolved about 200,000–300,000 years ago. Now we'll explore what such a human brain can do. The human brain typically weighs about three pounds, as opposed to a chimpanzee's, whose brain weighs about a pound[2] (Smithsonian Museum of Natural History 2016). The human brain has much greater connectivity and plasticity than a chimpanzee's, and at least twice as many neurons (Donald 2012, 271). An anatomically modern human brain contains 86 billion neurons (Azevedo et al. 2009, 535)! As we shall see, this capacity provides human beings with an extraordinary ability to process memories. Physicist Michio Kaku famously suggested, "The human brain has 100 billion neurons, each neuron connected to 10,000 other neurons. Sitting on your shoulders is the most complicated object in the known universe" (Egan 2015, 136).

Still, it would take this explosion of human mental capacity thousands of years to fully manifest itself. Memories, by their nature, don't suddenly appear; they form over time as we accumulate things to remember. Once we have memories worth preserving we need ways to preserve them for future generations. Everybody wasn't suddenly born with a library card! Human capacity for memory, may be the last to fully manifest itself evolutionarily, but, arguably, it is the one to have the largest impact on the development of civilization—and, of course, music and theatre.

We'll pick up our story in the Neolithic, or new stone age, about 10,000 years BCE. We'll explore the transition from hunter-gatherer societies to more sedentary, agrarian-based societies. We'll study the many kinds of memories necessary to the development of an oral tradition; stories full of ideas and music passed from generation to generation. All along the way, we'll explore how composers and sound designers in theatre use memory to carry and preserve the stories and ideas of playmakers.

The New Stone Age

Members of our genus, *Homo*, had been roaming the earth for almost two and a half million years when they finally started to settle down almost simultaneously all over the world—in the Levant, North and South China, New Guinea and Ethiopia, eastern North America, and Mesoamerica.[3] The shift was dramatic and swift: in a few hundred to a few thousand years, most humans settled down in primitive villages (Bocquet-Appel 2011, 560–561). Daniel Quinn famously dramatized the telling of this story in his 1995 book, *Ishmael*. In *Ishmael*, a telepathic gorilla tells the evolutionary story of biblical Cain and Abel. Abel was the hunter-gatherer "Leaver" displaced by Cain, the agrarian "Taker" (Quinn 1992, Part I, p. 41). Funny how biblical stories like this and Mitochondrial Eve[4] seem to resonate in significant events that could only have survived by being passed down in stories through oral traditions for millennia. Later in this chapter we'll discuss how music helps pass these stories down, and in the next chapter, what happens to the stories in the process.

Regardless, conventional wisdom has always been that this "settling down" originated in new farming practices of developing agrarian societies, but that may not be how it started at all. The oldest permanent structure known to us is the temple at Göbekli Tepe (pronounced ɟøbek'li te'pe).

It dates back to about 11,500 BCE. Archaeologist Klaus Schmidt discovered the site, and he and his team are convinced that it was the urge to worship that brought hunter-gatherers together at this site to build the temple (Dietrich et al. 2012, 679). Göbekli Tepe is rich with anthropomorphic figures that indicate a complex mythology, and a fairly advanced ability for abstraction and symbols (Dietrich et al. 2012, 684). The emerging consensus is that shepherds and farmers followed the building of these types of temples; the temple wasn't originally built by an agrarian society (Curry 2008, 58).

Of course, there is ample evidence of music that seems to always be associated with these early rituals. At Göbekli Tepe, Klaus Schmidt points out that "The stones face the center of the circle-as at 'a meeting or dance'"; a representation, perhaps, of a religious ritual. Pillars in the temple may represent priestly dancers at a gathering (Mann 2011). Schmidt's team points out more generally, "a rich repertoire of PPN (Pre-Pottery Neolithic) dancing scenes sheds some light on the

Figure 10.1 Location of Göbekli Tepe and Nevali Çori in Turkey.
Credit: Best-Backgrounds/Shutterstock.com. Adapted by Richard K. Thomas.

Figure 10.2 Excavation of Göbekli Tepe site.
Credit: iStock.com/tegmen.

nature of early Neolithic feasts"[5] (also see Garfinkel 2003). An especially good example is a bowl from a slightly later site, Nevali Çori, that shows two figures dancing with a turtle-like creature.

While we're on the subject, we can't help but note that the site is also known as possibly the birthplace of beer (Dietrich et al. 2012, 692), raising the specter of stone age "drugs, sex and rock and roll" type celebratory feasts releasing all sorts of dopamine in these early revelers.

Across the globe in Jiahu, China, more evidence has emerged about the role and prominence of music in prehistoric rituals and spirituality. Over 30 bone flutes have been discovered in Jiahu, China, with an increased number of finger holes dating to about 5700–7000 BCE.

The placement of these holes indicate that humans developed a much better understanding of the acoustic properties necessary to allow playing increasingly expressive and varied music. One of the flutes was so well preserved that a group of researchers was able to play it and analyze it, producing eight tones that closely resembled the modern melodic minor scale (Zhang et al. 1999, 366).

The discovery of a bunch of flutes may not seem like such a big deal to this discussion, but Zhang and his researchers remind us that

It is important in considering the possible role of these flutes in Neolithic society to recall that ancient Chinese tradition held

Figure 10.3 Dancing figures on either side of a turtle (a symbol of fertility) on a Pre-Pottery Neolithic bowl.

Credit: Image from Schmidt, Klaus, and Hauptmann, "Harald: Nevali Çori—Forschungen zum akeramischen Neolithikum im Vorderen Orient." doi:10.3203/IWF/G-264. Published by IWF Knowledge and Media GmbH, Provided by Technische Informationsbibliothek (TIB).

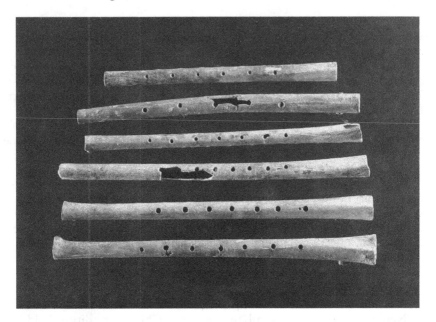

Figure 10.4 Bone flutes from the Jiahu early Neolithic site in China.

Credit: Reprinted by permission from Macmillan Publishers Ltd: *Nature*, "Oldest playable musical instruments found at Jiahu early Neolithic site in China," Juzhong Zhang, Garman Harbottle, Changsui Wang, Zhaochen Kong, *Nature*, 1999, Vol.401(6751), p. 366, copyright 1999. www.nature.com.

> that there were strong cosmological connections with music: that music is part of nature . . . mankind's earliest practices of musical expression . . . probably took place in a ritual setting.
>
> (1999, 367)

These very early examples of the relationship between music, rituals and spirituality continue throughout into the temples and the ritual practices of these early cultures. Henry George Farmer in the *New Oxford History of Music* suggests that "It is not improbable that music, or at least sound, stood at the cradle of all religion." Farmer bases this assertion on the origins of animism in sound. Animism is a belief system in which all animals, plants and inanimate objects possess a soul. In such a worldview, it would seem natural that if one would strike an object, or blow through a flute, one would hear the spirit of the object express itself through sound (Farmer 1957, 256). In the same volume, Marius Schneider elaborates on this basic concept, suggesting that for primitive humans there was no distinction between religious and secular life. Music may have had its pragmatic functions, but would have also simultaneously been offered "to appease the spirit of the felled tree or the gods of the water he is crossing" (Schneider 1957, 42). It's difficult to imagine in our fragmented lives such a holistic view of the world in which there were no divisions between music and the spiritual world, between music, dance and ritual. But this was a time when "gods were still wandering on earth." For these neo-stone-agers, thunder was as strong an evidence that the gods were "drumming" as it was that the "angels were bowling," which I was led to believe as a child.

The development of languages and more sophisticated music, would lead to the ability to tell more complex stories, which, in turn, led to elaborate mythologies. The only way to preserve these stories would be for each successive generation to learn them, to memorize them. Fortunately, anatomically modern *Homo sapiens* had that significantly larger brain, an almost unlimited ability to retrieve memories for our stone age performers. In the next section, we'll examine the complex ways in which our brain operates in order to store and retrieve memories, the role that music plays in memory, for us as composers and sound designers.

Memory

Introduction

In his extraordinary book, *This Is Your Brain on Music*, Daniel Levitin suggests that "Memory affects the music-listening experience so profoundly that it would not be hyperbole to say that without memory there would be no music" (2007, 166–167). We can make the same argument about the relationship between music, memory and theatre. We have seen the ability of the sleeping mind to conjure up memories on its own in our dreams. The sleeping mind constructs and fabricates dreams in seemingly random orders, and often for unknown purposes, presenting an altered reality that may or may not inform our waking world decisions. We have also seen in the rituals of the shamans the ability to induce dreamlike worlds, blending the unique memories of each audience member into new perceptions that bear a strong resemblance to the memories of everyone in the group—and those of their ancestors. Creating such memories must have provided shamans with extraordinary power to influence, control and shape the actions of large groups. This, in turn, may have allowed large groups to accomplish much more than smaller tribes could accomplish on their own. One way to create those group memories, and make them seem real, was by using music to carry the stories and emerging mythologies. Music and ritual surely must have had adaptive value that would ensure not just survival of our species, but the explosive growth that took place from the Neolithic age through the first large civilizations.

Distinguished professor James S. Nairne leads Purdue's Adaptive Memory laboratory. He suggests three possible characteristics of memory that our "stone age" brains must have developed in order to enhance our chances of survival. First, memory must be more than an ability to record the past; recalling memories must be useful for some present purpose. Second, in order to survive, we can't just randomly recall memories; there must be some mechanism that precipitates the appropriate memory for the current situation. Third, such a mechanism must have evolved in such a way so as to prove useful in recalling memories that are not just related to the present context, but that are useful in dealing with the present context (Nairne and Pandeirada 2008, 240). We could consider these principles as three questions one must ask oneself in scoring a play:

1. Why do we want to generate and subsequently recall this memory?
2. How will we cue this memory?[6]
3. How will recalling this memory enrich the audience experience in the present moment?

Keep these important characteristics in mind as we investigate each memory system.

There's not much difference in the basic requirements of the shaman and modern sound designers/composers when it comes to engaging our audience's memories in the perception of ritual or theatre. Basically, we must successfully manage three processes. First, we must provide sensory stimuli in such a way that the brain can process and encode it in a form useable by the memory systems of the human brain. Second, we must effectively be able to convince the brains of our audience to store the memory in useful ways. Finally, we must be able to manipulate the consciousness of our audience to retrieve the memory at appropriate moments both during the performance and afterwards, as they hopefully reflect on the experience. To do these three things, we must come to grips with how our anatomically modern *Homo sapiens* brains process memories.

In the next sections, we will examine the different types of memory systems commonly thought to be used by the human brain. We must point out before we do, however, that we are no longer dealing with individual, isolated components of the brain. We now investigate memory systems that utilize smaller components that may serve multiple functions: "Memory systems are organized structures of more elementary operating components," says Tulving (2002, 6). The simple fact that memory uses so many different components has made studying memory very complex, and there is still much more research to do. Many theories exist side by side, some mutually supportive of each other, some contradicting.[7] We'll try to stick to theories that have achieved some measure of validation and apply directly to the art of the sound designer and theatre composer. Of course, the advantage of having incorporated pragmatic conceptions of how memory works in my sound scores for 40 years will serve as an unlikely but hopefully welcome demonstration of the salient qualities of these theories. If not, they may still serve as interesting example of how these theories found their way into one person's aesthetic of theatre sound design and composition.

In 1968, R. C. Atkinson and R. M. Shiffrin proposed that there were three distinct parts of memory: sensory (echoic) memory, working memory, and long-term memory (Atkinson and Shiffrin 1968). While there has been an overwhelming amount of research into the different types of memories, the basic concept has survived in some form through the present day (albeit with its own share of variants and controversies). We'll consider each type of memory in the next sections.

Sensory Memory

We've introduced the auditory form of sensory memory, echoic memory, in Chapter 8, noting that the auditory cortex in the temporal lobe holds the sounds transmitted by the ear just long enough for other areas of the brain to process it, primarily for pitch, timbre, and to determine basic relationships such as consonance and dissonance.

Nishihara and others suggest that echoic memory has four defining characteristics:

1. You don't have to be paying attention to the sound in order for it to be stored in your echoic memory; it gets stored there whether you pay attention to it or not.
2. The information stored in echoic memory is sound only, transmitted directly from the sensory organ of the ear.

3. The information stored there has a finer resolution than other memory systems; this is the closest thing we have to a "tape recorder" in our brains.
4. Echoic memory does not last long (Winkler and Cowan 2005, 3; Nishihara et al. 2014, 1).

Recent research has suggested that sensory memory may be involved in a more sophisticated version of the habituation response we first encountered in Chapter 2. In one particular testing paradigm, called the *Mismatched Negativity Event Related Potential* (MMN), an auditory stimulus is presented repeatedly at relatively short intervals. The subject is typically engaged in a distracting activity and told to ignore the stimuli. After a pause in stimulus, which depends on the nature of the test, the stimulus is repeated once again as a reminder, and a different stimulus is then introduced that deviates from the original. Electrodes planted non-invasively on the scalp allow researchers to measure unconscious and conscious brain activity. From this test, researchers can tell how long the particular stimulus persists in echoic memory, and whether the deviant stimulus activates arousal; that is, whether other parts of the brain, particularly the frontal lobe, gets involved in bringing the deviant sound to our conscious attention.[8] Winkler and Cowan found that the limit of echoic memory under these circumstances was less than 11 seconds. Others have proposed different models, with different time limits based on how various stimuli were presented and analyzed (Winkler and Cowan 2005). MMN remains a somewhat controversial technique, but also continues to find many applications in cognitive neuroscience. Regardless, there does not seem to be much controversy that changes in pitch, duration, loudness and spatial location can all elicit a change-related cortical response, with subtler changes taking longer to register, and eliciting smaller amplitude responses (Näätänen et al. 1993, 436). In other words, when our auditory environment changes, we notice. The smaller the change, the longer it takes to attract our attention, and the less likely it will be to do so (Tiitinen et al. 1994).

In Chapter 2, we were dealing with the most primitive members of the animal kingdom when we considered unconscious, physiological startle response and habituation. We now see a much more sophisticated version than the unconscious physiological response of our more primal brain circuits. Much more subtle habituation responses occur when the sound persists in echoic memory without involvement of the frontal lobe. Likewise, arousal occurs when a major change in the sound environment grabs our attention, that is, involves other parts of the brain in a quick reaction. The stimulus enters our consciousness, where our frontal lobes get involved in analyzing the sound. In the hundreds of millions of years since startle and habituation first manifested themselves in primitive animals, our sensitivity to changes in our auditory environment has increased quite a bit. As sound designers and composers, we can arouse our audience with much subtler mass and dynamic effects than the startle effect. We can also use changes in color, rhythm, line, space and texture to arouse our audience and focus their attention. But still, the basic premise is the same: our attention is unconsciously aroused when our auditory environment changes.

The ability to use sound to grab the attention of an audience is both a tool and a pitfall for sound designers and composers. There are times when we need to draw the attention of our audience, and there are times when we need to avoid drawing attention. A playwright may introduce a new character into a scene, which introduces a new auditory rhythm and color and so forth, and that will draw focus. A composer or sound designer introducing a new sound, or changing the ambience in a scene will have the same effect—oftentimes distracting the audience from the dramatic scene. Putting the loudspeaker in the wrong place (e.g., on the side of the proscenium) can draw the attention of the audience (and the director!) to the sound without them even knowing why! As we discussed in Chapter 2, sound designers and composers need to be very cautious about where and when they introduce changes in the auditory environment. When used intelligently, however, changing the auditory environment can work as very powerful attention getting devices.

I remember my friend Abe Jacob telling me the story of how he got the building engineer to turn off the air conditioning system during *A Chorus Line* on Broadway, just before one of the quietest moments in the show, the Paul Monologue. The change in mass clearly drew the focus of the audience. Abe told me "it . . . made it a little bit uncomfortable in the house, a characteristic that director Michael Bennett loved, 'That's what we want them to feel—the same uncomfortableness that Paul is feeling onstage'" (Thomas 2008, 55). Usually we want to manipulate focus in just this way: unconsciously. The audience doesn't consciously hear the change in sound, but finds its attention suddenly more consciously focused. It's when the audience becomes aware of being manipulated that the emperor suddenly has no clothes and the audience is pulled out of the dramatic world of the play. Learning how to analyze the story and the text is one of the most significant abilities that we need to acquire in order to understand when to draw focus, and when to habituate, when to do it very consciously, and when to work one's magic very subtly.

Long Auditory Store/Short Term Memory/Working Memory

Sensory memory, which we discussed in the last section "allows the memory of . . . things to linger while we think about them" (Cowan 1997, 51). Cognitive psychologist Nelson Cowan suggests that the rich, highly detailed mental image of the sounds we hear only lasts for a few hundred milliseconds in this sensory memory. Cowan calls this *short auditory store*. However, some parts of it, such as color, pitch or loudness last significantly longer, up to as much as 20 seconds. Cowan called this *long auditory store*. Cowan considered both types of memory to be types of sensory memories.

Cowin's long auditory store bears some resemblance however, to another concept called *short-term memory*. George Sperling first proposed the concept of short-term memory in 1960, noticing in his experiments that subjects forgot visual stimuli within about a quarter of a second, but could remember about four specific bits of information like letters or numbers for longer periods of time (Sperling 1960, 8). Even though later experiments determined that the sensory memory was longer for auditory stimuli, the short-term memory for storage remained at about four items (Cowan 2015, 8). Cowan describes this short-term memory as "the subject's present mind" (Cowan 1997, 77). So we notice right from the start that there is some overlap, and, as always, controversy, between the concepts of sensory memory and short-term memory.

Beyond these limited capacities, the mind is capable of "juggling" a few different things at once, focusing first on one item, then on another, then on another, and then back to the first item. So the conscious mind is able to hold somewhat more than four items in its short-term memory. George Miller, in a landmark 1956 paper called "The Magic Number Seven, Plus or Minus Two," noted that human beings can maintain about seven discrete items in their brain at one time—plus or minus two (1996)! Baddeley and others discovered in 1975 tests that subjects could only recall as many items as they could repeat in about two seconds (1975, 575), and many others have subsequently confirmed these findings (Cowan 1997, 82). Robert Glassman suggests that the consensus today of cognitive psychologists is that we are able to hold about six items in what has come to be known as our *working memory* at a time. At any moment, our working memory will hold the last three or four items we heard (sensory memory). The other two items get refreshed as part of our two seconds of short-term memory, as long as we keep mentally repeating the items in our mind (Glassman 1999).

Atkinson and Shiffrin first proposed the concept of a *working memory*, which Baddeley defines as the "system or systems that are assumed to be necessary in order to keep things in mind while performing complex tasks such as reasoning, comprehension and learning" (Baddeley 2010, R136). Working memory differs from short-term and long auditory store in that working memory involves the entire "thinking" process, while short-term and long auditory store are simply the stored data. Baddeley overhauled the Atkison/Shiffrin concept of a working memory around the concept of the *Central Executive*, a system in the brain that controls how and where we focus our attention.

How long we are able to hold information in our working memory depends on how we attend to it. In 1984 Baddeley proposed a neural circuit that we now call the phonological loop.

The phonological loop allows us to repeat words over and over again subvocally, while our Central Executive system processes the information. Of course, there is also a visual correlate of the phonological loop that interacts with the Central Executive, called the Visuo-spatial Sketch Pad.

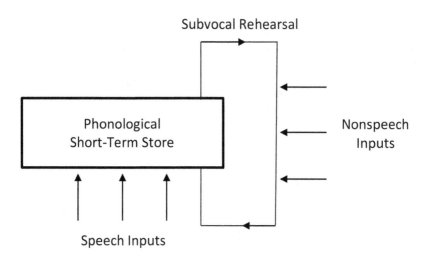

Figure 10.5 Baddeley's model of the phonological loop.

Credit: Derived from Baddeley, Alan, Vivien Lewis, and Giuseppe Vallar. 1984. "Exploring the Articulatory Loop." *The Quarterly Journal of Experimental Psychology*. Section A, 36: 2, 233–252, doi:10.1080/14640748408402157.

Levitin sets the capacity of our phonological loop at between 15 and 30 seconds (Levitin 2007, 155). You'll notice that you use your phonological loop all the time to do things like remember a phone number, mentally (subvocally) repeating the digits over and over until you are confident you have them memorized. This phonological loop even works with visual information—it doesn't make a difference whether you hear the phone number or see the phone number, when you try to remember it, you will typically subvocally repeat the digits over and over again—rather than attempt to visually keep the digits in your mind. Some research suggests that brain components that support the phonological loop include the right middle and inferior temporal lobe and the left hippocampus (Rudner et al. 2007).

The curious thing about this phonological loop is that David Kraemer and his team of cognitive psychologists have discovered evidence that the same phonological loop we use to rehearse those phone numbers into our long-term memories is where songs get "stuck in our heads," the auditory cortex and associated areas in the temporal lobe. Some people call them "earworms," from the German *ohrwurm*. The more scientific types describe earworms as *Involuntary Musical Images* (INMI) (Beaman and Williams 2010). Others describe the whole process of what gets stored in the phonological loop (including earworms) as *Auditory Images* (Kraemer et al. 2005, 158). But the interesting part is that while Baddeley's 1984 team just used words in their tests and research of the phonological loop, Kraemer's team found auditory imagery worked for instrumental music as well as words. But there was one important difference: when there is semantic meaning involved in the phonological loop, only the auditory association cortex got involved.[9] When the earworm was purely instrumental, the primary auditory cortex also got involved. Kraemer's team notes that the visual cortices function in a correspondingly similar way (Kraemer et al. 2005).

I've known about music getting stuck in this continuous loop in my brain since I was very young. Levitin suggests that musicians and people with OCD (obsessive-compulsive disorder) are more likely to experience earworms[10] (Levitin 2007, 155). From my very first experience with *The Effects of Gamma Rays on Man-in-the-Moon Marigolds*, I tried to incorporate "hooks" in my theatre music. I first wanted to make sure that the audience left the theatre with the hooks repeating in their phonological loops (of course I didn't know what to call it at the time), and then I wanted to attach important ideas in the play to the hook. In *Marigolds*, I co-opted Tillie's Theme into a repeating hook that underscored Beatrice's (Tillie's mom) descent into a nervous breakdown in the resolution of the play. I attached the lyric "What's left for me?" to the hook, and repeated it over and over again as the stage lights faded on the end of the play. The contrast between Tillie's tenacious idealism and Beatrice's self-destructive narcissism had given me a lot to think about, and I wanted to plant the same seed in the minds of the audience as they left the theatre. Beaman and Williams have a (pardon the pun) catchy name for the passing on of earworms such as this: *memetic transmission* (Beaman and Williams 2010, 638). In advertising, we typically attempt to attach a brand name to the earworm (meme); in theatre sound scores, we hope to attach the important ideas of the play.

I consider the opportunities to write music that I intend to insert into the audience's phonological loop on the way out of the theatre to be relatively few and far between. You get a lot of those opportunities if you write musicals, or if you compose for straight plays that have songs in them. Shakespeare is full of opportunities because virtually every one of his plays has a song in it from which you can parse themes and motifs. In straight dramas, you are more likely required to use hooks much more subtly, as you can't overpower dialog with underscore using a strong melody. You'll often have your only chances during scene changes and special moments in which there is no dialogue but strong emotion. Regardless of where the opportunity falls, the best advice I can give is: be careful.

Earworms are funny things, if you think about some of the ones you've had. I won't mention any names, but most everyone has experienced a really awful song that got stuck in their head at the grocery store or doctor's office. Earworms have no taste. Some of the melodies that get stuck are simply banal. Composers need to take care when writing hooks to keep them unique and interesting yet insanely memorable. The San Francisco–based Exploratorium website suggests using repetition and/or unique time signatures to create earworms (Exploratorium 2016). And there might be something useful in that advice. Repetition almost always helps to get something stuck in our memories; unique time signatures go a long way toward keeping a hook unique, fresh and interesting.

Daniel Levitin suggests that "style is just another word for repetition." It's not just the strict looping of precise auditory events that helps a tune get stuck in our phonological loop. The tune and the "hook" will observe very specific laws of music that we've heard before. It will reference in our memory all the music we've heard before that approximates the style of the tune and hook. Levitin describes this approximation as the *schema* of the style, the general set of rules that the style repeats. We take advantage of all this "hidden" repetition, just by virtue of writing in a particular style with which the audience is familiar (this is, by the way, one of the reasons I advocate composing underscoring using modern scoring techniques rather than following strict period; an unfamiliar period style may pull us ever so subtly out of total immersion in the scene).[11] Levitin goes on to suggest that it's not just strict repetition of the rules of a particular style that help us get a hook lodged into the phonological loops of our audience. It's the subtle variations that make our hook unique that help to create the arousal necessary; it's how we violate the schemas of the style (repetition) that help to set the hook. As they say in *This Is Spinal Tap*, "it's such a fine line between stupid and clever." Too much variation, and the hook will draw focus; too little and the hook becomes banal and doesn't set, or sets in a most irritating manner.

Early in my career, I crafted tunes while playing the guitar, like Tilly's Theme in *The Effects of Gamma Rays on Man-in-the-Moon Marigolds*. But I soon realized as I became more sure of myself as a composer and sound designer that sitting at a musical instrument was perhaps the worst place to develop a strong, memorable tune. I was a slave to my musical instrument, my facility on the instrument dictating melodic choices. Once I discovered this, a whole new world of composing tunes and themes opened up for me. I learned to take walks, go jogging, engage in some form of physical activity while turning the melody over in the back of my mind. The natural rhythms of my body would help structure the tune and teach me what worked and what didn't. The physical act of walking provides the mechanical tempo that forces the hook into an interesting rhythm. The physicalization of the rhythm also helps develop a hook that entrains the audience. If there's a lyric or text such as in Shakespeare, I'll memorize it before I head out so I can make sure to be true to its prosody. Often times both the dominance of the physical tempo of walking, and the scansion of the text of the language will force a hook into my mind with unusual rhythms and meters that nevertheless feel entirely organic. Those are the hooks that seem to stick the best and avoid the dreaded banality.

I have a rule that when I'm developing a hook, I don't write it down. If I don't remember it when I come back to work on it later, it wasn't good enough. A good tune will come back and haunt me, a good indication in my mind that it will do the same to my audience. Often when the melody does come back, the part that comes back is musically strong—a "hook," and the part I can't remember is the weak part. My thinking is that if it wasn't strong enough to stick in my mind, how do I expect it to get stuck in the phonological loops of the audience?

There simply are no explanations, however, for the moment when an amazing, memorable, hummable, catchy, extraordinary hook first appears. I never seem to remember the moment a great tune comes into my mind. I know that I often have to work it over and over again to get it exactly right, but my best tunes seem to have always come from inspiration, from deep within, not from craft. For me, the moment when the hook finally seats itself in my mind is always a special one. You massage and massage melodic ideas, and suddenly they appear, fully formed, and you know they are good, they are going to stick, and the audience won't mind them sticking. I remember the exact moment my hook for the ESPN Indy 500 television series first appeared. I had just walked past the University Bookstore close to our campus. Barely five seconds long, I found the hook outside the campus bookstore during a walk. It was just suddenly there; later my partner Michael Cunningham and I would develop that hook into all of the other scoring for the different shows in which it was used. A curious footnote to this ESPN story: I had planned a simmering chord progression that would create anticipation as it underscored the opening VO (voice-over). The idea was that the hook would erupt after the VO when the logo flew onto the screen. I thought my hook was strong and memorable and would not wear thin when it was repeated throughout the series at commercial breaks. Michael considered it and added a countermelody under and slightly after that exploded the energy exponentially. To this day, if that hook pops up in my phonological loop, Michael's countermelody is there as well. I credit Michael with making good brilliant.

There's no telling when and where the hook will happen; all I know is that I have to put the dramatic moment in my own working memory, and hold it there until the hook arrives. The tune for the opening theme for our Milwaukee production of John Pielmeyer's *Splatterflick* came to me in the shower (of course!). I was playing cards with my family when "The Doxie over the Dale" that Autolycus sings at the top of Act IV, Scene 3, in the Purdue production of Shakespeare's *Winter's Tale* came to me. What I have learned about creating melodies, themes and tunes, is to somehow hold them in my mind even as I go about my workaday life, and to hold them there until they come out right. This can take a couple of days or a week. It's usually the first thing I do for a show, if the show is going to require a hook, because so much other material will often derive in some way from that melodic material. And if I have learned one thing about being an artist, it's that a life as an artist will involve wonderful, thrilling hills of seemingly divine inspiration, in which you create sound and music beyond what you imagine you are capable of composing. You also learn that you do not bank on inspiration. In between the hills of inspiration, you make sure that you have learned your craft so meticulously that you can manage any deadline with something that may not be quite as brilliant, but will certainly be quality. Inspiration may make iconic composers such as Bach or Beethoven, but craft will keep a theatre composer working during the valleys.

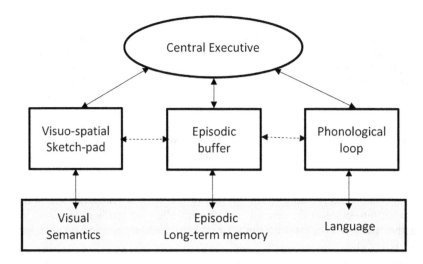

Figure 10.6 Baddeley's Model of the Central Executive has proved both "durable" and "widely used."

Credit: Derived from Baddeley, Alan. 2010. "Working Memory." *Current Biology* R136–R140.

You may have noticed that the length of an earworm is considerably longer than the two-second span that Baddeley and others discovered were able to be held in active memory in their 1975 tests, but about the same length as Cowan's long auditory store. How is it that we can hold so much more than two seconds in our active memories? To accommodate this characteristic, Baddeley modified his model of the working memory to include the ability to load long-term memories into an episodic buffer.

We store and load items to and from our long-term memories into a buffer that allows us to hold more items than in our immediate focus. Cowan proposed a similar solution, that the central executive could load items from long-term memory into the working memory while it needed them (Cowan 2015, 7). The trick here is that if we can organize smaller bits of information into a familiar group, our brain will only count the group as one item. In my classes, I offer up a simple example. I show the class the following for a couple of seconds:

FAT DOG EAT PIG

And ask the class to try to repeat what they just saw. Of course, they have no problem, after all, they only have to remember four words! I then show them the following:

FDEPAOAITGTG

And ask them to repeat that. Even the best have problems remembering more than about 7 (OK, +/–2) letters. Nobody gets all 12. Students are surprised, then, when I reveal that both examples contain the same letters. The test above is an example of a phenomenon called chunking. According to George Miller's 1955 hypothesis about the "Magic Number Seven, (+/–2!)" our working memory can hold a finite number of "chunks" of information at once, not bits: "the span of immediate memory seems to be almost independent of the number of bits per chunk" (Miller 1996, 349). Daniel Levitin defines chunking as "the process of tying together units of information into groups, and remembering the group as a whole rather than the individual pieces" (Levitin 2007, 218). This means that we don't remember all of the details (which takes up less space/time in our short-term memory), just the ones that are important to the chunk and the present situation.

What does all this have to do with sound scores and theatre? According to Michael Thaut, we use the same mechanisms of chunking in music as we use in language. Because of this, the tempos, meters and rhythms of music turn out to be a really good way to group and chunk verbal information. That's how children learn their ABCs, using the letters of the alphabet as the lyrics to a well-known melody. The melody and melodic rhythm of the song organize the letters of the alphabet into more easily remembered chunks, allowing music to facilitate learning that persists even beyond the song, when children use the alphabet in real life[12] (74–75).

The apprehension of such a large structure as plot successfully depends on manipulating and organizing structure to facilitate easy remembering of important elements of the play by the audience. Rhythm makes it easier for us to remember verbal material, and the elements of rhythm do their work entirely within our working memory (Thaut 2005, 6–8). When we use music to score lyrics and dialogue, we make it easier for listeners to chunk elements of the story together, first into smaller units of action. Chunking the individual scenes allows us to put those chunks together into larger units of scenes and acts, enabling us to hold the whole story in our minds as it unfolds. If you don't think we chunk plays together in this way, just ask somebody what the play was about, and watch how they piece the story into manageable chunks—not bits—of story. If you don't think chunking in plays is a musical phenomenon, imagine listening to the entire play unfold in a rhythmically unvarying monotone, and consider how much of that you would be able to remember—even of the part before you fell asleep from endless habituation!

Understanding how to organize the sound score of the play in a way that chunks the story in meaningful ways is perhaps the hardest task I encounter when helping new students learn about sound scores. Students instinctively concern themselves with how the sound cue works in the moment, which is a good and critical first step. Our most immediate chunking goal is to create a sound score that organizes the moment in such a way that the audience comprehends it in chunks rather than isolated bits of information. The sound that orchestrates the moment must work with the rhythm of the scene in order to create salient chunks of story. For example, we might describe the salient chunk in the opening scene of Hamlet as "those guys see Hamlet's father's ghost." In scoring this scene to embed the chunk into long-term memory, then, we must correctly identify where the most important parts of the key elements of the chunk start and end in the scene, and then make decisions about how we want to bracket the chunk with sound. We must identify the most important moments inside the chunk that will cement the gist into our memories. There's a lot to think about in terms of using sound to create a meaningful chunk in the first place.

But because students often have little understanding of dramatic and musical structures, thematic devices and the underlying experience of a play the author has in mind, they leave the individual chunk and treat the next one as if it exists in a wholly different play. Our next goal in creating an effective sound score is to put individual chunks together into a larger, more all-encompassing chunk, which will again make it easier to keep the whole story in one's mind in the present moment of the story. What does the first ghost scene have to do with later scenes in the play? If we can get the audience to effectively encode a story chunk into their memory, when and how do we recall it in subsequent scenes so that the audience codes the old and new chunks into a larger, more all-encompassing chunk? How do we vary the recurring chunk to code the new chunk we are forming?

Consider the later scene in Hamlet when the ghost reappears in Hamlet's mother's chambers and tells Hamlet: "Do not forget: this visitation is but to whet thy almost blunted purpose" (Hamlet, Act III, Scene 3, ll. 126–155). Now we have an opportunity to use music to recall the old chunk about when those "guys saw Hamlet's father's ghost," and that other one about "when the ghost told Hamlet to revenge the ghost's murder." We can then use our sound score to combine the earlier chunks with a new one about "don't forget to revenge the ghost's murder" into a larger chunk we might call "why doesn't Hamlet revenge his father's murder?"—which, coincidentally, is a subject that fills volumes of discussion in library sections of dramatic theory and criticism. But unless students know enough about theatre in the first place to visit this library section, or possesses strong play analysis tools, they might have a hard time understanding where and how to look. This is what we mean by sound being a powerful tool in telling the story. It's not just about finding a good sound effect for the moment.

As critical as chunking is to our ability to tell and comprehend stories in theatre, consider how important it must have been before there was modern theatre, with its scenery, costumes and lights. Consider how important it was before the advent of written language, where, without some extraordinary way to chunk the story into memorable units, the story would be lost to subsequent generations. In the time between the advent of oral language, and the introduction of written language, the chunking ability of music was an important component of what we now call the oral tradition.

It's not hard to imagine a progression then, from the first conceptualization of spirituality, expressed in ritual, propelled by the shaman's rhythm, and experienced through excursions into altered states of consciousness. Eventually these rituals produced stories, and over a long period of time, mythologies of gods who roamed the earth, preserved in the songs handed down from one generation to another through oral traditions. The evolutionary psychologist, Matt Rossano, carries this progression one step further, suggesting that ritual behavior did not just provide one of the roots of theatre, but led to the development and evolution of human working memory in the first place. In Rossano's view, ritual behavior "was a critical selective force in the emergence of modern cognition" (2009, 244). And up to this point, we have found very little to suggest that music was not as central to that ritual experience as human behavior can get. And eventually to theatre.

Long-Term Memory

If we rehearse (repeat) what's in our phonological loop long enough, we put it into long-term memory. On the other hand, a good scare will pretty much pop the event directly in. We'll come back to this later. Long-term memory is our ability to more or less permanently store our memories for a few days, weeks, months, years, or the rest of our lives. In the last section I suggested that the opportunity to create tunes, hooks and earworms that get stuck in the audience's phono- logical loops are few and far between, unless you are writing a musical, or plays that have a lot of songs in them, like Shakespeare. We will much more likely be required to compose sound scores in which we try to create a lasting memory of the dramatic moment rather than a lasting memory of a particular tune or hook.

Marilyn Boltz and others have demonstrated that for scenes involving back- ground music, it is more typical that our audiences cannot recall a given tune if it is played separately from the movie. However, they can recall it when it is played back with the movie attached to it (Boltz, Schulkind and Kantra 1991). It is the underlying mood that seems to become part of the long-term memory rather than the mechanics of a specific tune. Boltz and others' research demonstrated that background music effectively improved the ability of the audience to recollect a scene (1991, 602). We'll discuss why later in this chapter, but we should recognize that this is all a good thing. Why? Our working memories are hopefully focused on the dramatic moment, rather than the music itself. You will often hear sound designers suggest that most of our work goes unnoticed. With background music, when we do our jobs well, the full attention of our audiences focuses on the dra- matic moment. Unfortunately, it does make it easier for the good folks that pass out theatre awards to overlook our work, though.

Creating and Retrieving Long-Term Memories

Even if we are able to hold larger ideas in our minds through the process of chunking, we still must effectively store the chunk in the audience's long-term memories, so that we can trigger recollection later at an appropriate moment of the play. One effective way to create a lasting memory is to incite a strong emo- tional reaction to the moment. Michael Thaut states it plain and simple: "emo- tional context enhances learning and recall" (2005, 76). Baddeley seemed to get to the heart of the matter when he suggested that "processing a word in terms of its perceptual appearance or spoken sound is much less effective for subsequent learning than encoding the material on the basis of its meaning or its emotional tone" (Baddeley 2010, 5). The ideas are important, but if you really want your audience to remember something, escalate the emotion of the moment. And one of the best ways to escalate an emotional reaction is to infuse it with music. Music is all about emotions, and emotions are all about memories.

Thaut goes on to suggest that positive moods help us form and retain memo- ries better, and that musical memories have a powerful ability to trigger non- musical memories attached to the music (2005, 76). Marilyn Boltz and others have demonstrated this very effect in the ability of positive music (inciting feelings of lightheartedness, gaiety, relaxation) to enhance the ability of audience mem- bers to specifically recall scenes underscored by positive music as compared to scenes in which there was no underscoring at all, or even negative music (inciting feelings of anger, apprehension, melancholy) (Boltz, Schulkind and Kantra 1991, 603). However, episodes involving the emotion of fear appear to have a promi- nence all their own, and as LeDoux and others have reported in their studies, fear responses appear to get indelibly etched into our brains—the more traumatic, the more indelibly etched (LeDoux, Romanski and Xagorais 1989, 238). Cue the tense underscore leading up to the startle effect in the horror movie scene.

Our brain's emotional connection to memory is so critical that we have developed an organ in the oldest part of our brain largely devoted to processing emotional memories: our old friend the amygdala (see Figure 2.14). The amygdala sits adjacent to the hippocampus, and Daniel Levitin's research has consistently shown that the amygdala responds to music but not to random collections of sounds or musical tones (Levitin 2007, 167). What's more, remember that the path for music to our amygdala short-circuits the auditory cortex and the more consciously analytical centers of our brain in the neocortex. Our ears connect directly from the thalamus area to the amygdala in the subcortical structures of our brain (LeDoux, Romanski and Xagorais 1989, 238). We don't even get a chance to think about how we react before the music already stimulates our emotional memories! It's no wonder then that music is such a powerful conditioning influence to help etch elements of the story in our brains.

Marilyn Boltz and her team have also demonstrated that there are two important conditions in which we can use music to increase the ability of the audience to recall a scene. The first they call *Congruency Accompanying Music*. Music that incites the same emotional reactions as the ideas of the scene is more likely to increase the ability of the audience to remember the scene; sad music accompanies the death scene, and romantic music accompanies the love scene. Curiously, if the emotional content of the music scoring a scene does not match the emotions of the scene, the audience will still remember the scene better with music, as long as it is positive music scoring a scene with negative emotions (1991, 598). For example, I've done two productions of Shakespeare's *Twelfth Night*, one with my old friend Joel Fink at the Colorado Shakespeare Festival, and the other with my old friend Jim O'Connor at Purdue. In Act IV, Scene 2, Feste visits Malvolio in prison and promises to help him. Feste leaves and sings the song, "I Am Gone Sir." In the Colorado production, I wrote a sad accompaniment congruent to the general scene. However, in the Purdue production, I used the same melody, but contrasted the melancholy of the scene with an almost circus themed orchestration (happy).[13] Boltz and her team refer to this special case as *Ironic Contrast* (1991, 602). Curiously Boltz and others report that reversing this technique, that is, using sad underscore in a happy scene, does nothing to increase our ability to remember the scene. And, to be sure, I cannot remember any instances in my own work using this technique!

Boltz's second condition involves foreshadowing music. We use foreshadowing music at some point before a scene to create an emotional expectation of what is to come. Foreshadowing, it turns out, creates more memorable moments if the music creates an expectation that is not fulfilled by the dramatic moment the audience presumes the music to foreshadow (1991, 601). For example, director Joel Fink set our Chicago production of Shakespeare's *Henry V* in England during World War II, creating a natural resonance for Henry's triumph at Harfleur against the Normandy invasion. We ended with a symphonic orchestra playing the British national anthem ("God Save the Queen"), creating the expectation of a triumphant ending. Just as the theme climaxed, however, we punctuated the moment with the sound of the atomic bomb exploding over Hiroshima, a grim foreshadowing of the horror of war that followed both *Henry V* and World War II, hopefully made more memorable by the triumphant music that set up one of the more incongruent events in human history.

Once we have created a strong memory by attaching a dramatic moment to an emotionally strong musical stimulus, we are then free to chunk it and important elements of the play into a larger more significant experience by inducing the audience to recall it—either unconsciously without the audience bringing the memory to mind, or consciously, in which we attempt to bring a previous dramatic moment back into the working memory of each audience member. These two general types of long-term memories are called *implicit* and *explicit*.[14] Implicit memories are memories you have that you don't even consciously think about when you use them, the classic example being tying your shoelaces. You've done it so many times that you can do it without even thinking about it. Explicit memories are the ones you consciously think about, like remembering where you put your shoes in the first place ("I know I had them on when I came into the house"). Both of these types of memories can be activated simultaneously. Consider playing the piano. We practice scales for hours every day until we form what my piano teacher, Caryl Matthews, used to call muscle memory. That's implicit, we don't even have to think about how to play anymore, it just happens. At the same time, we may have to remember how that tune went either by remembering what was on our cheat sheet, or just by knowing the rules for that kind of tune, and thinking about all the other chord progressions that went like that. That's explicit memory. We'll consider both implicit and explicit memories, one at a time.

Implicit Memory

Morris Muscovitch and others describe three different types of implicit or non-declarative memory: perceptual priming, procedural, and conditioning. Perceptual priming refers to our perceiving something (such as a picture or a face) more quickly if we have been exposed to it (primed) before we see it again and are asked to recall it—even if we don't remember having ever seen it before. Procedural memory involves motor skills such as riding a bicycle that we learn as a result of repeating an activity over and over—even if we have no memory of the learning or repetitions. Conditioning is a type of learning that creates responses to something that is controlled by an unconscious memory, for example if I start feeling anxious around dogs because I was bitten by one as a child (I was, but I'm not). Researchers believe that implicit memories form in the areas of the brain where they are first perceived, for example, in the basal ganglia for motor skills such as playing that piano, or in the posterior neocortex (where we process vision) for visually induced memories such as seeing the picture or face (Moscovitch et al. 2005, 38–39). Larry Squire added the cerebellum and various reflex pathways (e.g., nerve responses in the spinal cord) to Moscovitch's list, as well as our old friend the amygdala, which can "modulate" the strength of just about any memory based on its emotional characteristics (Squire 2004, 173).

Merlin Donald suggested that the ability to voluntarily recall memories, a distinctive ability that separates humans from other animals, first appeared as an evolutionary adaptation in procedural memory. Such an adaptation allowed humans to systematically rehearse and recall memories in a manner that would lead to mimesis, the systematic ability to "initiate a specific pattern of learned action, review it, and then repeat it, or modify it, to improve performance." Early humans were able to consciously observe themselves, and critically review their actions, what Merlin refers to as the "review-rehearsal loop." The evolution of this "review-rehearsal loop" led directly to mimesis, pantomime, and eventually public performances and theatre (2012, 276–278). Donald insists that "mimesis and language were both impossible without voluntary recall from procedural memory" (2012, 282).

It probably doesn't seem like all this could have much to do with creating sound scores, but consider how we condition our audience using music and sound. Of course, we have already talked about how we use preshow music to "get the audience in the mood," or to condition them to enjoy the performance. We often do more—a lot more. Consider the old hero, heroine and villain themes from the old melodramas. The "Mysterioso Pizzicato" has been used so often to condition the audience about the villain being up to no good that it has become a cliché. Daniel Schacter, one of the earliest researchers of implicit memory, cites studies that demonstrate that a subject's attitude toward another person can be unconsciously influenced by exposure to hostile stimuli of which the subject is unaware (1987, 511). And, quite frankly, we do it all the time in scoring by using music to which we do not intend the audience to consciously attend, but nevertheless incite emotions in them that shape their impressions of the character.

We do this so much, however, that, like the villain's theme, character themes have become something of a cliché themselves. I remember having a conversation with my friend Tom Mardikes, an outstanding sound designer who succeeded me as the chair of the USITT Sound Commission in 1998. We were having coffee and I mentioned a student composer I was mentoring and the character themes he had developed for a show. "If I ever hear a character theme again, it will be too soon," Tom commented. I don't think I've used a character theme since.

The intent of the character theme is to influence the audience more or less subconsciously. The reality is that we often hit them over the head with our heavy-handedness, while everyone insists that the effect is subliminal. The problem, of course, is that character themes are often inherently one-dimensional, and the conflicts of our characters are (hopefully) multidimensional. We hope to use underscoring to incite a whole range of moods and emotions, in various combinations at various moments in the journey of the play. We try to attach these to multiple essential ideas related to (typically) the essential journey of the characters in the play. A simplistic strategy of "one size fits all" rarely seems to work.

Now, I tend to be much more selective about how I work to condition the audience toward the play by attaching important ideas of the play to a range and combination of emotions incited by the music. I do this rather than simply create a composite, individual character theme, which tends to oversimplify the complex emotions experienced by an individual character in a play, and the complex ways in which they might interact with the major ideas of the play. Typically, I might start by creating a number of chunks of music that incite a variety of the complex emotions we encounter in the play. I do this early on in the process, after I have chosen my color palette, but before we have spotted the cues in the script if at all possible. Sometimes I'll just write a "suite" of music that seems to generally trace the emotional journey of the play, knowing that I'll be able to later break the piece apart and use individual sections for specific cueing. This gives us a number of pieces that are very much "plug and play" for particular moods and moments. But it also gives us a number of related themes that get us in the ballpark, allowing us to quickly reshape each theme toward the given moment. For me, this approach seems to allow a more organic approach to tracing important ideas that surface in the course of the play.

A similar approach is to create a number of chunks using the color palette one has chosen for the play, and derived from the main motifs we have chosen to wrangle ourselves into a specific style. Composers who must work quick in rehearsals often use this technique so that they can quickly adapt a piece of music to a specific scene right in the middle of a technical rehearsal. When we created the music for the Indianapolis 500 productions, the producers had no idea what would happen down the road. They asked us to just provide them with as many different chunks as possible, from slow and reflective to fast and furious. Then the unimaginable happened. During one of the practice laps, a car crashed in turn one, killing the driver. My collaborator Michael Cunningham had an idea while we were creating chunks to create a slow dirge-like piece based on the ticking sound of a wheel slowly turning. I never imagined it would find a use in the fast-paced action of Indy car racing. The producers wound up using that piece under the footage of the crash in the daily show, *Road to Indy*. To this day, I cannot think of a more haunting moment of sound score composition in which I have been involved.

Inasmuch as we are able to subtly persuade our audience's impression of a character or idea, we should realize that with such a power comes responsibility. An important phenomenon we share with politicians when manipulating audiences is known as the *Illusion of Truth*. For many years, researchers have known that simply being familiar with a statement increases the chances that the audience will label the statement as true. Ian Maynard Begg and his collaborators trace discussion of the phenomenon back to Wittgenstein, who famously remarked that believing statements simply because they were repeated is like buying another copy of a newspaper to see if the first one is right[15] (Begg, Anas and Farinacci 1992, 446).

My friend Carrie Newcomer noticed a rather odd phenomenon as she toured her music through Germany in 2015. There was this strange fascination with folk music—Irish, American, Eastern European, just about any kind of folk music except . . . German folk music. Finally, she asked her hosts why the Germans didn't seem to embrace their own folk music. It turns out that the Nazis co-opted their nationalistic music from traditional German folk songs, reusing those songs to score the agenda of the Nazi party. The Nazi party knew what every religion, government and sports team has always known: the value of repetition in music and lyrics to make the cause at hand feel more true. And, in the right cause, the repetition of a musical theme can be a very powerful thing. I still get a tear in my eye when I sing the national anthem at the football game, remembering my father who sacrificed a great part of his life for our cause. But, as sound designers, we should also be careful, or at least cognizant about using such a power capriciously, adding validity to characters and causes we know to not be true.

Explicit Episodic Memory

We'd like to think that all of our underscoring goes unnoticed, and manipulates the heck out of our audiences, but the plain fact of the matter is that the audience is free to listen to anything they like in the theatre, and will undoubtedly be aware of the music score. Jack Smalley, who teaches film scoring at the University of Southern California and has scored many major movies, television series and cartoons, describes the idea that "the audience should not be aware that there is music" as "nonsense"[16] (Smalley 2005). I have already suggested that starting a sound cue in the middle of dialogue is asking for trouble, as audience attention will be drawn to the change in the auditory environment (the music), and may miss important dialogue. We already know that audience attention shifts in and out of the sound score, and we are hopefully going to work hard to shape the when and where of those shifts. When the sound score or its triggers become conscious, we open additional opportunities to manipulate explicit or declarative memory to enrich the dramatic experience.

Squire suggests that declarative (explicit) memory is the kind of memory we most often think about when we use the term "memory" in everyday language. It's all about the things we can consciously remember, and it comes in two basic flavors, semantic and episodic. Semantic memories are simply the facts we remember about the world, without memory for how, where or when we acquired the facts. For example, I know that a mile is 5,280 feet, but I'll be darned if I can remember the specific moment I learned that helpful tidbit. When we encode episodic memories, we not only memorize the raw facts, but we remember the whole experience, as if we were there again (Squire 2004, 173–174). We re-live the memory, mentally traveling back in time to it.

There are a couple of extraordinary biological differences between *recalling* semantic memories and episodic memories. Both semantic and episodic memories use cortical structures in the left hemisphere of the brain to *encode* memories. However, episodic memory *retrieval* activates the right hemisphere almost exclusively, while semantic memory retrieval activates the left hemisphere almost exclusively. Both types of memory require the hippocampus in the medial temporal lobe to encode the memories. However, once those semantic memories become embedded in our long-term memory, the hippocampus no longer activates when we recall them (Moscovitch et al. 2005, 39–40; Tulving 2002, 17–18). In contrast, activating episodic memories of our past life seems to always require activation of the hippocampus. If our hippocampus gets damaged, we can remember old facts, no problem, but we lose our ability to travel back in time and relive the experience (Moscovitch et al. 2005, 35, 52, 54, 59).

As lovely and important as semantic memory is—in truth it would be so hard to understand a play without it—it's our ability to manipulate consciousness around episodic memory that provides the most intriguing opportunities for this composer and sound designer. In a way, I tend to think about music being more related to episodic (both somewhat right-brained) and idea being more related to semantic (somewhat left-brained) in our equation of song = music + idea. Let's spend a little extra time considering some of the nuances of our episodic memories.

Endel Tulving first introduced the concept of episodic memory in 1972. He points to a couple of important characteristics that we have explored very early in this book. The first is the malleable concept of time that we discovered in Chapter 3 was inherently subjective and unique to each individual. Humans appear to be the only animals capable of perceiving anything other than the present time.[17] Other animal species appear to be unaware that their perception of time is hopelessly biased by their own subjective point of view. But it's Tulving's other major concept we raised earlier that really addresses another consideration of human consciousness: not only are we aware of the past and the future, but we have the ability to mentally travel into them, an ability Tulving describes as *autonoetic consciousness*.[18] Autonoetic consciousness is a special kind of consciousness in which we mentally travel back in time, but retain awareness that our physical selves have not "left the building," so to speak. Tulving called this uniquely human ability "mental time-travel." Tulving combined his conceptions of the subjective perception of time and autonoetic awareness with a third characteristic, the somewhat unique human sense of self, which Tulving called the "traveler," to describe three essential characteristics of episodic memories (2002, 1–3).

Here we have another model of human consciousness that closely resembles our special type of consciousness when we experience theatre. Tulving's model for episodic memory also resembles dreaming as we discussed in Chapter 3, except that in the "daydreams" of episodic memory, we maintain some awareness of our waking world. Tulving's description of episodic memory also bears a close resemblance to the shaman's altered state of consciousness that we described in Chapter 9, except that we relive our own experiences in these memory episodes, not the imagined experiences induced by the shaman's story. Our conscious experience in theatre also resembles both of these experiences, so we should not be surprised to find that episodic memory is closely related to how we experience theatre. Theatre artists create dramatic scenes that the collective audience experiences as if they were time-traveling into them—with varying degrees of autonoetic consciousness. At the same time, theatre artists have an opportunity to incite each member to mentally time-travel into their own unique episodic memories. It is the opportunity to connect the "collective dreaming" of the mise-en-scène with the unique "mental time-travel" of each audience member that gives theatre its extraordinary power.

In our particular case, we want to know how can we use music to enhance the collective dreaming of the entire audience, *and* cue each individual's mental time-travel. One key is using thematic sound, sound that recurs to first incite the audience to collectively experience the drama as if it were happening to them, and then to incite the audience to re-experience those same memories in the course of the story as episodic memories within the realm of the story. We stimulate a cohesive collective experience by inciting the audience to *involuntarily* recall prior dramatic moments in the story, creating what we refer to as *involuntary explicit episodic memories*. When we stimulate mental time-travel in each unique audience member by causing each audience member to re-experience prior events in their own life, and associate that with specific moments in the play, we create what we call *autobiographical memories*. We'll explore both involuntary explicit episodic memories and autobiographical memories in the next two sections.

Involuntary Explicit Episodic Memory

In the section on working memory, we described the process of using our sound scores to chunk individual dramatic moments into a larger outline of the story that makes it easier to hold the whole story in our conscious memory. Chunking the story, then, works in the same way as chunking our memories in real life: it allows us to fully engage in the moment, while bringing to mind only the memories that have the most critical bearing on the moment. As we discussed about the nature of entrainment in Chapter 6, our sound scores work primarily in the realm of experience—they don't use up any of the "seven +/– two" items in our working memory like symbols, signs and indexes do. Any use we make of music in our plays helps to create the time-travel experience. Associating the present moment with our chunked memories of prior dramatic moments not only helps to keep the whole story in our conscious minds, but also uses up the seven +/– two items we can consciously hold in our working memories at once. When our working memory fills up, we are, for all practical purposes, fully immersed in the dramatic story, fully time-traveled into the world of the play.

There may be moments in the script where we consciously ask the audience to retrieve prior memories in the play (Hamlet's ghost: "Do not forget: this visitation is but to whet thy almost blunted purpose"). With the sound score, however, we have an opportunity to plant the cues for recalling prior dramatic moments within the sound score, inciting the audience to involuntarily recall relevant chunks at the appropriate present moment in the play. A memory evoked by specific cues from an individual's past experiences is called an *Involuntary Explicit Episodic Memory*. Involuntary, because we don't use the executive functions of the right prefrontal cortex to make an effort to consciously recall the memory,[19] but we do otherwise use the same areas of our brain as in voluntary episodic memory recall (Hall, Gjedde and Kupers 2007, 262, 267; Berntsen 2012, 296). Explicit, because the memory enters our consciousness; and episodic, because we don't just remember the memory, we mentally "time-travel" back into it.

Dorthe Berntsen reviewed a number of studies of involuntary memories and discovered that they all tend to have four characteristics in common, which we will take the liberty of applying to our immediate dramatic context. First, the current dramatic moment should have "overlapping features" with the dramatic memory we are attempting to recall; in our Hamlet example, there is a ghost involved in every scene. Second, the cue to retrieve the memory is typically externally generated; in our case, we are specifically referring to external music used to score each ghost scene cueing the present memory. Third, the cue is often "peripheral to the ongoing activity"; the nature of underscoring is that it is non-diagetic;[20] that is, it is not a part of the dramatic world. Berntsen notes, however, that cueing could be diagetic but still peripheral; for example, a song playing on a radio while someone is studying. Such a method for cueing memories is also common in scoring. In our *Henry V* example, the entire play was presented under the guise of World War II soldiers listening to a broadcast of *Henry V* over the radio. The radio became diagetic to the soldiers' scenes, but that still allowed us to use the sound score to cue memories of prior scenes as the radio motif repeated itself. Finally, Berntsen notes that cueing these memories is most successful when the audience is not too focused on a particular task. A good example might be the stage manager calling the cues must concentrate very hard on each subsequent task, as one mistake can disrupt the entire show. We are typically not trying to cue the stage manager to retrieve involuntary explicit episodic memories! Rather, the nature of the theatre experience is one that is generally very conducive to what is called mind wandering, when our mind strays from the task at hand. Typically, we have no more complicated objective than simply following the story; this, as I'm often reminded, is NOT rocket science! Quite the opposite, we often encourage mind wandering during theatre, although we do attempt to exercise a significant amount of control over the direction in which the mind wanders. We might try to engage the audience enough that they don't think about the mundane ("I wonder if the baby's alright?"), but we do encourage their minds to wander into recollecting relevant past life experience (I remember that time when I couldn't make up my mind what to do, just like Hamlet). We will return to this last subject in the next section when we discuss autobiographical memories.

According to Berntsen, there are two keys to successfully cueing an involuntary memory: the first is emotion, the second is novelty. We have already discussed the undeniable power that music has to incite strong emotions, and the powerful memories created when we attach dramatic moments to the emotions generated by the music. When we repeat the music cue in a similar dramatic moment, we bring to bear much of the emotional power of the original scoring moment, perhaps even briefly causing the audience to time-travel back to that dramatic moment.

Once we start chunking thematic moments together, however, we are no longer concerned that the audience recall an exact, specific dramatic moment. Instead, we now hope the audience increasingly brings to mind the themes we wrestle with during the play that we attach to the music. In the larger form of theatre, we repeat our musical themes to attempt to get the audience to implicitly develop attitudes and emotions toward characters, situations or ideas, as we discussed in the last section, or to explicitly recall specific ideas, events, characters and so forth. Curiously, we can modify and develop our themes with a surprising amount of variation, and still have the themes exhibit their salient, cueing characteristics. Levitin reports on White's research, which suggests that we can recognize a theme in transposition, fragmented, with altered pitch relationships, changed rhythms and even reversed lines (retrograde melodic motion). Thematic variations allow us to adapt the theme to the emotional requirements of the moment, and yet still use the theme to cue the thematic chunk.

The second key to successfully cue an involuntary memory is novelty; the cue must be unique to both the immediate dramatic moment and to the memory we are attempting to recall. If our brains didn't rely on cues being unique to both the memory and the moment of retrieval, ubiquitous memories would constantly flood our waking life (Berntsen 2012, 297–299)! The likelihood of a cue providing access to one of our memories depends on the extent to which this cue is uniquely associated with the memory. Immediately this suggests that we would not want to use well-known music as a theme that attempts to cue an involuntary episodic memory from earlier in the play. Even if we were successfully able to cue a memory, we would have no control over which memory each audience member retrieved; it might be one from earlier in the play, it might be one from their own past history, or it might trigger nothing at all simply because the cue was not unique. Instead, we must create distinctive themes, conducive to memory, but not drawing focus away from the story. The theme I write to score the ghost scenes should be distinctive, but neither pull focus nor remind us of a theme in another movie.[21]

We should also not overlook the ability to incorporate diagetic sounds to increase the uniqueness of the theme. In the case of Hamlet's ghost, I created a low rhythm pulse underneath the scenes to which I would attach the ghost's footsteps as he walked. This was not a "sound effect" so diagetic that it was meant to convince the audience that the sound was how the ghost's feet sounded when they contacted the stage floor. Instead, it was a pulse that drove the tempo of the scene which we synchronized to the ghost's footsteps by literally pounding on a spring reverb device (remember this was way before digital audio, MIDI and modern technology). This sound was unique then, a sound the audience had presumably never heard before, played in that sort of way, reusable in other scenes in which the ghost did not walk, or even visually appear. I would later use a similar technique for the clock in the 1999 Chicago production of Edgar Allen Poe's "Masque of the Red Death" in Joel Fink's *An Unkindness of Ravens*. In this production, I focused on a more thematic sound for the clock chime that suggested the diagetic chiming, but was uniquely suited to the moment, rather than being a generic clock like one would find in a stock sound effects library. A unique sound that I could later recall in the guise of the masked figure's footsteps at the climactic moment of the play, thus chunking both the clock and the footsteps with the larger chunk of "death," as one audience member would later put it.[22]

A good theme will incite strong emotions in the audience and yet be unique; it will only be associated with the specific dramatic moments we choose in the play. If we do these two things, we stand a good chance of being able to involuntarily cue a memory of a prior dramatic moment or thematic chunk in the working memories of the audience.

Autobiographical Memory

The first thing we want to do in creating the sound score for a play is work to get the audience to "mentally time-travel" into the world of the play. All of the other elements of the play such as the story, the dialogue, the acting and the various designs also work together to transport the audience into this world. One thing we, as sound designers and composers, are really good at is infusing the story with strong emotions in a unique way that not only helps the audience to remember each scene, but to gather the story into manageable chunks that more or less fill up their working memories so that their entire consciousness exists in the world of the play; we help empower that mental time-travel. We attempt to do this with every member of the audience. But there is another important part of this journey that makes experiencing the play even more of a time-traveling experience: getting each member of the audience to infuse their own unique sense of self into the world of the play.

The concepts of episodic and autobiographical memory are so closely related that many researchers seem to use the terms interchangeably. But while all autobiographical memories include episodic memories, an episodic memory is but one part of an autobiographical memory. Robyn Fivush provides an excellent definition of an autobiographical memory in Berntsen and Rubin's book *Understanding Autobiographical Memories*: "Autobiographical memory is best defined as the construction of a coherent narrative woven from the fleeting memories of our past experiences" (2012, 226). In order to weave such a narrative of our life-story, Donald argues that autobiographical memories integrate pretty much all of our long-term memory elements—both episodic and semantic (explicit) and procedural (implicit) (2012, 270).

Fivush further argues that connecting all of our memories of the stories of our lives together into a connected narrative provides us with meaning and an identity. Our "narrative identity" goes beyond who we are individually, providing us with a sense of how we fit into the larger "socially and culturally constructed narratives" of the society in which we live. Donald further argues that it is our autobiographical memories that allow us to create, share and, most importantly, recall such narratives through our depicted stories.

Theatre, of course, is a primary activity in which we as a society engage that helps construct such social and cultural narratives in stories. The trick then, is for us to connect the unique individual narrative of each audience member with the narrative story of the play. It is not enough for each audience member to "time-travel" into the world of the play. We want to make them feel as if they are a character in the play itself. Most often, we want to make them feel as if they are at the center of the story. Theatre uniquely does this by creating a relationship between each audience member and the protagonist, or main character in the story. In typical stories, the relationship we develop between the protagonist and each audience member creates a certain sense of identification, in which each audience member in some ways becomes the protagonist in the journey of their mental time-travel.[23] Each audience member acquires the protagonist's memories as their own, subject to the unique life narrative each audience member has formed over the course of their lives, memories that are shaped by the *life scripts* of each audience member. Life scripts are the cultural templates for prototypical life events such as "when I was in high school" or "before I was married" (Fivush 2012, 237). They are unique to each individual, but because of the journey of the play, also shared with other members of the audience. By definition, then, this is the part of theatre that is unique to each individual yet shared with the entire audience. It is how we connect Tulving's traveler to the protagonist of the play.

Hopefully you can immediately see how the power of music to connect us to the story not intellectually, but viscerally, empowers such mental time-travel and identification. Music connects us to the journey of the protagonist in congruent underscore because the music incites the exact same emotions in us as it does in the protagonist. Remember the mirror neuron we explored in Chapter 5? Marco Iacoboni proposed a link between the "core circuitry for imitation and the limbic system" in his article "Imitation, Empathy, and Mirror Neurons" (2009, 665). Iacoboni's research suggested a "high road" for imitation that could incite "automatic" responses in the receiver, and found a "positive correlation between empathy scores and activity in pre-motor areas activated . . . while listening to action sounds" (2009, 665). Music entrains us to the protagonist and works toward synchronizing our physiological systems to those of the protagonist. When the protagonist gets nervous, we get nervous; when they feel happy, we feel happy; when they jump in fright from a startle effect, we jump. This has always seemed to me like a very powerful way to create such a state of identification in the mental time-travel of the story. In a song, we talk about how others think and feel. In theatre, we become those thoughts and feelings. It's the difference between sympathy and empathy. When we use music to create, store and recall autobiographical memories we tie the life-story of the protagonist to the unique narrative of the life-story of each audience member.

We may choose to do this through brute force, for example by associating a well-known piece of music with an action in the play. We attempt to elicit the unique long-term memories of each audience member by using a piece of music for which the audience shares a certain emotional reaction. Used in the right context, you can bring related, but unique-to-each-individual memories to a dramatic moment. As I mentioned earlier, I used the British national anthem in *Henry V*, just before we set off the atomic bomb, to sort of stir feelings of national pride. But this can be very risky because we don't control exactly which memories each audience member will recall. Some of them may not only be irrelevant to the play, but completely distracting! In my sound design class, I will ask each person to jot down the first thing that comes to their mind when I mention the "William Tell Overture." Some will write down "horse racing." Some will say "cartoons." Older students will write down "The Lone Ranger." And then I confess to them that the first thing that typically comes to my mind is the scene in Stanley Kubrick's *A Clockwork Orange* in which Alex brings home two girls from the record shop. Typically, we'll most often use such a brute-force device when the consequences of a mismatched long-term memory are small, or when the external reference is somewhat universal, for example, in satire.

A much larger aesthetic question for us as playmakers has to do with establishing a balance between the memories created by the elements of our story (theatre) and the individual life-story elements each audience member brings into the theatre (autobiographical memories). Tip the scale in the direction of providing every element to the story, such as in the style known as realism, and you risk giving up the sense of identification between each audience member and the story. You just might let the audience "off the hook," since the story clearly focuses on something that happens to other people, not to the audience. Tip the scale in the other direction, toward relying heavily on what each audience member brings to the story, and you risk their minds wandering so far away from the journey into their own life-story that they no longer share much communally. Neither approach is inherently right or wrong. Every artistic work demands its own balance, and every artist must develop their own unique aesthetic. Developing a balance between providing a common experience for every member of the audience, and providing stimuli that elicits unique reactions from each audience member is a critically important part of every artist's individual aesthetic, but not one we often consciously discuss.

Let's explore this a little further. In his book, *The Roots of Theatre*, Eli Rozik argues that the world of the play does not exist in the medium of theatre, but in the minds of the audience: "I contend that theatre is a specific imagistic medium (i.e., a method of representation or, rather, an instrument of thinking and communication), and as such its roots lie in the spontaneous image-making faculty of the human psyche"[24] (Rozik 2002, xi). The actor, set, costumes and lights are not the world of the play, but just mediate between the world that exists in the mind of the playwright and the minds of each audience member. This presents the production team with important choices about how to use that medium, the most significant of which is how much to mediate, that is, how much information to give the audience through our ideas and mimesis, compared to how much to allow the audience to bring to the drama from their own experience.

At one extreme, we have realism, in which theatre artists take great care to provide almost every single detail to our audience, in the hopes of creating very much the same story in each audience member's mind. I come from the other extreme, radio drama, in which, of necessity, we provide critical clues to each audience member, but because we do not provide defining visual referents, each audience member must create significant parts of their own story. For me, this has always been the most valuable theatre, because the parts of the story that the audience brings will be culled from their unique personality, history, psychology and so forth. By sharing the storytelling with each audience member, we have much greater potential to incite stories in unique and critically important ways. In my aesthetic, the more our audience identifies with the characters' stories because the audience consciously and continuously provide elements of the story from their own lives, the more our collective stories will resonate in their own life-story. Your mileage may—and should—vary, of course; that's what makes every artist unique! Regardless, determining the scope that theatre mediates between the composer's story and the story in the mind of each audience member is an important and critical element for every production team—from playwright to actor to designer—to consider in creating the medium of the physical production.

Music cuts both ways. Its immediacy creates an identification between each audience member and the story, particularly the protagonist's story. At the same time, we can use music to either incite strong emotions to which we attach dramatic moments, and chunk them into powerful working memories that enable the unique time-travel of each audience member, or we can incite the unique memories of each audience member through their association with well-known music. Creating sound scores for theatre is filled with aesthetic choices.

Conclusion: The Origins of Theatre and the Problems of the Oral Tradition

Early on in this book, we started Chapter 2 by noticing how the definition of a word could greatly impact philosophical discussions of a subject. In that case, how we defined the word "sound" had major implications for the answer to the

Memory

Sensory (Echoic)

Short Auditory Store

→

Long Auditory Store

Short Term Memory

The subject's present mind

→

Working Memory

←

→

↑ ↱

Phonological Loop

Sub vocal rehearsal

↰

↵

Long-Term Memory

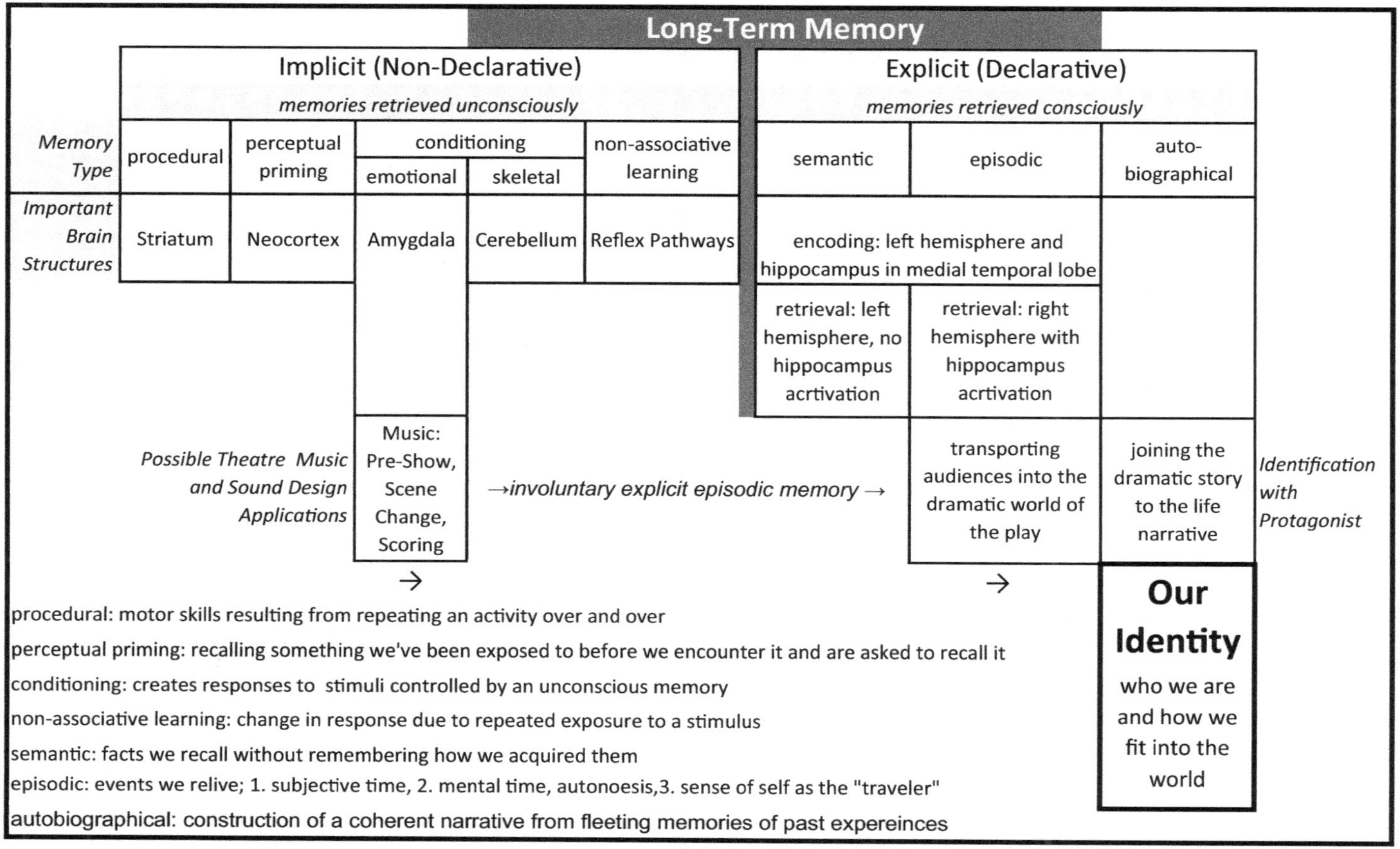

Long-Term Memory

	Implicit (Non-Declarative) *memories retrieved unconsciously*				Explicit (Declarative) *memories retrieved consciously*		
Memory Type	procedural	perceptual priming	conditioning — emotional	conditioning — skeletal / non-associative learning	semantic	episodic	auto-biographical
Important Brain Structures	Striatum	Neocortex	Amygdala	Cerebellum (skeletal) / Reflex Pathways (non-associative learning)	encoding: left hemisphere and hippocampus in medial temporal lobe		
					retrieval: left hemisphere, no hippocampus acrtivation	retrieval: right hemisphere with hippocampus acrtivation	
Possible Theatre Music and Sound Design Applications		Music: Pre-Show, Scene Change, Scoring				transporting audiences into the dramatic world of the play	joining the dramatic story to the life narrative

→ involuntary explicit episodic memory →

Our Identity — who we are and how we fit into the world

Identification with Protagonist

procedural: motor skills resulting from repeating an activity over and over

perceptual priming: recalling something we've been exposed to before we encounter it and are asked to recall it

conditioning: creates responses to stimuli controlled by an unconscious memory

non-associative learning: change in response due to repeated exposure to a stimulus

semantic: facts we recall without remembering how we acquired them

episodic: events we relive; 1. subjective time, 2. mental time, autonoesis,3. sense of self as the "traveler"

autobiographical: construction of a coherent narrative from fleeting memories of past expereinces

Figure 10.7 The taxonomic structure of human memory related to theatre.

Credit: Based on Larry R. Squire's diagram in "Memory Systems of the Brain: A Brief History and Current Perspective." 2004. *Neurobiology of Learning and Memory* 171–177.

age-old question, "If a tree falls in the woods, and there's no one around to hear it, does it make a sound?" If you define sound as something that requires processing by an ear, then the answer is no. However, if you define sound as simply the propagation of a mechanical wave, then the answer is yes. Definitions, it turns out, are important. That's why I have taken such care in proposing the definitions of music and theatre I have proposed in this book. In this conclusion, we'll explore the idea that one can have many definitions of music and theatre, and whole theories, and even more importantly, aesthetics, can be constructed around such definitions. At the end of the day, they may not all be so incompatible after all. Instead, they simply give us different insights into these sometimes not fully tangible concepts, and help us as artists to develop our own unique aesthetic. Curiously, the way our minds work to process memories may provide the insights we need to fully understand the nature of such seeming paradoxes as the many differing theories of music and theatre.

In this chapter, we have detailed the prominent theories about how the brain creates, stores and retrieves memories.

We've investigated the most immediate parts of our memory system, sensory memory, that memory prominently centered in the auditory cortex that processes incoming sound just long enough for us to discern some initial attributes such as pitch or timbre. We've articulated our working memory, the very limited part of both long-term memories and our phonological loop on which we can focus our attention at any given moment. And finally, we've considered our long-term memories, those that consciously come to mind, and those that we never even think about as we go about our daily chores. All of these aspects of memory involve an extremely complex array of elements of the brain, and research continues to provide new insights as to how exactly the human brain works. But are there any overriding theories that tie all of this together?

Of course there are, or I wouldn't have brought it up. In chapter five of his book, *This Is Your Brain on Music*, Daniel Levitin tells the story of how researchers came to their current understanding of how the brain processes memories. We used to think that the brain worked rather like a computer's hard drive, storing bits of data in specific locations until we needed to recall them. Levitin suggests however that there is an emerging consensus among memory researchers for two very similar models, the *exemplar* model and the *multiple trace memory* model. Both theories propose that rather than store each memory in a unique memory location such as would happen on a computer hard drive, every experience we have creates a pattern of neuronal firings in our brain (2007, 164–165). With close to 100 billion neurons, each connected to 10,000 other neurons, you can imagine that there is seemingly an infinite number of traces possible in the human brain.

In exemplar theory, every experience we have creates a unique trace in our brains—a unique pattern of neuronal firings that will forever be associated with that experience. Our brains, however, don't "record" those firings, but when called upon, recreate those firings. Some parts of the traces may be very similar to or even duplicated by other memories, creating "categories" that we use to relate similar experiences. We recognize a song by the Beatles because it triggers traces that more closely resemble traces we associate with the Beatles' songs than other types of music. Context is important to attaching ideas to particular categories. If I say the word, "play," you will need to know the context in order to decide if the category to which I refer is a children's activity or a dramatic work of art (Levitin 2007, 159–164). We've already seen specific parts of the brain, the auditory cortex, that deal with the large categories of hearing such as pitch and timbre, but research has shown that other parts of other big categories such as faces, animals, food and so forth all locate to specific regions of the brain (Levitin 2007, 163).

Presumably any experience we've ever had can be retrieved if we just have the right "cues" to reconstruct it. According to the multiple trace memory models, we should be able to recreate the memory trace if we just get the right cue that helps us set all those neuronal firings to the proper values. Music and theatre create very vivid memory traces, particularly because the emotional content is so strong that it tends to permanently burn those traces into our brain, making them like other strong emotional experiences, easier to retrieve. We might be able to vaguely remember being a sophomore in high school, but put on a song that was popular during that time, and you may be flooded with very detailed memories of your life at that time (Levitin 2007, 165–166).

In this chapter, we've explored some of the many ways we as sound designers and composers work to create specific memory traces that we will ask the audience to retrieve at a later date using cues that we will often provide. We've also explored how, by filling up the limited capacity of the working memory of each audience member, we are able to help them to mentally time-travel into the world of the play. Hopefully, we have tied together the earliest ideas of this book, from the subjectivity of time through all the various nuances that *Homo sapiens* evolved to perceive time as explored in the subsequent chapters of this book. We've arrived at the stunning sophistication that human consciousness is, and have tried to show in our very simple formulas:

Music = Time Manipulated

Song = Music + Idea

Theatre = Song + Mimesis,

both an evolutionary and a biological predisposition for our species to have arrived at theatre as a means of exploring the nature of our universe.

But we have not argued that this is the only way to think about theatre. When I subtitled this book "The Evolutionary Origins of Theatre in Time, Sound, and Music," I made a very conscious choice to not name it "The *Only* Evolutionary Origins of Theatre in Time, Sound, and Music." Levitin suggests that categories are not absolute, but relative to every situation, so when we attempt to trace the origins of theatre to a specific activity such as ritual, we immediately run into issues in that whether theatre evolved from ritual will depend a lot on how we define theatre. Levitin suggests rather than absolute categorizations, we use categories to suggest resemblance; that an activity, for example, ritual, has theatre-like characteristics, and an activity, for example theatre, may also have ritual-like characteristics. In this way, we don't have to worry about whether an activity is "absolutely" theatre; this doesn't help at all—perhaps echoing Schechner's controversial assertion that "origin theories are useless" (1988, 6). What is useful to us is to understand that a particular activity resembles the category we've created by defining theatre a certain way (i.e., it includes a strong mimetic component intended to communicate ideas carried into our hearts by music). What makes it theatre? Mimesis. When a dancer takes on a specific role in a dance, we would say that the dance has taken on theatre-like characteristics, just as we would not shy away from calling a dance in a play a "dance," or a song a "song."

In this book, we have suggested very distinct categories for theatre, starting out with the major category of theatre being a time art, then defining music as any art which organizes and manipulates time. From there we created a subcategory called songs, musics to which we've attached ideas. Finally, we've introduced a final category, theatre, in which songs are presented through mimesis. Along the way, we have attempted to show how these categories emerged as a result of the nature of space and time (astrophysics), the evolution of our ability to perceive space and time (anthropology, archaeology, genetics, etc.), the evolution of the human brain and the inherent ways in which it works (neuroscience, psychology), and my own lifetime of experience in which these common themes have continuously manifested themselves (aesthetics). The convergence of many streams of investigation into these very simple categories that distinguish theatrical types of activities from other artistic pursuits such as music, dance, painting, sculpture and so forth help to create a continuous through-line from the dawn of time to modern theatre, and tend to highlight the nature of our present predicament in which sound and music have often gotten disconnected from their fundamental a priori relationship to theatre. Embracing this categorization, this evolution and lineage will hopefully lead to reinforcing music as an organic component of theatre that opens new possibilities, new theatre experiences that we have yet to imagine.

By creating a categorization scheme such as this, we do not implicitly deny or support other categorization schemes. For example, Eli Rozik's categorization schemes stem largely from the categorization of ideas, in his case as expressed in elements reminiscent of Peirce's semiotic elements of signs, icons, indexes and symbols. Rozik's categorizations don't necessarily exclude mine, they are just of less use for sound designers and composers in theatre who are looking for insights in how music works in theatre. But they are hugely important for others who want to explore other elements of this large and wonderfully vague word, theatre.

Theatre today has capitalized on many schemes of categorization, all to its benefit. When Schechner wrote that "origin theories are irrelevant to understanding theatre," he hit the nail on the head: such theories could inherently limit the extraordinary possibilities of theatre by unnecessarily restricting theatre to certain activities, categorizations that resulted in the rise of styles such as twentieth-century realism. Yet Schechner considered six activities related to theatre: *ritual*, play, games, sports, *dance* and *music*—three of which inherently have music in their genes (1988, 6).

I have been drawn back to exploring the origins of theatre in music precisely because often in modern theatre, music has lost its way, particularly in the electronic tagging on to the play of sound scores that have not been derived from the play's obvious musical heart. In proposing these origins, I simply maintain that in any activity categorized as theatre, you will find music (as we've defined it in Chapter 4). You will also find ideas (as dissected by most dramatic theory and criticism), and mimesis (the first-person experience of music and ideas, as opposed to simply describing ideas in the third person). Such categorization acknowledges and embraces the possibility that we will find elements of theatre in a lot of other activities, for example in songs in which the singer takes on a character in performance, dance in which ideas are attached to the music and mimesis and so forth. We may also find moments in our "theatres" that distinctly do not fit our categories of music, idea and mimesis: parts of plays in which the actors do not engage in mimesis, for example. But stray too far from these three foundational components, and I suspect, you will no longer consider the experience to be theatre.

How do you define theatre? How you define theatre will have a lot to do with your aesthetic: how you perceive the world through your senses. How you define theatre will have a major impact on what sorts of categories you attach to your work, the rules by which you operate. How *do* you define theatre?

Ten Questions, Part I

1. Describe how the human brain differs from that of a chimpanzee. How much "connectivity" does the human brain have, and what does "plasticity" mean in terms of the brain?
2. Why are the temple at Göbekli Tepe and the flutes discovered at Jiahu, China, such important archaeological finds?
3. What is animism, and why is sound a particularly important element in the spiritual lives of Neolithic stone age cultures?
4. What three characteristics of memory must we have developed in order to increase the chances for our species to survive, and how does each serve as a useful characteristic to keep in mind when scoring a play?
5. Describe the process of using memories in sound scores in three steps.
6. Describe four characteristics of echoic memory, the relationship between echoic memory and habituation/startle responses, and briefly explain the significance of this biological process to sound designers and composers.
7. Describe the differences between short auditory store, long auditory store, short-term and working memory.
8. What is the phonological loop, what does it have to do with earworms, and where in the brain do earworms happen?
9. Give us five guidelines for creating effective "hooks" in theatre.
10. Define chunking, and give an example from a play or film soundtrack.

Things to Share, Part I

1. Now that you have a pretty good understanding of the element of line, it's time to explore your ability to use line to stir emotions in your audience. Imagine five melodic themes—great hooks, if you will, one for each of the following emotions: love, anger, fear, joy, sadness. Keep them short, less than about five seconds apiece, tops. Find a piano or keyboard and record these into five separate takes as audio files. We will play your five recordings back for the class, and the class will have to suggest which themes most incited which emotions in them. We'll poll the class to see which tracks they associated with each emotion, and then we'll ask you for the order you intended. We'll then tabulate the percentage of emotions you were able to correctly incite in each audience member, and discuss the results.

Ten Questions, Part II

1. What is one powerful way to get the audience to remember a dramatic moment, what can we as sound designers and composers do to help and

what is the name we typically give to the type of scoring we use to help? How does this compare to using ironic contrast to score a scene?

2. What part of our brain deals with emotional memories, why is it so important to sound designers and composers, and why is it so darn effective in inciting emotions?

3. Think up a new example of a common activity you undertake every day that involves both an implicit and explicit memory. Explain what makes each memory associated with the activity declarative or non-declarative. Decide which of the three types of implicit memory your example suggests, and explain why.

4. Give two examples of how sound designers and composers can use implicit conditioning to influence how the audience feels about the play. What is a very real danger about using music to condition an audience?

5. What are you doing right now that is a great example of semantic memory?

6. Explain how two of Tulving's concepts about episodic memory relate to concepts we explored in Chapter 2. What is the difference between what we discussed in Chapter 3 and autonoetic consciousness?

7. Briefly describe how we use music to incite involuntary explicit episodic memories, and how we use those memories to more fully coax our audiences into collective dreaming.

8. Describe Berntsen's four characteristics that involuntary explicit episodic memories have in common in terms that apply to creating sound scores.

9. What is the difference between an autobiographical memory and an episodic memory, and how does that difference empower the unique mental time-travel of each audience member? What can we as composers and sound designers do to effect this journey?

10. How on earth does the way the current consensus of researchers suggest our brain works help to explain how so many "origin" theories of theatre can exist without contradicting one another?

Things to Share, Part II

1. Find a movie that has won an Academy Award for sound editing or music composition. Pick a movie that you love and wouldn't mind seeing again. Now get hold of the movie (perhaps buy it, because you can use it for other projects in this class, rent it from Netflix, or even check it out from your local library). Watch it with an eye toward how the composer and sound designer use sound to create strong emotional attachments to dramatic moments and then recall those memories in other scenes. Play both the original scene, and the scene in which the musical theme is recalled. Identify the theme for us. Bring at least two examples with you in case someone uses your first example.

2. Having explored the wonderful world of line and melody, now it's time for you to explore these concepts in composition. Compose or design a 1:00–1:30 piece that explores line in all its glory: connecting individual sound objects into straight, curved, spiraling, angular and so forth, lines that weave in and out of one another in a composition. Stick to a relatively small color palette, so that your line will predominate, but, of course, feel free to modulate pitch and all the elements of rhythm, as these are fundamental characteristic elements of line.

As always, play and experiment, but still work to create a cohesive composition.

Notes

1   Remember that for the person traveling at close to the speed of light, time seemed to be passing normally; it's just when our traveler returned to earth, everyone had aged much more rapidly than our traveler.

2   Although we should keep in mind that what really matters here is the ratio of brain size to body size.

3   The region of North America extending roughly from central Mexico through northern Costa Rica.

4   See Chapter 7.

5   Keep in mind that dance is one of the visual manifestations of music. If you look at prehistoric art, one generally accepted clue that figures are dancing is that they will have their arms above their waists.

6   Please don't overlook the significance of the fact that both memory researchers and theatre stage managers use the term "cue" to refer to a signal given that triggers a change in the scene, either mentally or dramatically.

7   For a good overview of the most prominent memory theories and how they relate to each other, see Nelson Cowan's book *Attention and Memory, an Integrated Framework*, especially the introductory chapter, and the diagram on page 22 (Cowan 1997).

8   See Winkler and Cowan (2005) for a detailed explanation of Mismatch Negativity Event Related Potential paradigms, and the included references. Also see Nishihara et al. (2014) for more recent findings.

9   We first met part of the auditory associative area in Chapter 7; it's the large area that surrounds the primary auditory cortex including the secondary auditory cortex, or parabelt.

10 Note that Beaman and Williams question Levitin's claims in their study (Beaman and Williams 2010, 647–648).

11 A compromise that may serve both camps: in a 1995 production of *Dangerous Liaisons* for director Richard Sullivan-Lee, I deconstructed Mozart's *Requiem*, pulling out musical figures that seemed to resonate emotionally. I kept Mozart's color scheme (instruments of his orchestra), but then was able to rework the figures into underscores that were not too busy to pull focus, and also repetitive and simple enough to create tension and increase emotional gravitas. If the style demands that you nod to period, consider this approach.

12 Here's a curious footnote that demonstrates the close connection between chunking and music. Most of my theatre sound designer/composer friends know that I have used a digital audio workstation marketed by the Cambridge, Massachusetts, company Mark of the Unicorn (MOTU) since the dawn of MIDI sequencers. The software, called Digital Performer, varies from other software in the name it gives to audio sequences, curiously calling them "chunks." Digital Performer software found its niche in Hollywood where many well-known composers use it to score movies. As I thought about this, I realized that MOTU's approach to sequencing— one that has kept me using the software all these years—is how "chunks" conform to the concepts discussed in this chapter. I wrote to my old friend at MOTU, Magic Dave Roberts about this:

> Hi Dave . . . I'm writing a book on creating sound scores for theatre, and am exploring the psychological concept of chunking, "a familiar collection of

more elementary units that have been inter-associated and stored in memory repeatedly and act as a coherent, integrated group when retrieved" (Tulving and Craik 2000). In my book I talk about how we use music in scoring to create story chunks that allow us to hold the whole story in our mind at one time as we advance through the plot, etc. I've always thought it interesting that DP used the expression chunks to describe what others call sequences, etc. This got me to thinking, who came up with the name chunk (Johnson 2016)?

Dave responded:

Sometimes programmers are musicians. Programmers are always programmers (and therefore geeks). Your definition is 100% accurate and I'm fairly certain it is the reason Chunks got called Chunks in Performer.

Form follows function, as they say, and you will find many film and theatre composers swear by Digital Performer, as I do, because of its unique ability among DAW's (ed.: digital audio workstations) to allow the composer to manipulate multiple chunks within the same file.

13 For another example, see my discussion of Arthur Kopit's *Indians* in Chapter 8.

14 You may also hear explicit referred to as declarative memory (as in "declared in our conscious mind") and implicit referred to as non-declarative memory (as in "not declared in our conscious mind").

15 Although Begg credits Hasher, Goldstein and Toppino as the first ones to observe the phenomenon in 1977.

16 I strongly recommend his book, *Composing Music for Film*, the most succinct and useful treatise on the subject I have seen.

17 Donald, on the other hand, suggests that there are animals that can encode episodic memories, but are unable to voluntarily recall them (Donald 2012, 270).

18 Tulving also suggests that our ability to mentally time-travel applies to future events. For example, one famous patient, K. C., who had severe amnesia due to lesions in his medial temporal lobe (which includes the hippocampus), could not only not recall past events, but could not imagine future events (2002, 14).

19 Remember that we first met the executive functions of the brain, that part that controls how and where we focus our attention in the section on working memory.

20 Diagetic sound is sound that happens within the world of the play, for example a shepherd in a scene plays a pipe. Non-diagetic sound has no logical origin in the scene—underscore being a good example.

21 Full disclosure: when I composed my *Hamlet* score way back in 1984, the *Star Wars* movies were very popular. Completely separate from this, I wanted to explore the modern Phrygian mode (e.g., a scale starting on the white "E" key, and using each white key going up an octave, so that there's a half step between the first and second degrees of the scale, and a half step between the fifth and sixth degrees of the scale). Twenty years later when I went back to listen to the melody of my ghost theme, I discovered that I had almost perfectly replicated the first phrase of Darth Vader's theme from *Star Wars*! How I nor anyone else noticed this at the time is beyond me! Incidentally, my sound score for *Hamlet* was the first known public exhibition of a sound score, as part of the Scenography Exhibition at the 1984 USITT National Convention in Orlando, Florida, a testimony to how relatively new the discipline of theatre sound score design is as a recognized art form, compared to our central thesis, that the origins of theatre lie in music. It's a great example of the disconnect that occurred in the twentieth century between theatre and music that we discussed in the very first chapter of this book.

22 For a longer discussion of this particular series of cues, see my 2001 article, "The Function of the Soundscape" (Thomas 2001).
23 Video games take this notion one step further, by turning the gamer quite literally into the protagonist of the story.
24 Note that Rozik and I diverge into different paths of inquiry soon after he makes this argument. Rozik's theatre is largely based on text, visual images and semantics. My theatre is largely based on music, altered states of consciousness, and incitement of emotions. I will discuss why it seems like there is room for both aesthetic approaches more in the conclusion of this chapter.

Bibliography

Atkinson, R. C., and R. M. Shiffrin. 1968. "Human Memory: A Proposed System and It's Control Processes." Vol. 2. In *The Psychology of Learning and Motivation: Advances in Research and Theory*, edited by K. W. Spence and J. T. Spence, 89–195. New York: Academic Press.

Azevedo, Frederico A. C., Ludmila R. B. Carvalho, Lea T. Grinberg, José Marcelo Farfel, Renata E. L. Ferretti, Renate E. P. Leite, Wilson Jacob Filho, Robert Lent, and Suzana Herculano-Houzel. 2009. "Equal Numbers of Neuronal and Nonneuronal Cells Make the Human Brain an Isometrically Scaled-Up Primate Brain." *Journal of Comparative Neurology* 513 (5): 532–541.

Baddeley, Alan. 2010. "Working Memory." *Current Biology* 20 (4): R136–R140.

Baddeley, Alan D., Neil Thomson, and Mary Buchanan. 1975. "Word Length and the Structure of Short-Term Memory." *Journal of Verbal Learning and Verbal Behavior* 14 (6): 575–589.

Beaman, C. Philip, and Tim I. Williams. 2010. "Earworms ('Stuck Song Syndrome'): Towards a Natural History of Intrusive Thoughts." *The British Psychological Society* 101 (4): 637–653.

Begg, Ian Maynard, Ann Anas, and Suzanne Farinacci. 1992. "Dissociation of Processes in Belief: Source Recollection, Statement Familiarity, and the Illusion of Truth." *Journal of Experimental Psychology* 121 (4): 446–458.

Berntsen, Dorthe. 2012. "Spontaneous Recollections: Involuntary Autobiographical Memories Are a Basic Mode of Remembering." In *Understanding Autobiographical Memories: Theories and Approaches*, edited by David C. Rubin, 290–310. Cambridge: Cambridge University Press.

Bocquet-Appel, Jean-Pierre. 2011. "When the World's Population Took Off: The Springboard of the Neolithic Demographic Transition." *Science* 333 (6042): 560.

Boltz, Marilyn, Matthew Schulkind, and Suzanne Kantra. 1991. "Effects of Background Music on the Remembering of Filmed Events." *Memory and Cognition* 19 (6): 593–606.

Cowan, Nelson. 1997. *Attention and Memory, an Integrated Framework*. Oxford: Oxford University Press.

———. 2015. "Sensational Memorability: Working Memory for Things We See, Hear, Feel, or Somehow Sense." In *Mechanisms of Sensory Working Memory*, 5–22. New York: Academic Press.

Curry, Andrew. 2008. "The World's First Temple?" *Smithsonian*, November: 54–60.

Dietrich, Oliver, Manfred Heun, Jens Notroff, Klaus Schmidt, and Martin Zarnkow. 2012. "The Role of Cult and Feasting in the Emergence of Neolithic Communities. New Evidence from Göbekli Tepe, South-Eastern Turkey." *Antiquity*, 86 (333): 674–695.

Donald, Merlin. 2012. "Evolutionary Origins of Autobiographical Memory: A Retrieval Hypothesis." In *Understanding Autobiographical Memory: Theories and Approaches*, edited by Dorthe Berntsen and David C. Rubin, 269–289. Cambridge: Cambridge University Press.

Egan, James. 2015. *1000 Historic Quotes*. Raleigh: lulu.com.

Exploratorium. 2016. "Science of Music: Accidental Scientist." Accessed July 27, 2016. www.business.uc.edu/earworms.

Farmer, Henry George. 1957. "The Music of Ancient Egypt." In *New Oxford History of Music: Ancient and Oriental Music*, edited by Egon Wellesz, 255–282. London: Oxford University Press.

Fivush, Robyn. 2012. "Subjective Perspective and Personal Timeline in the Development of Autobiographial Memory." In *Understanding Autobiographical Memory: Theories and Approaches*, edited by Dorthe Berntsen and David C. Rubin, 226–245. Cambridge: Cambridge University Press.

Garfinkel, Yosef. 2003. *Dancing at the Dawn of Agriculture*. Austin: University of Texas Press.

Glassman, Robert. 1999. "Hypothesized Neural Dynamics of Working Memory: Several Chunks Might Be Marked Simultaneously By Harmonic Frequencies Within an Octave Band of Brain Waves." *Brain Research Bulletin* 50 (2): 77–93.

Hall, Nicoline Marie, Albert Gjedde, and Ron Kupers. 2007. "Neural Mechanisms of Voluntary and Involuntary Recall: A PET Study." *Behavioural Brain Research* 186 (2): 261–272.

Iacoboni, Marco. 2009. "Imitation, Empathy, and Mirror Neurons." *Annual Review of Psychology* 60: 653–670.

Johnson, Dave. 2016. Personal Email, July 28.

Kraemer, J. M., Adam E. Green, William M. Kelley, and C. Neil Macrae. 2005. "Sound of Silence Activates Auditory Cortex." 434 (7030): *Nature* 158.

LeDoux, Joseph E., Lizabeth Romanski, and Andrew Xagorais. 1989. "Indelibility of Subcortical Emotional Memories." *Journal of Cognitive Neuroscience* 1 (3): 238–243.

Levitin, Daniel J. 2007. *This Is Your Brain on Music*. New York: Penguin Group/Plume.

Mann, Charles C. 2011. "The Birth of Religion." *National Geographic* June: 34–36, 38–46, 48–49, 53–54, 56–59.

Miller, George A. 1996. "The Magical Number Seven, Plus or Minus Two: Some Limits on Our Capacity for Processing Information." *Psychological Review* 101 (2): 343–352.

Moscovitch, Morris, R. Shayna Rosenbaum, Asaf Gilboa, Donna Rose Addis, Robyn Westmacott, Cheryl Grady, Mary Pat McAndrews, et al. 2005. "Functional Neuroanatomy of Remote Episodic, Semantic and Spatial Memory: A Unified Account Based on Multiple Trace Theory." *Journal of Anatomy* 207 (1): 35–66.

Näätänen, R., P. Paavilainen, H. Tiitinen, D. Jiang, and K. Alho. 1993. "Attention and Mismatch Negativity." *Psychophysiology* 30 (5): 436–450.

Nairne, James S., and Josefa N. S. Pandeirada. 2008. "Adaptive Memory: Remembering With a Stone-Age Brain." *Current Directions in Psychological Science* 17 (4): 239–243.

Nishihara, Makoto, Koji Inui, Tomoyo Morita, Minori Kodaira, Hideki Mochizuki, Naofumi Otsuru, Eishi Motomura, Takahiro Ushida, and Ryusuke Kakigi. 2014. "Echoic Memory: Investigation of Its Temporal Resoulution by Auditory Offset Cortical Responses." *PLOS ONE* 9 (8): 1–9.

Quinn, Daniel. 1992. *Ishmael*. New York: Bantam.

Rossano, Matt. 2009. "Ritual Behavior and the Origins of Modern Cognition." *Cambridge Archaeological Journal* 19 (2): 243–256.

Rozik, Eli. 2002. *The Roots of Theatre*. Iowa City: University of Iowa Press.

Rudner, Mary, Peter Fransson, Martin Ingvar, Lars Nyberg, and Jerker Rönnberg. 2007. "Neural Representation of Binding Lexical Signs and Words in the Episodic Buffer of Working Memory." *Neuropsychologia* 45 (10): 2258–2276.

Schacter, Daniel L. 1987. "Implicit Memory: History and Current Status." *Journal of Experimental Psychology: Learning, Memory, and Cognition* 13 (3): 501–518.

Schechner, Richard. 1988. *Performance Theory*. Revised and expanded edition. New York: Routledge.

Schneider, Marius. 1957. "Primitive Music." In *New Oxford History of Music: Ancient and Oriental Music*, edited by Egon Wellesz, 1–82. London: Oxford University Press.

Smalley, Jack. 2005. *Composing Music for Film*. Third. JPS.

Smithsonian Museum of Natural History. 2016. "Human Characteristics: Brains." July 22. Accessed July 22, 2016. http://humanorigins.si.edu/human-characteristics/brains.

Sperling, George. 1960. "The Information Available in Brief Visual Presentations." *Psychological Monographs: General and Applied* 74 (11): 1–29.

Squire, Larry R. 2004. "Memory Systems of the Brain: A Brief History and Current Perspective." *Neurobiology of Learning and Memory* 82 (3): 171–177.

Thaut, Michael H. 2005. *Rhythm, Music, and the Brain*. New York: Routledge Taylor & Francis Group.

Thomas, Richard K. 2001. "The Function of the Soundscape." *Theatre Design and Technology Journal*, Winter: 18–29.

———. 2008. *The Designs of Abe Jacob*. Syracuse: USITT/Broadway Press.

Tiitinen, H., P. May, K. Reinikainen, and R. Näätänen. 1994. "Attentive Novelty Detection in Humans is Governed by Pre-attentive Sensory Memory." *Nature* 372 (6501): 90–91.

Tulving, Endel. 1972. "Episodic and Semantic Memory." In *Organization of Memory*, edited by Endel Tulving and W. Donaldson, 381–403. New York: Academic Press.

———. 2002. "Episodic Memory: From Mind to Brain." *Annual Review of Psychology* 53: 1–25.

Tulving, Endel, and Fergus I. M. Craik. 2000. *The Oxford Handbook of Memory*. London: Oxford University Press.

Winkler, István, and Nelson Cowan. 2005. "From Sensory to Long-Term Memory Evidence from Auditory Memory Reactivation Studies." *Experimental Psychology* 52: (1): 3–20.

Zhang, Juzhong, Garman Harbottle, Changsui Wang, and Zhaochen Kong. 1999. "Oldest Playable Musical Instruments Found at Jiahu Early Neolithic Site in China." 401 (6751): 366–368.

CHAPTER 11

THE BRONZE AGE AND THE INVENTION OF WRITING

Introduction: Theatre Becomes Drama

In 1985, I received a phone call from director Robert Cohen (author of the best-selling text, *Acting One*, among many others), asking me if I would like to compose a sound score for his production of *King Lear* at the Colorado Shakespeare Festival the following summer. Even in 1985 Robert had established a name for himself, so when one of the more prominent directors and authors in the American Theatre called, I gladly accepted, knowing that it was an invitation I did not want to screw up. I did what I often did with directors: I asked him what sorts of things he was reading to prepare for directing the play. Robert turned me on to a book, Marvin Rosenberg's *The Masks of King Lear*, one of a series of books Rosenberg wrote that traced the production history of Shakespeare's plays. *The Masks of King Lear* provided an extraordinary production history of *King Lear* from Shakespeare's original staging to modern times. Intricately woven into this history were detailed descriptions of all the diverse ways that Lear had been played over the centuries, from Edwin Booth to John Gielgud, and many more. It had never occurred to me before that in Shakespeare's play there could be *many* Lears.

I had always assumed that actors who took on the role sought to uncover *Shakespeare's* Lear. I was never so naïve as to think that there was only one way to play the extraordinary complexity of a character like Lear, but nevertheless labored under the belief that an actor sought to bring to life the character that Shakespeare first created. The book clued me in to something completely different: the seemingly endless possibilities the text suggested. But why? Why did the written text, passed down through many generations, fail so miserably in telling subsequent actors precisely how the role was to be played? One inevitable conclusion to which I arrived, was that the text failed to communicate the *music* of the character. Somehow, in the storing and recalling of the performance, the musical performance of the actors had gotten lost. But without printed music carrying the written ideas of the character's journey, the script left open a wide range of interpretations of the character of Lear. For the first time, it became clear to me how critical my score would be in bringing to life the emotional journey of the characters in the play.

I think most everyone would agree that the loss of this music in the printed word turned out to be a tremendous advantage for theatre. It freed every theatre company, every production team, every actor to create their own music to bring new life to the ideas in the script, each appropriate to the era. Such freedom to create that music allows the play to resonate in the present moment, allows us not just to consider the ideas of the play, but to live in the story and to emotionally experience the journey of the play in the present. Imagine if the only production of *King Lear* we could ever consider doing was the performance by the King's Men at Whitehall Palace on December 26, 1606 (Shakespeare Quartos Archive n.d.)! Film provides a clear record of the music of every production. In doing so, it tends to remove the ambiguity that allows the endless interpretations of the script that theatre allows. The ambiguity of the music in written play scripts allows endlessly new interpretations, such as the paper project of *King Lear* I developed with a group of students for the 2003 Scenofest at the Prague Quadrennial. In this production, *King Lear* was portrayed by a very troubled "Uncle Sam" wandering among the ruins of the World Trade Center in the years immediately following 9/11 (Thomas et al. 2002–2003).

Finding new music to carry ancient ideas keeps plays endlessly relevant for modern audiences. And yet, for all the advantages and advancements of civilization made possible by the advent of written language, we must stop and consider that something got lost along the way when idea first became separated from music in theatre, when theatre became *drama*, the written record of theatre. Anyone who has ever written an email that got misinterpreted because the reader imagined a music distinctly different from the music the author intended surely understands the potentially devastating consequences of such a separation. In many media, perhaps starting with opera, but certainly continuing through film, video, and even modern audio/video messaging applications such as FaceTime, music has been fundamentally reconnected with idea, leaving much less doubt about the author's intentions. Plays and scripts provide much

Figure 11.1 King Lear @ Ground Zero at the 2003 Prague Quadrennial.

Credit: Directed by Richard K. Thomas. Project members included Matthew Gowin, Kristy Lee McManus, Timothy J. Rogers, Justin Seward, Stephanie Shaw, David Swenson, and Jesse Dreikosen.

less specific indications. We must create the experience anew with each production, and my fundamental thesis in this book continues to be that we want to create in an environment in which music and idea come together in mimesis organically rather than one reacting to the other retroactively. Such an organic process occurs quite naturally for the actors, but not necessarily for the composer or sound designer. It is a process that is not always practical, but almost always highly desirable, and that's why many composers and sound designers have taken to sitting in rehearsals from the first reading through the opening. Fortunately, the tools we use to create sound scores have also advanced significantly to allow this to happen.

With that in mind, this chapter will explore how music and idea first became separated in the period immediately following the Neolithic or new stone age, a period that witnessed the tremendous explosion of invention and advancement in social order called the *Bronze Age*. The Bronze Age lasted very roughly from about 3000 BCE to 1000 BCE. The exact dates vary depending on the part of the world in which progress took place. We'll explore the development of musical instruments during this period, and their close connection to spirituality throughout the world. Then we'll consider the advent of writing itself. We'll explore how music finally separated from idea in our recorded history, even though both remained indivisible in the performance art of this age and the ages that would follow and led to the development of the first fully autonomous theatres.

The Bronze Age

Humans developed the ability to work with metals starting somewhere in the fourth to fifth millennium BCE. One of the first metals most humans made malleable was bronze, so the period is referred to as the Bronze Age. Actually, the first metal most humans made malleable was copper, about 7000 BCE in sites such as the Vinča culture site in eastern Serbia (Radivojević et al. 2010, 2775).

Later discoveries found that adding tin to copper produced a harder and more durable metal, bronze, and this became the predominant metal making technique for millennia. That's why the period is called the Bronze Age.

The early temples and villages of the Neolithic turned into cities, and the first four great civilizations arose during this period, all based around rivers.

Mesopotamia, which literally means "the land between rivers" arose in the land we now refer to as Syria and Iraq. Relatively nearby and closely connected was Egypt, a great civilization that arose around the Nile River. These two civilizations created the world's first "trans-regional civilization" that spanned from Anatolia (modern Turkey) in the northwest, to Central Asia (Turkmenistan and Afghanistan) in the northeast, to Arabia (Saudi Arabia) in the southeast, to the Sudan in Africa in the southwest (Wright 1989, 47). The third great civilization arose along the alluvial[1] plain of the Indus River and its tributaries in India and Pakistan. It stretched from Kashmir in the north to the Himalayas in the east, to Afghanistan to the west and the Indian Ocean to the south (Wright 1989, 96). The fourth great civilization arose along the Yellow River and its tributaries in China, where the first great Chinese dynasty, the Shang, arose, although some argue for an earlier dynasty, the Xia, based around a different ethnic group[2] (Liu and Xu 2007, 886).

It certainly can be argued that neither the ability to make bronze, nor the development of the first great civilizations, could have taken place without the aid of sophisticated means of communication. Human ability to manipulate language exploded during this period.

Figure 11.2 Map of Vinča culture in parts of Serbia, Croatia, Bosnia, and Romania.

Credit: Best-Backgrounds/Shutterstock.com. Adapted by Richard K. Thomas. Data from Vitezovic, S. 2017. "Antler Exploitation and Management in the Vinča Culture: An Overview of Evidence from Serbia." *Quaternary International*. Accessed July 21, 2017. http://dx.doi. org/10.1016/j.quaint.2016.12.048.

Thousands of Years Ago	Important Characteristics
1.9	Erlitou site along Yellow River in China
3.4	Papyrus texts preserved in sites along the Nile (Egypt) and Mesopotamia
5–2	The Bronze Age begins in various parts of the world
5	Near East (Egypt, Mesopotamia) settlements
7	Villages in valleys of the Indus River in India
7	Malleable use of copper in Eastern Serbia

Figure 11.3 Bronze Age timeline.

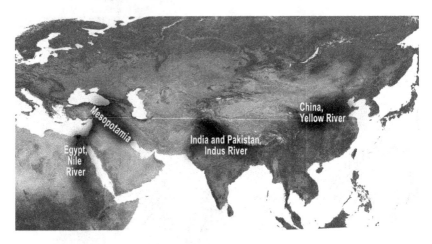

Figure 11.4 Map of the first four great civilizations of the world.

Credit: Best-Backgrounds/Shutterstock.com. Adapted by Richard K. Thomas.

Figure 11.5 Peter Bruegel's sixteenth-century depiction of the Tower of Babel.

Curiously, these languages all formed during the period of the biblical story of the tower of Babel, described in Genesis chapter 11.

Mallory and Adams argue that there were three specific biblical accounts widely accepted throughout history that governed the origin of language (2006, 4). The first was a single language—Hebrew—spoken by Adam and Eve, from which all other languages would derive. The second biblical account, found in

Genesis chapters 6–10, produces three languages spoken by the offspring of Noah's sons after the flood. The first included the descendants of Shem, mainly Arabic and Jewish people who spoke the Semitic language. The second were the descendants of Ham, the Hamites, who populated northern Africa, including the Egyptians. Finally, there was the offspring of Japheth, Gentiles who would eventually populate Europe. The final biblical linguistic event that describes the spread of languages around the world is the story of Babel. Babel is another name for Babylon, the civilization that arose in Mesopotamia around the twenty-fourth century BCE (Joshua 2011). The group that settled in Mesopotamia decided to build a tower to the heavens. The Lord came down from the heavens and said "not so fast," and "confounded" their language into many other languages while scattering them across the face of the earth.

The story of Babel is reflected in evidence that one common language, called the Proto-Indo-European, or PIE language suddenly (or at least suddenly as evolution goes) split into several hundred languages (Donald 1993, 158). Mallory and Adams describe the PIE language as "the world's largest language family" (2006, xxii), one that produced the languages that are today widely spoken in the Americas, Europe, and western and southern Asia (Violatti 2014). Of course, none of the archaeological evidence points to the single Indo-European language originating in Babylon. The particular Semitic branch of languages spoken in Mesopotamia and Babylon has largely died away (Encyclopaedia Britannica 2011). Two prominent theories place the origins of the PIE language either in Anatolia (Turkey) about 7000 BCE, or in the more temperate climates of the Ukraine and southern Russia around 4000 BCE (2006, 460–461).

The PIE languages are, of course, not the only languages that spread quickly around the world. Many "proto-languages" developed nearly simultaneously during the Bronze Age. The rapid development of language most certainly

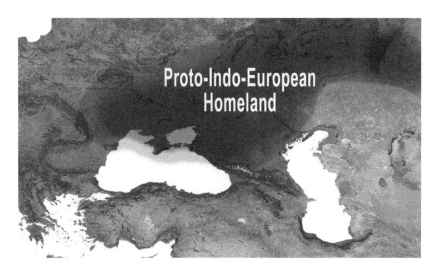

Figure 11.6 One proposed PIE migration, the Kurgan hypothesis.

Credit: Best-Backgrounds/Shutterstock.com. Adapted by Richard K. Thomas. Map based on data from Anthony, David W. 2007. *The Horse, the Wheel, and Language: How Bronze-Age Riders from the Eurasian Steppes Shaped the Modern World*. Princeton, NJ: Princeton University Press, 87.

significantly impacted the equally rapid spread of civilization around the globe. I mention the PIE family of languages specifically because it will be of interest in the next chapter.

By the third and second millennium BCE, musical instruments had also developed tremendously from the rattles, bone flutes, and primitive drums of earlier periods. Musicologist Curt Sachs identified two classes of musical instruments found in Paleolithic excavations and geographically scattered all over the world: idiophones (percussion instruments without a membrane) and aerophones (wind instruments).

The Neolithic period brought two additional classes of instruments, membranophones (percussion instruments with membranes) and chordophones (stringed instruments such as the lyre) (Sachs 1940, 63).

By the Bronze Age, a wealth and wide variety of instruments in these four categories all appear almost simultaneously (again, at least by evolutionary standards) in archaeological sites in all four civilizations. For the first time, the historical evidence is abundant.

All of these civilizations demonstrated a belief that there was a special relationship between music and belief systems. Religions developed from the Neolithic animism we discussed in Chapter 10, in which mimesis of sound conjured the presence of the imitated animal or object's spirit. According to Henry George

Figure 11.7 Nefertari, Queen of Egypt, holding a sistrum. A sistrum is a tambourine-like idiophone.

Credit: Image by Laban66 from the Abu Simbel Small Temple in Egypt.

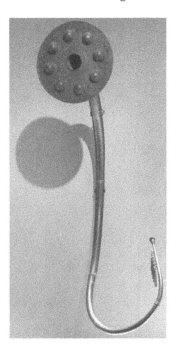

Figure 11.8 Danish Bronze Age lur (aerophone) from the thirteenth to fifth century BCE.

Credit: Photo by Anagoria. Accessed July 21, 2017. https://commons.wikimedia.org/wiki/File:-1300_Lure_Brudevaelte_anagoria.JPG. CC-BY-3.0. https://creativecommons.org/licenses/by/3.0/deed.en. Adapted by Richard K. Thomas.

Farmer, the presence of many gods was thought to be brought about through the mimesis of their sounds, and then later through music more abstractly. Such a belief is one example of totemism. Generally, totemism occurs all over the world, and involves a special relationship humans have developed with a spirit-being through, for example, an animal, an object or a plant (Haekel 2009). In our case, the sacred object or symbol manifested by a spirit would be the sound or music itself. In the urbanization of civilization, musical instruments diverged into popular instruments and professional instruments. The professional instruments largely followed the development of distinct classes, devoted especially to the practice of magic, religion and social purposes (Sachs 1940, 67).

In Mesopotamia, the oldest of the four civilizations, the god Ea had his name written with a sign that stood for drum. The dreaded sound of the drum signified his presence. Ramman commanded the thunder and the winds, and the reed pipe was his breath. The Egyptians built the elaborate temple services of Mesopotamia upon sounds and music such as these, the anima in all things (Farmer 1955, 231).

Gods ruled the world in Egypt before there were kings. The Egyptian god Osiris, taught the world the arts of civilization using discourse and music. His instrument was the sistrum (see Figure 11.7), an instrument specially dedicated to the goddess of music and dance, Hathor. Farmer describes clappers depicted in Egyptian pottery of the fourth millennium BCE being used to conjure the god of harvest, Min.

Farmer also describes two influences Egyptians believed music had over humans: one, purely physical sensation, and the other, a special power, called *heka*

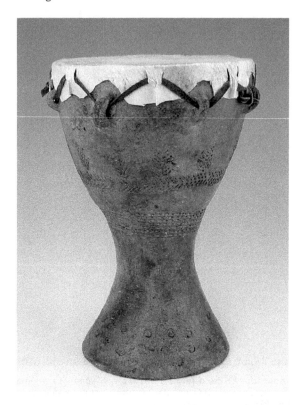

Figure 11.9 Upper Neolithic German clay drum from the fourth century BCE.

Credit: Museum für Vor- und Frühgeschichte, Staatliche Museen Berlin, Photo Claudia Plamp.

or *hike*, similar to "what we understand by 'spell.'" Farmer goes on to suggest that "it may be difficult to appreciate this hyperbole, and yet we still say 'enchanting' and 'charming' in our praise of music today without ever thinking that we are speaking in precisely the same way as did the ancient Egyptians, although they meant what they said" (Farmer 1957, 256–258). And yet, for everything we have explored throughout this book, we must note that, truth be told, we pretty much mean what we say: music certainly has the power to lead us into altered states of consciousness; it can literally be spellbinding. Theatre as a specific manifestation of music, has a similar power.

Ancient Chinese believed that sound and music possessed a "transcendent" power, way beyond the sound itself. According to Laurence Picken,

> The music of the seven-stringed zither tends constantly towards imagined sounds: a vibrato is prolonged long after all audible sound has ceased; the unplucked string, set in motion by a suddenly arrested glissando, produces a sound scarcely audible even to the performer. In the hands of performers of an older generation the instrument tends to be used to suggest, rather than to produce sounds.

Figure 11.10 Silver lyre from the Great Death Pit in Ur in Southern Iraq.

Credit: From *Ur Excavations, Volume II: The Royal Cemetery*. S.L. Wooley. Published for the Trustees of the Two Museums by the Aid of a Grant from the Carnegie Corporation of New York, 1934, 237.

Picken goes on to suggest the relationship between music and spirituality in ancient Chinese civilizations:

> The belief in the power of music to sustain (or if improperly used to destroy) Universal Harmony was but an extension of the belief in the magic power of sounds. As a manifestation of a state of the soul, a single sound had the power of influencing other souls for good or ill. By extension, it could influence objects and all the phenomena of Nature.

These influences eventually found their way into Taoist and Buddhist traditions, and Picken suggests that "to a considerable extent this view of the nature of music survives even to this day" (Picken 1955, 86–88).

Arnold Bake maintains that the development of a music system in India bears a strong resemblance to that of ancient Greece, and developed about the same time. The music system that developed in India was strongly tied to Indian culture, philosophy and religion. Even today Indian music students do not separate music from philosophy, religion and cosmology. Such music, when properly practiced, can even break the cycle between birth, death and rebirth. The belief that music can influence destiny goes back to the oldest surviving form of Indian music, the

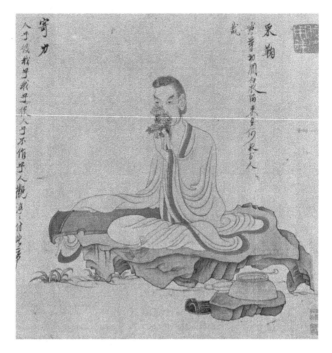

Figure 11.11 Seventeenth-century painting of fourth-century poet playing a qin, an ancient type of seven-stringed instrument.

Credit: Painting by Chen Hongshou.

music of the Vedas, centered around Vedic offerings and sacrificial rites. Such rites were considered to be of no value without not just the proper recitations, but also with the proper intonations.

The preceding sound is but one part of Indian cosmology, struck or manifested sound, or (áhatanáda). Struck and heard sounds cannot exist without their ideal counterparts, however. According to Bake, unstruck or unmanifested sound (anáhatanáda) "is identified with the creative principle of the universe in its transcendental form of the Hindu god, Shiva himself, as well as in its inherent form, the syllable OM, which is said to reside in the heart." Such unmanifested sound exists not for enjoyment, but for liberation, to break the cycle of existence, "merging of the individual self with the creative principle of the Universe" (Bake 1955, 195–198).

We see in the emergence of all of these earliest civilizations a fundamental and essential relationship between music and spirituality. This relationship transcends simple analogy. It suggests belief systems carefully attuned to the powerful effects that music had on individuals and the conscious states of listeners. It suggests a recognition of the ability of music to fundamentally alter human brain waves, and, in doing this, human consciousness. Whether this effect manifested itself in the animism of the Mesopotamian gods of thunder and wind, the spells of the Egyptian power of heka, the imagined sounds of the seven-string zither, or the unmanifested sound identified with the Hindu god Shiva, the close connection between cosmology, spirituality and sound and music provides diverse support that even our earliest civilizations understood: the tremendous power that music has over humans.

The ability of music to directly stimulate the mind, without conscious attention on the part of the listener, was a powerful component of proto-theatre activities. In the development of all cultures we see a relationship between music, ritual and spirituality that transcends simple analogy. This relationship stimulates fundamental states of perception and consciousness that are not part of our normal human perception (reality, for lack of a better word). Humans continued to access these states through the music of ritual in the great early civilizations. Altered states of consciousness may have first manifested themselves in the dreams of primitive animals, and were then subsequently consciously created by shamans in ancient rituals. But they continued to find manifestations in the relationship between music and the spiritual world of these earliest known civilizations. The ability of music to directly stimulate the human mind, to alter its fundamental electrical patterns, all without human conscious participation, continued to profoundly influence and empower the proto-theatre type activities of humans in the cosmologies and ritual of the earliest great civilizations.

The Emergence of Written Language

For thousands of years, then, the relationship between music and language was inextricably bound together, whether through the group singing of our ape ancestors, or the dance and songs of the shaman's ritual. This bond never undid itself as the oral tradition unfolded. However, those first drawings on cave walls and rock formations portended an extraordinary development in human cognition. They would pave the way for unparalleled advancements in our human ability to communicate. At the same time, such a development would require the pragmatic separation of music and idea necessary to achieve the most efficient communication.

The development of written language started with cave and rock drawings, and eventually those made on human-built structures. Eventually humans simplified the drawings into iconic images; that is, more generic versions that generally resembled the objects they represented, such as "man" or "woman." Before long, early communication connected icons together with symbols; visual objects that no longer resembled their counterparts in the real world, but instead, stood for something else. Archaeologists have discovered such symbols in the same Neolithic sites at Jiahu, China, in which archaeologists discovered the bone flutes we explored in the last chapter, but from a later period, between 7000 and 5700 BCE (Li et al. 2003) Other archaeologists discovered tablets containing symbols in a Neolithic settlement in Dipilio Kastoria in Northern Greece, dating back to 5260 BCE (Facorellis, Cofronidou and Hourmouziadis 2014). In still another Neolithic settlement, archaeologists discovered symbols in the Great Danube Basin in Romania, originating 6000 to 5000 years BCE (Merlini and Lazarovici 2008). It appears that the development of written symbols was a natural process that occurred independently in the early civilizations of Mesopotamia, Egypt, China and later in the Mayan culture of Mesoamerica. When a trait develops independently, it is a good sign that evolution has played a role, similar to those we found in the independent development of music.

Developing symbols such as those used in these early Neolithic settlements does not constitute communication in written language however. In the book *Visible Language, Inventions of Writing in the Ancient Middle East and Beyond*, editor Christopher Woods defines writing as

> a system of more or less permanent marks used to represent an utterance in such a way that it can be recovered more or less

> exactly without the intervention of the utterer. . . . One must be
> able to recover the spoken word, unambiguously, from a system of
> visible marks in order for those makers to be considered writing.
>
> (2015b, 18)

A more complex writing system is thought to have been created by the Sumerians of Mesopotamia around 3500 BCE (Sumer is the first urban civilization in southern Mesopotamia, today southern Iraq). Yes, these are the same Mesopotamians the Bible would later accuse of attempting to build the infamous tower of Babel. They used reeds to inscribe marks on wet clay in a system we refer to as cuneiform that used numerals, icons (the written form are called pictographs) and symbols (ideographs).

Archaeologists uncovered the earliest from of cuneiform, which date back to about 3200 BCE, at the temple in the precinct Eana in the sacred city of Uruk. Christopher Woods considers these earliest writings to be more administrative in nature, suggesting that the invention of writing was in response to practical, administrative needs (2015a, 33–35). These early writing systems were not invented to record speech. Jerold Cooper points out that "Livestock or ration accounts, land management records, lexical texts, labels identifying funerary offerings, offering lists, divination records, and commemorative stelae have no oral counterparts" (2004, 83). Hardly something worth singing about, unless performing from the phone book is your idea of a great time. To become fully formed writing, visible language would have to do a much better job of imitating its oral counterpart, speech. That would take hundreds more years.

Figure 11.12 Ancient Sumerian stone carving with cuneiform scripting.

Credit: Fedor Selivanov/Shutterstock.com.

The Transition from Oral Tradition to Recorded History

Over 500 years would pass before writing advanced to the point where it was capable of recording written speech (Woods 2015b, 20). Woods rightly describes writing as "one of humanity's greatest intellectual and cultural achievements. . . (it) enhances capacity, enabling recording of information well beyond the capabilities of human memory" (2015b, 15). The advent of written language allowed our ancestors to record and pass down their stories from generation to generation in a way that the oral tradition clearly did not.

It is a curious coincidence that the transition from an oral tradition to a written tradition coincided with the end of a time when gods roamed the earth, interacting freely with humans. Written language is not as conducive to developing mythology as is the oral tradition. The oral tradition is subject to many flaws, distortions, and reconstitutions, all of which better allow myths to be created out of the very real retelling of feats and accomplishments of normal human beings. The Greek mythographer, Euhemerus (around 300 BCE), was one of the first to assert that the ancient gods who roamed the earth were originally heroic men, greatly revered after their death. This interpretation of the emergence of gods is therefore known as Euhemerism, and we should note that not all researchers of the emergence of gods in all religions ascribe to this theory (Encyclopedia Britannica 2016).

It's not so hard to imagine how these myths would have been formed in the oral telling and retelling of stories passed down from generation to generation. However, experiments at Northwestern University reveal that the way our human brains process memories may help explain how the expansion of stories into mythologies helped our ancestors make sense of the world around them. As we explored at the end of Chapter 10, memories are not simply data stored in the hard drives we call our brains. Instead the brain works to retrieve memories by recreating the original traces, the unique collections of neurons connecting with each other, that formed the original sensory perception. Every time we retrieve a memory, we must retrieve it all over again. We don't typically get each reconstruction right. According to researcher Donna Bridge, a memory

> can be an image that is somewhat distorted because of the prior times you remembered it. . . . Your memory of an event can grow less precise even to the point of being totally false with each retrieval. . . . Memories aren't static. If you remember something in the context of a new environment and time, or if you are even in a different mood, your memories might integrate the new information.
>
> (Paul 2012)

And so, memory itself is like the old telephone game, in which a story is repeated from one person to another, and the story at the end of the chain is shown to have varied significantly from the one originally told.

Now imagine how our ancestors passed these stories down from one generation to another with only human memory providing "storage" along the way. Not only would the story morph as it passed from one person to another, but also from generation to generation. Eventually, the exact specifics would prove to be less important than the lessons to be learned, the big picture that made preservation of the story so important in the first place. Exceptional human beings became gods, and their exploits ritualized into stories that were crafted in such a way as to be easier to preserve.

Of course, the groups interested in passing their stories down from generation to generation had a huge interest in having them passed down correctly. But without writing, their options were limited. One such option that could help structure more precise recall was music. As we saw in Chapter 10, music turns out to be a pretty good aid in helping to organize memories for easier retrieval. Rhythm, tempo and meter, as we have seen in prior chapters, are particularly good tools to help organize ideas so that the traces can be correctly retrieved later. It's no wonder that music played so prominent a role in the passing of important stories from one generation to the next, and in the transition from ritual to autonomous theatre.

Nevertheless, in the later stages of the Bronze Age, written language would take on a significance absolutely necessary to the preservation of factual data. It ushered in the dawn of history, separating later times from *pre*historic times. It allows us to know so much more about our ancestors, and to help reconstruct the past with much greater certainty that our reconstructions are correct. But it's not very good at recording the music to which the ideas were originally attached. Somewhere along the way, the charioteer may have lost the chariot.

Conclusion: Lost in Translation?

In this chapter, we've considered the explosive growth of knowledge that accompanied the first four great civilizations of the Bronze Age. We considered how the spirituality of the Neolithic period manifested itself in the music of the gods of the Bronze Age, and we witnessed the near simultaneous development of the ability to more precisely record events in time afforded by the invention of writing. This transition from prehistory to history was neither fast nor homogeneous: while the oral tradition continued to be the primary method in which mythology developed and was passed down from generation to generation, writing took over as a more practical and efficient means to address the pragmatic needs of urban society. Eventually, however, writing advanced in a manner that allowed it to record human speech more precisely, and the oral tradition would slowly give way to written recordings of the ancient stories.

But something was lost in the transition from the oral tradition to written history. Oral traditions preserve the connection between music and idea. As Christopher Woods rightly points out "No writing system notates all of the linguistic structure of speech. Tone, stress, and loudness, for instance, are most often omitted in writing systems that are considered to be highly phonetic" (2015b, 21). Consider again, our discussion of the simple sentence we first presented in Chapter 1: "I'm going to the store." How we musically perform that sentence has everything to do with how it is received. While it is true that the separation of music from idea created in various degrees in all writing provides us with tremendous interpretive opportunities in theatre, one imagines that it will be hard to capitalize on those opportunities if music is not considered to be a fundamental, essential, and integral component of the story in our earliest consideration of the story we hope to bring to life. Music is the chariot that carries idea. Without careful consideration, when we separate music from idea, we leave open the possibility that we give up a shiny new Maserati for a '68 Rambler.

Ten Questions

1. Name the first four great civilizations of the Bronze Age, briefly describe where they flourished and then identify four classes of musical instruments that developed in the Bronze Age.

2. What is PIE, and how does it resemble the biblical story of the Tower of Babel?
3. What is totemism, and how does it differ from animism?
4. Name a Mesopotamian god that derived from animism and provided a voice for music. Tell us how to summon an Egyptian god.
5. Why is the special power of heka so relevant to our consideration of music in theatre?
6. Describe the transcendent power that the ancient Chinese thought sound to possess. How does this differ from áhatanáda and anáhatanáda in Indian music?
7. What is the difference between an icon and a symbol, and why is this important to the development of writing?
8. What is the most important characteristic of written language and what is its most important benefit?
9. What does Euhemerism have to do with the telephone game?
10. What is the advantage of writing over the oral tradition? What is the advantage of the oral tradition over writing?

Things to Share

1. Part I. Write a short story that documents a traumatic experience you had at some point in your life that has shaped your life in profound ways ever since. Provide as much specific details as possible, but keep the entire story between 300 and 400 words. Form a circle in a group. Tell your story privately to the person to your right, and then have that person repeat your story privately to the person to their right. Repeat this process until the story comes all the way around the circle to the person on your left. Now have the person to your left publicly share the story to the whole group.

   Part II. Turn your story into a ballad, that is, a song or poem narrating your story in short stanzas with a musical (sound) accompaniment. Consider adding a repeating chorus that stresses the most important ideas of your story, such as the important lesson you learned from the experience. Perform the ballad for the class after the person to your left shares the story with the group.

2. Bring a *secular* totem to class with you. It can be an individual totem that means something unique to you, or a group totem that you share with your family, social group or particular culture. Please do not bring religious totems, as we tend to have a harder time embracing, understanding and respecting religious totems than we do secular ones. You may discover that you have acquired an important totem that provides you strength in sport, in music, socially, or personally. Create a short, two- to three-minute ritual in which you share your totem with the class: lead us in a musical improvisation using whatever instruments are at your disposal, played by members of the group to celebrate your totem; give other members of the group iconic gestures associated with the totem that they can use to create improvisational dances to the music created by your musicians; write a short poem, song, or story to perform over the musicians and dancers' improvisations. Venerate the totem while reciting your text. Above all, try to help us not just *understand* the power of your totem, but *experience* it; *feel* it, *share* it in all its power and glory.

Notes

1 A large, flat area of land created by river sediment.
2 We should also give a shout-out to a fifth early civilization that arose quite independently from the other four, Mesoamerica. Mesoamerica extended from central Mexico all the way to northern Costa Rica. We won't include a discussion of this civilization here, largely because it emerged later than the first four civilizations, but in surprisingly similar ways: migration to the North American continent occurred around 20,000 years ago (National Geographic 2016); hunter-gatherer societies were in place by 11,000 BCE, the transition to a more sedentary agrarian society occurred about 7000 BCE, which gave rise to village farming by about 1500 BCE, and the first great Mesoamerican civilizations, the Olmec, from about 1200 to 400 BCE and the Maya, from about 1500 BCE until about 1000 CE (Klein 1971, 269; Encyclopaedia Britannica 2016). Amazingly, we find evidence of a parallel development of cave art, musical instruments, shamanism, animism, altered states of consciousness, and eventually, writing, in the Mesoamerican civilization as we saw in the other four. Most importantly, we see the close relationship between music, ritual, mimesis and altered states of consciousness develop that we have so closely associated with the development of theatre (Looper 2009, 58–61). In the next chapter, we will explore the development of Greek theatre out of these closely connected entities. Remarkably, Mayan theatre developed with extraordinary similarities to Greek theatre. And the plays "pulsated with sound, both natural and man-made," according to theatre historian Maxine Klein (Klein 1971, 272). The evolutionary forces that appeared to have given rise to music and theatre in the first four early civilizations appear to have also been at work in Mesoamerica!

Bibliography

Bake, Arnold. 1955. "The Music of India." In *The New Oxford History of Music: Ancient and Oriental Music*, edited by Egon Wellesz, 194–227. London: Oxford University Press.
Bridge, Donna J., and Ken A. Paller. 2012. "Neural Correlates of Reactivation and Retrieval-Induced Distortion." *Journal of Neuroscience* 32 (5): 12144–12151.
Cooper, Jerrold S. 2004. "Babylonian Beginnings: The Origin of the Cuneiform Writing System in Comparative Perspective." In *The First Writing: Script Invention as History and Process*, edited by Stephen D. Houston, 71–99. Cambridge: Cambridge University Press.
Donald, Merlin. 1993. "Human Cognitive Evolution: What We Were, What We Are Becoming." *Social Research* 60 (1): 143–170.
Encyclopaedia Britannica. 2011. "Akkadian Language." June 8. Accessed November 25, 2016. www.britannica.com/topic/Akkadian-language.
———. 2016a. "Euhemerus." Accessed October 16, 2016. www.britannica.com/biography/Euhemerus-Greek-mythographer#ref25747.
———. 2016b. "Mesoamerican Civilization." Accessed October 13, 2016. www.britannica.com/topic/Mesoamerican-civilization.
Facorellis, Yorgos, Marina Cofronidou, and Giorgos Hourmouziadis. 2014. "Radiocarbon Dating of the Neolithic Lakeside Settlement of Sidpilio Kastoria, Northern Greece." *Radiocarbon* 56 (2): 511–528.
Farmer, Henry George. 1955. "The Music of Ancient Mesopotamia." In *The New Oxford History of Music: Ancient and Oriental Music*, edited by Egon Wellesz. London: Oxford University Press.

————. 1957. "The Music of Ancient Egypt." In *Ancient and Oriental Music*, edited by Egon Wellesz. London: Oxford University Press.

Haekel, Josef. 2009. "Totemism." January 30. Accessed October 16, 2016. www.britannica.com/topic/totemism-religion.

Joshua, J. Mark. 2011. "Ancient History Encyclopedia." April 28. Accessed November 25, 2017. www.ancient.eu/babylon/.

Klein, Maxine. 1971. "Theatre of the Ancient Maya." *Educational Theatre Journal* 23 (3): 269–276.

Li, Xueqin, Garman Harbottle, Juzhong Zhang, and Changsui Wang. 2003. "The Earliest Writing? Sign Use in the Seventh Millennium BC at Jiahu, Henan Province, China." *Antiquity*, March: 31–44.

Liu, Li, and Hong Xu. 2007. "Rethinking Erlitou: Legend, History and Chinese Archaeology." *Archaeology*, 81 (314): 886–901.

Looper, Matthew. 2009. *To Be Like Gods*. Austin: University of Texas Press.

Mallory, J. P., and D. Q. Adams. 2006. *The Oxford Introduction to Proto-Indo-European and the Proto-Indo-European World*. New York: Oxford University Press.

Merlini, Marco, and Gheorghe Lazarovici. 2008. "Settling Discovery Circumstances, Dating and Utlization of the Tärtäria Tablets." *Acta Terrae Septemcastrensis*, VII. http://arheologie.ulbsibiu.ro.

Paul, Marla. 2012. "Your Memory Is Like the Telephone Game." September 19. Accessed October 6, 2015. www.northwestern.edu/newscenter/stories/2012/09/your-memory-is-like-the-telephone-game.html.

Picken, Laurence. 1955. "The Music of Far Eastern Asia." In *The New Oxford History of Music: Ancient and Oriental Music*, edited by Egon Wellesz, 83–194. London: Oxford University Press.

Radivojević, Miljana, Thilo Rehren, Ernst Pernicka, Dušan Sljivar, Michael Brauns, and Dušan Borić. 2010. "On the Origins of Extractive Metallurgy: New Evidence From Europe." *Journal of Archaeological Science* 37 (11): 2775–2787.

Sachs, Curt. 1940. *The History of Musical Instruments*. New York: W. W. Norton.

Shakespeare Quartos Archive. n.d. "King Lear—Shakespeare in Quarto." Accessed September 25, 2016. www.bl.uk/treasures/shakespeare/kinglear.html.

Thomas, Richard, Matt Gowin, Kristy Lee McManus, Timothy Rogers, Justin Seward, Stephanie Shaw, David Swenson, and Jesse Dreikosen. 2002–2003. "KingLear@Ground Zero." Accessed September 25, 2016. http://web.ics.purdue.edu/~zounds/KLAGZ/.

Violatti, Cristian. 2014. "Indo-European Languages." May 5. Accessed November 25, 2016. www.ancient.eu /Indo-European_Languages/.

Woods, Christopher. 2015a. "The Earliest Mesopotamian Writing." In *Visible Language: Inventions of Writing in the Ancient Middle East and Beyond*, edited by Woods, Christopher, Teeter Emily, and Geoff Emberling, 33–50. Chicago: Oriental Institute of the University of Chicago.

————. 2015b. "Introduction—Visible Language: The Earliest Writing Systems." In *Visible Language: Inventions of Writing in the Ancient Middle East and Beyond*, edited by Christopher Woods, Emily Teeter, and Geoff Emberling, 15–28. Chicago: Oriental Institute of the University of Chicago.

Wright, Henry T. 1989. "Rise of Civilizations: Mesopotamia to Mesoamerica." *Archaeology* January/February: 46–48, 96–100.

CHAPTER 12

CONCLUSION: EVOLUTION AND GREEK THEATRE

Introduction: A Case Study

In the last chapter, we saw the emergence of the first four great civilizations of the world, Mesopotamia, Egypt, India and China. Gradually, as human cognition develops, the culture of a civilization took over and it becomes harder and harder to determine when evolution was at work, when advances in culture led, or when both interacted as predicted by the various forms of Lamarckism. But here we are, at a point where we haven't experienced significant biological evolution for a couple of hundred thousand years, biologically 99.9% the same as our *Homo sapiens sapiens* ancestors. We've reached the end of our evolutionary journey in this book. But rather than conclude by merely telling you what I told you (as the old saying goes), let's conclude by exploring how all of these evolutionary adaptations may have manifested in a theatre that more closely resembles ours. And what better theatre to examine, than the one that is generally considered to be the first *autonomous* theatre, the theatre of ancient Greece (Brockett and Hildy 2007, 7). While only displaced 2,500 years or so from our culture, Greek culture provides us with the oldest substantial record of a theatre aesthetic. If the topics we've discussed throughout this book have any merit at all, we should find evidence of them in the development of Greek theatre, right? Well, I would be foolish to pick this approach if I wasn't sure we could!

Let's not forget that we started this book by remembering that we follow a very Greek definition and interpretation of the word *aesthetic*: our perception of the world around us through our senses. We accept the evidence presented in this book for what it is, understanding that much of it is, and will remain, controversial. But we expect every artist in every culture to apply it consciously or subconsciously according to their own unique aesthetic, according to how they perceive the world. That not only goes for you and me, but, in this chapter, provides us with an opportunity to examine the various aesthetics of ancient Greek music and theatre artists in the context of their evolutionary underpinnings.

We begin by reviewing the main thesis of this book for which we will be searching for evidence about evolutionary influences in the development of Greek music and theatre. Our thesis, of course, is that theatre is a *type* of music. It is not words written in a book. It is an experience that has more in common with dreaming than words on a page. It seems possible that separating music from theatre by writing words on a page may even undermine the theatre experience. We traced this thesis through a series of simple formulas that served as major sections of this book:

Music = Time Manipulated

Song = Music + Idea

Theatre = Song + Mimesis

We should find evidence of these formulas at work in the development of Greek theatre that we found in astrophysics, anthropology, biology, neuroscience, and all of the other disciplines we've explored throughout this book.

Several themes have emerged as we have explored this thesis. We have learned that our perception of time itself is subjective, and the unique way we experience time has a lot to do with the unique way that music moves from composer through mediated performance and into each audience member. Music affects us at the subconscious level through various types of entrainment and other processes. It arouses our interests and interacts with our memories. All of these processes combine to fundamentally, and often, subconsciously manipulate our emotional states. They lead us into altered states of consciousness that have their basis in dreaming, the shaman's trances, and primitive ritual. They are perfectly suited to carrying ideas into the conscious and subconscious minds of audience members. Music as a Chariot.

The Origins of Greek Music: Music = Time Manipulated

We start our journey by observing that to the Greek mind, music was a gift of the gods. This should not surprise us. Throughout our journey, music and sound always connected deeply to the cosmology of our *Homo* ancestors. As far as the Greeks were concerned, Zeus, the king of the gods on Mount Olympus, and son of Kronos, god of *time*, slept with his aunt Mnemosyne, the goddess of memory, for nine nights. The result of that brief affair was the birth of nine Muses (Hesiod 1983, 25–26).

Think about that for a second. The king of the gods was the son of the god of *time*! And he hooked up with the goddess of *memory*. This would be the same memory that we quoted Daniel Levitin in Chapter 10, saying that without it, music could not exist! Zeus and Mnemosyne's progeny were the nine Muses. Each Muse,

Figure 12.1 A sarcophagus from the first half of the second century CE shows the nine Muses.

Credit: Photo by Jastrow, original located in the Louvre Museum, in Paris, France.

a goddess in her own right, inspired a different *temporal* art: Klio, the Muse of history, things that take a long time; Thalia, the Muse of comedy; Melpomene, the Muse of tragedy; Terpsichore, the Muse of dance; Erato, the Muse of love poetry; Polyhymnia, the Muse of choral poetry and religious hymns; Kalliope, the Muse of epic poetry. Then there's Euterpe, the Muse of music, the temporal art we most often associate with the audible form of music produced by musical instruments. The Greeks often depicted her holding an aulos (a type of Greek flute) or a lyre (a stringed instrument). Finally, there's Ourania, the Muse of astronomy.[1] The Muse of astronomy? We'll come back to that later in this chapter, but rest assured that the Greeks perceived a very fundamental and temporal relationship between music and astronomy. Most importantly, we see that the Greeks developed a very fundamental understanding of the unique relationship between time, certain arts, and hearing very early on, just as we explored in Chapter 2.

And so, in the very earliest manifestations of Greek culture upon which much of western civilization would be built, we see a fundamental recognition that Music = Time Manipulated.

But there is one more element of the mythology of the Muses that we must not overlook. The Muses did not simply govern the temporal arts, they inspired them. In Greek cosmology, we see a rather sophisticated understanding of how music transmits from one entity into another. It doesn't use symbols or signs. It doesn't reference anything. It simply connects, like entrainment, startle, habituation and other physiological and neurological processes we have investigated. The Muses helped the Greeks explain the unique way that music incites responses in listeners— the same phenomena we have explored throughout this book, especially in Chapter 9, where we examined the role of sound in altering the conscious states of the shaman and the shaman's subjects.

Much later, Plato would describe the essence of this process brilliantly in his *Ion*:

> The gift which you possess of speaking excellently . . . is not an art, but . . . an inspiration. There is a divinity moving you, like that contained in the stone which Euripides calls a magnet, but which is commonly known as the stone of Heraclea. This stone not only attracts iron rings, but also imparts to them a similar power of attracting other rings; and sometimes you may see a number of pieces of iron and rings suspended from one another so as to form quite a long chain: and all of them derive their power of suspension from the original stone. In like manner, the Muse first of all inspires men herself; and from these inspired persons a chain of other persons is suspended, who take the inspiration.
>
> (Vol. I, p. 501)

The mythological view of the Muses identifies several very important concepts we have explored in this book:

1. It identifies the predominantly temporal arts and organizes them together.
2. It predicts the close relationship between memory and music (the Muses were the progeny of Mnemosyne, the goddess of memory).
3. It describes how the process of musical inspiration works (from composer/playwright, through performer to listener).

The Development of Greek Song: Song = Music + Idea

The earliest agricultural settlements in Greece occurred about 7000–5000 BCE in Sesklo, Dimini and Crete (Thomas 2014, 10).

One group, the Minoans, named after the legendary king Minos settled on Crete about 3000 BCE. In about 1600 BCE, a gigantic volcanic eruption on the nearby island of Thera disrupted the Minoan civilization (Thomas 2014, 21–22). This made them pretty much sitting ducks, easily overtaken by a much more aggressive and warlike group from Mycenae on mainland Greece. The Mycenaeans appeared in Greece around 2000 BCE, and are best known for their siege on the city of Troy in retaliation for the Trojan kidnapping of Helen, the wife of the Spartan king, Menelaus. The whole escapade resulted in the brilliant deception known as the "Trojan Horse," in which the Greek army hid a number of men in a large wooden horse, and left it as a gift for the Trojan army after an unsuccessful siege. The men, once inside, opened the gates so the rest of the Greek army entered and destroyed the city of Troy (Kanopy Streaming, 5:42).

Out of the Minoan and Mycenaean cultures comes the first evidence we have for a distinctly Greek language that descended from the Proto-Indo-European language we first met in Chapter 11. Written language appears on thousands of tablets known as the Linear A (Minoan) and Linear B (Mycenaean, derived, from the Minoan) writing systems (Thomas 2014, 21; Mallory 2006, 28). The Linear B tablets give us a record of Greek mythology that dates back to the Bronze Age. But these tablets rarely provided more than simple records of how many sheep produced wool, or the number of chariots—and spare wheels, of course! Spoken

Years BCE	Important Characteristics
534–400	Golden Age of Greek Drama (see separate timeline)
534	Great Dionysian Festival established; Thespis wins first tragedy competition and introduces first actor
542	Pythagoras settles in Greece
600–500	Modes develop characteristic sound/emotion, less reliant on distinct dialect; music separated from written language; dithyrambs develop from processions to tragedy (see separate graph of Greek Dramas); Pythagoras and the Pythagoreans
700–600	Seven-string lyre introduced; more homogenized modes based on dialects; citharodes, komasts on vases; dithyrambs first performed; slow transition to writing
800–700	Homer and Hesiod, four-string lyre; isolated ethnic dialects
800	End of the Greek Dark Ages
1200	Dorian invasion and beginning of Greek Dark Ages
1400	Mycenaeans conquer Minoans; Linear B Tablets
2000	Mycenaeans settled in Greece
3000–2000	Minoans settled in Crete; Linear A Tablets
7000–5000	Earliest settlements in Seklo, Dimini and Crete

Figure 12.2 Timeline of ancient Greek civilization.

Figure 12.3 Map of ancient Greece shows earliest settlements, Minoan and Mycenaean civilizations.

Credit: Best-Backgrounds/Shutterstock.com. Adapted by Richard K. Thomas.

language, on the other hand, diverged geographically and developed separate dialects, the unique music of the spoken word.

Oral traditions developed specifically to each ethnic group and geographical area. And when these early Greeks mused about the gods, they "sang" in a way that closely resembled the dialects, a practice that the classical scholar M. L. West contended may have originated in the Proto-Indo-European language. West also contended that the Greeks may have inherited a very basic method of music notation from the Indo-Europeans in which marks are placed above the text that indicated one of three possible pitches that might be sung—although no extant examples exist (West 1981, 115).

Around 1200 BCE, a variety of disputed causes ranging from invasion by a people from the north known as the Dorians to environmental catastrophe, thrust Greece into a period of famine and hardship known as the Dark Age.

The Mycenaean Linear B writing disappeared and only Athens survived. Athens had a fortress called the Acropolis that was fortified with walls and its own water supply (Kanopy Streaming, 3:19; Thomas 2014, 31–32). Curiously, Greece descended into its Dark Age just as the next archaeological period, the Iron Age, began in other parts of the world. As you can imagine, during the Iron Age, humans learned the superior qualities of iron over bronze.

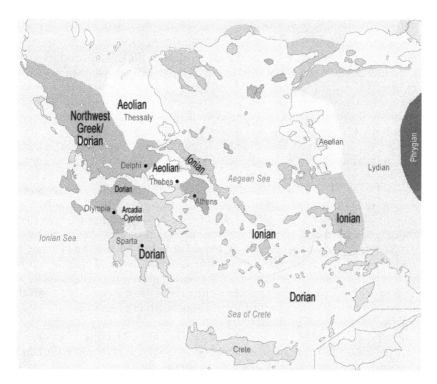

Figure 12.4 Derivation of Greek languages and dialects from Proto-Indo-European.

Credit: Map Adapted by Richard K. Thomas from original by Fut.Perf. Based on source map by Roger D. Woodard. 2008. "Greek Dialects." In *The Ancient Languages of Europe*, 51, edited by Roger D. Woodard. Cambridge: Cambridge University Press.

Three distinct tribes emerged: the Mycenaeans, who would eventually become associated with the Ionian dialect and Athens; the Dorians of Northwest Greece, who eventually became associated with Sparta among many other areas; and the Aeolians of the northeastern territory that become known as Thessaly.

Of course, if you asked the Greeks of the period, Zeus destroyed the men of the Bronze Age, and allowed Prometheus's wife, Pyrrah, and son, Deucalon, to repopulate the planet by throwing stones over their heads, which turned into men and women (Appolodorus 1921, I-7.1–3).

In the absence of a written record of language in the Greek Dark Age, the oral tradition continued. Myths and language morphed into many different stories and dialects in many different locations. Politics and rivalries deeply divided the different tribes, especially the cities of ancient Greece (Encyclopedia Britannica 2016). In these early ethnic groups, music and language were so closely associated with one another that particular speech melodies (i.e., pitches and rhythms) would be named after their home region, for example, Ionian, Dorian or Aeolian. Although scholars have long debated the issue, it appears that singing also became stylized according to the dialect of the particular race or geographical area. The music of language would become a critically important aspect of ethnic culture, just as it often is today.

By the end of the Greek Dark Age, about 800 BCE, the singing and recitation of poetry were often accompanied by the four-string lyre (West 1981, 116). The four notes that each of the strings provided limited the notes the performer could sing. So, how one tuned the lyre had a lot to do with the possible melodies. The meter of the poem dictated the rhythm and the pulse. We must imagine that the story itself dictated the tempo. The lowest string and the highest string were typically tuned a fourth apart, providing an opportunity for consonance. The inner notes depended on the particular type of scale, providing different opportunities for more or less consonance or dissonance with each scale used.

Playing the lyre also became stylized according to the dialect of the particular race or geographical area, because, as West suggested: "instrumental accompaniment went in unison with the voice" (West 1981, 115). In addition to the Ionian (Athens), Dorian (Sparta) and Aeolian (Thessaly) dialects, other dialects become known to the Greeks; the Lydian (western Anatolia, or Turkey), and Phrygian (west-central Anatolia, see Figure 12.4), sharing its western border with Lydia. Without a written language, the burden of passing down ideas from one generation to another fell to the oral tradition, requiring a close association between language (idea) and music (emotion). As we discovered in Chapter 10, using music to carry and preserve ideas was much more than just a pleasantry. Tempo, meter and rhythm provided a vital method to chunk ideas into more memorable forms that could be more robustly transmitted from one generation to another.

Two voices emerged in the late eighth/early seventh century BCE that would forever alter the worlds of music and theatre: Hesiod and Homer. It was Hesiod who first told us about the origins of the Muses. Scholars largely credit Hesiod with writing the poems that set down the stories of the Greek gods that proliferated during Greece's Dark Age. The Greek poet Homer set his stories to verse in two works: the *Iliad*, which describes the end of the Trojan War and the legend surrounding the famous siege, and the *Odyssey*, which covers Odysseus's (Ulysses's) long journey home after the Trojan War.

Both Hesiod and Homer are most likely to have composed and passed down their poems orally, even though the Greeks had commandeered the Phoenician alphabet as early as 800 BCE. This was a period of transition from the oral tradition to fully written out works in ancient Greece, although, it would seem that both Homer and Hesiod developed their works during a period of the oral tradition and only would have written them out later in life (Hesiod 2004, xii–xiv). Originally, artists called "rhapsodes" created their vocal performances on the four-string lyre, but West still considers their singing to be a "stylized form of speech, the rise and fall of the voice being governed by the melodic accent of the words" (West 1981, 115). Eventually, the Greek alphabet would improve on the Phoenician alphabet by adding vowels—α (a), ε (e), ι (i), ο (o), υ (u)—that allowed a more faithful representation of actual speech (Encyclopedia Britannica 2016).

The classical Greek musical system developed by attempting to match the speech melody as closely as possible. It's not hard to imagine, then, that they would develop melodic systems based on the various dialects, such as Dorian or Phrygian. These melodic systems, called modes, were scales constructed from varying combinations of intervals between successive notes. Melodies were based on the consonant interval of the fourth, in between were notes of varying dissonance that made the scale more closely resemble the dialect stylistically. Notice how the scales developed on the basis of the consonant and dissonant relationships we examined in Chapter 8.

In the seventh century, a seven-string lyre would be introduced—conveniently right when the various musical melodies in the Dorian, Lydian and Phrygian modes spread throughout Greece.

As necessity is the mother of invention, the seven-string lyre possibly arose as a solution to the problem of performing different poems based on the different ethnic dialects. Rather than laboriously retuning between each song, the rhapsode could tune the seven-string lyre to multiple modes at once, and simply change the strings played depending on the needs of the song. Most modern folk singers recognize this problem—but they have precisely engineered tuning pegs, capos and digital electronic tuners to speed up the process! The expansion of the scale from four notes to seven not only solved the technical problems of performing poems written in different "dialects," but allowed for much greater virtuosity of performance.

The seven-string lyre eventually gave way to the larger, more professional cithara (also spelled *kithara*—notice the resemblance to the word guitar).

Curiously, a split developed between rhapsodes and citharodes at the same time the words—but not the music—started getting written down. Rhapsodes were more concerned with the faithful transmission of the lyrics; citharodes were more concerned with virtuosic musical improvisation (West 1981, 120–125). In Chapter 7 we discussed how music and language shared some neural networks in their processing of sound, how some parts of the brain used parallel systems that

Figure 12.5 Muse playing a seven-stringed lyre, 440–430 BCE.

Credit: Photo by Bibi Saint-Pol. Original located in the Staatliche Antikensammlungen in Munich, Germany.

Figure 12.6 Sir Lawrence Alma-Tadema's nineteenth-century painting, *Sappho and Her Companions Listening to Alcaeus Play the Kithara*. Sappho was a Greek poet who lived from about 630–580 BCE.

Credit: iStock.com/Nastasic.

Figure 12.7 Komasts dancing circa 575–565 BCE.

Credit: Photo by Jastrow, original located in the Louvre Museum in Paris, France.

process speech in the left hemisphere and music in the right, and how some areas of the brain process music and language in distinctly different ways. It seems possible, then, that as Greek music developed, the artists became more consciously aware of the possibilities created by a brain that processed music and language differently, and increasingly learned how to make use of the diverging nature of the processing mechanisms of each.

Decorative vases started to appear in the middle of the seventh century BCE, that depicted scenes of choric rituals.

A couple thousand of these vases have been uncovered, depicting male dancers called *komasts*, generally in large groups. These vases are important for they depict iconically the world of the Greeks during a time when textural fragments are few and far between. Without exception, the komasts dance, and often their musical accompaniment is shown with them (typically flutes).

The Dorians in Corinth produced most of these vases and exported them to all parts of the Greek world. Significantly, Corinth is also said to have birthed a choral hymn called the *dithyramb* during this same period, although this is not the whole story. Archilochus, a poet from the island Paros credited with inventing lyric poetry, appears to have sang personal dithyrambs in 640 BCE. Archilochus may also have been the first person to use music as "underscoring," that is, rather than always having the music follow the speech melody, the performer would speak the words with music "below the song" (Mathiesen 1999, 72). But it was Arion, a professional musician on the cithara, who is credited with composing, naming and teaching a public dithyramb in Corinth (Caspo and Miller 2007, 11).

During the course of the sixth century, dithyrambs developed as a processional ritual danced and sung to honor the god Dionysus (Caspo and Miller 2007, 11). Its origins may have included erotic elements and not been very far removed from phallic songs (Pickard-Cambridge 1962, 1–2). Thomas Mathiesen cites several ancient Greek writers who describe the dithyramb in similar ways: the dithyramb was "full of passion," "tumultuous and appears in a highly ecstatic manner . . . hurried along by its rhythms," and its use of "simpler diction . . . discovered from . . . merriment in drinking" (Mathiesen 1999, 71–74). It's hard not to notice the similarities of this to the shaman's art we have explored in the last few chapters. One way or another, these early audiences were constantly being led into altered states of ecstasy invariably grounded in musical stimuli. Wine was also a major theme depicted on the komast vases, so one can imagine the original qualities of these drunken orgiastic processions. Combined with music, they certainly would form a certain archaic fulfillment of the "drugs, sex and rock n' roll" neurological entanglement we explored in Chapter 9.

As we shall see, the dithyramb holds a very special place in our story.

Greek language and culture became more homogenized as the Greek ethnic groups increasingly interacted in the sixth century BCE. Types of poetry that had originated in various dialects spread orally to other groups and morphed to include linguistic characteristics of other cultures. Epic poetry, particularly Homeric epics, became a highly stylized artificial mixture of dialects. Homeric epics were thought to be based on the Ionic dialect, but in actuality were an artificial dialect based on Ionic but included Aeolian and Mycenaean elements (Encyclopedia Britannica 2016; Mallory 2006, 28). Homeric epic language would, in turn, influence other types of poetry, such as choral lyric. Personal poetry would naturally retain the dialect of its creators, be it Ionic, Lesbian, Boeotian or others. The effect of the telephone game we discussed in Chapter 11 was to blend and combine different ethnic groups over a long oral tradition into a more homogeneous environment.

Dialects from different regions eventually became more associated with different types of literature and music. A good example of such a homogenization of cultures is the dithyramb we met earlier that Arion first performed publicly in Corinth. Corinth is more natively Dorian, but dithyrambs were performed almost exclusively in the Phrygian mode (Phrygia being a central Anatolian dialect). Aristotle tells us that Philoxemus tried to compose a dithyramb in the Doric mode, and simply couldn't—he had to revert back to the Phrygian mode to get it to sound right (Aristotle 2009c, Book Eight, Part VII)!

The spread of the Greek language and the mixing of ethnic groups in the sixth century led to each mode developing a "characteristic sound"—probably at the expense of faithful imitation of the dialect from which the mode originated. An oft-cited quote argues, however, that "When Lasus (a sixth-century poet) . . . referred to the Aeolian harmonia, he was probably thinking less of a scale pattern than of a melodic style that had become localized among Greeks who spoke the Aeolic dialect" (Anderson and Mathiesen 2007–2016). But how much we can expect these Greek modes to reflect the actual dialects of a people, morphed over hundreds of years, is open to much speculation and debate.

Eventually, the Greek alphabet spread not only to the Greek races, such as the Dorians, Ionians and Aeoleans, but also to the other nearby races, including the Phrygeans and Lydians. Writing further enabled the referential power of language to become separated from the musical characteristics of spoken words. Eventually, the Homeric epics, the *Iliad* and the *Odyssey*, transitioned from an oral tradition to a written tradition as the Greeks further developed their alphabet.[2] Music and language parted company, palpably manifested in the separation of prose and poetry. Isobel Henderson describes the consequences of this in the *New Oxford History of Music*: "The spread of books may even be thought to have pushed music out of education, for the mutual aide-memoire of verse and melody was no longer indispensable when the words were easily available in written copies" (1955, 338). Recall how in Chapter 10 we explored how organizing our memories according to principles of music helped make recalling text easier. Remember FAT DOG EAT PIG? In the absence of a written tradition, the music of language, especially when stylized into the meter and verse of poetry could have been an essential tool in storing Homer and Hesiod in the collective conscious. Written language would have cut the cord on that particular partnership.

This slow separation of music and language may be of greater significance than we initially imagine. Let's remind ourselves of how we got started all the way back in Chapter 1. We began this book by lamenting the disassociation between sound design and music from theatre, and blamed the phenomenon on the fact that "electronic theatre sound design as we now know it, came to the theatre table pretty late." That may be true, but let us now consider the separation of music and theatre brought on by the emergence of written language, and the subsequent disassociation of the experience of theatre and what is written in a published play. In such a system, we suspect a problem much more pervasive and undermining: our tendency to treat the written text of a play as the experience of the play itself. Theatre production has become a process of reverse engineering: attempting to find the music of a play by studying the written language of a play. Musicals (and opera!), of course, reversed this trend, and we can plainly see the positive effects this has had on the theatre experience: musicals run on Broadway for years; plays for months. There can be no denying that the essence of the theatre experience rooted in the underlying music has a magnetic attraction that draws modern audiences in substantial and demonstrable ways. Worth keeping in mind as we proceed. We'll notice a similar phenomenon in Greek theatre.

Later in the sixth century, the various modes more fully morphed into scales bearing the name of their origin, but each having its own characteristic rhythm and pitch structures as we discussed in Chapters 6 and 8. Eventually, each mode became associated with a specific type of character and/or emotion. For example, the Lydian scale seemed to be good at expressing sorrow. The Aeolian, which, as we mentioned before, bore some relationship to Homer's dialect, had a nice quality that existed between "tense and relaxed." It was perfectly suited, according to "the outspokenly conservative poet, Pratinas of Phlius . . . to braggarts in song" (Anderson and Mathiesen 2007–2016). Compare this to Robert Thayer's components of mood we discussed in Chapter 9 (calm to tense, and tired to energetic). Notice how the Greeks slowly developed a system of melodies and lines, each more suited to creating and experiencing one mood over another.

Over a long period of time that extended well into the fifth century, styles began to become separated from their geographic origin, and began to be associated with particular musical patterns, the prosody of the rhapsodes. Poets eventually emerged that favored a particular musical style without necessarily following the dialect or the language. Sappho (see Figure 12.6) and Alcaeus favored the Aeolean style, Pindar was said to have a Lydian manner. Pindar also composed in both Aeolean and Dorian styles—and apparently sometimes confused them. Pratinas called his music Dorian (Henderson 1955, 382–383).

As the performance of poetry developed and flourished, the particular mood of a poem or song would become associated with an emerging concept, ethos. Ethos is a complex subject with many different meanings but Anderson and Mathieson connect it directly back to music: "When indications of ethos occur in poetry, they almost always concern mood rather than morality." By the end of the sixth century BCE, the strange ability of music to influence mood also became associated with mimesis, and mimesis would thereafter become associated with ethos.

Here we have one of the great paradoxes of the close relationship between music and theatre: for the Greeks, even mimesis had its roots in music. In its original conception, mimesis involved imitating sound, but it meant much more; Plato would later make that clear (Mathiesen 2016). Mimesis had more to do with the power of sound and music to reach the inner recesses of the soul and affect a person's ethical and moral states, their ethos. Gerald Else ascribed the origin of the term to the expressive primeval power of "mousikē" in music and dance. Else argued that the interpretation of imitation was a later, and inappropriately applied use of the term to such art forms as painting (Else 1958, 73). Like the iron rings that took on the characteristics of Plato's magnet, the Muses permeate through the composer, then the performer and finally into the listener, inciting particular moods in each along the way. It's hard to imagine that the genesis of the word mimesis itself, as we use it in our more modern sense, had its origin in music.

Could the moods created by music actually cause specific moral or ethical states to develop? So began a discussion about the relationship of mimesis (the mysterious power of music attached to ideas) to ethos (the manner in which ethics and morality were instilled in virtuous citizens). The Greeks slowly became aware of the special power of Music as a Chariot, when we use music to carry ideas into the hearts of humans. They explored it specifically in their consideration of mimesis and ethos. And it made a lot of them very, very nervous. Consider the "drugs, sex and rock and roll" excesses of the Dionysian festivals, and one can quickly imagine why. That debate still carries on today, and it strikes at the heart of our discussion about the nature of the experience of music. We will return to it later in this chapter as we explore the difference between how Plato viewed the phenomenon, and how Aristotle viewed it.

Music as Math Made Audible: The Greeks Revisit Consonance and Dissonance

One of the earliest Greek scholars to tackle the complex subject of the relationship between music and ethos was the sixth-century Ionian mathematician Pythagoras, and the cult that followed him, the Pythagoreans. Pythagoras was born in Syria around 575 BCE, and studied in Egypt for 21 years before being captured and taken to Babylon, where he studied music and mathematics for 12 more years, among other disciplines. He then settled in Samos, a Greek island in the North Aegean Sea. It was there that he founded a cult that promoted theories about the harmony of the spheres that detailed relationships between the harmonious ordering and movement of the planets and harmony in music.

Pythagoras and his cult taught about mathematical relationships between the order of the planets and the order of notes found in music. They thought that the same simple harmonic structures we've discovered that govern consonance and dissonance in Chapter 9 appear in the movement of planets in the heavens, in the seasons of the year, in all of the universe. A couple of hundred years later, Aristotle, in his *Metaphysics*, would describe this worldview:

> since, again, they [the Pythagoreans] say that the attributes and ratios of the musical scales were expressible in numbers; since, then, all other things seemed in their whole nature to be modeled after numbers, and numbers seemed to be the first things in the whole of nature, they supposed the elements of numbers to be the elements of all things, and the whole heaven to be a musical scale and a number.
>
> (Aristotle 2009a, Book I, Part 5)

Aristotle claimed that the Pythagoreans believed that the heavenly spheres actually produced sound:

> the motion of bodies of that size must produce a noise, since on our earth the motion of bodies far inferior in size and speed of movement has that effect. Also, when the sun and the moon, they say, and all the stars, so great in number and in size are moving with so rapid a motion, how should not produce a sound immensely great? Starting from this argument, and the observation that their speeds, as measured by their distances, are in the same ratios as musical concordances, they assert that the sound given forth by the circular movement of the stars is a harmony.
>
> (Aristotle, 350 BCE, Book II, Part 9)

For the record, Aristotle thought that they were a bit off on this one. Still, we should not underestimate the importance of this connection. Remember that we promised to return to the subject of Ourania, the Muse of astronomy? For the Greeks, astronomy was not only a time art, but also more closely connected with music than visual arts and space. Jamie James sums up those relationships: "It is clear that the Pythagoreans did not simply discern congruities among number and music and the cosmos: they identified them. Music was number, and the cosmos was music" (1995, 30–31). Michael Thaut explained the predominant view that "In ancient Greece, music was considered in many ways to be a part of the natural sciences . . . one could study music to gain insights into important aspects of the physical world" (2005, 28–29).

It is not hard to understand, then, that, given that worldview, the Pythagoreans imagined a very close relationship between the ethos of the modes—in the context of the ability of music to influence moods—and ethical states. Henry Farmer goes on to explain in the *New Oxford History of Music*:

> music, being a cosmic ingredient, possessed qualities and sensibilities which could evoke the like if the appropriate and related kind of music were used. Thus, one species would banish depression, another would assuage grief, a third would check passion, while yet another would dispel fear.
>
> (Farmer 1957, 247)

Anderson and Mathieson suggest that while the origins of the belief in the "magically potent" power of music to affect ethos was born in the Near and Middle East, "the liberating force was Pythagorean theory, whereby musical phenomena were brought under the control of number and of proportionate relationship" (Anderson and Mathiesen 2007–2016).

The influence of Pythagoras on the Greek worldview was pervasive. It reflected an element of society that was somewhat preoccupied with mathematics and science—to the point that it was suspicious of anything that challenged its logic and rigor. As we shall see, the Greeks grew especially suspicious of the mysterious power of music to stir the emotions and moods of its audience and to alter the conscious perception of the individual. These would increasingly be considered real threats to the state. Over a long period of time, music came to be seen as a way to influence morality, one that should be used specifically to carry "good" ideas. As we discussed in our section on implicit memory in Chapter 10, the Greeks understood not just the power of music to carry ideas, but the power of music to create an impression of truth magnified by the mood induced by the music. Music as a Chariot.

The First Autonomous Theatre: Theatre = Song + Mimesis

Pythagoras arrived in Greece in the mid to late sixth century to find a strong performative element that had already emerged out of a long oral tradition thriving in ritual festivals all over Greece. The dithyramb was but one genre of festivals that sprang up and featured competitions of epic poems dedicated to particular deities, first perhaps in Sparta or Delphi, and then spreading to the rest of Greece (Henderson 1955, 379). By this time, dithyrambs had branched out from purely Dionysian rituals to poems that honored other gods and more serious subject matter. Dithyrambs contained a strong narrative component and were accompanied by the aulos (Henderson 1955, 379). Throughout this transition from story-telling and ritual enactment to a completely autonomous theatre, tension existed between referential language, and emotional music. Rozik notes this tension early on suggesting that Lasos may have inaugurated a "predominance of the music over the words against which . . . Cratinas shortly afterwards protested" (Rozik 2002, 246; A. W. Pickard-Cambridge 1927, 50).

The stage was set for the birth of theatre, and Athens was ground zero. While the Greeks developed their conception of mimesis and ethos, a big party was breaking out in Athens. Two dithyrambs were known to have been performed at the Great Dionysian festival that was established in 534 BCE (Mathiesen 1999, 79). Thespis, a singer of dithyrambs, won his first contest in Athens that year (Brockett and Hildy 2007, 11). Eli Rozik notes how this coincides or slightly predates Lasos' institution of dithyrambic contests in Athens with "some elaboration of the rhythms and the range of notes employed in the music of the dithyramb" (2002, 146). Caspo and Miller also credit Lasos for introducing the circular chorus to the dithyramb that would later serve as the foundation for the Greek theatre chorus (Caspo and Miller 2007, 11). Rozik suggests that dithyrambs and tragedy were most likely very similar at their start and probably existed side by side for some time. Indeed, Mathieson describes dithyrambic performances that were apparently full of dramatic "sound effects" provided by the audience in the form of onomato-poeic neighing horses, or hisses of snakes, and percussion toys such as crotalas or clappers (Mathiesen 1999, 76–77). The differences between dithyrambs and tragedy are most likely not as well divided as the names might suggest. The development of tragedy most likely took place over some time, rather than emerging full-blown one fine day. Rozik describes a significant connection between the two:

> As a choral, danced, and sung performance, dithyramb could indeed have been a source of tragic theatre. . . . The imitation of a serious-sublime action is a property common to both storytelling and drama. This view is congruent with the continuity and sup-posedly smooth transition from dithyramb to tragedy, since both share the presentation of heroes and their actions in a serious and lofty or, rather, tragic style.
>
> (2002, 150)

Tragedy (which derives from the Greek τραγῳδία, meaning "goat *song*") required one more critical invention in order to become theatre, the invention of the actor. Rozik argues that the main difference between dithyrambic choral performances and tragedy was "the introduction of actors, who represent characters by enact-ing them and their doings" (2002, 150). Thespis is generally credited with intro-ducing the actor to tragedy—a character that speaks directly to the chorus, and thus creates dialogue (Brockett and Hildy 2007, 11). The introduction of an actor who portrayed characters in first person, rather than told their stories in third person as storytellers did, so fundamentally changed the auditory experience that a new art form was born, theatre. Theatre = Song + Mimesis.

With the addition of the actor, the essential tools for achieving the dramatic experience were in place: language, music, and a very specific type of mimesis. Language provided the referential information necessary to imagine the world and all its details, music subconsciously aroused, manipulated time (especially through rhythmic entrainment) and incited emotional responses. The actor anchored the language and music in a tangible, physical organism that bore such a strong resemblance to the character portrayed that audiences no longer per-ceived themselves in their theatrical surroundings, but began to perceive them-selves in the world of the dramatic performance. This experience of course also occurred to a certain extent in storytelling, because both theatre and song have their basis in music.

At the very end of the sixth century BCE, the ritual processions of the dithyrambic performers found an important end to their procession in the Theatre of Dionysus of Athens. Prior to this, performances had been held in the central market square (agora) or a public park on the southeast slope of the Acropolis (Brockett and Hildy 2007, 16). But the Theatre Dionysus was a permanent theatre, built around the "dancing space," the circular orchestra. Theatre now had a home, and it was built around a fundamentally musical type of performance.

In the beginning, these performances were filled with music. The chorus sang as many as half the lines. Much of the remaining dialogue was sung or delivered as recitative, and dance was part of many scenes (Brockett and Hildy 2007, 18). Even at this late date, music and language, united in speech were typically inseparable. The earliest dramatic performances were centered around one unique individual who wrote the play, composed the music and dances, trained the chorus, played the single acting role established by Thespis, and oversaw every aspect of the production. As an actor this uber-creator did not focus on reproducing the attributes of the character so much as they did on inciting emotion. The chorus comprised 50 amateur members of the community. There was no scenery, no lighting, and the vases of the period do not even make convincing arguments for much in the way of costumes (Brockett and Hildy 2007, 18–20). Essentially, there was the actor and the chorus, music and dance, and language, with music clearly a dominant force arousing strong emotions.

In the fifth century BCE, music, idea and mimesis flourished in the newly discovered music form, theatre. Theatre continued as an oral tradition throughout much of the fifth century (Henderson 1955, 336). Most of the plays that we now know from Greek theatre—from playwrights such as Aeschylus, Sophocles, Euripides and Aristophanes—were written in the fifth century BCE.

The fifth century BCE was also the period of the great philosopher, Socrates, who was not only very suspicious of Greek democracy, but also of any form of writing things down. Unlike Merlin Donald in Chapter 8, Socrates suspected that the offline storage of writing things down could lead to replacing human memory, making human memory weaker, which, in turn would lead to a lack of wisdom (Vol. I, p. 485).

But the handwriting was on the wall. As the fifth century went on, the role of instrumental music started to wane, in favor of the ideas of the play. Aristotle tells us that Aeschylus (525–426 BCE) introduced a second actor and then diminished the role of the chorus. Sophocles (495–405 BCE) introduced the third actor (about 468 BCE, according to Brockett) (2007, 12). Plot took on greater

Years BCE	Important Characteristics
427–388	Aristophanes (446–406) wrote a number of plays including *Lysistrata* (411)
429–406	Euripides (480–406) wrote a number of plays including *Medea* (431)
468–456	Sophocles (497/496–406/405) introduced the third actor
458	Aeschylus wrote the Oresteia about Agamemnon
499–468	Aeschylus (525–456) introduces the second actor
534–532	Thespis "invents" tragedy

Figure 12.8 Timeline of major Greek plays.

and greater importance and the rhythms of dancing were replaced by the more "natural" rhythms of colloquial speech. "Nature," as Aristotle would much later say, "herself discovered the appropriate measure" (Aristotle, Poetics (350 BCE) 2009, Part IV).

What could have caused such a drastic shift away from a form that had such strong evolutionary ties throughout human and animal history? The obvious answer would seem to be that the more "natural" style of theatre, with its greater emphasis on plot and dialogue, was more popular with its audiences. However, there may have been other forces at work here.

One must remember that a significant part of Greek society was quite suspicious of the power of music to sway human emotion, and felt that the purpose of music was more properly related to its mathematical connection to the cosmos, as the Pythagoreans believed. Henderson describes the interest of Greek theorists "not to analyze the art of music but to expound the independent science of harmonics" (1955, 336). Government was skeptical of the ability of music to affect ethos, and was not anxious to return to the hedonistic ways of satyrs and Dionysian excess. The government needed to co-opt the festivals in order to assure that they improved the moral and ethical disposition of the citizens and inhabitants of Greece.

The government provided the theatre space, prizes, and payments to the actors and possibly dramatists (Brockett and Hildy 2007, 17). An author wishing to present a play had to apply to the archon, the "chief magistrate" of the Greek city-state. It is no wonder that the plays produced would increasingly focus on the psychological and ethical attributes of their personages, a far cry from the ritualistic excesses of the early Dionysian rites (Brockett and Hildy 2007, 12). Only the more ribald satyr plays, about half the length of the tragedies, and only performed after trilogies of tragedies, were allowed to appeal to the baser side of human nature.

Further complicating matters was the problem that the words of the plays were apparently written down, but there did not appear to exist a similar technique for recording music—Greek writers constantly quote literary texts, but not musical ones; figures on vases perform music, but none reference written music (Henderson 1955, 337–338). Music remained a prisoner of the oral tradition, largely improvised, whereas language was stored outside the memory in written form. Cartwright goes even further, suggesting that "scripts regarded as classics, particularly by the three great Tragedians, were even kept by the state as official and unalterable state documents" (Cartwright 2013). I don't mean to be a conspiracy theorist here, but a government that had developed a deep and abating suspicion of the negative power of unchecked musical expression on an unsuspecting populace, would have a particular interest in supporting and preserving the "good" ideas, and would be just as happy to see music disappear altogether. Or, it was just a matter that no one invented a music notation system that caught on. Regardless, eventually the music of the great plays would inevitably be lost, while the written record of the ideas of the plays would be preserved. In the process, *drama* was born. Drama is the written down text of the performance. It's good at recording ideas, very poor at recording music. Theatre is the actual performance, and includes every aspect of the performance, especially the music upon which it is based.

One final important development Mathiesen notes is the "rising importance of the instrumental virtuoso." As music became further separated from written text, the musicians found a new sense of freedom for self-expression that also would eventually lead to a further parting of ways with the spoken word (Mathiesen 1999, 75). One would think, then, that advancements in writing would have produced a plethora of new dramatic works, each logged meticulously in written form, and recorded and resurrected throughout the ages. Yet, by the time Plato arrived on the scene, the great works that have been passed down to us through the centuries had just about all been written. And Plato was firmly of the mind that the purpose of music—that which we call song and includes its offspring, theatre—should be carefully controlled by the state to ensure it helped ennoble virtuous men.

Plato and His World

Up until now, we've met Plato and Aristotle primarily as historians who happened to be a couple of the best authorities closest in time to early historical events. But in reality, both Plato and Aristotle came much later than most of the events we've been describing. Plato was born around 428 BCE, fully 100 years after Thespis was said to have introduced the first actor.

Plato's earliest dialogues didn't appear until the next century, when he was deeply affected by the trial and execution of his mentor, Socrates in 399 BCE (Meinwald 2016). Plato may have known the great playwright Aristophanes; at least that's what's implied by including him as a character in Plato's *Symposium*. Aristotle was Plato's student, so he was even further removed from the age of the great classic theatre.

Plato followed the Pythagoreans. The influence of Pythagoras on the Greek worldview was pervasive. It reflected an element of society that was somewhat preoccupied with mathematics and science—to the point that it was suspicious of anything that challenged its logic and rigor. As we have seen, the Greeks grew especially suspicious of the mysterious power of music to stir the emotions of its audience and to alter the conscious perception of the individual. These would increasingly be considered real threats to the state.

Both Plato and Aristotle were largely writing about what was quickly becoming a bygone era, about what made the "old" plays great—not about their contemporaries. Anderson and Mathieson describe Plato as "manifestly out of touch with his own times" (Anderson and Mathiesen 2017b), but Plato was also reacting to what he perceived to be the decay of the education system and culture of fifth-century Greece. Aristotle was somewhat more adaptive to his own times. Both Plato and Aristotle wrote descriptively about the past, but both also wrote prescriptively, prescribing what they thought good music, good theatre—and, by extension, good citizenship, should be.

At the end of the fifth century, in 404 BCE, Sparta conquered Athens in the Peloponnesian War and the so-called Golden Age of Greece ended (Encyclopedia Britannica 2015). By then, the oral tradition that produced the great music-theatre of the fifth century was all but obliterated. Anderson and Mathieson report that Timotheus of Miletus had so altered the dithyramb by making the text an elaborate libretto, and adding frequent modulations to the musical accompaniment, that any possible connection to ethos was lost (Anderson and Mathiesen 2007–2016). Musicians were making up melodies and playing them with no regards for the words, and were often more popular than the poets themselves. Mathiesen asserts that, at least as far as the dithyrambists were concerned, the improvisatory ability of the performers became so popular that "the name of the aulete himself sometimes precedes that of the poet and choregos, and this provides further

Figure 12.9 Plato.

strong indication of the popularity of the virtuoso instrumentalists associated with . . . the dithyramb" (Mathiesen 1999, 81). But as far as Plato was concerned, and as Jamie James points out in his book *The Music of the Spheres*: "cultivated Greeks did not listen to purely instrumental music, but rather considered it to be only a vehicle for song—that is, poetry—or dance" (1995, 57).

From the fourth century BCE on there was a significant division between poet and composer. This may be attributed to several causes, beyond the obvious problems caused by written plays that were passed down in history, while unannotated musical compositions separated and were lost for all time. First, as drama and music became more sophisticated, it became increasingly difficult for one person to become accomplished in more than one area (see Chapter 1). Second, the drama was no longer considered to be strictly a teaching device, but was increasingly accepted purely as an entertainment. Third, these two factors together created a need for specialists who strove to appease an audience. Fourth, there was an increasing dependence on financial reward to attract new talent to the field. Henderson writes that these factors produced a revolution in art: "when the classical unity of Music was broken, the 'music' . . . was supplied by a professional engaged in the performance. The modern figure of the pure composer, who is neither poet nor player, was unknown to antiquity" (Henderson 1955, 400). New styles of accompaniment arose, such as the use of sound effects like wind, hail, rain, thunder and so forth. The organic unity that had once been the ideal, now took second place to pandering to public opinion.

Plato's history of the musical revolution in the mid-fourth century BCE relates the bastardization of style to the downfall of the democracy itself. And, just in case you think I'm kidding, consider this sample from Plato's Laws:

> let us speak of the laws about music—that is to say, such music as then existed—in order that we may trace the growth of the excess of freedom from the beginning . . . the directors of public instruction insisted that the spectators should listen in silence to the end; and boys and their tutors, and the multitude in general, were kept quiet by a hint from a stick. . . . And then, as time went on, the poets themselves introduced the reign of vulgar and lawless innovation. They were men of genius, but they had no perception of what is just and lawful in music . . . ignorantly affirming that music has no truth, and, whether good or bad, can only be judged of rightly by the pleasure of the hearer. And by composing such licentious works, and adding to them words as licentious, they have inspired the multitude with lawlessness and boldness, and made them fancy that they can judge for themselves about melody and song. . . . in music there first arose the universal conceit of omniscience and general lawlessness;—freedom came following afterwards, and men, fancying that they knew what they did not know, had no longer any fear, and the absence of fear begets shamelessness. . . . Consequent upon this freedom comes the other freedom, of disobedience to rulers; and then the attempt to escape the control and exhortation of father, mother, elders, and when near the end, the control of the laws also; and

at the very end there is the contempt of oaths and pledges, and no regard at all for the Gods.

(Vol. 5, pp. 82–83)

Plato lamented the old school of the oral tradition, and the development of new styles in which music and drama gradually become separated. To understand Plato's problem (and Socrates, since Plato often wrote in Socrates' voice), one must understand how music shaped his core belief system. For Plato, the essence of the most fundamental entities in the universe all proceed in accordance with the harmonious nature of the universe as described by Pythagoras. Plato developed a "Theory of Forms" that attempted to explain universal attributes such as beauty in their exemplars. In Plato's theory, for example, the beauty of Achilles or Helen would somewhat approximate examples of the ideal form of beauty. Plato's theory eerily reflects the exemplar theory we examined in Chapter 10 that describes how the brain fires unique patterns of neuronal firings for each experience, yet how some aspects of those firings are similar or duplicated by other memories, creating categories. In Plato's worldview, proportion and harmony, in the Pythagorean sense, are aspects of the first principle of everything, which Plato called "The Good." So, in his *Timaeus*, Plato describes how the Demiurge (i.e., creator) created the world in strictly Pythagorean terms:

> And he proceeded to divide after this manner: First of all, he took away one part of the whole [1], and then he separated a second part which was double the first [2], and then he took away a third part which was half as much again as the second and three times as much as the first [3], and then he took a fourth part which was twice as much as the second [4], and a fifth part which was three times the third [9], and a sixth part which was eight times the first [8], and a seventh part which was twenty-seven times the first.

Plato keeps manipulating the numbers until he comes up with the mathematical ratios necessary to produce an almost perfect major scale covering five octaves!

> After this he filled up the double intervals [i.e. between 1, 2, 4, 8] and the triple [i.e. between 1, 3, 9, 27] cutting off yet other portions from the mixture and placing them in the intervals, so that in each interval there were two kinds of means, the one exceeding and exceeded by equal parts of its extremes [as for example 1, 4/3, 2, in which the mean 4/3 is one-third of 1 more than 1, and one-third of 2 less than 2], the other being that kind of mean which exceeds and is exceeded by an equal number. Where there were intervals of 3/2 and of 4/3 and of 9/8, made by the connecting terms in the former intervals, he filled up all the intervals of 4/3 with the interval of 9/8, leaving a fraction over; and the interval which this fraction expressed was in the ratio of 256 to 243.

(Vol. III, p. 454)

Now, it wouldn't have occurred to anyone to actually "play a few bars of the World Soul on the lyre," as James reminds us (1995, 48). It was "just a theory," as we are fond of saying now. But Plato definitely connected the world soul to the soul of each individual, and, in doing that created a connection between the mathematics of music and the ethereal power that music has to influence and create human emotion, an awareness of the strange power of consonance and dissonance as we discussed in Chapter 8.

Music was, for Plato, and for Greek citizens, an essential element of education. In his Republic, Socrates gets Thrasymachus to admit that a musician is wise, and one who is not is foolish!

Socrates:	And now to take the case of the arts: you would admit that one man is a musician and another not a musician?
Thrasymachus:	Yes.
Socrates:	And which is wise and which is foolish?
Thrasymachus:	Clearly the musician is wise, and he who is not a musician is foolish.
Socrates:	And he is good in as far as he is wise, and bad in as far as he is foolish?

(Vol. III, p. 28)

Socrates goes on to suggest that a better education could not be found for heroes than in the two divisions of gymnastics for the body and music for the soul:

Socrates:	And our story shall be the education of our heroes.
Adeimantus:	By all means.
Socrates:	And what shall be their education? Can we find a better than the traditional sort?—and this has two divisions, gymnastic for the body, and music for the soul.
Adeimantus:	True.

(Vol. III, pp. 58–59)

For one thing, Plato lived in a time when music was still considered to consist of the inseparable elements of referential words and non-referential music, not as we defined it in Chapter 4. But Plato was keenly aware of this separation and spoke of it explicitly:

Socrates:	And when you speak of music, do you include literature or not?
Adeimantus:	I do.

(Vol. III, pp. 59)

But Plato also calls this combination of words and music, song, as we have throughout this book, and makes no distinction between the words that are set to instrumental music and words which are not:

Socrates:	You can tell that a song or ode has three parts—the words, the melody, and the rhythm; that degree of knowledge I may presuppose?
Glaucon:	Yes, so much as that you may.
Socrates:	And as for the words, there surely be no difference between words which are and which are not set to music; both will conform to the same laws, and these have been already determined by us?

Glaucon: Yes.
Socrates: And the melody and rhythm will depend upon the words?
Glaucon: Certainly.

(Vol. III, pp. 58–59)

So, here we see Plato consciously reflect the definition of music we so carefully detailed in Chapter 4: the referential aspects of language and ideas that include the words, plots and stories of literature, and the non-referential parts of music, which include melody and rhythm. Sound familiar? Outside of this oddity of whether to include words in the actual definition of music, Plato shares our broader conception of mousikē—any activity governed by the Muses—in many ways, the same wide view that we have taken of "song" we first introduced in Chapter 7.

Plato understood that when you attach ideas to music, it can have a profound effect upon the listener. Plato really, really distrusted that special power of music. Like many philosophers of his and subsequent days, he needed to reconcile the undeniable power of music, idea and mimesis—especially when they got together in theatre—with the cultural milieu of his day. Isobel Henderson describes the situation: "It is true that to classical Greek minds music was like a second language, capable of expressing almost all that could be said in words, and of bringing out the moods or passions latent in them" (1955, 385). Plato was, in fact, suspicious of all the musical aspects of poetry, particularly rhythm and melody (line), because of the way these found their way into the human soul and affected a person's ethos:

> musical training is a more potent instrument than any other, because rhythm and harmony find their way into the inward places of the soul, on which they mightily fasten, imparting grace, and making the soul of him who is rightly educated graceful, or of him who is ill-educated ungraceful.

(Vol. III, p. 88)

The solution was to insist that music subordinate to language, and this was easy to justify. Since musical styles had evolved from the dialects of the various ethnic groups, these should only be employed as they best served the state. Or at least that would be the story that Plato would eventually advocate.

Plato first wanted to seriously control what sorts of things children learned in school, starting with the ideas in literature:

Socrates: And literature may be either true or false?
Glaucon: Yes. . . .
Socrates: The first thing will be to establish a censorship of the writers of fiction, and let the censors receive any tale of fiction which is good, and reject the bad . . .

(Vol. III, p. 59)

Socrates: Some tales are to be told, and others are not to be told to our disciples from their youth upwards, if we mean them to honour the gods and their parents, and to value friendship with one another.

(Vol. III, p. 69)

Then Plato insisted that students needed to be taught how to match the music to the text in the classical tradition:

Socrates: And the melody and rhythm will depend on the words?
Glaucon: Certainly. . . .
Socrates: The teacher and the learner ought to use the sounds of the lyre, because its notes are pure, the player who teaches and his pupil rendering note for note in unison; but complexity, and variation of notes, when the strings give one sound and the poet or composer of the melody gives another—also when they make concords and harmonies in which lesser and greater intervals, slow and quick, or high and low notes, are combined—or, again, when they make complex variations of rhythms, which they adapt to the notes of the lyre—all that sort of thing is not suited to those who have to acquire a speedy and useful knowledge of music in three years.

(Vol. III, p. 84)

Because music was so powerful in stimulating emotions, Plato felt a strong need to ban any modes that did not promote a strong ethos or character disposition. Plato rejected both the bass Lydian and the tenor Lydian scales. These expressed "sorrow" and were "useless . . . even to women." (!) Also out were the Lydian and the Ionian. These are the modes of drunkenness, softness and indolence, and "unbecoming the character of our guardians" (Vol. III, p. 84). This just left the Dorian—for times of war, which require the "strain of necessity . . . the unfortunate . . . and courage," and the Phrygian, for times of peace, which demand "the strain of freedom . . . the fortunate . . . and temperance."

In the color department, Plato would ban any instruments capable of producing the banned melodic modes, including many stringed instruments and the flute. Okay was the simple lyre and the pipe for shepherds in the country (Vol. III, p. 85). Also out were sound effects:

Socrates: Nor may they imitate the neighing of horses, the bellowing of bulls, the murmur of rivers and roll of the ocean, thunder, and all that sort of thing?
Adeimantus: Nay, he said, if madness be forbidden, neither may they copy the behavior of madmen.

(Vol. III, p. 81)

Plato wasn't so sure about which rhythms expressed which emotions (he decided to leave that job to his contemporary, the Greek music theoretician, Damon). But he was sure that complex rhythms would lead to no good. Simple rhythms were "the expression of a courageous and harmonious life. . . (and) grace or the absence of grace is an effect of good or bad rhythm" (Vol. III, p. 85).

Plato, of course, was writing in an era in which the old laws of music and language intrinsically interwoven into poetry, were no longer followed. Plato felt an increasing need to address that growing trend to ignore the important moral and ethical ideas that had been embedded in poetry and Greek theatre, and, instead, to simply create music for its own sake. By the time he wrote his Laws, Plato had refined his thinking that music was divinely transmitted by the Muses through the composer to the performer to the audience like the rings of Heracles's magnet:

Athenian Stranger: Do we not regard all music as representative and imitative?
Cleinias: Certainly . . .
Athenian Stranger: And will he who does not know what is true be able to dis-
                        tinguish what is good and bad?

(Vol. V, p. 47)

Plato argued that if one did not truly know what the thing was that was imitated, that one could not be sure that what was imitated was good. And if one imitated bad things, then one could inadvertently transmit and incite a "bad" disposition. So, there must be laws to prevent musicians from imitating any old thing. It would not be enough to simply assert that one was "inspired by the Muses":

Socrates: Then let us not faint in discussing the peculiar difficulty of music. Music is more celebrated than any other kind of imitation, and therefore requires the greatest care of them all. For if a man makes a mistake here, he may do himself the greatest injury by welcoming evil dispositions, and the mistake may be very difficult to discern, because the poets are artists very inferior in character to the Muses themselves.

(Vol. V, p. 48)

Plato adopted the emerging conception of mimesis, an admittedly ambiguous term even in fourth-century Greece, to explain human intervention in the creative process. This included so many of the modern inventions that Plato protested against, instrumental music, the indiscriminate mixing of modes and language, unorthodox use of musical instruments, etc. However, according to Anderson and Mathiesen, Plato

> repeatedly failed . . . to reconcile the component of musical ethos which is mimetic of human attitudes with the rhythmic and melodic component of ethos. . . . He saw music as a vehicle of ethos through mimesis; and he held to this practical view even if it had to be at the expense of Pythagorean theories of number and cosmic harmony.

(Anderson and Mathiesen 2007–2016)

For Mathieson, Plato's interest in musical mimesis had to do solely with the ability of music to affect ethos. For Plato, music could only be mimetic that joined and carried text. Instrumental music was not mimetic.

Plato felt so strongly about this that he wanted to ban any advances in music. He thought that unregulated departures from approved music would destroy civilization (Vol. III, p. 112). But the cat was already out of the bag in ancient Greece: composers and performers were all making music with no thought of what they were "imitating." They were simply expressing themselves, allowing the inspiration of the Muses to pass through them to the listener. Plato is not the only major public figure to make this claim throughout history: jazz, rock and roll, hip hop and many other forms of music have all been accused of portending the end of civilization.[3] Here, in a very real and somewhat elegant argument, was an exploration of the effects of conditioning using implicit memory as we discussed in Chapter 10.

The concept of mimesis and ethos remains controversial. Some, such as Gerald Else, argue that the basis of mimesis lies in imitation: "What we can infer with some confidence is that the original sphere of mimesis—or rather of mimos and mimeisthai was the imitation of animate beings, animal and human, but the body and the voice (not necessarily the singing voice)." But if we follow this argument, we must simultaneously consider the evidence presented earlier of the beliefs that drove animism, in which someone who could imitate, such as an animal or deceased human, was thought to be possessed by the soul of that person. At what point did the shaman stop imitating animals and humans, and truly believe that they were channeling the souls of animals and humans? In such a world, what does it really mean to "imitate"? Else appears to recognize this when he says:

> the key to the puzzle . . . is the psychological premise (that) the thing which dramatic imitation (in Plato's sense, i.e., impersonation) and musical imitation have in common is assimilation of one's soul to the character of the person or "life" which is imitated. . . . Plato brought together mimesis, with its dramatic connotations, and the concept of assimilation which was at home in music.

Else suggests that the unique conception behind this complex interaction between music, idea (language) and mimesis was Plato's (Else 1958, 85).

Hermann Koller, on the other hand, argued that the origin of the word mimesis lay in the primitive expressive power of music, and that imitation was a much later development. Mimesis had to do with those rings of Plato, that unique ability of humans to express themselves and incite in others similar states through the experience of music. Koller argues that Plato introduces this concept specifically so that he could use its derivation to condemn certain types of poetry, in the same sense that we have explored how Plato felt a strong need to use government to control the extraordinary power that music had on an individual (Else 1958, 84).

In any case, we find a culture squarely becoming aware of the unique power of music, and attempting to understand it, and even to develop governmental systems to control it. The core concept is that simply translating the term mimesis to mean imitating something undermines both the Greek worldview and the very fundamental conceptions we have examined in this book. Even Merlin Donald's discussion of mimesis as an evolutionary adaptation, as we discussed in Chapters 5 and 6, implies not just the imitation of an action, but the internalization of the action itself. Music is not simply an imitation of someone else's colors, rhythms, melodies and so forth. The music experience involves the transmission of the actual experience of music from the composer through the performer and into the listener. It involves the powerful evolutionary physiological and psychological systems that we explored in Chapter 9, often without our conscious awareness of the process. Successful mimesis unleashes something almost frighteningly more powerful: the ability to transport the listener into the world of the performer, whether strictly emotional and temporal in the case of instrumental music, or more powerful and complete when ideas become attached to music in song, and actors bring the characters to life in theatre. This process seems to occur in much the same way that shamans embodied the souls of passed ancestors as we explored in Chapter 9 and that developed into animism in Chapter 10. And that was precisely what Plato was worried about.

This problem of imitation versus mimesis is not simply one that the ancient Greeks wrestled with in order to form a better democracy. It lies at the very core of the art of theatre, and, inasmuch as theatre is a type of music, at the core of the challenge facing the sound designer and composer. Remember that we examined the biological base behind true mimesis and indicating in Chapter 8. In acting as well as composing, there are two ways to get at an emotion: by imitating the emotion, or by genuinely generating the emotion. Twentieth Century Fox acting coach Scott Rogers describes the problem of indicating: "One of the most common problems for actors tends to be the temptation to indicate emotions. There is only one way to convincingly act real emotions in film, and that is, to actually FEEL the emotion" (Rogers 2014). In my classes, and throughout this book, we have offered a series of exercises (Things to Share) in which students attempt to isolate a particular design element (e.g., color, mass, rhythm, space, line, or texture) for a range of emotions (love, anger, fear, joy, and sadness). They then attempt to incite that emotion in the listener by manipulating only one specific design element. But in every class, we eventually get to the discussion about whether the example is truly "inciting" the emotion, or simply representing or "indicating" the emotion. We accept the reality that there is a lot of indicating, especially among beginning composers and sound designers who are still learning their craft.

It might be useful to consider an example of a time when I first became consciously aware of the difference between the two concepts, imitation and mimesis. I was composing a score for our original work, *The Creature*, and working with my good friend and former student, Cory Kent. This was in the 1990s, and the band Limp Bizkit was very popular. We had conceived of the production stylistically as a series of MTV music videos, and Cory and I wanted to explore Limp Bizkit's style. In theatre, unless you are really famous like Stephen Sondheim or Philip Glass, you will have to learn to compose in a variety of styles, so I knew just what to do. The first thing we did was to simply mock up a Limp Bizkit song— imitate it. Then, as is typical for me, we threw that away, and worked to create in that style, but from the honest emotional well of the scene. But we reached an impasse. We could not find a drum fill for a particular moment in the sequence. Finally, I simply rewound the sequencer and just pounded out an almost totally impulsive explosion of random drums. It worked. We edited a little, took a few bad hits away, quantized a little more to tighten up the style, and suddenly we had the exact emotion the moment required. I was amazed how, when I let my conscious self go, and immersed myself in the moment, I could trust I had enough craft to channel my impulses through the style of the piece.

I learned a valuable lesson from this. Often times now I'll create an underscore or a strong emotional musical moment in a scene by simply turning on the recorder, finding a versatile patch (strings with a velocity-controlled variable attack work well), and just playing in the emotion as much as I can for as long as 20 or 30 minutes, typically around a short motif of a few notes. Of course, I'll drift in and out of the most powerful and honest expression of the scene. But then I can come back and edit virtually all the bad stuff out, keep the honest and true moments, assign colors to various parts, flesh out the orchestration and so forth. I do all of this knowing that I'm building on a true and honest foundation in which I'm not imitating an emotion, but living in one.

Composing sound scores without indicating requires a rather complete mastery of one's craft. We visited this subject in Chapter 10 when we talked about how tying one's shoes passed from a consciously recalled imitation we called explicit memory and into the unconsciously recalled implicit memory where we no longer imitate, but simply tie our shoes. Let's consider a couple of examples. Having worked with a number of international students, I always check in with them to find out when they started thinking and even dreaming in English rather than mentally translating into their native language. Typically, this seems to take place about four to eight months after they become totally immersed in the language. They have mastered conversational English, and now they can simply exist in it. In sports, If I were to teach a child how to hit a baseball, I would show the child how to hold the bat, how to swing it, etc. The child would then imitate me. At first, the child's imitation would not be very good. Flash forward 20 years to the child now playing in the major leagues. He no longer imitates swinging the bat. The craft of swinging a bat is so deeply ingrained that the major league slugger is no longer imitating. Instead he feels it deep inside, and incites that musical motion of a great swing from deep within—like the source magnet of Plato's rings. At that point, we could hardly say the man was imitating. Although he got to where he was through imitation.

Most musicians have the same experience learning to play piano. At first, we imitate, by reading notes on a page, and struggling to get our fingers to conform to the patterns the composer indicated. But in every piece, there comes a time when we have stopped doing that—we've learned the piece—and then we just start being the piece, fully immersed in its emotional journey. For example, I can attest to having emotion incited in me when I learned to play Chopin— the moment in which I stopped trying to imitate anything, and just became immersed in the music, genuinely feeling the strong emotions Chopin elicits. As an audience member, I've spoken quite a bit in this book about memorable moments where I've felt the emotions of the performance deeply. But the problem with teaching scoring is that we are asking composers to write to an emotion. We are asking them to empathize with a character, scene or theme of a story rather than merely sympathize. That turns out to be very hard to do for some composers. It requires an actor's process coupled with the craft and genius of the composer.

As one perfects one's craft, one no longer concentrates on imitation; instead one works to develop the emotion, let it out through music, where it can then incite a similar emotion in both the actors and the audience. Indicating in sound scores, is perhaps as distracting as indicating in acting. But young sound designers and composers should not shy away from learning the "craft" of composing to a specific emotion through imitation, in the same way that they would not shy away from learning how to hit a baseball properly.

For Plato, the problem was that the young upstart composers had learned their craft very well, and were composing whatever they felt. They were no longer imitating virtuous states Plato thought necessary to create virtuous citizens! There were no longer any rules about what could be attached to these compositions either, and this was an even greater threat to the state. So, by the time Plato laid down his Laws, he had developed a conception of music that of necessity considered "all music as representative and imitative"—as it did in the old days of the classics, when the melody of the lyre must follow the same inseparable core as the prosody of the actor.

Aristotle's Theatre

Isobel Henderson describes the Peloponnesian war that ended in 404 BCE as "the decisive event" that included "the revolt against (music's) former intellectual elite . . . musical incompetence, once the mark of the cad, became a plume of the new snobbery. It was asked whether the citizen should practice music at all" (Henderson 1955, 339–340). It was into that postwar world that Aristotle, perhaps the greatest mind ever, was born.

Aristotle (384–322 BCE) would have a profound effect on the disciplines of "biology, botany, chemistry, ethics, history, logic, metaphysics, rhetoric, philosophy of mind, philosophy of science, physics, poetics, political theory, psychology, and zoology" (Britannica.com 2013, 1). He was, perhaps, the first to truly begin to understand the unique nature of the human mind to categorize knowledge as we described in Chapter 10, and he did so continuously and relentlessly throughout his life.

In 366 BCE, at the ripe old age of 18, Aristotle traveled to Athens where he became a member of Plato's Academy. He studied there with Plato for the last

Figure 12.10 Aristotle.

Credit: Photo by Jastrow of a Roman copy in the National Museum of Rome of a Greek bronze; original by Lyssippos from 330 BCE. Adapted by Richard K. Thomas.

20 years of Plato's life, and developed a philosophy that bridged Plato's primarily classical view and the realities of fourth-century Greece. Both Plato and Aristotle are thought to have discussed and written their own unique opinions on mimesis and ethos during that 20-year period they spent at the academy together: Plato in his Laws, and Aristotle, primarily in his *Politics* and *Poetics* (Britannica.com 2013). Aristotle's thinking, then, was displaced by at least three-quarters of a century from the part of the classical age that Plato pined for; the era of classical Greek theatre from which almost all of our extant plays come. Henderson argues that Aristotle wrote in an age that had all but forgotten the music from that classical period. Music for the plays before the Peloponnesian war was composed for each play. It was not written down and, after the war, musical illiteracy became commonplace. Aristotle suggested that it be left to professionals (Henderson 1955, 337–340). Imagine trying to perform the music of the Beatles or stage a theatre performance of *Oklahoma!* if we didn't have any recordings, no written down music, and no one remembered any of the tunes—all that was left were the words.

By the end of Plato's time, and in Aristotle's prime, the relationship between music and theatre had changed. Dislodged was Pythagorean intellectual discourse, which apparently never really caught on with the lower classes, since they needed to be kept in line with "the hint of a stick." Audiences loved the way the new music made them feel, and it was only a matter of time before its emotional power won out over didactic formalities. From a government's point of view, emotionally inciting mass audiences rather than teaching them the ins and outs of ethics was not a good development. This was the age in which Aristotle wrote, and to which history has placed such an extraordinary emphasis on his teachings.

Like many of you reading this book, Aristotle believed a lot of things his teacher taught him, and didn't buy into some of it at all. In Chapter 4, we started to define the word "music" based on Plato's conception, who used the word mousikê and included language as a part of music. We then narrowed that definition to exclude referential ideas as expressed in language. Aristotle did the same thing, forever changing the meaning of the word "music" to conform to how most people perceive the word today. He used the neuter, plural form of the term, "ta mousika," which roughly corresponds to our English term, "music" (Anderson and Mathiesen n.d.). Without having any of the evolutionary evidence we uncovered in Chapter 7, Aristotle separated language from music in much the same way we have throughout this book. We found a neurological basis for separating music from language in some of the right-brain and left-brain neurological processes in Chapter 7. Aristotle simply discerned them logically.

In his "Rhetoric," Aristotle divided the modes of persuasion into three parts:

1. *Ethos*, the personal character of the speaker
2. *Pathos*, the ability of speech to stir emotions
3. *Logos*, using reason or logic to prove a truth or apparent truth (Aristotle 2000, Book I Part 2).

Note the same division between logos (idea) and pathos (music) we have carefully separated throughout this book, because we think that they use such fundamentally different techniques to accomplish their ends.

Aristotle agreed with Plato that music could influence a person's ethos, but differed with Plato in that he didn't perceive a direct connection between the experience of music and ethos. Aristotle never ascribed to Plato's idea that the effects of music were originated by the Muses and then transferred from composer to listener like the power of a magnet. Aristotle doesn't appear to have placed much stock in inspiration being provided by the Muses at all. He rarely refers to them, and then, typically as mythological figures. Plato thought that only virtuous music should be allowed, Aristotle did not think that music had such a permanent ability to alter the "ethos" of the listener. For Aristotle, music was a skill, not a virtue (Anderson and Mathiesen 2007–2016). Plato wanted to ban the professional instrumentalists that so appealed to the popular masses. Aristotle embraced them. Simply listening to bad music wouldn't make you bad. Aristotle agreed with Plato that ethos was a disposition to which you habituated. He differed with Plato in that Aristotle thought this habituation took place over a long period of time, and was not the result of simply listening to music (Anderson and Mathiesen 2007–2016). Once again, we see this difference debated endlessly in our modern culture: should music and movies be censored if they incite good people to do bad things? As we discussed in Chapter 10, how does implicit memory conditioning affect our worldview. To which Aristotle added, "and how does that conditioning take place?"

Aristotle had no problem with music existing simply to provide pleasure. In Chapter 9 we asked, "What's so good about feeling bad?" Aristotle was compelled to wonder what was so bad about feeling good: "the pleasure given by music is natural, and therefore adapted to all ages and characters" (Aristotle 1885, 252). Music makes us happy, so why shouldn't it be part of our educational system? Aristotle thought that education in music would prove beneficial later in life when one listened to music. He did not think that what one listened to directly resulted in noble living (Anderson and Mathiesen 2007–2016).

Aristotle also differed substantially from Plato in his conception of mimesis. Whereas Plato understood the emotions generated in the performer and in the listener to be real (and induced like the magnetism in iron rings), Aristotle thought that music was more imitative because the poet, the performer, and the listener all did not experience music in the same way. Aristotle argued that everyone experiences the emotional content of music in "exact proportion to their susceptibility to such emotions." For example, if the music expressed anger, the composer would not become angry in the same way that the performer would become angry or the listener would become angry. Music, in and of itself, was not angry (Sorbam 1994, 43). Here we find Aristotle making what is perhaps a direct and astute connection between the dreamlike experience of music and theatre, and the mental process of combining the dreamlike experience with the totality of our memory, as we discussed in the section on autobiographical memory in Chapter 10.

Cognitively, we have already explored this dichotomy between Plato's and Aristotle's perception: music does have extraordinary power to incite emotions in us without conscious participation on our part (especially in our primitive brain). At the same time, we also possess the ability to employ the newer part of our brain, the cerebrum, to consciously analyze and regulate our emotional responses to music, and to make these judgments in light of our memories. In doing so, we are perfectly capable of imitating emotional reactions without really experiencing the emotions themselves. In this sense, we can see that both Plato and Aristotle explored differing aspects of human response to music, most likely under the strong influence of the culture that shaped their worldview.

In Aristotle's case, he correctly identified that an actor or a musician could imitate an emotion, and this might have the effect of creating an emotion in a listener. But my experience and the development of both musician and actor performance styles have both shown that the most powerful emotional performances are ones in which the actor or musician do not simply "imitate" an emotional state, but experience it as a real and true state of consciousness. It would be hard to imagine an audience member being able to have much of an emotional experience if either they or the actor were simply imitating emotional states. As David K. O'Connor argues in the *Routledge Guide to Ancient Philosophy*, "if we merely contemplate the protagonist, and even if we learn an important general truth about human beings from the example on stage, the tragedy has not succeeded. Such contemplative cognition of an example is fundamentally different from identification with a protagonist we take as an exemplar" (O'Connor 2014, 385). For Aristotle, pathos, especially as provided by the experience of music, provided a special kind of mimesis that went beyond simple imitation.

In his "Rhetoric," Aristotle specifically addresses how the manner of delivery (music/pathos) affects the content (language/logos):

> The proper method of delivery; this is a thing that affects the success of a speech greatly; but hitherto the subject has been neglected. Indeed, it was long before it found a way into the arts of tragic drama and epic recitation: at first poets acted their tragedies themselves. It is plain that delivery has just as much to do with oratory as with poetry. . . . It is, essentially, a matter of the right management of the voice to express the various emotions-of speaking loudly, softly, or between the two; of high, low, or intermediate pitch; of the various rhythms that suit various subjects.
>
> These are the three things—volume of sound, modulation of pitch, and rhythm [n.b., mass, color and rhythm, respectively]—that a speaker bears in mind. It is those who do bear them in mind who usually win prizes in the dramatic contests; and just as in drama the actors now count for more than the poets, so it is in the contests of public life, owing to the defects of our political institutions. No systematic treatise upon the rules of delivery has yet been composed; indeed, even the study of language made no progress till late in the day. Besides, delivery is—very properly—not regarded as an elevated subject of inquiry. Still, the whole business of rhetoric being concerned with appearances, we must pay attention to the subject of delivery, unworthy though it is, because we cannot do without it.
>
> The right thing in speaking really is that we should be satisfied not to annoy our hearers, without trying to delight them: we ought in fairness to fight our case with no help beyond the bare facts: nothing, therefore, should matter except the proof of those facts. Still, as has been already said, other things affect the result considerably, owing to the *defects of our hearers* [italics mine]. The arts of language cannot help having a small but real importance, whatever it is we have to expound to others: the way in which a thing is said does affect its intelligibility. Not, however, so much importance as people think. All such arts are fanciful and meant to charm the hearer. Nobody uses fine language when teaching geometry.
>
> (Aristotle 2000)

"The defects of our hearers." What could these defects be? They seem to translate rather directly to our definition of music from Chapter 4: "Speaking loudly, softly, or between the two" (mass); "of high, low or intermediate pitch" (color); and "the various rhythms that suit various subjects" (rhythm). Notice how Aristotle describes these "defects" purely in terms consistent with our definition of music!

Aristotle spent some amount of time investigating those "defects of our hearers." Like Plato, he struggled to reconcile the extraordinary power of music with the prevalent worldview of his day. He thought, as Merlin Donald did in Chapters 5 and 10, that imitation was a natural instinct:

> the instinct of imitation is implanted in man from childhood, one difference between him and other animals being that he is the most imitative of living creatures, and through imitation learns his earliest lessons; and no less universal is the pleasure felt in things imitated.
>
> (Aristotle 2009a, Section I, Part IV)

Aristotle suggested that like a picture, which is an imitation of a real thing, music must also be an image of a real thing, or as Plato put it, "Do we not make one house by the art of building, and another by the art of drawing, which is sort of dream created by man for those who are awake?" (Vol. IV, pp. 403–404). Aristotle thought that music must be an image of human character, for example, an imitation of anger, or joy, or fear or sadness:

> Rhythm and melody supply imitations of anger and gentleness, and also of courage and temperance, and of all the qualities contrary to these, and of the other qualities of character, which hardly fall short of the actual affections, as we know from our own experience, for in listening to such strains our souls undergo a change.
>
> (Aristotle 2009c, 252)

Already we see Aristotle hedging his bet: "which hardly fall short of the actual affections." He goes on to note that this quality is quite unique to music: "The objects of no other sense, such as taste or touch, have any resemblance to moral qualities" (Aristotle 2009c, 252) This ability of music to cause "our souls" to "undergo a change" perhaps compelled Aristotle to consider the nature of the relationship between the audience and the protagonist. He quite specifically describes the nature of the protagonist in drama: "we must represent men either as better than in real life, or as worse, or as they are . . . for Comedy aims at representing men as worse, Tragedy as better than in actual life" (Aristotle 2009b, Part II). Is this because the audience will identify with the protagonist—to become so immersed in the dreamlike nature of the play that they begin to imagine themselves in the role of the protagonist actively involved in the action of the play? Certainly, this is a concept that has been taught with some regularity in beginning theatre courses for some time. And, if we are going to identify with the protagonist, to enter that dreamlike state in which we find ourselves powerfully involved in the actions and events of the drama, it does seem to be in our best interest for our noble self to suffer the outrages of the injustices of fate in tragedy, and our ignoble self to witness the consequences of our foibles in comedy. Perhaps any other way would be too cruel, and maybe, even personally devastating.

Much is made in literature about Aristotle's thoughts about the nature of the audience's identification with the protagonist, the very specific type of mimesis involved in acting and singing that we discussed in Chapters 5 and 10. In the dreamlike world of the play that we first discussed in Chapter 3, we have argued repeatedly that music, by the nature of its neurological processes, lures us into an empathetic (rather than sympathetic) response similar to the characters in the play, especially the protagonist. For Plato, this was such a strong response that he felt music should only be used for virtuous characters. To use music to score the not-so-virtuous characters opened a very real door to creating less than virtuous citizens. But Aristotle recognized the tug of war that went on within the minds of the theatre audience. On the one hand, music continuously pulls us into this sense of identification—to the extent that we share the same subjective sense of time, mood and emotions as the protagonist. In such a process, our episodic memories may merge the experience of the play into the mental time-travel of autonoesis that we discussed in Chapter 10. On the other hand, Aristotle understood that everyone experienced music in "exact proportion to their susceptibility to such emotions" (Aristotle 2009c, VIII). In our more modern thesis of Chapter 10, autobiographical memories may introduce other elements of our memory that force a more analytical distancing of ourselves from the protagonist.

Thus, as artists, we find ourselves faced with creative opportunities provided by yet another continuum. On one hand, we experience the play as a dreamlike journey, more Platonic and, in modern times, carried to the extreme by the first-person camera technique used by master filmmakers such as Alfred Hitchcock. On the other hand, we may consciously want to distance our audience from the dreamlike identification with the protagonist, a concept Aristotle clearly wrestled with in his exploration of the required characteristics of the protagonist, and taken to its logical extreme in Bertolt Brecht's approach to theatre.

Aristotle clearly struggled with the concept of mimesis as applied to music, and by extension, to theatre. Anderson and Mathieson commented on Aristotle's mimesis problem: "The proofs throughout are strikingly empirical, however, with very little theory of any kind as a balance; the evidence is derivative; and the reader is left with no explanation either of the 'likenesses' or of the affinity of the soul with mode and rhythm" (Anderson and Mathiesen 2017a).

Plato, Aristotle and others of their day had precious little to go on other than their own very limited empirical ability to study the human condition. Still, they made amazing observations that correlate quite well with much of the evolutionary evidence we have uncovered throughout this book. In all cases, our concern is that music works its way into the "inner soul," where it then joins, and becomes a part of each person's unique life narrative, their autobiographical memory. Plato felt that this joining was so complete, and so influential, that he wanted to ban advances in music and seriously control the stimuli in the first place. Aristotle gave humans a lot more credit to analyze the incoming stimuli, but still was keenly aware of the power of music and theatre to affect the life narrative.

In the end, as far as music goes, we must circle back to Plato's rings; you do not need to think about music to have it affect you. Harold Burris-Meyer's famous comment "you can shut your eyes, but the sound comes out to get you" suggests a different experience the audience has with music than it has with language and ideas, and the imitations thereof. Aristotle correctly suggested that an actor or a musician could imitate an emotion, and this might have the effect of creating an emotion in a listener. Anyone who has performed over a long run understands this problem. While it is hard to determine the extent that performances in Aristotle's time were inwardly motivated or outwardly imitated, our knowledge of how emotion is incited suggests that the strongest emotions are created more like Plato's rings than the low road of simple imitation. This is important to understanding how the more complex concept of mimesis works with the more primeval power of music. It's important to understanding that when you combine music and acting you create a very powerful ability to transport your audience into the dreamlike world of theatre.

Aristotle elaborates about the powerful effect that music and mimesis have on the ethos of the audience. He elaborated on this in his "Politics," suggesting that music also had an important therapeutic effect:

> In education, the most ethical modes are to be preferred, but in listening to the performances of others we may admit the modes of action and passion also. For feelings such as pity and fear, or, again, enthusiasm, exist very strongly in some souls, and have more or less influence over all. Some persons fall into a religious frenzy, whom we see as a result of the sacred melodies—when they have used the melodies that excite the soul to mystic frenzy— restored as though they had found healing and purgation. Those who are influenced by pity or fear, and every emotional nature, must have a like experience, and others in so far as each is susceptible to such emotions, and all are in a manner purged and their souls lightened and delighted. The purgative melodies likewise give an innocent pleasure to mankind.
>
> (Aristotle 2009c, 257)

What does Aristotle mean by "all are in a manner purged and their souls lightened and delighted. The purgative melodies likewise give an innocent pleasure to mankind"? Unfortunately, Aristotle promised to give a better description of this "purging" in his "Poetics," but never did. And that's too bad, because the underlying concept of this purging, which we first encountered in Chapter 7 in its more commonly used term, catharsis, has created controversy pretty much ever since. Letwin, Stockdale and Stockdale cite a dissertation that revealed "over ninety different interpretations" of the term (2008, 99).

What Aristotle seems to be saying here is eerily prescient of the phenomenon we first uncovered in Chapter 9. Aristotle appears to have asked the same awkward question we asked there, "what's so good about feeling bad?" and responded in terms of "pity and fear, and every emotional nature." Why would the audience subject themselves to that? Aristotle suggested, "all are in a manner purged and their souls lightened and delighted." Did Aristotle make a connection that reflects our more modern understanding that the end result of a musical experience is the pleasurable release of dopamine in the brain? Could this be Aristotle's "innocent pleasure" given to mankind? Well, there are 90 different interpretations of catharsis. Make it 91.

If theatre developed from music, as Aristotle—and we—contend, then it is reasonable to presume that the same catharsis that manifested itself in the music of Aristotle's "Politics" also subsequently manifested itself in his "Poetics."

Nowhere else does Aristotle mention the term other than in the realms of music and theatre. And why not? When the first actor stepped out of the chorus and took on the image of another, the audience would have pretty much the same emotional experience from the actor's performance as from the poet's. The only real difference was the level of mimesis. Aristotle makes this very clear in his "Poetics":

> Epic Poetry and Tragedy, Comedy also and Dithyrambic poetry, and the music of the flute and of the lyre in most of their forms, are all in their general conception . . . produced by rhythm, language, or "harmony," either singly or combined.
>
> (Aristotle 2009b, Section I Part I)

It should come as no surprise, since Aristotle ascribed to the belief that theatre grew out of music, that he then extended his application of catharsis in music from his *Politics* to his definition of tragedy in the *Poetics*:

> Tragedy, then, is an imitation of an action that is serious, complete, and of a certain magnitude; in language embellished with each kind of artistic ornament, the several kinds being found in separate parts of the play; in the form of action, not of narrative; through pity and fear effecting the proper purgation of these emotions. By "language embellished," I mean language into which rhythm, "harmony" and song enter. By "the several kinds in separate parts," I mean, that some parts are rendered through the medium of verse alone, others again with the aid of song.
>
> (Aristotle 2009b, Section 1, Part VI)

Here, Aristotle once again directly ties catharsis (pity and fear effecting the proper purgation of these emotions) to music (rhythm, "harmony" and song). Later, Aristotle directly references back to the power of music to create catharsis in Part VI of Section I: "The power of Tragedy, we may be sure, is felt even apart from representation and actors." And, in another section tells us that: "the plot ought to be so constructed that, even without the aid of the eye, he who hears the tale told will thrill with horror and melt to pity at what takes place" (Aristotle 2009b, Part XIV). Of course, it is not necessary to have actors or scenery to experience the "power of tragedy" and the pleasurable release of dopamine in the brain as any folksinger can confirm. But try to do that without music!

To create this cathartic experience, Aristotle spent a lot of time in his "Poetics" talking about structure and how to trigger arousal. Aristotle's discussion of the play's structure bears a strong resemblance to the activation structures we examined in Chapter 9. He recognized that our brains like structure: "Such an effect is best produced when the events come on us by surprise . . . [but] Even coincidences are most striking when they have an air of design" (Aristotle 2009b, Part IX).

Aristotle, of course, was the first writer to specifically discuss the unique musical structure of theatre. His system, called Aristotelian analysis, has become something of a standard teaching tool in theatre appreciation courses ever since. He started with the obvious, describing the basic structural components of a plot as a whole that has a "beginning, middle and end." Aristotle's beginning corresponds with our modern "given circumstances," which include elements of the story that begin before the action of the play begins and "point of attack," or where the play begins relative to the larger story that includes the given circumstances. Aristotle's middle includes our modern "rising action," subsequent actions that further arouse the audience, creating tension, and suspense. It typically begins at the inciting incident, or as I like to put it for my students, "what makes this day different from any other, and sets a course in motion that inevitably leads to the climax." The climax typically marks the end of the "middle" or rising action. Aristotle's end corresponds to our modern "resolution," or the new order of the world that results as a consequence of the climax of the play.

Of course, Aristotle, and most modern teachers of theatre, consider these features of a play to be related to intellectual ideas in the plot. But if that were truly the case, then they would not typically occur in the same places in every play. Rather, I maintain that these elements are the typical structures of the musical form we call theatre. They operate similarly to sonata-allegro form, or the form for a three-part invention in other types of music. Their musical basis lies in the activation structures of music we explored in Chapter 9. Aristotle's beginning establishes a form of habituation in which we become accustomed to the world of the play. His middle consists of a series of smaller units that employ arousal, anticipation and (sometimes temporary) resolution leading to new tentative habituations. These small segments combine together in a larger form of slowly escalating arousal and anticipation leading to the climax of the play. Aristotle's end is typically a period of final habituation as we become accustomed to the new order of the world established by the events of the play and the resolution of the climax.

It's worth noting for sound designers and composers that one of the main differences in sonata form and theatre form is that sonata form typically ends in a recapitulation, or reiteration of the main theme in the home key. Theatre typically ends with the "new order of the world." We have discussed the neurological basis for this difference in Chapters 9 and 10. In the resolution of the play, we often reiterate one of the main themes of the play as a type of "recapitulation," but rendered in a style more immersed in the new world of the play. In this way, we are able to bring back the emotional baggage of memories as we discussed in Chapter 10 into the new order of the world. Of course, there are as many variations on this musical formula as there are variations of musical formulas in any form of music. In the modern theatre, this is especially true. As structure has become increasingly explored, understanding how music works may be the surest way to create a satisfying theatre experience for our audience!

One final point worth noting: Aristotle limited the length of this main structure to a "single revolution of the sun." Why? According to Aristotle, "in the plot, a certain length is necessary, and a length which can be easily embraced by memory" (Aristotle 2009b, Section I, Book V). While Aristotle conceded that epic poetry allowed for "no limits of time," the mimesis of tragedy required the particular Muse to operate under greater restraint of the mother ship, Mnemosyne, the goddess of memory. In Chapter 10 we discussed the ability of the human brain to chunk information. Aristotle appears to have been aware of the limitations of the Greek theatre production system to chunk information into easily memorable units. In modern times, we no longer feel constrained to strictly adhere to the "unity of time." This may be because we simply have a much more sophisticated arsenal of tools available that help us more effectively chunk salient elements of the play together into a more meaningful whole. This may also have something to do with a more Lamarckian evolution that has taken place between now and the classical age of Greek theatre.

Conclusion of the Conclusion

After Aristotle's death in 322 BCE, the great classical styles of ancient Greece became a distant—and sometimes completely forgotten—memory. A new wave of what Isobel Henderson calls "popular classics" and "a flood of transient stuff" all "petered out in the backwoods of Arcadia" after the Roman conquest (Henderson 1955, 337). Music took over, and it was the musicians who became rock stars. In the ancient world, drama, separated from music by the invention of writing, would not again achieve the lofty status held fast by a time in which the oral tradition reigned, and, in which music and idea were inseparable.

But we witnessed the development of the autonomous theatre exactly as evolution predicted it: musical expression coupled with ideas inseparably merged into a lengthy oral tradition of song that eventually developed specific genres in a special partnership with mimesis: choral poetry (comedy) and dithyrambs (tragedy). Theatre = song + mimesis. We witnessed the songs of Homer turn into the rituals of the dithyrambs, phallic songs, and Dionysian festivals, and these in turn develop into the first autonomous theatre. We saw how, from the earliest times, ancient Greeks explained the unique relationship between music and time that we laid out in Chapters 2 and 3: nine Muses, each a goddess of a different temporal art. We discovered how Aristotle gradually developed an understanding of the unique nature of music that separated music and language, ta mousika, that we proposed in our definition in Chapter 4 and further explored in Chapter 7. For Aristotle, as for us, separating music and idea (language) proved much more useful in understanding the unique power of each than Plato's mousikē, which combined language and music into one inseparable art (that we would later describe as song). And yet, we cannot deny another fundamental thesis of this book, the need to reunite music and idea as Plato conceived, in order to maximize the expressive power that theatre has to transport us into other realms.

We saw how the Greeks wrestled with mimesis, a concept that, as we explored in Chapter 5, turned out to be much more than simple imitation. We explored its unique relationship to music, the process of going from a simple imitation to becoming the thing imitated, to possibly enabling empathetic responses such as those elicited by music. In Chapter 5 we also witnessed some of the earliest evidence of ritual, perhaps a byproduct of mimesis, in our ancient primate animal ancestors. It should not surprise us then, that we discovered elements of mimesis in ritual prominently featured in an apparently unbroken chain in our family tree from monkeys through to the earliest civilizations on earth to the mythological roots of Greek theatre. And where there was ritual, there was always, music, at least in the broad terms we define music in this book.

We saw how Aristotle correctly identified some of the same fundamental elements of music that we have, whether loudness, pitch and rhythm, as Aristotle called them, or the more ubiquitous mass, color and rhythm of our expanded definition of music. Even more importantly we found both Aristotle and Plato wrestling with the mysterious properties that these elements possess, which we have identified in the neuroscience of subconscious entrainment of rhythm (Chapter 6), consonance and dissonance (Chapter 8) and phrasing (Chapter 9), as well as the arousal stimuli of startle, habituation and other mass effects we considered in Chapters 2 and 9.

Going even further, we discovered that Aristotle may have put his finger on the fundamental reason we love music and its progeny theatre so much: the neurological reward provided by the experience of music that we first examined in Chapter 9. Aristotle called it an "innocent pleasure," and we linked the effect to the pleasurable experience that makes the human brain such an "arousal seeking organ." For Plato, the pleasures were not so innocent, however. He wanted the government to carefully control them, lest the theatre contribute to a society of less than "virtuous" citizens.

We saw in that mythology of the Muses, a very primal and innate understanding of the unique relationship between music, consciousness and memory that we explored in Chapters 9 and 10. The same nine Muses that each inspired a different temporal art were the progeny of the "timeless mind" of Zeus, king of the gods and son of the god of time, Kronos, and Mnemosyne, goddess of memory. The implications of the special power that music has to manipulate human consciousness underscored Greek aesthetics, cosmology and philosophy, from the Muses and the mind of Zeus through Pythagoras and Plato, through Aristotle's "defects of our hearers."

Both Plato and Aristotle wrestled with the unique way that music affected the listener that we have explored throughout this book. Plato described them as being like the effect of a magnet on iron rings and Aristotle attempted to explain them in his description of mimesis, pathos, ethos and catharsis. The Greeks were at odds over the specific nature and mechanisms of mimesis, and how music worked its way into "the inward places of the soul." But the Greek concepts of mimesis and ethos speak to the very heart of the unique effect that music and theatre has on an audience. They are fundamental ideas that have and will continue to be debated in so many fields of inquiry: anthropology, neuroscience, psychology, history, art, sociology, and many more. When an audience participates in the emotional, dreamlike state of the characters, but simultaneously blends that state with their own unique autobiographical journeys, extraordinary insights and changes to our worldview are possible. And, some would argue, not all of them are indisputably good. No wonder the Greeks were so obsessed with the power of music and theatre to profoundly affect the moral and ethical foundations of our human species!

But, as we first argued in Chapter 1, something often happens when music becomes separated from the ideas of the play. In Chapter 1, we suggested that a separation in the modern theatre was caused by the slow introduction of the electronic control of sound to a mature theatre of ideas and spectacle. But in Greek theatre, we discovered that the problem may have a more deeply ingrained origin than we first suspected. In Chapter 11, we witnessed the development of writing, a method of recording ideas that did not simultaneously record the music. But it was music that had a primal tactile connection to human spirituality. It should not surprise us that the Greeks used a mythical cosmology such as the Muses to explain such a fundamental human adaptation. That phenomenon of the relationship between music and spirituality appears to have held true across all cultures and civilizations all over the world as we discussed in Chapter 11. Each culture expressed spirituality differently, to be sure, but every culture developed a close association between sound and music and the unknown. Greek civilization was no different, but when the music was lost and only ideas were passed down through written words, a situation very similar to the problem we examined in Chapter 1 revealed itself: when the music is divorced from the ideas written down in the drama, bad things can happen unless the artists involved are careful to scrupulously discover and incite the inner music of the play.

And that, friend, has been the journey of this book. Thank you for coming along!

Eleven Questions, Part I

1. Review the main arguments of Chapter 1 and discuss how they manifest themselves in the origins and development of Greek theatre.
2. Review the main arguments of Chapter 2 and discuss how they manifest themselves in the origins and development of Greek theatre.
3. Review the main arguments of Chapter 3 and discuss how they manifest themselves in the origins and development of Greek theatre.
4. Review the main arguments of Chapter 4 and discuss how they manifest themselves in the origins and development of Greek theatre.
5. Review the main arguments of Chapter 5 and discuss how they manifest themselves in the origins and development of Greek theatre.
6. Review the main arguments of Chapter 6 and discuss how they manifest themselves in the origins and development of Greek theatre.
7. Review the main arguments of Chapter 7 and discuss how they manifest themselves in the origins and development of Greek theatre.
8. Review the main arguments of Chapter 8 and discuss how they manifest themselves in the origins and development of Greek theatre.
9. Review the main arguments of Chapter 9 and discuss how they manifest themselves in the origins and development of Greek theatre.
10. Review the main arguments of Chapter 10 and discuss how they manifest themselves in the origins and development of Greek theatre.
11. Review the main arguments of Chapter 11 and discuss how they manifest themselves in the origins and development of Greek theatre.

Eleven Questions, Part II

1. Review the main arguments of Chapter 1 and discuss how they manifest themselves in the philosophies of Plato and Aristotle.
2. Review the main arguments of Chapter 2 and discuss how they manifest themselves in the philosophies of Plato and Aristotle.
3. Review the main arguments of Chapter 3 and discuss how they manifest themselves in the philosophies of Plato and Aristotle.
4. Review the main arguments of Chapter 4 and discuss how they manifest themselves in the philosophies of Plato and Aristotle.
5. Review the main arguments of Chapter 5 and discuss how they manifest themselves in the philosophies of Plato and Aristotle.
6. Review the main arguments of Chapter 6 and discuss how they manifest themselves in the philosophies of Plato and Aristotle.
7. Review the main arguments of Chapter 7 and discuss how they manifest themselves in the philosophies of Plato and Aristotle.
8. Review the main arguments of Chapter 8 and discuss how they manifest themselves in the philosophies of Plato and Aristotle.
9. Review the main arguments of Chapter 9 and discuss how they manifest themselves in the philosophies of Plato and Aristotle.

10. Review the main arguments of Chapter 10 and discuss how they manifest themselves in the philosophies of Plato and Aristotle.
11. Review the main arguments of Chapter 11 and discuss how they manifest themselves in the philosophies of Plato and Aristotle.

Things to Share

1. Having explored the wonderful world of the elements of design throughout this book, now it's time for you to explore all of these concepts together in composition. Find a Shakespearean sonnet that you would like to turn into a short theatre piece. Record the text, and then, being mindful of the prosody (feel free to manipulate that, of course!), orchestrate the sonnet using the techniques you have learned in this book. Find ways to exploit the elements of design—color, rhythm, mass, line, texture and, yes, even space! Compose or design a piece that explores the elements most appropriate to immersing your audience in the world of the sonnet and providing them with a deep and rich emotional journey. As always, play and experiment, but still work to create a cohesive composition.

Notes

1 Note that we have used Fraser's spellings from the *Theogony* of Hesiod (Hesiod 1983, 26).
2 The written records that have survived give us insights into the development of various Greek dialects, but keep in mind that when Homer's poems were actually written down is a subject of much debate. The earliest extant example we have is from the third century BCE (The University of Chicago Library 2014).
3 For more on government censorship of music, visit Freemusic.com.

Bibliography

Anderson, Warren, and Thomas J. Mathiesen. 2007–2016. "Ethos in Oxford Music Online." Accessed January 7, 2017. www.oxfordmusiconline.com:80/subscriber/article/grove/music/09055.
———. 2017a. "Aristotle." Accessed January 15, 2017. www.oxfordmusiconline.com:80/subscriber/article/grove/music/01247.
———. 2017b. "Plato." Accessed March 26, 2017. www.oxfordmusiconline.com:80/subscriber/article/grove/music/21922.
———. n.d. "Aristotle." Oxford University Press. Accessed April 2, 2017. www.oxfordmusiconline.com/subscriber/article/grove/music/01247.
Appolodorus. 1921. *The Library*, edited by Sir James George Frazer. Cambridge, MA: Harvard University Press. www.perseus.tufts.edu/hopper/text?doc=Perseus%3Atext%3A1999.01.0022%3Atext%3DLibrary%3Abook%3D1%3Achapter%3D7%3Asection%3D3.
Aristotle. 1885. *The Politics of Aristotle*. Translated by Benjamin Jowett. Vols. I, II. London: Henry Frowde.
———. 2000. "Rhetoric." The Internet Classics Archive. Accessed January 22, 2017. http://classics.mit.edu/Aristotle/rhetoric.html.
———. 350 BCE. "On the Heavens." Daniel C. Stevenson. Accessed July 21, 2009. http://classics.mit.edu/Aristotle/heavens.html.

————. 2009a. "Metaphysics." The Internet Classics Archive. Accessed December 26, 2016. http://classics.mit.edu/Aristotle/metaphysics.html.

————. 2009b. "Poetics (350 BCE)." The Internet Classics Archive. Daniel C. Stevenson. Accessed January 21, 2017. http://classics.mit.edu/Aristotle/poetics.html.

————. 2009c. "Politics (350 BCE)." The Internet Classics Archive. Accessed December 27, 2016. http://classics.mit.edu/Aristotle/politics.8.eight.html.

Britannica.com. 2013. "Aristotle Greek Philosopher." September 30. Accessed January 15, 2017. www.britannica.com/biography/Aristotle.

Brockett, Oscar G., and Franklin J. Hildy. 2007. *History of Theatre.* Foundation Edition. Boston: Allyn and Bacon.

Cartwright, Mark. 2013. "Greek Tragedy." March 15. Accessed March 26, 2017. www.ancient.eu/Greek_Tragedy/.

Caspo, Eric, and Margaret C. Miller. 2007. *The Origins of Theater in Ancient Greece and Beyond.* New York: Cambridge University Press.

Else, Gerald F. 1958. "'Imitation' in the Fifth Century." *Classical Philology* 53 (2): 73–90.

Encyclopedia Britannica. 2015. "Peloponnesian War." April 27. Accessed March 26, 2017. www.britannica.com/event/Peloponnesian-War.

————. 2016. "Greek Language." October 20. Accessed November 27, 2016. www.britannica.com/topic/Greek-language.

Farmer, Henry George. 1957. "The Music of Ancient Egypt." In *Ancient and Oriental Music,* edited by Egon Wellesz. London: Oxford University Press.

Henderson, Isobel. 1955. "Ancient Greek Music." In *The New Oxford History of Music: Ancient and Oriental Music,* edited by Egon Wellesz, 336–403. London: Oxford University Press.

Hesiod. 1983. *The Poems of Hesiod.* Translated by R. M. Frazer. Norman: University of Oklahoma Press.

————. 2004. *Theogeny, Works and Days, Shield.* 2nd Edition. Baltimore: Johns Hopkins University Press.

James, Jamie. 1995. *The Music of the Spheres.* New York: Copernicus.

Kanopy Streaming. 2015. *Timelines of Ancient Civilizations: Greek Part 1.* San Francisco: kanopy.

Letwin, David, Joe Stockdale, and Robin Stockdale. 2008. *The Architecture of Drama.* Plymouth: Scarecrow Press.

Mallory, J. P., and Adams, D. Q. 2006. *The Oxford Introduction to Proto-Indo-European and the Proto-Indo-European World.* New York: Oxford University Press.

Mathiesen, Thomas J. 1999. *Apollo's Lyre: Greek Music and Music Theory in Antiquity and the Middle Ages.* Lincoln: University of Nebraska Press.

————. 2016. "Mimesis." Accessed December 24, 2016. www.oxfordmusiconline.com/subscriber/article/grove/music/18722.

Meinwald, Constance C. 2016. "Plato." January 29. www.britannica.com/biography/Plato.

O'Connor, David K. 2014. "Aristotle's Aesthetics." In *The Routledge Companion to Ancient Philosophy,* edited by James Warren and Frisbee C. C. Sheffield, 377–390. New York: Routledge/Taylor Francis Group.

Pickard-Cambridge, Arthur W. 1927. *Dithyramb, Tragedy and Comedy.* Oxford: Clarendon Press.

————. 1931. *The Dialogues of Plato.* 3rd Edition. Translated by M.A.B. Jowett. 5 vols. London: Oxford University Press.

————. 1962. *Dithyramb Tragedy and Comedy.* 2nd Edition. London: Oxford University Press.

Rogers, Scott. 2014. "Indicating." August 11. Accessed January 21, 2017. http://scottsactingtips.blogspot.com/2011/08/indicating.html.

Rozik, Eli. 2002. *The Roots of Theatre.* Iowa City: University of Iowa Press.

Sorbam, Goran. 1994. "Aristotle on Music as Representation." *Journal of Aesthetics and Art Criticism* 52 (1), 38-46.

Thaut, Michael H. 2005. *Rhythm, Music, and the Brain.* New York: Routledge Taylor & Francis Group.

Thomas, Carol G. 2014. *Greece: A Short History of a Long Story, 7,000 BCE to Present.* West Sussex: John Wiley & Sons.

The University of Chicago Library. 2014. "Homer Before Print." January 13. Accessed March 19, 2017. www.lib.uchicago.edu/e/webexhibits/homerinprint/preprint.html.

West, M.L. 1981. "The Singing of Homer and the Modes of Early Greek Music." *The Journal of Hellenic Studies* 101: 113–129.

INDEX

Italic page references indicate figures.

3D film 35

absorption property of waves 17
acetylcholine neurotransmitter 202
Acheulean stone tools 115, *116*
acting beat 215–216
acting and music 316
activation 201, 215–216, *215*, 317
actors: Aristotle and 312–313; dialogue
  of 6, 122, 178; pacing and 4; physical
  performance of 6; protagonists 314–315;
  rhythm of 4, 122–123; tempo of 205
Adams, D. Q. 268
adaptation 88
Adeimantus 303, 305
Ad Infinitum 70, 217
ADSR of sound 73, 146–147
aerophones 270, *271*
Aeschylus 297
aesthetic 3–4, 7–8, 63, 66, 282
Alcaeus 293
Allen, Janet 124–125
alpha frequency region 174
Altamira cave 192, *192*, *193*
altered states of consciousness 196–197,
  199–200, 211
American Idiot (Green Day) 217
aminergic system 202, 210–211
amniote clade 44
amplitude of sound wave 167, *167*
amygdala 30–32, *31*, 44, 84, 174
ancient Chinese civilization 272–273
Anderson, Warren 293, 295, 299, 301,
  306, 315
Anisimov, 198–199
anthropomorphism 195–196, *195*, 225
apes 92

Appia, Adolphe 133
Arion 290–291
Aristotelian analysis 317–318
Aristotle: actors and 312–313; adaption
  of, to times 299; birth of 310; catharsis
  and 316–317; comedy and 11, 314;
  death of 319; defects of hearers and
  314; dithyramb of Philoxemus and
  291–292; dreaming and 49; epic poetry
  and 318; influence of 310; language
  and 298; math and music and 294;
  mimesis and 312–314, 316–317; Muses
  and 311–312; music and 311–316,
  319–320; musicians and 312–313;
  music versus song and 67; pathos and
  313; persuasion and, modes of 311;
  Plato and 310–311; protagonists and
  314–315; purgative melodies and 316;
  Pythagoreans and 294; sculpture of *310*;
  theatre and 317–319; tragedy and 11,
  314, 317–318
arousal: activation and 201; Berlyne's
  theory of 214–216, *215*; curtain times
  and 213–214; defining 201; Mozart
  effect and 205; music and 202–206;
  neuroscience of 201–202; tempo and
  205; Thayer's model of 211–214, *212*
Arrival at a Train Station (film) 69
art: cave 191–192, *191*, *194*, *195*,
  195; evaluating 63; musical line and,
  development of 160–165; sound, terms
  of 34; timeline of earliest *160*; visual
  34–35, 68–69, 71, 72, 165; visual line
  and, development of 164
Atapuerca cave 134–135, *136*, *137*,
  138, 165
Atkinson, R. C. 230, 233

For Product Safety Concerns and Information please contact our EU
representative GPSR@taylorandfrancis.com
Taylor & Francis Verlag GmbH, Kaufingerstraße 24, 80331 München, Germany

www.ingramcontent.com/pod-product-compliance
Lightning Source LLC
Chambersburg PA
CBHW070932050326
40689CB00014B/3174